KU-790-964

ening." —Cal McCrystal, *Financial Times*

"Hiro . . . is a model political analyst. His approach is as incorrigibly nonpartisan as it is methodical." —Justin Wintle, *Sunday Times*

"Necessary . . . reading for anyone interested in the contemporary history of two 'rogue' states." —*Kirkus Reviews*

"Engaging, readable, and jargon-free book . . . Hiro combines first hand information with a keen sense of political knowledge of the region . . . Highly recommended for academic and public libraries."
—Nader Entessar, *Library Journal*

Iraq: A Report from the Inside (2003)

"For a rigorous and nonpartisan analysis of Iraq's recent history, you could hardly do better than pick up Dilip Hiro's *Iraq* which traces the path of its relationship with the West and its neighbors."
—Nicholas Lezard, *Guardian*

"A clear account of recent developments in Iraq by a writer renowned for his scholarship on Iraq and Islamic fundamentalism"
—Martin Bright, *Observer*

"A scrupulous and discerning vest-pocket contemporary history of Iraq from a writer with a well-earned reputation for even-handedness. Hiro does an elegant job." —*Kirkus Reviews*

"Whence my change of heart [on Iraq]? For one thing . . . I've been listening and reading particularly Dilip Hiro's book *Iraq: In the Eye of the Storm.*" —William Raspberry, *Washington Post*

"Highly readable and provocative book . . . Hiro offers a critical analysis of both the Iraqi regime and the West's duplicitous role in buttressing Saddam Hussein." —Nader Entessar, *Library Journal*

Also by Dilip Hiro

Nonfiction

Secrets and Lies: The True Story of the Iraq War (2005)

Iraq: A Report from the Inside (2003)

The Essential Middle East: A Comprehensive Guide (2003)

War Without End: The Rise of Islamist Terrorism and Global Response (2002)

The Rough Guide History of India (2002)

Neighbors, Not Friends: Iraq and Iran after the Gulf Wars (2001)

Sharing the Promised Land: A Tale of Israelis and Palestinians (1999)

Dictionary of the Middle East (1996)

The Middle East (1996)

Between Marx and Muhammad: The Changing Face of Central Asia (1995)

Lebanon, Fire and Embers: A History of the Lebanese Civil War (1993)

Desert Shield to Desert Storm: The Second Gulf War (1992)

Black British, White British: A History of Race Relations in Britain (1991)

The Longest War: The Iran-Iraq Military Conflict (1991)

Holy Wars: The Rise of Islamic Fundamentalism (1989)

Iran: The Revolution Within (1988)

Iran Under the Ayatollahs (1985)

Inside the Middle East (1982)

Inside India Today (1977)

The Untouchables of India (1975)

Black British, White British (1973)

The Indian Family in Britain (1969)

Fiction

Three Plays (1985)

Interior, Exchange, Exterior (Poems, 1980)

Apply, Apply, No Reply & A Clean Break (Two Plays, 1978)

To Anchor a Cloud (Play, 1972)

A Triangular View (Novel, 1969)

IRAN TODAY

DILIP HIRO

POLITICO'S

First published in the United States 2005 by
Nation Books
An Imprint of Avalon Publishing Group Inc.
245 West 17th St., 11th Floor
New York, NY 10011

First published in Great Britain 2006 by
Politico's Publishing, an imprint of
Methuen Publishing Limited
11–12 Buckingham Gate
London SW1E 6LB

Copyright © 2005 Dilip Hiro

Methuen Publishing Limited Reg.3543167

A CIP catalogue record for this book is available from the British
Library.

This book is sold subject to the condition that it shall not by way of
trade or otherwise be lent, resold, hired out or otherwise circulated
without the publishers' prior consent in writing in any form of binding
or cover other than that in which it is published and without a similar
condition, including this condition, being imposed on the subsequent
purchaser.

ISBN-10: 1 84275 158 1
ISBN-13: 978 1 84275 158 9

10 9 8 7 6 5 4 3 2 1

Book design by Maria E. Torres
Printed and bound in Great Britain by
Bookmarque Ltd, Croydon, Surrey

Contents

Maps • viii

List of Photos • xii

Main Characters • xiii

Chronology • xvii

Preface • xxxiii

Introduction • xxxvii

ONE: The Iranian Bazaar: A Crucible of Trade,
Religion, and Politics • 1

TWO: Majlis: Voice of the People • 25

THREE: Mussadiq: The Rise and Fall of a Nationalist
Democrat • 63

FOUR: The Pahlavis: Modernizing Dictators • 85

FIVE: Khomeini, the Pioneer, and Khamanei • 113

SIX: Qom: The Religious Capital of Islamic Iran • 151

SEVEN: Oil: Life Blood of Modern Iran • 183

EIGHT: Iran and Iraq: Neighbors, Not Friends • 209

NINE: Iran and America: Allies Turned Adversaries • 241

TEN: Iranian Youth and Women: The Future • 295

Overview • 339

Epilogue • 363

Notes • 395

Glossary of Foreign Words and Shia Islam • 419

Select Bibliography • 425

Index • 429

TURKMENISTAN

⊛Ashgabat

○Tejan

Serakhs

Mashhad○

AFGHANISTAN

PAKISTAN

I R A N

○Iranshahr

Gulf of Oman

0　　　　　　200 mi

0　　　　　　200 km

BRITISH AND RUSSIAN ZONES OF INFLUENCE 1907-1917

0　　　　300 mi

0　　　　300 km

Caspian Sea

RUSSIAN INFLUENCE

NEUTRAL

BRITISH INFLUENCE

Persian Gulf

N

BRITISH-SOVIET OCCUPATION OF IRAN 1941-1946

0　　　　300 mi

0　　　　300 km

Caspian Sea

SOVIET OCCUPATION

○Tehran

BRITISH OCCUPATION

Persian Gulf

N

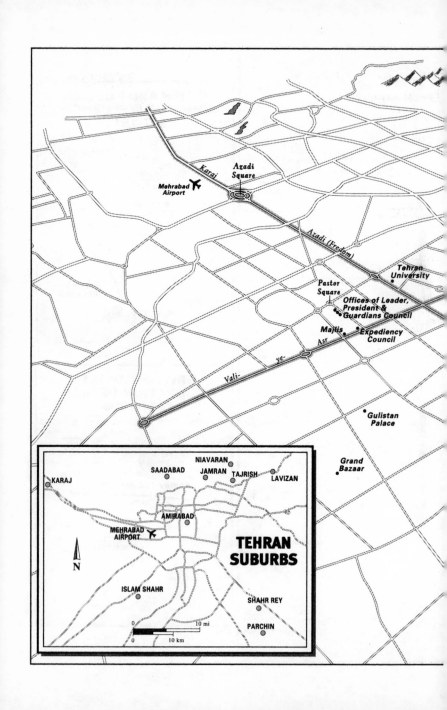

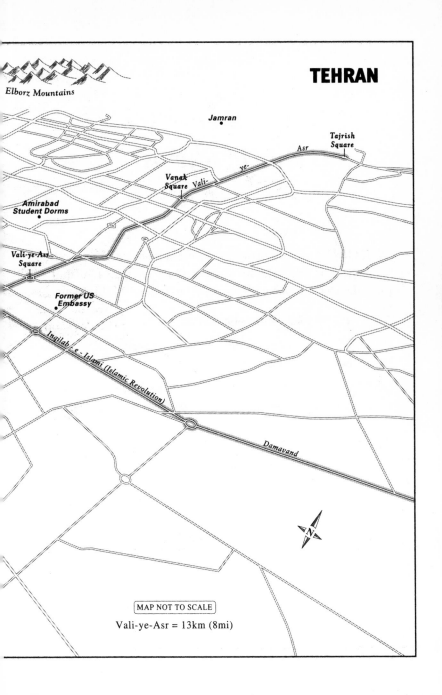

Elborz Mountains

TEHRAN

Jamran

Asr

Tajrish Square

Vanak Square

Vali-

ye-

Vali-

Amirabad Student Dorms

Vali-ye-Asr Square

Former US Embassy

Inqilab-e-Islami (Islamic Revolution)

Damavand

N

MAP NOT TO SCALE

Vali-ye-Asr = 13km (8mi)

List of Photos

All photographs © Dilip Hiro 2006

CHAPTER 1—Ali Duroosh Beheshti, the oldest trader in the Grand Bazaar, Tehran. Behind his back, below the framed sign of "Allah," (in Arabic) hangs a picture of Imam Ali, the founder of Shia Islam.

CHAPTER 2—The Majlis in session, Tehran

CHAPTER 3—Iranian Prime Minister Muhammad Mussadiq at the Liberty Bell, Philadelphia, 1952

CHAPTER 4—An Iranian bank note with the portrait of Muhammad Reza Shah and the official logo of a pre-Islamic symbol of a gryphon

CHAPTER 5—Ayatollah Ruhollah Khomeini blessing a gathering at his official residence in Jamran, Tehran, 1983

CHAPTER 6—The shrine of Fatima Massoumeh, Qom

CHAPTER 7—The site of Oil Well Number One in Iran and the Middle East, 1908, Masjid-e Suleiman

CHAPTER 8—The aftermath of an Iraqi surface-to-surface missile strike on Dezful, April 1983

CHAPTER 9—A perimeter wall of the former U.S. embassy portraying the top the Statue of Liberty capped with a skull

CHAPTER 10—Women at a library near Vanak Square, Tehran

Main Characters

MAHMOUD AHMADINEJAD, President of Iran, 2005–Present

MADELEINE KORBEL ALBRIGHT, U.S. Secretary of State, 1993–97

SHAHPUR BAKHTIAR (1914–91), Prime Minister of Iran, 1978–79

ABOL HASSAN BANI-SADR, President of Islamic Republic of Iran, 1980–81

MUHAMMAD EL BARADEI, Egyptian Director-General, International Atomic Energy Agency, 1998–Present

MAHDI BAZARGAN, (1905–95), Prime Minister of Islamic Republic of Iran, 1979

GEORGE HERBERT WALKER BUSH, U.S. President, 1989–93

GEORGE WALKER BUSH, U.S. President, 2001–Present

JIMMY CARTER, U.S. President, 1977–81

BILL CLINTON, U.S. President, 1993–2001

WILLIAM KNOX D'ARCY, British financier of first successful oil strike in Iran, 1908

DWIGHT EISENHOWER, U.S. President, 1952–63

SADDAM HUSSEIN, President of Iraq, 1979–2003

AHMAD JANNATI, Chairman of Iran's Guardians Council, 1999–Present

AMIR KABIR (a.k.a. Mirza Taqi Khan) Chief Minister of Iran, 1848–51; first modernizer

ABOL QASIM KASHANI, (1884–1962), Iranian radical religious-political leader

ALI HUSSEINI KHAMANEI, President of Iran, 1981–89; Leader of Iran, 1989–Present

MUHAMMAD KHATAMI, President of Iran, 1997–2005

MUHAMMAD REZA KHATAMI, Leader of Islamic Iran Participation Front, 1997–Present

RUHOLLAH KHOMEINI (1902–89), Leader of Islamic Republic of Iran, 1979–89

MUHAMMAD MUSSADIQ (1881–1967), Prime Minister of Iran, 1951–53

MUHAMMAD REZA PAHLAVI, Shah of Iran, 1941–78

REZA PAHLAVI, Shah of Iran, 1925–41

AHMAD QAJAR, Shah of Iran, 1909–25

MUFAZZAR AL DIN QAJAR, Shah of Iran, 1896–1906

NASSER AL DIN QAJAR, Shah of Iran, 1848–96

MUHAMMAD ALI QAJAR, Shah of Iran, 1907–09

ALI AKBAR HASHEMI RAFSANJANI, Speaker of Iran's Majlis, 1980–89; President of Iran, 1989–97; Chairman of Expediency Council, 1997–Present

MASUD RAJAVI, Leader of Mujahedin-e Khalq Organization, 1978–2003

RONALD REAGAN, U.S. President, 1981–89

GEORGE REYNOLDS, British geologist who first struck oil in Iran, 1908

CONDOLEEZZA RICE, U.S. Secretary of State, 2005–Present

KERMIT ROOSEVELT, executor of United States' coup against Muhammad Mussadiq, August 1953

HASSAN ROUHANI, Secretary-General, Iran's Supreme National Security Council, 1989–Present

YUSUF SAANEI, Iranian grand ayatollah

MUHAMMAD HASHEMI SHAHROUDI, Head of Iran's Judiciary, 1999–Present

MUHAMMAD KAZEM SHARIATMADARI (1903–86), Iranian grand ayatollah

ABDUL KARIM SOROUSH, leading dissident Iranian Islamic thinker

MAHMUD TALEQANI (1910–79), leftist Iranian religious-political leader

Chronology
1501–2006

Safavid, Afshar, Zand, and Qajar dynasties (1501–1925)

1501:

After capturing Tabriz in Azerbaijan, Shah Ismail I Safavi extends his domain from Baghdad to Herat, Afghanistan, and adopts Twelver Shia Islam as state religion. The subsequent Safavid dynasty lasts 235 years.

1524:

Shah Tahmasp succeeds Shah Ismail. In 1547 he rebuilds the dome over Fatima's grave in Qom, the winter capital of the Safavids.

1577:

Shah Muhammad Khudabande follows Shah Ismail II's brief reign of one year.

1587:

Shah Abbas I moves capital from Tabriz to Isfahan. He constructs an extensive complex around Fatima's grave in Qom.

1629:

Shah Safi transforms two of the courtyards of Fatima's shrine into Faiziya Seminary which would become the largest theological college in Iran.

1642:

Shah Abbas II ascends the throne.

1666:

Shah Suleiman I succeeds Abbas II.

1694:

When Shah Sultan Hussein tries to convert Sunni tribes in Afghanistan to Shia Islam by force in the late 1710s, they rebel. Led by Mahmoud, they capture Isfahan in 1722.

1722:

Mahmoud tries to reimpose Sunni Islam in Iran, but fails. He is replaced by Nadir Quli, an Afghan noble belonging to Afshar clan, in 1729.

1732:

Shah Abbas III reclaims the throne, but is overthrown by Nadir Quli in 1736, who establishes the Afshar dynasty.

1736:

During his foray into northern India in 1739, Nadir Shah loots the treasure of the Mughal dynasty, including the Peacock Throne, which he brings to Iran.

1747–50:

Brief rules by Nadir Shah's two successors end with the founding of the Zand dynasty by Karim Khan Zand.

1779:

Karim Khan Zand is defeated by Muhammad Khan Qajar, a Twelver Shia, who conquers most of Iran by 1790.

1790:

Founding of Qajar dynasty, with its capital in Tehran, lasts 135 years. Qajar rulers continue the Safavid tradition of placing royal and noble mausoleums in Fatima's shrine complex in Qom.

1797:

Fath Ali Shah, nephew of Muhammad Khan Shah, embellishes the cupola of Fatima's shrine with golden leaf and turns Qom into a leading place of Shia pilgrimage.

1834:

Muhammad Shah succeeds Fath Ali Shah. Influence of Britain and Russia in Iran grows.

1848:

Start of long reign of Nasser al Din Shah. In 1872, he grants exclusive rights for railroad and streetcar construction, almost all minerals, a national bank, and many industrial and agricultural projects for small royalty and initial payment of £40,000 to British Baron Julius de Reuter, and then withdraws it when there is popular outcry. In 1883, he reconstructs some parts of the Fatima complex in Qom. In 1890, he gives a monopoly on tobacco to a British company and then revokes it when faced with popular protest.

1896:

Muzaffar al Din Shah gives oil concession to British citizen William Knox D'Arcy in 1901. In August 1906, he decrees that a Majlis of delegates be elected. In December he signs a set of Fundamental Laws passed by the Majlis.

1907:

Muhammad Ali Shah signs the Supplementary Fundamental Laws, specifying a parliamentary form of government. James Reynolds, financed by D'Arcy, finds oil at Masjid-e Suleiman in 1908. Following a failed assassination attempt on him in mid-1909, the Shah orders his palace guard to bomb the Majlis building. In the ensuing civil war, he loses and abdicates in favor of his twelve-year-old son, Ahmad.

1925:

Ahmad Shah is overthrown by Reza Khan in October 1925 who establishes Pahlavi dynasty.

Pahlavi Dynasty (1925–79)

1925:

Reza Shah crowns himself king in April 1926.

1941:

Reza Shah is forced to abdicate by the invading Soviet and British troops in favor of his son Muhammad Reza.

April 1951:

Prime Minister Muhammad Mussadiq nationalizes the British-owned Anglo-Iranian Oil Company and establishes the National Iranian Oil Company.

August 1953:

In his tussle with popular Prime Minister Mussadiq, the Shah loses, and flees to Baghdad and then Rome. Following a coup by the U.S. Central Intelligence Agency, working with the British MI6, against Mussadiq, the Shah is restored to his throne after three days. He represses all opposition brutally, and lets Western oil consortium run Iran's oil industry.

June 1963:

Qom-based Ayatollah Ruhollah Khomeini addresses the Shah as "You miserable wretch" and attacks him for his pro-American policies. Following his arrest, there is a nationwide insurrection. Its suppression by the military results in thousands of deaths.

November 1964:

The Shah expels Khomeini. After spending a year in the Turkish city of Bursa, he moves to Najaf, a Shia holy place in Iraq.

October 1973–January 1974:

Following the quadrupling of petroleum oil prices in the wake of the October 1973 Arab-Israeli War, the Shah's ambition rises, and the Iranian economy becomes overheated.

January 1978:

A scurrilous attack on Khomeini in a progovernment newspaper inflames popular feelings and leads to demonstrations by theology students in Qom in which dozens are killed by police firings.

August 1978:

Nonviolent protest intensifies during the fasting month of Ramadan, starting on August 5, with the faithful breaking their fast in mosques and listening to smuggled audiotaped speeches of Khomeini.

September 8, 1978:
Following declaration of martial law, troops—armed with tanks and helicopter gunships—attack a crowd of fifteen thousand who, unaware of the freshly declared curfew, have gathered in Tehran's Jaleh Square. Some sixteen hundred people lie dead.

October 6, 1978:
Expelled from Iraq at the Shah's behest, Khomeini takes refuge in France, settling in Neuphle-le-Chateau, a Paris suburb, and gives several interviews to the international media daily.

December 2, 1978:
Start of the ten-day mourning for Imam Hussein, on Muharram 1.

December 5, 1978:
An indefinite strike by oil workers causes crippling fall in government revenue.

December 11, 1978:
On this day—Ashura in the Shia calendar—nearly two million people in Tehran march through the city center and adopt a seventeen-point charter by acclamation, demanding an end to monarchy, acceptance of Khomeini as their leader, and establishment of an Islamic government.

January 16, 1979:
The Shah leaves for Aswan in Egypt for vacation after appointing Shahpur Bakhtiar as the Prime Minister.

February 1, 1979:
Khomeini returns to Tehran to a tumultuous reception.

February 5, 1979:
Khomeini appoints Mahdi Bazargan as the Prime Minister of the Provisional Islamic Government.

On February 10–11, 1979:
Clashes between armed revolutionaries and thousands of military deserters on one side, and pro-Shah Imperial Guard on the other side, result in the defeat of the Guard. Declaring its neutrality, Military Supreme Council orders troops to return to their garrisons. The Shah's 414,000 strong military is reduced to about 100,000.

Islamic Republic of Iran (1979–)
Ruhollah Khomeini (1979–89)

April 1, 1979:
In a referendum, Iranians vote almost unanimously for an Islamic republic.

August 1979:
Elections are held to Assembly of Experts to draft a constitution.

October 22, 1979:
Violating its promise of denying the Shah entry into the U.S., the Jimmy Carter administration allows him to register at a New York hospital for cancer treatment.

November 4, 1979:
Militant students seize the U.S. Embassy in Tehran and take

diplomats as hostages, offering to exchange them for the Shah. The Carter administration dismisses the offer.

December 1, 1979:
In a referendum, Iranians endorse Islamic constitution, which names Khomeini as Leader of Islamic Republic of Iran.

January 1980:
Abol Hassan Bani-Sadr is elected President of Iran.

April 24–25, 1980:
The Pentagon's mission to rescue American hostages in Tehran is aborted after three of the eight helicopters are disabled in a desert in central Iran, and the presence of the team is noticed by the passengers of a passing bus.

May 1980:
The Majlis elections result in a majority for the Khomeini-backed Islamic Republican Party.

July 27, 1980:
The Shah dies of cancer.

September 22, 1980:
Iraq, ruled by President Saddam Hussein, invades Iran.

November 4, 1980:
On the first anniversary of the American Embassy seizure in Tehran, Jimmy Carter is defeated in the U.S. presidential poll by Ronald Reagan.

January 20, 1981:
The American hostages are flown to Algiers and released a few

minutes after Reagan is sworn in as U.S. President, thus ending 444-day crisis.

June 1981:
Khomeini dismisses Bani-Sadr as President after his impeachment by Majlis.

October 1981:
Ali Khamanei is elected President of Iran.

June 1982:
After recovering their lost territory from Iraq, Iranians forces enter Iraq.

October 1983:
Iraq uses chemical weapons against the Iranian troops.

January 1984:
Washington adds Iran to its list of countries that support international terrorism.

November 1984:
After Reagan's reelection as U.S. president, his administration removes Iraq from list of countries sponsoring international terrorism and resumes links with Baghdad in January after eighteen-year break.

March 1985:
Iraq initiates a "War of Cities" by hitting civilian targets, and Iran reciprocates. It ends in June.

August 1985:
Khamanei is reelected President of Iran.

November 1985:

Ayatollah Hussein Ali Montazeri is named by Assembly of Experts as successor to Khomeini.

February 1986:

Iran captures Fao Peninsula in southern Iraq.

November 3, 1986:

A Beirut-based magazine reveals Iran-Contra scam, exposing how Reagan White House had conducted clandestine operation to fund Contra guerrillas against leftist government in Nicaragua with profits from illicit arms sales to Iran in return for release of American hostages held by pro-Tehran groups in Lebanon.

January 1987:

Iran's major offensive to capture Basra leads Iraq to resort to "War of Cities." Iran fails to retain much Iraqi territory. "War of Cities" ends in February.

July 1987:

A comprehensive United Nations Security Council Resolution 598 calls for a ceasefire in the Iran-Iraq War.

April 1988:

While Iraq regains Fao Peninsula by large scale use of chemical weapons, U.S. Navy mounts multiple attacks on Iranian targets.

July 3, 1988:

American cruiser USS *Vincennes* shoots down an Iran Airbus with 290 people on board, mistaking it for a U.S.-made F-14 warplane.

July 18, 1988:
Iran accepts UN Security Council Resolution 598 unconditionally.

August 20, 1988:
The Iran-Iraq War ends with a ceasefire after ninety-five
months.

March 1989:
Khomeini decides that Montazeri is unsuitable to succeed
him as Leader of Iran.

June 3, 1989:
Khomeini dies of cancer. The Assembly of Experts elects
Khamanei as Leader by sixty votes to twelve.

Ali Khamanei (1989–)

July 1989:
Ali Akbar Hashemi Rafsanjani is elected President of Iran; and
Iranians endorse the 1979 constitution with forty-two
amendments by an overwhelming majority in referendum.

August 2, 1990:
Iraq invades Kuwait. Iran condemns Iraq's aggression.

March 1991:
Iran's attempt to direct Shia uprisings in southern Iraq, following U.S.-led coalition's defeat of Iraqi forces in Kuwait, fails.

April–May 1992:
In first post-Iran-Iraq War elections for Majlis, conservatives
emerge as majority at expense of their leftist opponents.

May 1993:
U.S. administration of Bill Clinton unveils its policy of "dual containment" toward Iran and Iraq.

June 1993:
Rafsanjani is reelected President of Iran.

Mid–1994:
After 134 members of Writers Association have signed a letter calling for an end to censorship, several of them are assassinated or die in suspicious circumstances.

March 1995:
Clinton imposes trade embargo on Iran.

August 1996:
America passes Iran-Libya Sanctions Act, banning investment in oil industries of these countries.

May 23, 1997:
Muhammad Khatami is elected President of Iran in a landslide win over his rival Majlis Speaker Ali Akbar Nateq-Nouri favored by religious establishment.

December 1997:
Iran hosts fifty-four-member Islamic Conference Organization summit in Tehran. It is the first Shia-majority country to do so.

January 7, 1998:
Khatami expresses regret over American hostage taking in Tehran and proposes people to people exchanges to dissipate "walls of distrust" between Iran and America.

June 17, 1998:

U.S. Secretary of State Madeleine Albright says that Washington is ready to draw "a road map for normalization of relations."

July 7, 1999:

Against the background of number of publications doubling since Khatami's victory, conservative-dominated Fifth Majlis passes first reading of bill to amend 1985 Press Law, requiring journalists to reveal their sources, and authorizing Press Court to conduct summary trials. The judiciary bans leftist *Salaam* newspaper.

July 8–13, 1999:

Nonviolent protest by university students in Tehran escalates when their dormitories are attacked by right-wing vigilantes and police, and spreads to universities in seventeen other cities. In Tehran student unrest turns violent when disgruntled nonstudents join.

October 12–November 11, 1999:

Jury in Special Court for Clergy finds Hojatalislam Abdullah Nouri, a former Vice President, guilty of publishing anti-Islamic articles in his newspaper *Khordad* and judge sentences him to five years in jail, later reduced to two years.

February 18, 2000:

In first round of Sixth Majlis poll, reformist candidates win large majority.

April 17, 2000:

Conservative-dominated Fifth Majlis tightens up Press Law further, banning criticism of constitution and Leader.

May 5, 2000:

Despite closure of many reformist publications, reform candidates win two-thirds majority in Majlis.

September 2001:

Following 9/11, Khamanei and Khatami condemn terrorist attacks on New York and Washington.

January 29, 2002:

U.S. President George W. Bush declares Iran, Iraq, and North Korea to be part of "an axis of evil."

April 2003:

Following overthrow of Saddam Hussein's regime by Anglo-American troops, Iran demands that peacekeeping and holding of elections should be turned over to UN.

June 16, 2003:

International Atomic Energy Agency's report says that Iran has failed to meet its nuclear Non-Proliferation Treaty obligations by failing to report acquiring some uranium in 1991 and naming facilities where it processed the material.

October 10, 2003:

The Nobel Committee awards Peace Prize to Shirin Ebadi, an Iranian lawyer specializing in human and civil rights, and political and social freedoms.

October 21, 2003:

According to deal signed by Iran with Britain, France, and Germany, Iran promises to fully resolve questions raised by IAEA, and agrees to voluntarily suspend its uranium enrichment and reprocessing activities in return for European nations' assistance in providing Iran with access to modern technology in all areas.

March 2004:
IAEA Board of Governors deplores Iran's failure to declare "potentially arms-related nuclear activities to the IAEA."

May 2004:
In elections to Seventh Majlis, conservatives win 190 seats and reformists are down to 50.

July 2004:
Claiming that European Troika (EU3) has failed to deliver its side of the agreement, Iran resumes its uranium-enrichment activities.

November 5, 2004:
Khamanei declares that developing, producing, or stockpiling nuclear weapons is forbidden under Islam and our Islamic nation.

November 29, 2004:
IAEA Board of Governors welcomes Iran's decision to continue and extend its suspension of all enrichment-related and reprocessing activities following its fresh deal with the EU3 to this effect until a "grand agreement" is concluded between the two sides.

January 2005:
The *New Yorker* reveals that secret U.S. Special Forces units had infiltrated Iran from Pakistan and placed remote detection

devices to sample radioactivity.

February 2005:
The *Washington Post* reveals that the Pentagon had been flying drones over Iraq since April 2004 to test Iran's defenses. Bush describes Iran as "the world's primary state sponsor of terrorism—pursuing nuclear weapons."

June 24, 2005:
Mahmoud Ahmadinejad defeats Rafsanjani in the second round of the presidential poll by a factor of nine to five.

August 5, 2005:
Iran rejects the EU3's Framework for a Long Term Agreement due to its denial of all aspects of peaceful nuclear technology to Iran, and resumes conversion of yellow cake into uranium gas under IAEA supervision.

September 24, 2005:
IAEA Board decides that Iran is in noncompliance of the nuclear NPT.

February 4, 2006:
IAEA Board decides to "report" Iran to the UN Security Council for its "many failures and breaches of its obligations" under the nuclear NPT.

Preface

Since the 1979 revolution I have visited Iran a dozen times on news reporting or op-ed assignments for the *New York Times*, *Washington Post*, *Wall Street Journal*, *Boston Globe*, *Toronto Star*, and *Nation* in North America; and the *Economist*, *Sunday Times*, *Observer*, and *Guardian* in Britain.

As someone born in the northern region of the Indian subcontinent, I am always struck by the cultural impact Iran has had on that part of the world. This is most apparent in architecture, languages, and cultural mores. Since Persian was the court language of the Afghan and Mughal dynasties, which ruled most of the Indian subcontinent for seven centuries, the regional languages are overlaid with Persian words.

The word "bazaar," (market place) is a prime example: it is used throughout the northern Indian subcontinent. Along with the term goes the associated art of haggling between the seller and the potential buyer.

A bazaar in Iran, however, is more than a market. It is a place where commerce, religion, and politics intersect. That is why this book opens with a chapter on the Iranian bazaar—more specifically, the Grand Bazaar of Tehran—and describes the crucial role it has played in the country's chronicle.

Bazaar merchants were an important part of the coalition that helped launch the Constitutional Revolution of 1905–6, which resulted in the establishment of a parliament, called Majlis (lit., Assembly). Despite the many instances of dramatic turmoil Iran has experienced since then, the Majlis as an institution has survived. Chapter Two outlines the vicissitudes of the Iranian parliament over the past century.

As a vigorous voice of the people in the late 1940s, the Majlis threw up a charismatic politician, Muhammad Mussadiq, as Iran's first truly popular leader in modern times. Chapter Three, centered round Mussadiq, ends with the overthrow of his government in a coup masterminded by the United States Central Intelligence Agency (CIA) and the restoration of Muhammad Reza Pahlavi as the Shah of Iran.

The next chapter traces the rise and fall of the Pahlavi dynasty, ending with the revolution in 1979, led by Ayatollah Ruhollah Khomeini. Chapter Five starts with the story of Khomeini, and provides a detailed account of how and why the revolutionary movement headed by him succeeded. It continues with a description of the rule of his successor Ayatollah Ali Khamanei.

Senior Iranian clerics are almost invariably graduates of the seminaries in Qom, the Shia holy place in Iran. That is why Chapter Six offers a history of the city and explains the significance of Shia Islam in the Iranian society and state. In the latter part of this chapter, I outline the performance of the two Qom clerics—Hojatalislams Ali Akbar Hashemi Rafsanjani and Muhammad Khatami—who were both elected President. Interestingly, Qom also figures prominently in Iran's petroleum industry: it is an important junction for oil and gas pipelines between the petroleum-rich Khuzistan province and Tehran, and has a large oil field nearby.

Starting with a visit to Masjid-e Suleiman, where oil was discovered in commercial quantities in 1908, Chapter Seven outlines a history of Iran's crucial petroleum and gas industry, ending with a visit to the oil city of Khorramshahr on the Shatt al Arab (Arvand Rud, to Iranians) waterway which forms part of the Iranian-Iraqi border and which was at the root of the war between Iraq and Iran.

Chapter Eight deals with the 1980–88 Iran-Iraq armed conflict, describing it in its nine distinct phases, and outlining the escalating support given to Iraq, ruled by President Saddam Hussein, by the United States.

The following chapter, devoted to relations between Iran and America since the two countries established diplomatic links in 1883, also covers Iran's nuclear programs that the U.S. has done much to highlight in the international arena. In contrast to the hostility shown toward the U.S. by high officials of the Islamic Republic of Iran, many young Iranians are favorably disposed to America.

Chapter Ten focuses on the young people of Iran, furnishing details of the student protest of July 1999, as well as the status of women.

The final chapter is an overview of the several aspects of Iranian society and state covered in the earlier text, with a hint of where Iran is headed in the near future. Overall, in this book, I have attempted to navigate—what seems to most Westerners, particularly Americans—a challenging labyrinth, fascinating and infuriating in equal parts, as a reporter and historian. I have done so by blending travelogue, history, and sociopolitical analysis.

Since I have constructed the book thematically some overlap between chapters is inevitable. I have, however, avoided duplication by mentioning different facts and insights of the same event in different chapters.

A word about the place names and the spellings of Persian and Arabic words. I have used the term "the Gulf" that divides Iran from the Arabian Peninsula, and "the Persian Gulf," interchangeably. There is no standard way of transliterating Persian names. I have chosen one of the most widely used spellings in the English-language print media—except where the spelling of the book author is different from mine. While using an index, a particular difficulty arises where different spellings of a proper noun, or an object, begin with a different letter—as in Koran/Quran. I have solved this problem by using one spelling in the text but including others as well in the Index.

Iranians tend to use "e" where others use "i" ("Esfahan" rather than "Isfahan"); "o" instead of "u" ("Hossein" rather than "Hussein"); and "gh" instead of "q" ("Ghom" rather than "Qom"). That explains why they spell "Mussadiq" as "Mossadegh."

A foreign word, written in italics at the first mention, later appears in roman. I have provided a glossary of foreign words and Shia Islam at the end of the book.

A list of the main characters and a chronology appear at the beginning of the volume.

The epilogue in this edition takes the narrative to January 2006 and deals at length with Iran's ongoing nuclear issue, and the unexpected victory of Mahmoud Ahmadinejad in the presidential poll of 2005 and its causes and consequences. The epilogue is not indexed.

Though Ayatollah Ali Khamanei is described in the Western media as the Supreme Leader of Iran, his official title is merely Leader, *Rahbar* (of the Islamic Republic). Since I spell this title consistently with 'L', all other official titles too start with a capital letter—e.g., President, Speaker and Minister.

Unlike in the west, Iranian women do not change their given and family names after marriage.

My special thanks to Carl Bromley, my editor at Nation Books, New York, for his extra interest in the manuscript, and his meticulous attention to detail.

—Dilip Hiro
February 2006

Introduction

Iran is unique in geography, history, and culture. Its shoreline runs all along the eastern side of the oil-rich Persian Gulf and about 300 miles (480 km) of the Arabian Sea. It is a neighbor of the six Arab Gulf monarchies. It has land borders with the Indian subcontinent, Afghanistan, Turkmenistan, Azerbaijan, Armenia, Turkey, and Iraq; and it shares its Caspian Sea littoral with Kazakhstan and Russia. It is the only country in the region with shorelines along the Caspian Sea and the Indian Ocean. Thus Iran, half the size of India, is probably the most strategic country on this planet.

It is also richly endowed with oil and natural gas. At the current rates of extraction, its petroleum deposits of nearly ten billion barrels will last another sixty-five years, and its natural gas reserves of 23,000 billion cubic meters 450 years.

"Iran encompasses some of the most critical geography in the world," said United States President Ronald Reagan in his television address to the nation on November 13, 1986. "Iran's geography gives it a critical position from which adversaries could interfere with oil flows from the Arab states that border the Persian Gulf. Apart from geography, Iran's oil deposits are important to the long term health of the world economy."[1]

Archaeological excavations show Iran's history stretching back six thousand years. Zoroastrianism, a religion originating in Iran, impacted on Christianity and Islam. In the sixteenth and subsequent centuries the Persian Empire competed with both the Ottoman and the Tsarist Empires. It was his rivalry with Sunni Ottoman Turks that drove the Safavid ruler of Iran in 1501 to adopt Shia Islam as state religion, thus carving out a distinctive place for his country in the Muslim world. Later, finding itself on the periphery of the expanding Tsarist Russia and the recently established British Empire in the Indian subcontinent in the nineteenth century, Iran became a buffer between two competing empires.

Iran's language, culture, and architecture have influenced not only the regions to its north and west—modern Central Asia and Turkey—but also the Indian subcontinent to its east. The Taj Mahal is a shining example of Iranian architecture at its most refined. Persian was the court language not only of the Ottoman Turks but also the Afghan and Mughal dynasties that ruled the Indian subcontinent for seven centuries. Apparently, this is what led U.S. President Bill Clinton to refer to Iran, in a speech in March 2000, as "one of the most wonderful places in all of human history, one of the most important places culturally in all of human history."[2]

Iran's recent history makes it uniquely distinctive. It was the first country in the Middle East to find oil in commercial quantities (1908, at Masjid-e Suleiman); to experience a constitutional revolution (1905–11), which led to the first parliament in the region, called Majlis (lit., Assembly), meeting in 1907; to evolve into a constitutional monarchy with a multiparty system in 1941—until 1953, when a coup masterminded by the U.S. Central Intelligence Agency (CIA) reimposed royal dictatorship; to challenge Western economic imperialism in the form of the Anglo-Iranian Oil Company (AIOC) by nationalizing it (1951); to become a victim of the CIA's machinations against a legitimate government, and turn into a template for a series of coups that the CIA later mounted against progressive, nationalist regimes throughout the Third World; and to experience a genuine revolution, in which millions of ordinary citizens participated, but which was inspired primarily by religion, an unprecedented phenomenon.

The 1979 Iranian revolution generated a process that shaped the history of the region to a large extent in the succeeding decades—profoundly affected as it would be by three major wars from 1980–2003—which in turn impacted directly on the U.S. presidential elections twice, in 1980 and 1992. In the latter case the source was the 1991 Gulf War against Iraq. Following it, the popularity of U.S. President George Herbert Walker Bush Sr. soared so high that leading Democrats chose not to enter the presidential race, thus creating a vacuum, which the comparatively unknown Governor of Arkansas, Bill Clinton, filled.

Three major wars in less than a quarter century—the first, between Iran and Iraq, ending up as the longest conventional armed conflict of the last century, the second inaugurating hi-tech warfare by the U.S., and the final one unveiling America's newly adopted doctrine of preventive wars—all of them are inter-related.

Had there been no Iran-Iraq War (1980–88), with Iraqi President Saddam Hussein claiming victory, he would not have felt so overconfident as to invade Kuwait, and the Gulf War of 1991 would not have ensued. And it was the aftermath of that conflict that dragged on for a dozen years in the form of United Nations economic sanctions on Iraq, and culminated in the Anglo-American invasion of Iraq and the overthrow of Saddam Hussein's Baathist regime.

What lay behind Saddam's invasion of Iran in September 1980, which in turn led to the subsequent wars? First and foremost, his determination to preserve his presidency of Iraq—acquired in July 1979 by elbowing out his predecessor, Gen. Ahmad Hassan Bakr—which was threatened by the rising militancy of Iraq's majority Shias, who were inspired by the victorious Islamic revolution in the predominantly Shia Iran five months earlier.

Further a field, the impetus to curb Iran's Ayatollah (lit., Sign of Allah) Ruhollah Khomeini came from Washington where U.S. President Jimmy Carter, feeling humiliated by his failure to gain the release of the American diplomats taken hostage in Tehran, was desperate to see the Islamic regime either overthrown or destabilized.

Conveniently, Saddam's foreign masterminds (Carter and the Gulf monarchs) overlooked the fact that his claim of unfairness about the demarcation of the fluvial border between Iraq and Iran along the midchannel of the Shatt al Arab (lit., Arab Waterway), which he used as the casus belli, was spurious: it was he who had signed the border agreement with Muhammad Reza Shah of Iran as Iraq's then Vice President, in 1975.

The roots of the Islamic revolution lay in the coup mounted by the CIA and the British Secret Intelligence Service, code-named MI6, in conjunction with certain Iranian military leaders in August 1953. They did so to restore Muhammad Reza Pahlavi Shah on the Peacock Throne after his flight from Tehran following his failure to dismiss Prime Minister Muhammad Mussadiq, the country's first truly popular leader.

A land-owning aristocrat, who studied law in France and Switzerland, Mussadiq was a nationalist, constitutionalist, and democrat who, as a Majlis deputy, voted against the accession of Reza Shah in 1925 and was imprisoned by the new autocratic monarch. With his election to parliament in 1944, he began his second political career. By nationalizing the British-owned Anglo-Iranian Oil Company seven years later, and setting up the National Iranian Oil Company (NIOC), he ended London's economic imperialism, and opened the way for Iran to pursue a nonaligned foreign policy.

Following the 1953 coup, the Shah, advised by Washington, retained the nationalization law but reduced the NIOC to a paper organization. It leased the rights to, and management of, Iranian petroleum for the next twenty-five years to a consortium of Western oil giants. Over the next two decades, this Western consortium exported twenty-four billion barrels of crude at the paltry price of $1.80 a barrel. No C.I.A.-driven coup since then has proved so lucrative to Western economies.

In the end, though, this bonanza ended so dramatically—with the Shah's ignominious departure from Tehran ostensibly for "holiday" in January 1979—that it had a traumatic impact on Western economies, with the oil price spiraling to $31 a barrel.

Furthermore, from being an integral part of the Iran-Israel-Saudi Arabia triad on which Washington's anti-Soviet strategy in the Middle East rested, the emergent Islamic Republic of Iran not only expelled the American influence from its own territory but also attacked the pro-American Gulf monarchies and inspired Muslims throughout the region to challenge the hegemony of the U.S. It was then that the image of Iran as a land of fundamentalist mullahs took hold in the West, particularly in America. As the 1990s unrolled, however, the role of exhorting Muslims in the oil-rich region and elsewhere to wage a religious and political struggle against Washington was taken over largely by Al Qaida and its leader Osama bin Laden.

As an instance of poetic justice, however, by triggering the American hostage crisis from November 1979 to January 1981, Khomeini became the first foreign leader to impact directly on a U.S. presidential poll, bringing about the defeat of Carter in November 1980.

I witnessed Iran in a feverish state when I arrived in Tehran in November 1979 as a correspondent of the (London) *Sunday*

Times to report on the crisis caused by the militant Islamic students taking hostage sixty-seven American diplomats at the sprawling United States Embassy.

The Islamic regime of Khomeini exploited the event to mobilize the population and establish its anti-imperialist credentials. Day and night, processions of students, merchants, clerics, workers, and housewives, carrying portraits of Khomeini—white-bearded, black-turbaned, stony-faced, with a middle-distant stare—marched past the embassy, shouting slogans such as "America, Mother of Corruption on Earth" and "Vietnam shows America is nothing."

While the militant students maintained a twenty-four-hour vigil in the full glare of American and other Western television cameras outside the embassy, inside scores of their comrades painstakingly assembled—with carpet-weaving skills—tens of thousands of shreds of the secret documents that the diplomats had pushed hurriedly into the shredding machines during the three hours it took the raiders to seize full control of the embassy.

Since Tehran had been the Middle Eastern headquarters of the U.S. Central Intelligence Agency for many years, the documents that the militant students retrieved and captured proved to be cornucopia for the new regime. It showed the U.S. Embassy courting dissident military officers as well as ethnic Kurdish and Azeri leaders. After the revolution the hostage takers would go on to publish these documents in fifty-four volumes, a few of them revealing—embarrassingly—the personal quirks and weaknesses of such Israeli leaders as Shimon Peres and Yitzhak Rabin as noted by the local CIA operatives.

The failure of the subsequent rescue mission by the Carter administration to retake the embassy in Tehran in April 1980, and the interminable captivity of the American hostages paved the way—along with a weak economy—for the defeat of Carter in the presidential election seven months later and the inauguration of the presidency of Ronald Reagan. The 444-day hostage crisis left a deep scar in the popular American psyche, and turned Khomeini into a demonic figure to the extent that even Fidel Castro or Soviet leader Nikita Khrushchev—with his menacing boast, "We'll bury you"—had failed to achieve.

Fast forward—around the twentieth anniversary of the Islamic revolution in 1999. Sitting near a window of the third-floor restaurant of Mashhad Hotel facing the former U.S. Embassy, its walls covered in images and slogans, "America can't do a thing!"—now Imam Hussein University and the Organization of the Islamic Revolutionary Guard Vocational School—I fell into conversation with Amir Zarkesh, a plump kitchen worker. He remembered the embassy takeover vividly. He remembered too the American guests at the hotel before the revolution, swimming half naked in the pool and being boisterous. He expressed himself without emotion or nostalgia, a sign that the revolution had reached a turning point as all revolutions do when a new generation, unfamiliar with the ancien regime, comes of age.

About midway through this period came the end of the bloody Iran-Iraq War and the death of Khomeini. The image that Iran had embossed on America and Europe as the hotbed of Islamic fundamentalism began to soften somewhat as the successors to Khomeini tried to build bridges with neighbors and revive the economy shattered by a decade of revolution and war while maintaining a system of representative government, which draws its popular mandate at regular intervals[3] within the parameters of Islam, which, besides being a religious faith, is also a sociopolitical ideology.

So the image that 1990s Iran came to project in Europe and America changed from black to gray. Inside the country, on one hand were the unrelieved figures of veiled Iranian women clad in a chador—almost invariably charcoal black, forbidding and melancholy, designed to obliterate distinctions between one female and another—stamping gloomy conformity on the streets, on the other were veiled women skiing on the slopes of Elborz Mountains north of Tehran. Western travelers, depressingly familiar with the restrictions imposed on women in Iran, arrived at Tehran's Mehrabad Airport only to find themselves facing female immigration and customs officers.

By the beginning of the twenty-first century, the education of girls in sex-segregated schools and universities had risen so sharply under the Islamic regime that the majority of university students were female. And, the triennial Olympics for women from Muslim countries, initiated by Iran, had become a regular event.

The landslide victory in 1997 of moderate Hojatalislam (lit., Proof of Islam) Muhammad Khatami—more of a well-read intellectual, fluent in English and German, than a politician—over a conservative cleric, favored by the religious establishment, softened Iran's image further not only in Europe but also in America then under the presidency of Clinton. It proved that the Iranian claim of democracy was not a sham—a point U.S. Secretary of State Colin Powell would make seven years later.

By expressing regret over the taking of American hostages in a CNN interview in January 1998, Khatami made the first move to break "the wall of distrust" between Iran and America. However, it was not until March 2000 that U.S. Secretary of State Madeleine Albright reciprocated by owning up the "significant role" Washington had played in "orchestrating the overthrow of Iran's popular Prime Minister Muhammad Mussadiq" in 1953, describing the C.I.A.-backed coup as "a setback for Iran's political development."[4] However, that did not change the fact that the first nationalist Third World leader to be pilloried in the Anglo-American alliance and its media after World War II was Mussadiq, to be followed by Gamal Abdul Nasser of Egypt, Fidel Castro of Cuba, Ho Chi Minh of Vietnam, and Khomeini.

Later in 2000 came the victory of George W. Bush in the American presidential election; and with it, the ascendancy of the neo-conservatives in formulating policies toward Iran and other Middle Eastern countries. Iran, declared Bush, was part of the "axis of evil" along with Iraq and North Korea.

But major European powers, including Britain under Prime Minister Tony Blair, did not deviate from mending their fences with Tehran. They were in the forefront of trade with Iran, well aware that it had the largest population in the region, and possessed huge deposits of oil and natural gas. For many years now, European petroleum corporations have been participating actively in Iran's oil and gas industry. The European Union began negotiating a Trade and Cooperation Agreement (TCA) with Iran in mid-2003.

Outside of diplomacy, Iran has been making a mark in the world of cinema. Iranian films are regular fare at film festivals around the world. Such movie directors as Jafar Panahi (*Crimson Gold, White Balloon*) and Abbas Kiarostami are highly respected by cinema critics and audiences outside Iran. The awarding of the Nobel Peace Prize to Shirin Ebadi, an Iranian human rights lawyer, in 2003 put Iran in international limelight.

Iran's domestic politics, as exemplified by the shenanigans of the conservative bloc who wield power through the Guardians Council and the judiciary, and intent on stopping or slowing down political reform that was backed by both President Khatami and the Majlis were dramatic enough to engage the readers of the quality press in America and Britain.

Such is the nature of this ongoing battle that pessimists can argue that Iran's sociopolitical system is authoritarian to the core and is beyond redemption while optimists can argue that the conservative-reformist struggle is the dynamic of Islamic democracy that Iran's leaders are attempting to create as a working model for the rest of the Muslim world—the first attempt of the kind.

To interested Westerners, the extraordinary image of dozens of parliamentary deputies staging a sit-in in the corridors of the Majlis—an episode without parallel in the Middle East, except in Israel—and live broadcasts of the chamber's proceedings on the state-run radio, conveyed the vigor and civility of Iranian politics.

It was this political culture that led Colin Powell to remark in July 2004: "Remember that the President of Iran is freely elected. President Khatami was elected by his people . . . in an election that essentially tapped into the desires of the people."[5]

The Iranian Bazaar:
A Crucible of Trade,
Religion, and Politics

✦ CHAPTER 1 ✦

Atraditional Eastern bazaar[1] is an unrivaled place of exotic sights, smells, and sounds. And the Grand Bazaar in southern Tehran is one such. Yet it has neither the grandeur of the Covered Bazaar of Istanbul nor the religious aura of the one in the Muslim Quarter of East Jerusalem's Old City or the ascetic simplicity of Damascus's centuries-old bazaar. The term "grand" applies to its sprawling size—covering 5 miles (8 kilometers) of warrenlike alleyways, more than a dozen mosques, including an impressively spacious one named after Ayatollah Ruhollah Khomeini, the Armenian St. Thaddeus Church, and a fire station—and not to its architecture. At some places, it appears as if two- or three-story-high structures of brick, stone, plastic, and glass are tenuously held together with rope and black electric wire and telephone cable.

All Eastern bazaars have one thing in common, though. They are compact, urban community centers, complete with mosques, religious schools, restaurants and teahouses, public baths, courtyards with fountains, private banks, guesthouses, and transportation facilities. It is here that information and technical know-how travel swiftly, and the law of supply and demand rules supreme.

Behind its shabby, higgledy-piggledy appearance, Tehran's Grand Bazaar is a massive shopping mall of thousands of stores and stalls, a commodities market where nationwide prices of staples are determined daily, a stock exchange, and banking network, where credit and investment are organized with little fuss and less paperwork than in corporate banks. The term *bazaari*, therefore, includes all those who work there: affluent wholesalers, bankers and workshop owners at the top, and peddlers and porters pushing wheelbarrows at the bottom and artisans and craftsmen, shopkeepers, commission agents, and brokers—providing supplies and distribution channels—in the middle. In the Iranian chronicle, bazaaris have been as important as clerics and soldiers.

Different sections of the bazaar are clustered around individual products or commodities—footwear, textiles, garments, spices and herbs, paper, plastic goods, books, hardware—or guilds of craftsmen, such as blacksmiths, bookbinders, carpet weavers, tailors, saddlers, tinsmiths, coppersmiths, and goldsmiths. Their hole-in-the-wall stalls and open front stores are ideal for gossip and instant communication, commercial or political. Indeed, many of these establishments are mere showcases, with the owners maintaining large warehouses elsewhere, the primary function of a shop being a site for an ongoing contact with brokers, suppliers, and buyers, wholesale and retail, in Iran and abroad.

Ever since its inception a century and a half ago out of the amalgamation of smaller craft markets, the Grand Bazaar, located near the Gulistan Palace of the ruling Qajar dynasty (which moved its capital from Isfahan to Tehran in 1785) has been a major player in Iran's history. Initially, it was the focal point not only of commerce but also social events and politics.

Past its battered, dun-colored entrance archway, inconspicuously merging with the surrounding structures, you enter a world that has changed little over centuries, save for dangling electric cables, neon lights, and telephones. Through its narrow, labyrinthine, dusty alleyways and arcades, passes a ceaseless stream of veiled women, robed clerics, and men in open-neck shirts, periodically nudged aside to let heavily laden porters pass by, or trolleys overloaded with goods pushed by sturdy men, warning of their approach with piercing whistles. Reflecting Iran's imperial past, here you see the faces of Persians, with classically sharp features, as well as those of Azeri Turks, pale and fleshy, and Mongols, leathery-skinned and narrow-eyed. Indeed, an estimated third of the merchants here are speakers of Azeri— a language they share with Leader Ayatollah Ali Khamanei. Yet all are united in their love of the Eastern art of haggling.

What you encounter first is the Grand Bazaar's dazzling section, the gold market, with goldsmiths' shops crowded with women in black chadors, scrutinizing necklaces, chains, bangles, rings, bracelets, brooches, and pendants—all the more lustrous in the covered, dingy surroundings—to be acquired for personal embellishment, or as part of a family savings scheme or a dowry. Next follow, in an unwittingly logical sequence, stores selling white bridal gowns, followed by the ones stocked with chadors.

An adjoining section of the bazaar is permeated with a variety of aromas—from irritatingly pungent to sickly sweet—emanating from the multicolored cone-shaped heaps of whole cardamoms, red chilies, cloves, coriander, sticky dates, dried ginger, ground nutmeg, parsley, black peppercorns, raisins, shimmering rock salt, saffron strands, sage, and turmeric. The picturesque display of these spices and herbs often overwhelms the first-time visitor's senses of sight and smell.

The experience of ambling through the copperware section, with its cacophonous sounds generated by an army of coppersmiths rhythmically hammering out kitchenware, is likely to linger long after a foreign visitor has left the Grand Bazaar and Tehran to return home.

On straying into the textiles area, a visitor will find the stores filled with broadcloth on enormous bolts which a shop assistant flings out for display with a sure touch—exceeded only by a carpet salesman in another section of the Grand Bazaar as he unrolls carpet after carpet, peeling them off a huge pile like the sheets of writing paper, surprising his prospective foreign buyer with one that is handwoven to replicate a giant $100 bill carrying the image of Benjamin Franklin.

* * *

Historically, Tehran's Grand Bazaar, the commercial backbone of Iran, has intricately woven the vital strands of trade, Islamic culture, and politics. Built on the foundation of traditional trade or crafts guilds, the bazaar has pursued its interests tenaciously by opposing foreign imports and undue government regulation, both of which have been regular features in Iran ever since free trade was foisted on Asia in the early nineteenth century by Britain and Russia. In the 1830s, Iranian craftsmen and merchants protested against the rising tide of factory-made European imports that were wrecking their businesses, and demanded a ban, but failed due to the rising influence of foreign powers, particularly Britain. Following the 1857 anti-British uprising in India, the British government secured permission from Nasser al Din Shah (r. 1848–96) for telegraph lines to provide an overland link between Britain and India. The system began functioning in 1865, and was extended into internal Iranian lines so the central government could learn quickly what was happening in the provinces.

In March 1890, the Shah granted a concession to a British company (which later became Imperial Tobacco) for the production, sale, and export of tobacco. This proved to be a very unpopular move. Merchants, organized into guilds, wanted to circumscribe the Shah's power to award economic rights to aliens. Their delegation protested against the tobacco deal—a trigger that escalated into a nationwide agitation and the withdrawal of the concession within two years. This was the first successful mass protest, backed by bazaaris, clerics, intellectuals, and ordinary folk. It was facilitated by telegraph, which enabled city dwellers to stay in touch with one another, a role that would be played eight decades later by audiotapes which disseminated exiled Ayatollah Ruhollah Khomeini's speeches in Iran.

The Constitutional Revolution

In December 1905, it was the public beating of several of the Grand Bazaar's wholesale sugar merchants for not lowering prices as decreed by the local governor—arguing that high import prices militated against a reduction—which sparked the Constitutional Revolution.[2] The wholesalers' punishment—their feet were caned—led to an instant closure of the bazaar. Later, some two thousand merchants, theological students, and clerics took sanctuary inside the Royal Mosque of Tehran. When they were expelled from there by government agents, the clerics decided to retire to the shrine of Shahzadeh Abdul Azim outside Tehran. There the assembly demanded that the Shah should enforce the Sharia (Islamic law) and establish the House of Justice, a religious concept in Shia Islam. Muzaffar al Din Shah (r. 1896–1906)—a big hulk of a man with florid cheeks and a luxuriant mustache running across his face—held out for a month while Tehran was crippled by a general strike. Finally, he conceded to the demands. But he failed to keep his promise.

Matters came to a head in the holy month of Muharram after the arrest of radical Sayyid Jamal al Din Isfahani. In the capital, now under military rule, fourteen thousand merchants and clerics sought refuge in the spacious garden of the British Embassy in north Tehran. The protestors raised their demand from a House of Justice to a National Majlis (*lit.*, Assembly). Negotiations ensued between the Royal Court, the religious leaders in the holy city of Qom, and merchant elders in Tehran. Faced with a continued strike, the Shah capitulated. On August 5, 1906, he issued a decree that an Assembly of Delegates be elected by six categories of electors: "princes, ulama [i.e., clerics], the Qajar family, nobles and notables, landowners, and merchants and the guilds."

The constitutional movement was backed by property owners as well as religious and intellectual leaders. The propertied classes, consisting of landowners, administrators, merchants, and artisans wanted Iran to be free of European domination so that they could develop their own potential, unfettered by the Shah's practice of granting economic concessions to Europeans. Senior clerics reckoned, rightly, that diminution in the monarch's authority would increase their power in manipulating tribal chiefs, feudal aristocrats, and the junior clergy.

During the six-year life of the Constitutional Revolution (1905–11), bazaar merchants were steadfast in their loyalty to the new constitution. When Muhammad Ali Shah (r. 1907–9) attempted to circumvent or abrogate the constitution, the bazaar shut down in protest. Finally, Muhammad Ali Shah was forced to abdicate in favor of his twelve-year-old son Ahmad.

The bazaar's links with the mosque go back to early Islam. Prophet Muhammad was a merchant, and so was his first wife Khadija, who financed caravans trading between Mecca and Damascus via Jerusalem. In Iran, as well as in the rest of the Muslim world, clerics and merchants often came from the same families. Traders were the leading contributors of Islamic taxes and presents to clerics, who used them for charitable, educational, and religious ends, which in turn raised clerical influence in society, and reinforced mercantile-clerical ties. In Shia-majority Iran, merchants often acted as intermediaries between the believers and leading clerics—called *marja-e taqlid* (source of emulation)—by letting their names be used by ordinary Shias seeking an audience with the marja. Many merchants held religious meetings at their spacious homes where the assembled discussed politics and political tactics. Also bazaar guilds funded the communal celebration of religious ceremonies conducted by clerics. Even the traders and entrepreneurs outside the bazaar—running village workshops, commercial farms, and shops outside the bazaar—were related to the clergy.

Modernization

The centralizing and modernizing drive by the secular-minded Reza Shah Pahlavi (1925–41) who, as Reza Khan, a mere military officer, had managed to catapult himself to Iran's famed, bejeweled Peacock Throne, met resistance from bazaar merchants and clerics. Unsure of being accepted as a successor to the Qajar dynasty due to his non-aristocratic pedigree, he toyed with the idea of turning Iran into a Republic. The clergy rejected the idea: they associated Shiaism with monarchy because it was the Safavids, claiming lineage from a Shia Imam, Mousa al Kazem, who had adopted Shia Islam as state religion at the turn of the sixteenth century. The bazaar shut down, and repeatedly resisted the Shah's attempts at reopening. Some affluent merchants approached Khomeini, then a respected religious teacher in Qom, to produce a book opposing the ruler's plans. The result was an anti-secularist work, *The Secrets Revealed* (1942), published anonymously,[3] which upheld the sanctity of private property in Islam—a theme that endeared him to the mercantile class.

Responding to the needs of the Allied forces stationed in Iran during World War II (1939–45), and a virtual absence of Western imports, Iran's bazaars expanded, and merchants thrived. Due to the accelerated economic activity caused by the rise in demand in goods and services, stemming from the presence of a large number of foreign troops and their war-related activities, including the urgent task of supplying U.S.-made military hardware to the hard-pressed Soviet Union from the Gulf ports of Iran, the size of the modern middle class grew.

With the end of the war, though, came a dramatic contraction in demand coupled with resumed imports. A flood of cheap imports allowed by Muhammad Reza Pahlavi Shah (r. 1941–79) during the late 1940s and early 1950s bankrupted a substantial segment of bazaaris and generated strong support for nationalist economic policies of Prime Minister Muhammad Mussadiq. The alienated bazaar merchants allied with the enlarged middle class rallied round the shared aim of achieving economic and political independence for Iran, and reducing foreign—chiefly British—competition and control in Iran's economy.

Among bazaaris, artisans and retailers suffered more than wholesalers and bankers. They were particularly close to the clergy who, after years of anti-clerical autocracy of Reza Shah, sensed an opportunity to reclaim some of the social-political status they had lost during the reign of Reza Shah, whose rule is described at length in Chapter Four. In Abol Qasim Kashani (1884–1962), a bearded, stern-looking, black-turbaned cleric, they found a charismatic leader.

Kashani

During my visit to Tehran's Grand Bazaar in July 2004, I found ninety-year-old Ali Duroosh Beheshti referring to Kashani in glowing terms. A tall, lean man, straight as a rod, Beheshti, wearing a clipped white beard and walrus mustache, ran a one-man hole-in-the-wall teashop, in a short alleyway that led to a theological school, its classrooms lining a rectangular courtyard open to the sky, with a fountain at its center. "Kashani was a fine man, honest and uptight, a patriot," Beheshti told me while I sat, cramped, on the only chair available, sipping tea from a dainty little cup, shaped like an hourglass, as the sun's rays penetrated through the holes in the grimy plastic roof above. "Kashani had a clothing shop in the bazaar. And he is remembered today for the hospital in this neighborhood that he unveiled."

Born into a religious family in Tehran, Kashani grew up in Najaf, Iraq, where he pursued theological studies. He returned to Iran in 1921 after Iraq was placed under the British Mandate, in wake of the collapse of the Ottoman Empire. During the inter-war years, he emerged as a radical, who opposed senior clerics' advice to juniors to stay away from politics. He became popular with second-rank clerics and itinerant mullahs. He was arrested for his anti-British activities after Britain had occupied Iran in August 1941 during World War II.

On his release after the war, he founded a political party,

Mujahedin-e Islam, which demanded abrogation of all secular laws passed by the regime and reintroduction of the veil for women, abolished by Reza Shah. He was sent into forced internal exile in Qazvin until late 1947. His third arrest, followed by his expulsion to Lebanon, followed the failed assassination of Muhammad Reza Shah in February 1949. He was permitted to return home a year later.

The issue of the nationalization of the Anglo-Iranian Oil Company dominated the general election held from July 1949 to February 1950, in which Kashani participated. Elected to the Majlis, he advocated oil nationalization. In March 1951, the Majlis voted for it and then for the appointment of Mussadiq as Premier. On May 1, after giving his assent to the oil nationalization bill, the Shah called on Mussadiq to form the next government.

Kashani's followers, drawn mainly from Tehran's Grand Bazaar, were prominent in the pro-Mussadiq demonstrations before and after his elevation to premiership. Kashani was moved as much by anti-imperialist feelings as by an Islamic vision of fusion of politics and religion. "Islamic doctrines apply to social life, patriotism, administration of justice, and opposition to tyranny and despotism," he said. "Islam warns its adherents not to submit to foreign yoke. This is the reason why the imperialists are trying to confuse the minds of the people by drawing a distinction between religion and government and politics."[4] In this, he foreshadowed another ayatollah—Khomeini.

But when Mussadiq's Minister of Economy decided on opening new bakeries to lower food prices, which had spiraled due to the economic crisis created by the West's boycott of Iranian oil, Kashani encouraged the Grand Bazaar guilds to protest against the government's intervention in a free-market system. The Kashani-Mussadiq alliance started to deteriorate. It broke down when, in order to survive politically, Mussadiq began to rely increasingly on secular leftists. In January 1953,

Kashani opposed Mussadiq's request for an extension of his emergency powers by a year. He was then courted by Gen. Fazlollah Zahedi, a Shah loyalist. In April, when Zahedi was implicated in the killing of a policeman trying to arrest the kidnappers of the Tehran's pro-Mussadiq police chief, Gen. Mahmoud Afhartus, Kashani provided him refuge in the Majlis.

After the Shah's flight from Iran on August 16, 1953, CIA field officer Kermit Roosevelt laid his plans for an anti-Mussadiq coup. He was advised by his local cohort, Assadollah Rashidian, to co-opt Islamic leaders who were adept at providing large mobs swiftly. To win over Ayatollah Kashani, Roosevelt sent $10,000 [worth $450,000 today] to Kashani's confidante Ahmad Aramesh to be handed over to the ayatollah.[5] It is not known whether Aramash did as instructed. But Kashani was among those who turned up to greet the Shah at the airport when he returned to Tehran from Baghdad on August 22.

Kashani, however, did not have the backing of the majority of the Grand Bazaar's merchants and guild leaders, who remained loyal to Mussadiq, and never reconciled themselves to Washington's restoration of the Pahlavi dynasty. Time and again, the bazaar played an important role in countering and checking the Peacock Throne. In 1960, they closed the bazaar in protest against the blatant rigging of the Majlis poll and compelled the Shah to call on the parliamentarians to resign. They did, paving the way for fresh elections in early 1961.

Two years later, bazaaris throughout Iran played a pivotal role by shutting down the marketplace and demonstrating against the Shah's referendum on socioeconomic reforms, called the White Revolution, and leading mammoth protests against Khomeini's arrest on June 5, 1963, following his virulent attack on the White Revolution and its sponsor, the Shah himself. To quell the protest in and around the Grand Bazaar, the army troops resorted to firing on protestors, many of whom were killed.

Indeed, during his exile in Najaf from 1965 onward, Khomeini maintained close ties with the local mercantile community. A wealthy merchant was his chief financial supporter. And when he prepared a series of lectures on religious administration of Muslim countries between January and February of 1970—later published as *Hukumat-e Islam: Vilayat-e Faqih* (Islamic Government: Rule of the Faqih)—he delivered them at the main mosque of the bazaar.

Toward Revolution

The dramatic oil price rises in 1973–74 bolstered state income and fueled frantic economic activity in Iran, causing an unprecedented population shift from villages to cities. This, naturally, created a greater need for retailers, wholesalers, and bankers, and enlarged the bazaari, but it also fueled runaway inflation.

To tackle soaring inflation, the government passed an anti-profiteering law, which empowered special guild courts to enforce the application of the prices fixed by fiat by the central government nationally, requiring shopkeepers to display the mandated prices, which were also published in newspapers. Hundreds of young recruits of the ruling Rastakhiz (*lit.*, Renaissance) Party, mostly students and housewives, started checking prices in bazaars. Soon the total of such vigilantes reached ten thousand nationwide.

By the end of 1975, besides collecting 250,000 fines from traders, the guild courts had handed out further punishments to another one hundred and eighty thousand offenders, banished twenty-three thousand shopkeepers to internal exile away from their stores, and imprisoned eight thousand traders.[6] That is, a majority of half a million bazaaris were punished one way or another by the authorities. To add insult to injury, the Shah began favoring foreigners and big, modern Iranian commercial enterprises such as department stores and supermarkets. Feeling pressured, bazaar merchants turned to their age-old allies: clerics. But they too were under attack.

Being economically independent of the government, bazaaris were in the same category as students and intellectuals. They were also a formidable economic force. Despite the Shah's onslaughts, they and their business partners and affiliates controlled more than two-thirds of domestic wholesale trade and about a third of imports in 1978. Another estimate put the bazaari lending at 15 percent of all private credit.[7] Assured by clerics that Islam was committed to free enterprise, and that there was no place for price controls in it, bazaaris became early and ardent supporters of the anti-Shah movement, both morally and materially. Allied to clerics, students, and intellectuals, they propelled the anti-Shah protest in 1978 into a popular movement.

After the Revolution

A year later, during my visit to the Grand Bazaar, I found every single shop and stall displaying a flattering portrait of Khomeini. Those run by Azeri Turks hung up an additional picture of Grand Ayatollah Muhammad Kazem Shariatmadari, a fellow Azeri—the twinkle in his eyes penetrating his spectacles. Carpet merchants talked glowingly of doing brisk business in small carpets carrying Khomeini's image, bought for decorating walls at home and office. Traders told me that policemen had stopped harassing them and that they had discontinued their pay-offs to them, which had become an established practice after the Shah's anti-profiteering campaign.

On the other hand, with a slump in factory output caused by the last year's strikes and revolutionary turmoil, the economy was down and business had slumped. Even carpet sales had declined because, following a ban on their export, Iranians could no longer take money out of the country in the form of expensive carpets. So carpet prices fell steeply. Alcohol was a different matter altogether.

In the aftermath of newly enacted prohibition laws, the price of a bottle of whiskey shot up from Iranian Rls 900 ($11) to 5,000 ($63), to be consumed strictly at home.[8]

Nonetheless, the bazaari-clerical alliance remained intact. Bazaar merchants were keen to see the postrevolution situation stabilize, a process hampered by the terrorist activities of the Mujahedin-e Khalq (People's Mujahadin) Organization (MKO), which reached a peak with a bombing that killed seventy-four Islamic leaders in June 1981. Bazaar merchants urged a determined action by the government, thus favoring the hard-line faction within the ruling Islamic Republican Party (IRP).

They rallied behind the government in April 1982 when the elders of the Faiziya Seminary stripped Shariatmadari of his religious title after he had confessed knowledge of a failed coup attempt in which his son-in-law Ahmad Abbasi was involved. Long before that, Shariat0madari's portraits in Iran's bazaars had disappeared because of the disclosure of his contacts with the U.S. Central Intelligence Agency, as revealed by the confidential documents seized at the American Embassy in Tehran by the militant Iranian students in November 1979, and publicized by the Khomeini government. In late 1982, bazaar merchants applauded the Guardians Council's vetoing of a parliamentary bill specifying limits on land ownership: many of them had purchased agricultural land to enhance their social standing and had become absentee landlords.

The long-running war with Iraq, however, created conditions that ran counter to the interests of mercantile leaders. To divert scarce foreign exchange, derived solely from oil exports, for war materials, the government curtailed civilian imports, instituted rationing, thus interfering with the consumption patterns of the upper and middle classes, and introduced a complicated, three-tier exchange rate for the Iranian rial, which favored the state and penalized private traders.

A battle ensued between conservatives and leftists on foreign-trade nationalization. In May 1981, the government, led by left-of-center Prime Minister Mir Hussein Mousavi—a bearded, bespectacled architect with a degree in interior design from a British university—introduced a nationalization bill to the Majlis, well aware that Article 44 of the 1979 constitution placed foreign trade in the public sector and that replacing commercial middlemen would increase state revenue. Khomeini ratified it in November.

The following May, after passing it unanimously, the Majlis submitted it to the Guardians Council—composed of six theologians authorized to judge whether a bill is compatible with Islamic precepts and the constitution, and six legal jurists entitled to rule only on the bill's compatibility with the constitution. The council's theologians declared the bill un-Islamic, reasoning that total nationalization barred privately financed imports, thus contravening Islamic principles which regard private trading sacrosanct. They proposed that the foreign exchange earned by the private sector should be used to pay for imports by the traders' guilds. In practice, as exports of oil, a public sector industry, accounted for 98 percent of Iran's foreign exchange earnings, the private sector had to make do with a meager 2 percent of foreign currencies. This brought little comfort to affluent merchants and other rich Iranians.

When Iran's oil sales increased in late 1982 due to the price discounts it gave, the government eased the restrictions somewhat on the imports by the traders' guilds. By then, bolstered by the crushing of the MKO challenge and the expulsion of the Iraqis from the Iranian territory in the ongoing war, the Islamic regime acquired confidence.

Given this, and the pleas to Khomeini by bazaaris, Khomeini issued an Eight-Point Decree on Civil Liberties. It forbade arrest without warrant and curtailed the authority of Revolutionary

Courts by transferring the anti-Islamic crimes of morals from their jurisdiction to the Justice Ministry's public courts. Once the threat of arbitrary arrest by the local Revolutionary Komitehs[9] was removed, bazaaris took to large scale hoarding and profiteering, thus giving ammunition to religious leftists' arguments that, if given a chance, bazaaris would fatten themselves at the consumers' expense. It was only when Khomeini had addressed a special meeting of bazaaris' representatives that the latter exercised restraint in their pricing policies out of their profound reverence for the ayatollah.

In a climate of falling living standards caused by the war, affluent merchants became the butt of criticism by politicians. Prominent among those who criticized "the amassing of wealth by a small minority" was Hojatalislam Ali Akbar Hashemi Rafsanjani, Speaker of the Majlis, whose Mongoloid features and paucity of facial hair accorded him a distinctive look among the top leaders. Although a cleric, he did not spare religious institutions. In his Friday prayer sermon in March 1983, he followed his assertion that the Islamic endowments possessed the bulk of Iran's wealth with a proposal that their affairs be "put right."[10] In practice, nothing came of it.

Yet this was enough to move bazaar merchants to petition Khomeini, requesting him to instruct Rafsanjani to "refrain from making provocative statements against the business community and wealthy persons which were contrary to Islamic principles and were inspired mostly by Marxist thoughts." Rafsanjani ignored these moves, as did Khomeini. But thousands of theological students in Qom signed a petition, describing Rafsanjani as "the worthiest personality analyzing Islam in the path of the Islamic revolution." Fakhr al Din Hejazi, a radical parliamentarian, said, "Whenever the Majlis seeks to take a step for the welfare of the oppressed masses, it is accused of being 'socialist.' "[11]

Such actions and statements worried bazaar merchants, who

were fearful of the growth of state-aided consumer cooperatives, which they saw as a direct threat to their interests. The government had resorted to promoting them in its drive to curb profiteering by traders, encouraged by the shortages caused by the Iran-Iraq War and import controls. It combined this tactic with periodic appeals and threats directed at traders. In an interview with Tehran Radio on July 10, 1983, Mousavi said, "We have hundreds of thousands of shops in Tehran . . . Can one imagine that some three hundred to four hundred consumer cooperatives can take over all these services . . . Cooperatives are one of the revolutionary foundations of our society. So they are being strongly supported by the deprived people." At the same time the Prosecutor-General of the guilds court threatened "Islamic justice" to hoarders and profiteers, and warned that the guilty would be executed.[12]

The pro-bazaar Commerce Minister Habibollah Asghar-Owaldi, a rich merchant, resigned when his decision to transfer rice distribution to the private sector, resulting in a steep price rise, was reversed within days. His resignation combined with the state-sponsored campaign against "economic terrorists" created a gap between the bazaar and the administration.

Given the long history of the merchant-clergy alliance, the alienation between the bazaar and the Islamic government was unprecedented. It worried Khomeini, who had earlier reaffirmed his interpretation of Islam thus, "As long as there is Islam there will be free enterprise."[13]

Among the wide variety of select groups that were invited to Khomeini's headquarters in the north Tehran suburb of Jamran, where he appeared weekly to deliver a short speech, bazaar merchants were at the top. Addressing an assembly of bazaar elders on January 2, 1984, he said, "If bazaaris are not in step with the Islamic Republic, the public will suffer defeat . . . We should ignore our grievances for the sake of Islam."

Nine months later, Khomeini intervened in the debate on the public, private, and cooperative sectors thus: "The things that the government is not able to do, the government should not do. But do not prevent the bazaar from doing the things it can do."[14] He followed this up by issuing an Eight-Point Decree in March 1986, which was viewed as strengthening the foundation of the private sector.

However, the basic conflict between the interests of the better off and the worse off remained unresolved. Nor did it improve the living standards of ordinary Iranians whose annual population growth rate, according to the 1986 census, soared to 3.9 percent, one of the highest in the world. The per capita income declined by 45 percent between 1977–78 and 1989–90, a year after the end of the Iran-Iraq War.[15]

In that conflict, the Iranian bazaar contributed mightily in money and men. I discovered this when, during my visit to Tehran's Grand Bazaar in 1989, I arrived at a mosque, situated behind a two-story building sandwiched between shops along a narrow alleyway. It was the base of a unit of the *Niruyeh Muqawamatt Baseej* (Resistance Force Mobilization), commonly called the Baseej, a volunteer force established by Khomeini in 1981, primarily to bolster the manpower of the military. It was placed under the command of the Islamic Revolutionary Guard Corps (IRGC). Since there was no age limit to join the Baseej, its volunteers were aged fifteen to sixty-five years, and belonged to both sexes. Following the rationalization of the military and sundry security forces after the war, the Baseej, still commanded by the IRGC, became an auxiliary to the Law Enforcement Forces (LEF), which combined the police, gendarmerie, and Revolutionary Komitehs.

Sitting in a barely furnished room on the first floor, and sipping black tea sweetened by a sugar cube held between my lower lip and gum, I chatted with Sadiq Yazdani, a muscular man of twenty-three with a fleshy face and a thin black beard. "From this mosque there were twenty-five martyrs during the war with Iraq," he said. "The Baseej volunteers are all from the local area. Fifteen of them are university students. We meet two or three times a week. We do military training inside the mosque. There is no salary. We join for Islam and the Islamic system."[16]

On the fringes of the Grand Bazaar is the Marvi Seminary which, despite the abundance of computers on its premises, is a hotbed of hard-liners. Run by Ayatollah Muhammad Reza Mahdavi-Kani, leader of the conservative *Jame-e Rouhaniyat-e Mubarez* (Association of Combatant Clergy), it made a substantial contribution to the ranks of a regiment of clerics in the army formed during the Iran-Iraq War.

After the War

Once the war ended, the attention of the government—led by President Rafsanjani from 1989 onward—turned to reconstruction. He began liberalizing the economy. This had a beneficial effect. In 1990–91, the annual growth rate rose to 10.5 percent while inflation declined to 8 percent. At first, when Rafsanjani's liberalization drive focused on the domestic scene, he had the backing of the social conservatives—allied to bazaaris—in the Majlis. But when he extended the process to the economy's external dimension—abolishing the rial's three-tier exchange rate (Rls 70 to U.S. $1 for essential imports; Rls 600 to U.S. $1 for the industrial sector; and a floating rate for trade and services, which fluctuated around Rls 1,500–1,800 to U.S. $1), devaluing the local currency, securing foreign loans, setting up free-trade zones, and encouraging foreign investment and return of the exiled Iranian capital and expertise—his Majlis support split into economic nationalists, who gained the backing of Leader Ali Khamanei, and free-trade internationalists.

Rafsanjani's phased rationalization plan for the Iranian rial culminated in a single exchange rate on March 21, 1993, a few months before the presidential poll, when the rial devalued by 95.6 percent. As the government's foreign revenue consisted almost exclusively of income from oil sales paid in American dollars, the rial's devaluation had no effect on its income. But the cost of imports skyrocketed, and the annual inflation rate of 23 percent hurt salaried employees, including two million civil servants and some six hundred thousand soldiers.

Ahmad Tavakoli, the leading rival of Rafsanjani in the 1993 presidential contest, raised the slogan, "Less luxury and more austerity for leaders." It was targeted at the luxury cars and spacious villas of influential clerics in the affluent north Tehran, which increasingly set the leadership apart from their less fortunate compatriots. Many among the Islamic hierarchy, far from emulating the Spartan life of Khomeini, had succumbed to the lures of high living and corruption in an environment of rising unemployment (officially put at 14 percent) and soaring inflation, caused by the removal or curtailing of the subsidies on basic goods and services, a drastic devaluation of the rial, high-budget deficits, and low oil revenue, due to falling prices. The depressed living standards were confirmed by the Central Bank's per capita income estimate of $540 in 1993, which, though better than at the end of the war, was still 22 percent lower than under the Shah in 1978.[17]

Rafsanjani got reelected albeit on a much-reduced plurality. He persisted with his economic liberalization, despite its unpopularity, aware that he was constitutionally barred from running for presidency for the third time. The World Bank report in December 1995 stated that the previous six years had registered an impressive advance in the implementation of structural reform in the economy, and commended Tehran for being vigilant in repaying its foreign loans on time.

As the next presidential poll in May 1997 approached, there

was much speculation on the successor of Rafsanjani, in which bazaaris joined. Given their conservative leanings, they favored the religious establishment's favorite, Hojatalislam Ali Akbar Nateq-Nouri. But his rival, Hojatalislam Muhammad Khatami, won.

After Khatami's victory, the public debate shifted to political reform. It continued, despite a faltering economy caused by falling oil prices—at the lowest in four years—triggered by the severe downturn in "the tiger economies" of Southeast Asia in the summer of 1997, compounded by the decision of the Organization of Petroleum Exporting Countries (OPEC) in November to raise output by 10 percent to 27.5 million barrels per day. Khatami's lack of experience in economic policy or public finance made matters worse. At an annual growth rate of 1 percent and inflation at 25 percent, the economy was stagnant. It was creating only about half the jobs needed to absorb the rising number of graduating students.[18]

I was in Tehran a month after the massive university protest of July 1999, which escalated into the most widespread street violence nationwide since the revolution. During my visit to the capital's Grand Bazaar, the downbeat mood of those I interviewed was palpable.

"During the student protest, the rioters attacked the Bank Melli here," said Agha Shahi, a slim, young, bespectacled tailor with a diploma from a vocational college. "Yet the bazaar closed only for one day. These people were just expressing themselves." But, according to spice merchant Hamid Madani, a stocky man of forty-five, with bulging eyes, "The rioters were not students; they belonged to a special group paid to disturb the peace."

Abdul Karim Hadavi, a heavy-set textile merchant in his mid-thirties, blamed the riots for the recent weakness of the rial. Resting his elbows on the glass case displaying imported watches, the lean, intense-looking thirty-seven-year-old Jamal Gharazi, with his mind on the next year's assembly elections, said, "The

Majilis elections won't be real, they will be rigged." He added, "Khatami is good himself, but not other politicians. They want to make money for themselves. Look at Rafsanjani. He controls everything. He is involved in politics, but he is a very rich man."

Shahi the tailor was despondent about political reform and its impact. "Even if the Majlis goes the Khatami way, not much will change." He would prove prescient.

In the Majlis election, reformists performed well, capturing almost two-thirds of the seats. But their initial hopes of furthering political reform were frustrated by the conservatives controlling the Guardians Council and the top echelons of the judiciary. By 2002, it was clear that the reform movement had run into sand.

The following year, the Anglo-American invasion of Iraq engaged bazaaris as well as all other Iranians not only because Iraq is a neighboring country but also because it has the Shia holy cities of Najaf and Karbala, the respective burial places of Imam Ali, the cousin and son-in-law of Prophet Muhammad, and his son Imam Hussein.

President Saddam Hussein's overthrow, followed by the chaos that ensued, paved the way for pious Iranian Shias to make pilgrimage to Najaf and Karbala. Among the first merchants from Tehran's Grand Bazaar to take advantage of the changed situation was forty-year-old clothier Hajji Muhammad Ibrahim Khiyat, a small, stout man, pale-faced, with a crew cut and a close shave that left intact a barely visible mustache. His "Hajji" title meant that he had done the hajj pilgrimage to Mecca. During his trip to Iraq, he visited not just Najaf and Karbala but, being a Twelver Shia[19] also Samarra, where the eleventh Shia Imam Hassan al Askari is buried and the last Imam Muhammad al Qasim disappeared—he told me during my last visit to Tehran's Grand Mosque in July 2004.

"My textile shop is twenty years old," he said, moving the olive green beads in his rosary with his thumb. "My father has a shop in another part of the bazaar. We have been trading in the bazaar for six generations." In other words, his family has been trading ever since the Grand Bazaar was established some 150 years ago.

His shop, overfilled with rolls of broadcloth displayed the pictures of Imam Ali, Khomeini, Khamanei, and Khatami. As a stream of fellow-traders, mullahs, and sundry friends passed by his shop, he nodded pleasantly and exchanged the latest prices and rumors. "Iran's oil revenue does not impact on my business," he said. "People buy clothing because it is their second basic necessity after food. My business is seasonal. Now is high season and business is good."

He proudly declared himself to be a member of the five thousand-strong Baseej unit based in the Grand Bazaar. "Not all Baseejis are bearded, wearing scruffy clothes," he said with a smile. "The Baseej work with the police to safeguard the bazaar, and mount joint patrols at night."

A staunch supporter of the Islamic regime, Khiyat regards voting as his religious duty. He has not missed any of the twenty-one elections and three referendums held in Iran since the revolution, when he was fifteen.[20] He even participated in the 2004 Majlis poll when only one out of three Tehranis bothered to vote. He assured me that bazaaris voted in strength as before.

"After all," I said, "bazaar merchants had played a leading role in getting Muzaffar al-Din Shah to establish the Majlis, the first parliament in the region." He nodded in agreement, saying, "The First Majlis was convened near the Grand Bazaar, and today the modern Majlis building is only a kilometer and a half from here."

Majlis:
Voice of the People

◆ CHAPTER 2 ◆

A striking feature of the domed, three-story building of Iran's parliament—called Islamic Majlis[1]—standing on a vast platform at the top of a short flight along Khomeini Road in south Tehran is its façade: thick marble planks running horizontally and vertically, forming large empty squares. What could possibly be the purpose of such a bizarre structure, you wonder.

The answer lies in the thirty-four line sketches you see inside the chamber that embellish the semicircular press and visitors' gallery along its circumference[2] and represent the members of the First Majlis (1980–84) of the Islamic Republic who were blown up by a bomb in June 1981 planted by the opposition Mujahedin-e Khalq Organization (MKO). The purpose of the strange façade is to protect the building from a bomb blast from the street.

To get to the visitors' and press gallery, a visitor will have to undergo three body searches—at the outer entrance of the Majlis complex, where he/she will be shorn of all things metallic, including rings and any other jewelry; then at the entrance to the Majlis building; and, finally, before entering the chamber, through a corridor emblazoned with the slogans: " 'Neither East nor West' should be our internal and external policy"; "Islam without clerics is like a country without doctors"; and "Majlis is the guardian of Islam."

The chamber, which housed the Senate during Muhammad Reza Shah's reign, is furnished with a deep royal-blue carpet and a vast chandelier hanging from a high roof, and decorated with elaborate interiors designed by the Parisian House of Jansen, reflecting the Shah's love of French art and design. On its floor, the first two semicircular rows with red-plush seats, reserved for ministers and top civil servants, are followed by seven expanding concentric rows for the deputies—each with a glass-topped desk and a microphone—to accommodate 350 representatives.

Facing them, on the day of my first visit there in April 1983, was the presiding officer on a podium, Deputy Speaker Hojatal-islam Muhammad Yazdi, a chubby-faced man of fifty-two, with a neatly trimmed beard, wearing clerical robes and a white turban. Of the 234 sitting deputies, 171 were present—the figure displayed on the screens to the right and left of Yazdi as well as on the one facing him across the vast hall.

Elected in 1980, members of this Majlis proved their independence from the executive by exercising their right to accept or reject the Prime Minister recommended to them by the President, who was head of the executive branch. They rejected President Ali Khamanei's first choice for Prime Minister—conservative Ali Akbar Velayati—and favored Mir Hussein Mousavi, a left-of-center politician, by a majority of three to one.

While the three women deputies wore standard black chadors, men were dressed variously, with Kurdish members in long shirts and billowing trousers, and some deputies in business suits with open neck shirts. It was hard to spot a single male representative who was clean shaven. Even though clerics were a minority in the Majlis, the overall visual impression was of a place dominated by turbans.

The deputies discussed flooding caused by overflowing rivers along the border with Iraq. Some suggested that the Agriculture Ministry should plant trees to tackle the problem. Next, they debated the labor welfare bill's provision of the transferability of insurance and medical care of a worker. It was passed by ninety-eight votes to seventy-seven, the figures appearing on the electronic indicator on the wall facing the deputies. The proceedings were being broadcast live on the state-run radio.

The main event of the day, however, was the grilling that the deputies gave to the Commerce Minister, accusing him of mal-distribution of basic necessities sold through the rationing system introduced due to the war with Iraq. Looking harassed, the Minister, wearing a business suit, an open-neck shirt, and the ubiquitous stubble—a de rigueur for public officials of the Islamic Republic as a sign of modesty—promised to do better and distribute the staples properly and rationally. The deputies gave him two months to submit a progress report. It would prove unsatisfactory and he would end up resigning. Ministers and senior bureaucrats are also questioned vigorously by several Majlis committees behind closed doors.

No wonder that over years the Iranian Majlis came to be described by many Western reporters as the liveliest parliamentary forum in the Middle East, surpassed only by the Israeli Knesset (*lit.*, Assembly). If further evidence of this was required, it came twenty-one years after my first visit to the chamber.

In January 2004, the alcove on the top floor of the Majlis building became the site of a sit-in not by protesting citizens but their parliamentary representatives. Between 50 and 120 deputies participated, and their protest went on for three weeks, five days a week. All along the atmosphere was relaxed, with some parliamentarians bringing their children in tow. They also fasted from sunrise to sunset in protest, and broke the fast together. They were protesting against the Guardians Council's decision to bar eighty-three of them from contesting the next parliamentary election.

Of the 8,200 applicants for 290 seats, the Council had rejected nearly 3,600. President Muhammad Khatami and Majlis Speaker Haojatalislam Mahdi Karrubi intervened on their behalf, and Leader Ali Khamanei publicly instructed the council to reconsider the cases. They reinstated 1,160 applicants, but increased the number of the rejected incumbents by six to eighty-seven.

This was the most severe crisis that the Majlis had faced since the founding of the Islamic Republic. Yet, while the state-run Islamic Republic of Iran Broadcasting (IRIB) continued to air the Majlis proceedings on one of its radio channels, it ignored the deputies' unprecedented sit-in.

Majlis Under Monarchy

Ever since a Majlis was conceded by Muzaffar al Din Shah in August 1906, it has been the stage where the drama of a tug-of-war between the ruler and the ruled has been played out, and where the still unresolved issue of sovereignty has been debated time and again: does it lie with God, the Twelfth Imam, senior Shia clergy, or the people?

Clerics have been a regular feature of the Majlis ever since its inception. As many trade guilds elected them as their representatives, they occupied a majority of the elected 106 seats in the First Majlis under the monarchy.

During the two month-long session, a debate raged between the purist clerics and the pragmatic—all of them being Twelver Shias, who believe that the last Shia Imam, Muhammad al Qasim, the infant son of the Eleventh Imam, went into occultation in Samarra, Iraq in 873 AD, and will end his concealment at the end of time, and institute justice and order in the world. The purists argued that in the absence of the Twelfth Imam, the present "Government of the Cruel" should be replaced by a constitutional government of the Just Mujtahids, those clerics entitled to practice interpretative reasoning regarding the Sharia, Islamic law.

The pragmatists, forming a large majority in the Majlis, agreed with the purists' sentiment, but found it impossible to implement it. The moderates within their ranks wanted to check the monarch's arbitrariness along the lines laid out in such European constitutions as Belgium's, while the radicals advocated limiting the ruler's power within an Islamic framework. On sovereignty, the radicals argued that since it had been delegated by God to the (Twelfth) Imam, and then to the mujtahids, it did not rest with the people. Their view was opposed by moderate clerics and secular constitutionalists. The latter group won. "Sovereignty is a trust confided [as a Divine gift] by the People to the person of the King," stated Article 35.[3]

While following the Belgian model, with its separation of powers between the legislative, executive, and judicial organs of the government, the Majlis deputies framed the constitution within an Islamic context. Article 1 declared Jaafari or Twelver Shiaism as state religion.[4] Only a Jaafari Shia could become king, minister, or judge. Article 39 enjoined upon the monarch to "promote the Jaafari doctrine" and to "seek the help of the holy spirits of the Saints of Islam to render service to the advancement of Iran." Article 20 declared the press to be free within the framework of the Sharia. Article 22 required the right of free association to be dependent on an organization's stand toward Islam. Article 29 confirmed the right of Sharia courts to exist.

The Majlis deputies passed these Fundamental Laws unanimously and rushed them to the seriously ill Muzaffar al Din Shah. He ratified them on December 30, 1906, and died five days later. His son, Muhammad Ali Shah, tried to emulate his dictatorial grandfather, Nasser al Din. So the Majlis produced the longer Supplementary Fundamental Laws, which outlined the citizens' bill of rights, and a parliamentary form of government, with power concentrated in the legislature—composed of a 136-member Majlis with a two-year term and a sixty-member Senate also with a two-year tenure[5]—at the expense of the executive, with the cabinet being responsible to the Majlis.

Significantly, Article 2 specified that no bill passed by the Majlis was valid until a committee of five mujtahids—elected by the Majlis from a list of twenty submitted by the Shia clergy—had judged it to be in conformity with Islam. In practice, however, this Article was never implemented. The Qajar rulers ignored it, as did the Pahlavis.

Muhammad Ali Shah signed the new document in October 1907, but only after widespread demonstrations and the assassination of his Prime Minister. The two sets of Laws, forming the Iranian constitution, ushered in the Constitutional Revolution.

The Shah was still reluctant to become a figurehead monarch. He used an attempt to assassinate him in mid-June 1908 as a pretext to mount a coup against the elected government. On June 23, he ordered his palace guard to bomb the Majlis building, which was being defended by seven thousand lightly armed constitutionalists. In the ensuing fight, over 250 people were killed. He dissolved the First Majlis, declared martial law, and waged a campaign of terror against his opponents. A civil war ensued. By mid-July, he had lost and secured refuge in the Russian Embassy. He abdicated in favor of his twelve-year-old son, Ahmad (r. 1909–25), in whose name a Regent exercised power.

In November 1909, the Second Majlis approved the appointment of William Shushter, an American economist, as the Treasurer-General to increase the state's falling revenue. He organized a special tax-collecting force and deployed it everywhere, including the northern region, then regarded as a Russian zone of influence. In November 1911, having ordered his troops to occupy Iran's Caspian Sea ports of Enzali and Rasht, the Russian Tsar gave an ultimatum that failure to remove Shuster within two days would lead to the Russian occupation of Tehran. But it was only after the deadline had passed, and the Russian troops had begun marching toward Tehran, that the Majlis decided to dismiss Shuster. To placate the Tsar, the Iranian Regent dismissed the Majlis for having defied Moscow's ultimatum. Though the Regent did not abrogate the 1906–7 constitution, his dismissal of the Majlis marked the end of the Constitutional Revolution.

However, it was not long before the Majlis was revived. It

performed a vital role at pivotal points during the monarchical rule—in 1920 when it preserved Iran's independence by rejecting the Anglo-Persian Agreement of the previous year, in 1925 by deposing Ahmad Shah, and in 1951 by compelling Muhammad Reza Pahlavi Shah to appoint nationalist Muhammad Mussadiq his Prime Minister.

During World War I, Iran's neutrality meant little to Russia and Britain, the two Great Powers that had loomed large on the Iranian horizon. Moscow forced Ahmad Shah to dissolve the Third Majlis in 1915. But the predominantly anti-Russian, pro-German majority in the Majlis refused to accept the royal decree, moved to the holy city of Qom, and set up a parallel government there. It lasted until 1917 when Qom fell to the advancing Russians.

By the end of the war, the Iranian government was in such dire financial straits that only British subsidies kept it solvent. This encouraged Britain's Foreign Minister, Lord Curzon, to realize his dream of turning Iran into a British protectorate. He concluded a secret agreement with the Tehran government in 1919 that gave Britain enormous political, economic, and military control over Iran. When the terms of the agreement were disclosed on the eve of a debate in the Fourth Majlis, there was furor not only in Iran but also in America and Bolshevik Russia. The Majlis refused to ratify it, and this led to the downfall of the government of pro-British Hassam Khan Vossuq al Dawla.[6]

Britain then tried to supplant the monarchical authority with a new and strong force in the persona of Col. Reza Khan, commander of the powerful Cossack Brigade, formed originally in 1879 and led by Russian officers. In February 1921, he overthrew the government of Prime Minister Fathollah Gilani, and had the Shah appoint a pro-British journalist Zia al Din Tabtabai his Prime Minister. Tabtabai was soon eased out and, in the subsequent cabinet, Reza Khan became Minister of War. By late 1923, he had moved up to premiership.

In February 1925, when Ahmad Shah was on a European tour, Reza Khan secured the emergency powers from the Majlis, including the title of the Commander in Chief of the military. Eight months later, the Fifth Majlis (1924–26) voted by eighty votes to five, with thirty abstentions, to depose Ahmad Shah and appoint Reza Khan as Regent. He ordered the convening of the Constituent Assembly of 260 members. Packed with his backers, the Constituent Assembly proclaimed him Iran's monarch in December 1925. He thus became Reza Shah.

The Majlis Under the Pahlavis

Since the dictatorial Reza Shah needed a pliable Majlis to implement his policies, he resorted to manipulating elections. With the help of the police chiefs of the capital and the provinces, he would draw up a list of desirable candidates for the benefit of the Interior Minister in charge of the polling. The Minister would then forward these names to Provincial Governors-general, who would pass them on to the local Electoral Councils, charged with supervising the balloting. As these councils consisted mainly of men who were close to the Interior Ministry, they complied readily. In line with Reza Shah's antipathy toward the clergy, the number of mullahs in the Majlis declined rapidly. The Eleventh Majlis (1936–38) did not have a single well-known cleric.

This pattern continued until Reza Shah's overthrow by Britain and the Soviet Union in 1941, due to his refusal to end his neutrality in World War II, when he named his son, Muhammad Reza, as his successor. Following the failed attempt on his life in February 1949, the Shah convened a Constituent Assembly with a view to increasing his powers. At his behest, the Constituent Assembly stripped the Majlis of its power to appoint the Prime Minister for endorsement by the Shah and gave it to the Shah, with the Majlis relegated to endorsing his nomination. The Constituent Assembly also resolved to establish a Senate, thus implementing a provision in the 1906–07 constitution, and authorized the Shah to nominate half of its sixty members. Due to these changes, the poll for the Sixteenth Majlis dragged on from July 1949 to February 1950.

The election campaign, dominated by the nationalization of the oil industry monopolized by the British-owned Anglo-Iranian Oil Company (AIOC)—whose history is outlined in Chapter Seven—led to the new legislature being dominated by the pro-nationalization deputies. On March 7, 1951, while the nation was in the grip of a heated debate on the subject, Khalil Tahmasibi, a member of the clandestine Fedaiyan-e Islam (*lit.*, Self-Sacrificers for Islam), assassinated the pro-British Premier Gen. Ali Razmara inside a Tehran mosque.

Reflecting the national mood, the Majlis followed up its passing of a motion on nationalization with the specifics of the takeover of the AIOC on April 28. The Senate too adopted the nationalization bill. In an unprecedented move, the Majlis recommended by a large majority that Mussadiq, leader of the National Front—a secular, nationalist party committed to ending Britain's economic imperialism in Iran—be appointed the Premier. On May 1, the Shah signed the oil nationalization bill, and named Mussadiq his Prime Minister. Over Britain's loud protests, AIOC passed into Iranian hands.

London found a way of striking back. During the run-up to the elections to the Seventeenth Majlis, Britain's Iranian agents, flush with cash, bribed candidates and provincial elders. Yet Mussadiq's National Front secured all the twelve seats in Tehran. Elsewhere, in the absence of proper monitoring of ballots, results proved contentious, with violence erupting in several provincial cities. Once the Mussadiq government was convinced that some of the elected parliamentarians were henchmen of the British agents, it decided to halt the poll after seventy-nine results had been announced—to stop "the destabilization of Iran, plotted by foreigners"—until the return of Iran's delegation, led by Mussadiq, a trained lawyer, from The Hague: it had gone there to argue the case for oil nationalization before the International Court of Justice. (Due to the crisis that developed soon after, elections to the remaining fifty-seven seats were not held.)

This Majlis too broke new ground by asserting a right for the government that the Shah had usurped earlier. On July 13, when Mussadiq insisted on appointing his War Minister, a privilege hitherto exercised by the monarch in his capacity as the active Commander in Chief of the military, the Shah refused to yield. Mussadiq resigned. But the Shah's nomination of Ahmad Qavam al Saltane as Premier met with strikes, riots, and demonstrations for five days. Relenting, the Shah recalled Mussadiq.

On August 3, the Majlis gave Mussadiq emergency powers for six months to tackle the deteriorating economic situation due to the boycott of the Iranian oil by the West. And in late October, the Majlis voided the pro-Shah Senate's vote to extend its life unilaterally by another four years. In mid-January 1953, Mussadiq secured a yearlong extension of his emergency powers from the Majlis. He appointed himself acting War Minister. The Shah objected. To dramatize his disapproval, he threatened to leave Iran immediately, wanting to galvanize his forces and confront Mussadiq. Unwilling to confront the Shah then, Mussadiq backed down.

To conciliate the Prime Minister and the Shah, the Majlis appointed a committee. It ruled that since the constitution put the military under the government's jurisdiction, the Shah should cede his active command of the military. He refused. On May 24, all but three of the fifty-seven deputies present voted to implement the committee's recommendation. The Majlis thus asserted its constitutional rights.

In July 1953, Mussadiq called on his Majlis supporters to resign so that he could call fresh elections without the Shah's concurrence. All but twenty-three did so, thus depriving the Majlis of a quorum and causing a de facto dissolution. On July 27, Mussadiq ordered a referendum on the dissolution of both houses. Since the opposition boycotted it, he won almost all the votes. He then formally dissolved the Majlis and the Senate.

Following his return to power on the coattails of the CIA coup in mid-August within a few days of his flight from Iran, the Shah tried to turn the Majlis into his echo chamber as his father had done, and succeeded. In the wake of the 1956 census, he expanded the Majlis from 136 members to 200, and the following year he extended its tenure to four years. He rigged the election to the Nineteenth Majlis in August 1960 so blatantly that there was mass protest in which the outlawed National Front played an important role. The Shah called on the deputies to resign, and thus prepare the ground for a fresh poll in early 1961.

The general election to the Twentieth Majlis too was fraudulent, though not to the same extent as the one before. The emboldened National Front called for the dissolution of the Majlis. This happened. But the subsequent poll for the Twenty-first Majlis too was marred by electoral irregularities. A further dissolution followed. As the government of Prime Minister Ali Amini resorted to ruling by decree, the opposition became restless. On the other hand, the absence of the Majlis fueled the Shah's dream of becoming an absolute ruler.

The White Revolution

This was the backdrop to the Shah's launching of a six-point socioeconomic reform package, including votes for women, called the White Revolution, in January 1963. He called a referendum on the White Revolution. The National Front urged a boycott not because of the content of the package but because of its unconstitutionality since the Shah had bypassed the Majlis and issued it as a royal decree. Its stance led to a fresh jailing of its leaders. After his release from jail in 1957, Mussadiq was placed under house arrest with thirty guards to keep watch on him.[7] As expected, the referendum revealed an almost unanimous support for the White Revolution.

Following the enfranchising of women in 1963, the Shah ordered a general election. The resulting Twenty-second Majlis saw the emergence of the officially sponsored New Iran Party in the chamber. The opposition was represented by an earlier, Court-sponsored group, Mardom (People's) Party. The Twenty-third Majlis, elected in 1967, was housed in a newly built building. In the wake of the dramatic oil price rise in 1973 to 1974, the Shah noticed that the ruling New Iran Party was taking all the credit for an impressive economic achievement, and giving no quarter to the Mardom. Fearing that the minority party might become the base for genuine and open opposition to his regime, he decided to include it in the government as well. That meant creating a single political entity.

So, on March 8, 1975, came the inauguration of the Rastakhiz Party with Amir Abbas Hoveida as its leader. In the election for the Twenty-fourth Majlis in June, the Rastakhiz polled nearly five million votes out of 7 million cast.

It proved to be the last legislature under the 1906–7 constitution.

After the Islamic Revolution

In the era of the Islamic republic, the Islamic Majlis has emerged as one of the main political actors. It made its mark by impeaching the first popularly elected President Abol Hassan Bani-Sadr in 1981 for incompetence—a charge he failed to rebut by refusing to appear before the Majlis, which had earlier passed a law setting out a procedure to judge his competence and provide him with an opportunity to defend himself.

Soon after, it rejected President Khamanei's first nominee, Velayati, as the Prime Minister. Its tightening of the 1985 Press

Law in July 1999 triggered the student protest that shook the Islamic regime. A year later it became the focus of public debate on press freedom.

After the proclamation of the Islamic Republic of Iran on April 1, 1979, in the wake of a 98 percent "yes" vote in a referendum under universal suffrage on the subject, Khomeini decreed the election of a seventy-three-member Assembly of Experts—each member representing about half a million people—on June 30. The three non-Muslim members were to represent the Christian, Jewish, and Zoroastrian communities. Among the seventy Muslim members elected in early August, forty-five were clerics: four-fifths of them either belonged to or were sympathetic to the governing Islamic Republican Party (IRP). Among the lay members, almost half were either IRP members or in sympathy with it. The IRP was established within a month of the February 1979 revolution by Iran's leading clerics, with the main aim of guarding the revolution and infusing Islamic principles into political, economic, cultural, and military spheres of society. As well as encouraging individuals to join it, the founders of the IRP urged the existing Islamic Associations in offices, schools and universities, factories, and bazaars to affiliate to it.

Starting August 19, the Assembly finished the job of producing a 175-Article constitution within two months.

The draft document presented to it did not contain the *Vilayet-e Faqih* (Rule of Religious Jurisprudent) doctrine because the group of clerics and nonclerics, informally appointed by Khomeini to produce a draft, felt that this concept was more of an ideal to be achieved in the future rather than something to be implemented straight away. However, once the election to the Assembly of Experts resulted in producing a large majority of clerical members, most of them affiliated to or sympathetic with the IRP, the leaders of the Islamic Republic lost their initial hesitancy, and came to perceive this doctrine as essential to laying a sound foundation of theocracy. It was therefore introduced, discussed, and adopted in the course of the debate that followed. This doctrine, developed by Khomeini in his book *Hukumat-e Islam: Vilayet-e Faqih* (*Islamic Government: Rule of the Faqih*), stated that an Islamic regime required an Islamic ruler who is thoroughly conversant with the Sharia and is just in its application: a Just Faqih. He should be assisted by jurisprudents at various levels of the legislative, executive, and judicial bodies. The function of a popularly elected parliament, open to both lay believers and clerics, is to resolve the conflicts likely to arise in the implementation of Islamic principles. However, judicial functions are to be performed only by the jurisprudents conversant with the Sharia. Such jurisprudents also oversee the actions of the legislative and executive branches. The overall supervision and guidance of parliament and judiciary rests with the Just Faqih, who must also ensure that the executive does not exceed its powers. Khomeini's vilayet-e faqih doctrine became the backbone of the Iranian constitution.

At the apex of power was the Leader of the Islamic Republic who was the Commander in Chief of all armed forces, and had the authority to declare war or peace. He had the power to approve presidential candidates, and appoint the President on his election by popular vote, or dismiss him after the Supreme Court had found him politically incompetent and in violation of his duties, as determined by the Majlis. He was empowered to appoint the highest judicial authorities and the Islamic jurists to the Guardians Council charged with vetting all legislation in the light of Islamic precepts and the constitution.

The Guardians Council consisted of six faqihs, (Islamic jurisprudents), conscious of current needs and the issues of the day, to be appointed by the Leader, and six jurists, specializing in different branches of Islamic law, to be elected by parliament from a list of qualified candidates submitted by the head of the judiciary, and appointed by the Leader. All guardians voted on the compatibility of a bill passed by the Majlis with the constitution, but only the six faqihs ruled on its compatibility with Islamic precepts. The Council also vetted all candidates for public office at the national level for their loyalty to the constitution and Islam, and the results of the elections.

On the vexatious question of sovereignty, the Islamic constitution provided a compromise. "Absolute sovereignty over the world and man belongs to God, and it is He who has placed man in charge of his social destiny," read Article 56. "The people exercise this God-given right by the paths specified in the Articles below." The next Article stated that "These [legislative, executive, and judicial] powers are independent of each other, and communication between them will be ensured by the President of the Republic."

Article 113 specified that the President was "responsible for implementing the constitution," and described him as the head of the executive power, except for the affairs pertaining directly to the Leader. Elected directly for a four-year term, the President nominated a suitable person as Prime Minister who then had to win the endorsement of the Majlis before taking up office. Of the 270 Majlis seats, four were allocated to non-Muslims: two to Christians and one each to Jews and Zoroastrians.

The incorporation of the Vilayet-e Faqih doctrine into the constitution went down badly not only with secular and leftist parties and groups but also the quietist school among Shia clerics, the most prominent among them being Grand Ayatollah Muhammad Kazem Shariatmadari, who opposed clerical participation in state administration, except in the judiciary. They called on their followers to boycott the referendum on the constitution to be held in early December 1979. But their plans went awry when militant students stormed the U.S. Embassy in Tehran on November 4 and took dozens of diplomats as hostage—the details of which are given in Chapter Nine. This event enabled the Khomeini government to rally the nation in its dramatic conflict with America, and drained away support from those opposing it, whether religious or secular—all the more so as the authorities rushed to publish the sensational material the militant students discovered inside the embassy showing clandestine contacts between the U.S. mission and many of the Islamic regime's opponents. In this politically charged atmosphere, any detractor of the Khomeini's government came through as a stooge of the highly unpopular U.S. administration of President Jimmy Carter. The Islamic government thus succeeded in securing an overwhelming popular support for the constitution. As for those who opposed the constitution, they became ineligible for contesting the presidency or Majlis seats, so declared the Guardians Council.

In the First Majlis, clerics exceeded nonclerics by a small margin. The party-wise breakdown was: the IRP, eighty-five; IRP allies, forty-five; the Liberation Movement of Iran, twenty; and independents, eighty-four.[8] Since the main aim of the IRP—to guard the Islamic revolution and infuse Islamic principle into political, economic, cultural, and military spheres of society— was much too general, it was more a movement rather than a party with specific aims and objectives. While encouraging individuals to join it, the founders of the IRP urged Islamic Associations to affiliate to it. These associations were formed voluntarily at workplaces, educational institutions, neighborhoods, and military garrisons during and after the revolution. They identified un-Islamic elements, guarded the security of military units, strengthened Islamic culture, and encouraged voter participation in elections and referendums. On the socioeconomic issues, the IRP did not have a coherent socioeconomic ideology or program. It contained those who favored strong public sector and active governmental intervention in the economy as well as those who held contrary views. When the differences between the two factions became irreconcilable, Khomeini acted as an arbiter, and alternatively favored one or the other.

The Liberation Movement of Iran, formed in 1961, by Mahdi Bazargan, a pious layman, and Ayatollah Mahmoud Taleqani, a left-of-center cleric, to link Shia Islam with modern political ideas and movements. After the revolution, Khomeini appointed Bazargan Prime Minister of the provisional government, which lasted about nine months.

But the discipline in the ruling IRP was not so tight as to ensure the endorsement of President Khamanei's first nominee, Velayati. The fact that left-of-center Mousavi—a British-trained architect and interior designer, who became the chief editor of the IRP's newspaper *Jumhouri-ye Islami* (Islamic Republic)—won the deputies' vote of confidence by three to one showed that the Majlis had more leftists than conservatives. Most of the rest would be Independents. Confusingly, while pursuing different agendas, many conservatives and leftists (including Mousavi) belonged to the IRP. When it came to impeaching President Bani-Sadr on June 20, 1981, for pursuing policies considered harmful to the fledgling Republic when he defied the orders of Khomeini, the constitutional Leader of the Republic, and lost the loyalty of military commanders, then engaged in a war with Iraq, who publicly swore their allegiance to Khomeini and the constitution, both factions closed ranks and, assisted by many independents, produced 177 votes. Within two years of its formation, the IRP and its allied groups occupied all political space.

On the other hand, IRP factions had become so deeply divided on socioeconomic issues and foreign policy, between pro-private sector conservatives who favored increased diplomatic and economic links with the West (except America) and pro-public sector leftists who opposed closer ties with the West that their infighting impeded the workings of the executive and the legislature. The pressing demands of the war with Iraq favored those who wanted governmental management of the economy in order to deploy the scarce resources more efficiently. This ran against the traditional bias of clerics in favor of the bazaar and free-market economy. Hence the Iranian government was bedeviled by tensions it could not resolve one way or the other, and had to resort to seeking the mediation of Khomeini, who was aging fast. He would go on to establish an Expediency Council in January 1988 to formally resolve differences between the Majlis, the President, and the Guardians Council.

In the Second Majlis (1984–88), where only two-fifths of sitting deputies were reelected, neither faction had a majority. Yet the Majlis again endorsed Mousavi when President Khamanei presented him as his choice after his own reelection in 1985—chiefly because Khomeini, keen to maintain a balance between the two factions, favored Mousavi, and conservative Khamanei had to go along with what Khomeini wanted. That uneasy cohabitation did not lessen the friction that existed between the executive headed by Khamanei and the legislature to which Mousavi was beholden.

Indeed, by mid-1986, the tension between two IRP factions had become so acute that Khomeini appointed a mediation council to conciliate them. It failed. So he ordered the party's dissolution in July 1987.

To provide political alternatives to the people, Khomeini encouraged the radicals—those who gave priority to social and economic justice at the expense of free enterprise—within the long-established Association of Combatant Clergy to break away and form the *Majma-e Rouhaniyoun-e Mobarez* (Society of Combatant Clerics) in March 1988, and set up its own religious network, to be activated on the eve of elections and referendums. Led by Hojatalislam Mahdi Karrubi, a small, dapper man of fifty-one, noted for his meticulously trimmed beard and undiminishing glimmer in his eyes, it fared well in the general election.

43

In the Third Majlis (1988–92), the leftist camp—including the Society of Combatant Clerics and the older Mujahedin of the Islamic Revolution, established soon after the revolution as a leftist group, providing an alternative to the young Iranians who belonged to secularist Marxist groups—which had co-opted moderates—claimed the loyalty of two-thirds of the deputies. It legalized chess and amateur boxing, created an environment that encouraged growth in the theater, and revived traditional Iranian and Western classical music. It also exempted soccer players and wrestlers from a ban on wearing shorts or other "immodest" clothing as well as spectators from watching these sports.

Article 109 in the old constitution required the Leader to be a *marja-e taqlid* (source of emulation)—a status accorded to Khomeini—and possess "political and social perspicacity, courage, strength, and the necessary administrative abilities for leadership." This article, amended in 1989, required the Leader to be merely scholarly in different fields of fiqh (religious jurisprudence); and possess "right political and social perspicacity, prudence, courage, administrative abilities, and adequate capability for leadership." In other words, the Leader did not have to be a marja-e taqlid, a grand ayatollah. (At any given time, there were about a dozen grand ayatollahs among an estimated 150–180 million Shias worldwide.) This provision therefore caused a disjunction between the constitutional position of the Leader and the traditional Shia religious hierarchy.

The amended Article 110 increased the Leader's powers, authorizing him to delineate "general policies after consultation with the Expediency Council"; supervise "the proper execution of the general policies of the system"; resolving problems "which cannot be solved by conventional methods, through the Expediency Council"; and appoint the Chief Commander of the Islamic Revolutionary Guards Corps (IRGC) and the Head of the radio and television network, the Islamic Republic of Iran Broadcasting (IRIB).

By dispensing with the Prime Minister's post—prescribed by Article 124 of the 1979 constitution—which had hindered efficient administration, and authorizing the President to appoint one or more Vice Presidents, the amended document ushered in an era of executive presidency.

On July 30, 1989, Iranians voted on the constitutional amendments as well as for one of the presidential candidates. They endorsed the new constitution almost unanimously, and elected Ali Akbar Hashemi Rafsanjani as President by a plurality of 95 percent. The voter turnout of 14.2 million amounted to 70 percent of the total.

The leftist-dominated Majlis resisted Rafsanjani's plans to liberalize the economy to the extent that he collaborated with Khamanei, now elevated to Leader, to ensure the fall of leftists in the elections to the Fourth Majlis in April 1992 by getting the Guardians Council to do their bidding. The Council's Competence and Qualification Committee disqualified a third of the prospective candidates, including 45 sitting deputies.[9]

As it was, an aspiring candidate had to be cleared by the Provincial Supervisory Body and the Ministry of Interior before his/her application reached the Guardians Council. In a Friday prayer sermon in March, Khamaeni upheld the vetting system used by the Guardians Council, and backed Rafsanjani and his cabinet. He urged the electorate to vote for the candidates favoring economic reform.[10]

The election campaign was quite lively with many outdoor rallies and colorful posters. But most of the leftists, who were allowed to contest, lost. This was due to the common perception that leftists were inclined to be more ideological and slogan-eering rather than pragmatic, and the public mood after many years of revolution and war had turned decidedly against slogans. Also, in the postwar period, popular opinion turned increasingly against a strong public sector, which had emerged as a result of the revolution, when the regime had no choice but to take over the properties and industries owned by the super-rich Pahlavi Foundation and many affluent families who fled. The war with Iraq accelerated the direct role the Iranian state was playing in Iranian life.

In the first round on April 10, 18.8 million electors, forming 70 percent of the total, voted; and in the second, held in May, 7.5 million. Interestingly, the number of clerical deputies fell sharply, from 122 to 71, about a quarter of the total. Winning 150 seats, economic reformers, who were also social conservatives, emerged as the majority. And their leftist opponents were reduced by half, to ninety. Hojatalislam Ali Akbar Nateq-Nouri, an oval-faced man of forty-nine with a prematurely white beard, and a leader of the conservative Association of Combatant Clergy, became the Speaker.

From the floor, conservative deputies, opposed to "Westoxication" (their term for Western cultural imperialism), began attacking Hojatalislam Muhammad Khatami, who had been Minister of Culture and Islamic Guidance since 1982, for his failure to tackle the threat posed by the encroaching Western culture, and indulging Westernized Iranian intellectuals and artists. Their views were given wide publicity by the largely conservative press. Yielding to this pressure, Khatami resigned in July 1992.

However, the parliamentarians, favoring a strong private sector and economic liberalization split, when Rafsanjani, reelected in 1993 on a much-reduced mandate (63 percent on a voter turnout of 56 percent), extended reform to the economy's external dimension—with economic nationalists in the conservative camp opposing his moves. Their resistance to Rafsanjani's plans led to the President's supporters to drift away from the traditional right-wing camp and, in January 1996, sixteen top technocrats and politicians published an open letter, calling on the electorate to vote for those Majlis candidates who were dedicated to prosperity and modernization of Iran as exemplified in Rafsanjani's policies. This led to the founding of the *Kargozaran-e Sazandegi* (Servants of Construction, SOC) to contest the forthcoming poll.

In its national economic policies, the SOC was for curtailing state subsidies and lifting foreign currency restrictions, which had been endemic since the revolution. It proposed economic regeneration through industrial capital, not mercantile, which had been a consistent backer of the traditional right. A proponent of détente in foreign policy, the SOC wanted to expand contacts with the West to which conservatives were opposed.

Whereas the SOC was for political liberalization, the traditional Right, with its belief in "society under a religious guardian," argued that the degree of political freedoms should be determined by senior clerics, not the popularly elected Majlis or President.

The remaining major political force, consisting of leftists was for political reform, and for retaining a strong public sector and state subsidies, the removal of which, it argued, would hurt the needy, who should be the prime beneficiaries of the Islamic revolution.

In the election campaign, Nateq-Nouri asserted that a liberal Majlis and cabinet would destroy revolutionary precepts, and accused his (disparate) opponents of establishing dialogue with America. In his (Iranian) New Year speech on March 21, 1996, Leader Khamanei warned electors not to be deceived by candidates who wanted to enfeeble the foundation of Islamic thought under the guise of "freedom and liberalism." Following this, the Guardians Council—taking its cue from the Leader—rejected as many as 35 percent of the prospective candidates. The unstated, but commonly known, reasons for rejection were breaking the law, insufficient educational qualifications, taking drugs, lack of full commitment to Islam, and disloyalty to the Leader. Demoralized by this, many leftists who had been allowed to contest the poll decided not to run.

One of the driving forces of the Islamic revolution was the alliance between bazaar merchants and the lower social strata. During the election, the conservative faction successfully revived this alliance. But in the process it lost the support of the modern middle class which switched its loyalty largely to the mainly centrist SOC.

Consequently, the conservatives' strength in the Fifth Majlis (1996–2000) declined to 120. Yet they outnumbered the combined strength of the left-wingers and centrist SOC members at seventy. The rest were independent. The number of women rose from four to nine. But the figure for clerics in the new Majlis fell to forty-nine, the lowest statistic since the revolution as more and more voters realized that clerical politicians were no better than their nonclerical counterparts. More remarkably, only twelve of the deputies of the First Majlis survived, an indication of how competitive the position of a parliamentarian had become.

In the 1997 presidential poll, Khatami scored a remarkable landslide victory on a reformist platform. Despite this, he reached an understanding with conservatives inside and outside the Majlis, resulting in his defeated rival, Nateq-Nouri, being reelected Speaker for a year. Another consequence of Khatami's win was that the term "leftist" almost disappeared from the vernacular, giving way to "reformist/reformer," which covered everybody who was not a conservative or hard-line fundamentalist.

With the major battles on running the economy seemingly settled, the different factions had converged on such vital issues as further privatization (to include railways and petrochemicals) and maintenance of highly popular subsidies on essential items like foodstuffs, fuel, and medicine. It was in the arena of political reform that differences arose. Fundamentalists and right-wingers wanted to maintain the status quo while centrists and leftists advocated widening of the freedom of expression, association, and assembly within the constitution. They invoked Chapter Three of the 1989 constitution, entitled "People's Rights," containing Articles 19–42. "Publications and the press have freedom of expression except when it is detrimental to the basic principles of Islam or the rights of the public," stated Article 24. "The details of this exception will be specified by law." And, according to Article 27, "Public gatherings and marches may be held freely provided arms are not carried and they are not detrimental to the basic principles of Islam."

On paper this was a vast improvement on what transpired during the Shah's reign, when censors sat in the offices of newspapers and the state-run radio and television. Following the revolution, freedom of speech and expression thrived, albeit briefly. As the Mujahedin-e Khalq Organization mounted deadly terrorist attacks and the country faced the invading troops of Iraq, newspapers were urged by officials to emphasize the virtues of the Islamic revolution and exercise self-censorship—a practice which, given the siege mentality engendered by a seemingly endless war with Iraq, editors seemed to have adopted without protest.

This was the case until 1985 when Minister of Culture and Islamic Guidance Khatami piloted the first Press Bill in the midst of the Iran-Iraq War, drafted within the framework of the above-mentioned Article 24 of the constitution, which barred publications that conflicted with Islamic principles.

Following the end of the armed conflict and death of Khomeini in 1989, the political climate changed. Preeminent among those who started to push at the boundaries of the Press Law was leftist Ayatollah Muhammad Mousavi Khoeiniha, a chubby-faced man of fifty, with a long gray beard and tainted glasses. In 1991, his daily newspaper *Salaam* (Peace) introduced a column, "Hello, Salaam," inviting its readers to air their complaints and questions. The column became hugely successful, with the readers complaining bitterly of rampant inflation, stagnant incomes, hoarding and profiteering, and mullahs flaunting their newly acquired foreign luxury cars. Other newspapers followed.

As the decade progressed, in the absence of well-organized and properly structured political parties, newspapers became their surrogates, their circulations indicating the size of their support. Their number multiplied after Khatami's victory. "Before the 1997 presidential poll there were several restrictions on the press," Muhammad Soltanifar, the genial managing director of the English language *Iran News*, established in 1994, told me. "After Khatami's victory journalists realized the importance of the Press Law; and so did the Fifth Majlis. Both felt that it was time to amend the legislation. But reformist deputies wanted to do so to open up the press, conservatives to control it."[11]

Press freedom was part of a wider demand for political and social liberalization. As expected, conservatives resisted this not only in the Majlis but also in the judiciary where they were in a majority. Given this, and the unprecedented student protest in July 1999 which focused on political freedoms, economics did not figure prominently in the public debate as the country prepared for the elections to the Sixth Majlis in mid-February 2000. Reformists feared that the conservative Guardians Council would veto candidates from their camp on a large scale. But this did not happen.

Of the 6,800 aspiring candidates for 290 Majlis seats, only seven percent were barred.

A dozen conservative groups, dominated by the Association of Combatant Clergy and the Miscellaneous Islamic Committees—an umbrella organization of various bazaar merchant and guild groups—formed an alliance called the Followers of the Imam's and Leader's Line. It emphasized improvement in economic conditions rather than political reform. On the other side, eighteen reformist factions—ranging from the reformist Society of Combatant Clerics to the leftist Islamic Iranian Participation Front (IIPF, popularly known as *Mosharekat*, Participation) to the centrist SOC—formed the Second Khordad/May 23 Front, named after the (Iranian) date on which Khatami scored his landslide victory. The IIPF's program included greater media freedom, including privately owned radio and television channels, and reform of government bureaucracy. Whereas it favored encouraging private investment in industry, it was opposed to privatizing state-owned oil, power, telecommunications, and tobacco industries, and giving tax incentives to companies. With many of its activists being journalists, the IIPF had a substantial presence in the press.[12]

After a slow start, the election campaign picked up as Khatami toured Iran's provincial capitals, culminating in a mammoth rally on February 11, Revolution Day, in Tehran to urge people to participate in the poll, well aware that a large voter turnout would favor the reformist May 23 Front coalition.

By contrast, the state-run radio and television, whose head was appointed by Leader Khamanei, treated the elections in a determinedly low-key manner. Given the legal prohibition of campaigning by electronic media, the public surmised that those given exposure on the broadcasting media were favorites of the conservative establishment.

Both camps put much stress on public rallies, which were well attended, and widely reported in the print media, which played a crucial role. With pro-reform newspapers being more popular, reformists had a clear lead over their rivals. In the absence of conventional political party organization, newspapers became the central nervous system of the reform movement. They played a vital role in molding public opinion. The ambiance of most public rallies was well encapsulated by Howard Schneider of the

Washington Post on February 18, 2000. "Establishment figures are booed," he reported. "Catch phrases involving freedom, prosperity, and 'Iran for all Iranians' have replaced religious militancy in slogans from the Right, Center, and Left. Readings from the Quran still start the typical gathering, but they are followed by once-banned nationalist anthems and ancient Persian poetry. Summing up the electoral scene, a Tehran-based Western diplomat said, "A free and fair election. No holds barred. An open debate. This is supposed to be a clerical theocracy, and it is transformed, before our eyes, into a pretty lively democracy."

On the polling day, with thirty-two million electors participating, the turnout was 83 percent, a record for Majlis elections, and 12 percent higher than in the previous poll. Winning almost two-thirds of the seats, the May 23 Front emerged as the clear victor. The conservatives' score was sixty, and the independents' fifteen. There were less clerical winners than ever before whereas the number of women deputies rose to a record eleven. (Only 14 percent of the deputies were clerics, down from 53 percent in the First Majlis.) Karrubi became the new Speaker by a huge majority with nobody voting against him, and sixty-two deputies abstaining. The breakdown of the 186 deputies voting for Mahdi Karrubi was: ninety-five members of the Islamic Iranian Participation Front, thirty of the Society of Combatant Clergy, ten of the longer-established Mujahedin of Islamic Revolution, made up of leftist laypersons, thirty of the Servants of Construction, and fifteen independents.

In Tehran, reformists made a clean sweep—with IIPF leader Muhammad Reza Khatami, the president's younger brother, aged forty-three, topping the list. A dapper British-trained urologist, with a trimmed salt-and-pepper beard, prematurely silvery hair, and a pleasant demeanor, he was a former Deputy Health Minister, who had set up the IIPF as a platform for his elder brother's reformist ideas in late 1998. At the bottom of the list appeared

Rafsanjani despite the fact that, on the eve of the election, he had splashed full-page advertisements in newspapers and distributed two million flyers. Later, when his election was challenged, Rafsanjani decided to withdraw his name rather than face possibly embarrassing scrutiny by neutral auditors. "Rafsanjani did not grasp the political climate and the democratic reforms," wrote Hamid Reza Jalaipour, executive director of the *Asr-e Azadegan* (Era of the Free), a leading pro-reform daily. He accused Rafsanjani of "relying on political tricks and his traditional sources of power, and failing to understand that the time had come for the will of the people to prevail."[13]

Nasser Hadian, a sad-eyed, thickly bearded political scientist at Tehran University, interpreted the reformers' victory as "the revenge of the outsiders—groups marginalized over the years, women, youth, and the modern middle class." He noted that, "These are the groups whose standard of living—culturally, politically, and economically—has declined since the revolution. They have been increasingly alienated from the political system. They voted against the status quo when they elected Khatami and they've done it again [in 2000]. For these groups, demonstrations, riots, and strikes would have costs; voting is a cost-free way to register their demand for change."[14]

While reformists were euphoric, conservatives were crestfallen, surprised, and depressed by the extent of their defeat. Among those who lost was Muhammad Reza Bahonar, a prominent Tehran deputy. "We will not change our principles and positions, but it is natural that we should reconsider our policies and methods," he declared. Muhammad Reza Taraqi, a leading conservative deputy, said ominously, "We must not make a new religion of elections. If they help strengthen Islam they are good. If they weaken it they are evil." Among those who agreed with him was Masoud Dehnamaki, a leader of the *Ansar-e Hizbollah* (lit., Helpers of the Party of God) and editor of the *Jebhe* (front) weekly. He told a public rally in Tehran that Ansars should go on the offensive and "scare the bourgeois classes back into their homes."[15] According to such radical right-wing ideologues, divine edicts authorizing violence in defense of Islam overrode the laws of the state.

Between the parliamentary poll and the dissolution of the Fifth Majlis in late May 2000, the conservative majority, taking its cue from Khamanei's vehement attack on the reformist press—which in some cases had provided a platform to those advocating separation of politics and religion—moved fast to pass the latest batch of clauses in the Press Law in an ongoing process dating back to July 1999. These extended the responsibility for press violations from journalists to the publication's managing director, and, most importantly, outlawed criticism of the constitution and the Leader. Between the first and the second run of the Majlis election, the judiciary closed down fourteen pro-reform publications with a total circulation of one million, for insulting Islam and spreading corruption.

To reverse the conservative move, reformist deputies of the Sixth Majlis prioritized amending the restrictive Press Law they had inherited. But to their surprise and disappointment, on August 6, the scheduled date for debating and voting on the amendments to the Press Law, Speaker Karrubi read out a letter he had received from Leader Khamanei the night before. "If the enemies of Islam, the revolution, and the Islamic system take over or infiltrate the press, it will be a big danger to the country's security and the people's religious beliefs," said Khamanei. "Therefore I cannot allow myself and other officials to keep quiet in respect of this crucial issue. The bill is not legitimate and not in the interest of the system and the revolution." Reformist leaders had reckoned that the Guardians Council would veto the bill and that it would end up with the Expediency Council headed by Rafsanjani since 1997. But neither they nor their ranks had anticipated that Khamanei would make this drastic, unprecedented intervention at this early stage. His vetoing of the bill meant indefinite suspension of the matter. There were angry and shouted protests in the chamber. Scuffles broke out between reformists and conservatives.

But Khamanei had acted within his powers as described in Article of 110 of the constitution, which charged him with "delineation of the general policies" of the Islamic Republic. "Our constitution has the elements of the absolute rule of the Supreme Clerical Leader, and you all know this and approve of this," said Speaker Karrubi. "We are all duty bound to abide by it."[16]

The next day, thousands of raucous conservatives assembled outside the Majlis complex to demonstrate their backing for Khamanei's edict. The situation was so surcharged that many onlookers felt that the chanting crowd might storm the building. It did not.

As the existing Press Law banned direct criticism of the Leader, the reformist bloc directed its anger at its conservative rivals. On August 13, a motion pledging to advance reform and accusing the conservative bloc of manipulating Khamanei's letter was signed by 161 deputies (out of 274).

The following day, Ayatollah Ahmad Jannati, the arch conservative, stern, gaunt-faced, seventy-four-year-old head of the Guardians Council, spoke. "You cannot save Islam with liberalism and tolerance," he declared. "I am announcing clearly and openly that the closure of the [pro-reform] newspapers was the best thing the judiciary has done since the revolution."[17]

Faced with this reactionary onslaught, the reformist centrist-leftist majority in the Sixth Majlis decided to lower its horizons. It knew only too well that the institutions directly controlled by the Leader, and functioning outside the purview of the Majlis, included the Ministry of Intelligence, the judiciary, the military, the Islamic Revolutionary Guard Corps, the state-run radio and television, and the richly endowed foundations which controlled a substantial segment of the economy.

During the four-year tenure of the Majlis, reformists found their modest attempts at liberalization quashed repeatedly by the Guardians Council. It vetoed bills guaranteeing freedom of speech as well as political dissidents' rights, barring security forces from university campuses, and establishing an independent arbitration body to settle challenges to the Council's decisions on candidates' eligibility for elected public offices.

As stated earlier (in this chapter), the Guardians Council rejected more than two-fifths of the applicants wishing to win a seat in the Seventh Majlis (2004–08). The intervention by Khatami and Karrubi—followed by Khamanei's public call to the Council to reconsider the rejected cases with a specific guideline that a sitting deputy must not be disqualified unless there was something serious and specific against him/her—still left about a third of the applicants, including eighty-seven incumbents, barred.

But when disqualified deputies staged a sit-in at the Majlis complex, disappointingly, there was not a single public demonstration in their favor. "The general public witnessed four years of constant bickering between the Majlis and other organs of the government and got fed up," Jim Muir, the BBC's longtime correspondent in Iran, told me. "They thought this was a quarrel among politicians, and took little interest."[18] That weakened the reformists' hand.

Yet they did not surrender. On February 1, 124 deputies rushed to the Speaker's podium and handed in their resignations one by one to him after a leading reformist, Muhsin Mirdamadi, had read aloud his letter of resignation—broadcast live on state-run radio. He said that that the totalitarians planned "to eliminate the republicanism of the system and turn its Islam into a Taliban version of Islam [as in Afghanistan, from 1996 onward]."

Another deputy, Rajab Ali Mazrsoui, said, "An election whose results is decided beforehand is treason to the rights and ideals of the nation."

Some in the reform movement proposed that the Khatami government's Interior Ministry should refuse to conduct the general election or include the rejected candidates' names on the contestants' list, or postpone the poll to gain time to resolve the crisis satisfactorily. But Khamanei decreed that the poll must be held on February 20 as scheduled. Khatami complied.

The reformist camp split. Eight of the twenty-two groups in it decided to participate, including the Society of Combatant Clerics to which Khatami and Karrubi belonged. These groups formed a coalition called the Construction and Development of Iran. After co-opting moderate conservatives and independents, it fielded candidates for all the seats. Khatami and Karrubi appealed to the electorate to vote while fourteen reformist groups, including the IIPF, boycotted the poll. Because of this, the voter turnout became a crucial element in the upcoming contest, with Hamid Reza Tarraqi, leader of the conservative Islamic Coalition Association, asserting that 50 percent voter turnout would satisfy Khamanei's call for a successful election.

The conservatives, contesting under the umbrella of the *Abadgaran-e Iran-e Islam* (Builders of Islamic Iran), led by Gholam Ali Haddad-Adel, which included the bazaar-based Miscellaneous Islamic Committees, were in a buoyant mood. Tarraqi argued that instead of chanting "such ambiguous slogans as freedom, reform, and civil society," the new Majlis should concentrate on inflation, unemployment, state control of the economy, and social justice. "If the government increases supervision over the economy, without being directly involved, social justice can come alongside privatization."[19]

According to the reformist-run Interior Ministry, 50.6 percent of the forty-six million voters participated in the poll. In Tehran the turnout was 30 percent versus 63 percent in 2000, which was also the national figure.

The national statistic on the voter turnout was twice the reformist camp had predicted. At the same time, since the figure was marginally above 50 percent, conservatives claimed legitimacy.

Little wonder that the general mood was of disillusionment and apathy, not of revolt.

Reformists were down to fifty deputies, back to their strength in the Fifth Majlis, with Karrubi failing to win a seat. They would go on to rename themselves Followers of Imam Khomeini. The 189 conservatives were divided into pragmatic (about 10 percent), mainstream (roughly 75 percent), and ideological hardliners (10 to 15 percent). The number of women parliamentarians at eleven was about the same as before; and that of clerical deputies fell to thirty, a record low.

When the Seventh Majlis met on May 27, it elected Adel, a conservative with the largest vote in Tehran, its Speaker. A slim, bespectacled, oval-faced man with a straggly beard, he was a philosophy teacher and member of the Academy of Sciences, whose daughter Bint al Hoda was married to Mujtaba Khamanei, a son of the Leader.

Having won the legislature, the conservative camp relaxed somewhat. The conservative-dominated Guardians Council finally approved the bill banning the use of torture, and the judiciary chief Ayatollah Muhammad Hasehmi Shahroudi issued a circular to all concerned to avoid abusive and illegal actions, including torture, while carrying out arrests and detentions.

The IIPF, the preeminent reformist group, was in a self-critical mood, with its chief strategist, Saeed Hajjarian—a bespectacled, fifty-year-old man of medium build, with graying stubble—in the lead. "While reformists with seats in the Majlis were often thinking of compromise, those outside, the rank and file, were thinking of challenging the system in an extremist way," he said.

"We should have struck a balance between challenge and compromise which we did not." Then, with rare candidness, he pointed out that the IIPF represented the interests of the new middle class. "So what is our relationship with the working class?" he asked rhetorically.[20]

It was the first time a leading intellectual-politician had introduced class analysis into the political discourse since the Islamic revolution deploying a phraseology in common use outside Iran, where, due to the political-ideology monopoly enjoyed by Khomeini—who shunned such terms used worldwide by the secular Left as proletariat, capitalist, feudal, etc.—there was an almost total absence of sociopolitical analysis based on class interests. Emulating Khomeini, those Islamic leftists who tried to advance the interests of the working class and the lower-and-middle middle class invariably referred to the *mustazafin* (needy).

Addressing the seventh annual congress of the IIPF in July 2004, Muhammad Reza Khatami blamed the failure of the reform movement on lack of strong party organization, and recommended rebuilding the IIPF.

"Since countries such as ours are experiencing limited opportunities for establishing home-grown democracy and do not want to submit to democracy from outside, probably by use of force, we have no alternative but to continue the difficult course of democracy in Iran," he said. He rejected the alternatives of "tearing down all the legal foundations of the system," and "playing behind-the-scene games [of compromise] even at the price of losing the people's trust so that we obtain some concessions." He recommended a policy of détente to pursue the overall objective of administering society according to the views of the majority.

"An important challenge for democracy in Muslim countries is the interpretation of mixing of religion and politics," he continued. "We consider a religious government to be democratic since a majority of Muslim citizens want it. We believe in the independence of religious institutions from political institutions, which does not mean separation of religion and politics, because we consider religious institutions to be separate from religion, which is not the case with traditionalists: they equate religion with religious institutions and exploit them to achieve their political and party objectives. Whereas religious institutions like the clergy, mosques, and religious centers are sacred, they must not practice politics with special privileges."

Thus Muhammad Reza Khatami excluded himself from the column of those who advocated separation of politics and Islam—a concept to which Iran's governing establishment is implacably opposed. It associates this view not only with Abdul Karim Soroush, a political scientist and thinker, but also with Muhammad Mussadiq, a towering figure of the recent past.

The founders of the Islamic Republic remember only too well that within weeks of the Islamic revolution on February 12, 1979, more than half a million people assembled in Ahamdabad, the home village of Mussadiq, to commemorate the anniversary of his death on March 5. The vast rally, addressed among others by leaders of the old National Front, resolved to form the National Democratic Front open to all groups and individuals believing in a democratic and anti-imperialist struggle, and appointed an eight-member committee led by Hedayatollah Matine-Daftari, a grandson of Mussadiq, to accomplish the task. He made some progress while the government led by Mahdi Bazargan, in which the National Front shared power, lasted. With its fall in November in the wake of the takeover of the U.S. Embassy by militant students—an action it disapproved but could not reverse—however, the situation changed abruptly.

As the confrontation between the uncritical followers of Khomeini and others escalated in the spring of 1981, the role and importance of Mussadiq in Iran's recent history became a bone of contention between Khomeini and his estranged President of the Republic Bani-Sadr, an ardent admirer of Mussadiq. In Khomeini's eyes, when—ignoring a message from his office to refrain from visiting Mussadiq's estate in Ahmadabad on May 19, 1981, the centennial of his birthday—Bani-Sadr went to Ahmadabad, he crossed the Rubicon. Since Khomeini considered Mussadiq a flawed nationalist who hobnobbed with secular leftists, he regarded Bani-Sadr's hero worship of Mussadiq unforgivable.

Mussadiq:
The Rise and Fall of a
Nationalist Democrat

◆ CHAPTER 3 ◆

Among the oddest pieces of recent Iranian history I discovered during my July 2004 trip to Iran was a set of rusting gates resting against the compound walls of the house of Muhammad Mussadiq in Ahmadabad, a village 60 miles (100 km) west of Tehran.

Once part of Prime Minister Mussadiq's house in north Tehran, the gates—made of blue-painted sheet steel—were unhinged after a Jeep carrying an army officer and a gang leader from south Tehran, Shaaban Jaafari, nicknamed *Bemukh* (Brainless), smashed its way in on February 28, 1953, while a crowd gathered outside. The protestors were angered by the rumor—falsely spread by pro-Shah partisans alleging that in their dispute over who should run the military, the Prime Minister was pressuring Muhammad Reza Shah to depart as a prelude to ending the monarchy.

By the time the intruders entered the house, Mussadiq had safely escaped by climbing a back garden wall. In retrospect, the event would prove to be a dry run for what followed six months later when the Mussadiq government was overthrown in a coup organized by the CIA and Britain's MI6.

Though only an hour's drive from the outskirts of Tehran, Ahmadabad proved an uncommonly· difficult destination to reach. My inquiries with Iranian journalists and foreign diplomats drew a disappointing, monotonous response: "Don't know." Once, an overly confident driver, fluent in English, took me to a place called Ahmadabad-Musafi. Nobody there had a clue about the unhyphenated "Ahmadabad." Evidently, Mussadiq had disappeared into a memory hole of the present regime. It is hard to believe now that in the immediate afterglow of the revolution, Tehran's municipality renamed Pahlavi Avenue—an

8 mile (13 km) long thoroughfare, connecting Reza Shah's palace in southern Tehran with his summer palace in Saadabad in the north—after him (later renamed Vali-Ye Asr), and that the post office issued a Mussadiq commemorative stamp after him.

Arriving at the right Ahmadabad, it was easy to locate the house of its most famous son, called Qalah Ahamadabad, where Mussadiq and his wife lived after his release from prison in 1957. Behind the high steel-plated gate, past tall trees and lawns, at the end of a graveled pathway stood a modest two-story house with broken windows, their frames painted garish blue. The only impressive object on his estate was his olive green Pontiac, now stored in a garage next to the main residence. When we arrived at Qala Ahmadabad—escorted by the caretaker living nearby, Zahra Tukrosta, a small, plump, lively matron with a prematurely lined face and covered in a flowered wraparound—it was being renovated by Dr. Mahmoud Mussadiq, one of the dead leader's Tehran-based grandsons.

Weirdly, the small, carpeted reception room, decorated with the drawings, etchings, and photographs of Mussadiq—the most memorable is of him gazing at the Liberty Bell in Philadelphia, Pennsylvania, with his hand resting on the barrel; a few framed quotes from the Quran, including "Allah is the light of heaven and the earth" in elegant Arabic calligraphy, and his statement nationalizing Iranian oil industry—doubles as his mausoleum with a gravestone carrying his death date in the Iranian era: 14.12.1345 (Iranian Year)/March 5, 1967 AD. "Roses and soil were brought from Najaf [the Shia holy place in Iraq] to his grave," Tukrosta told us.[1]

Going through other rooms, we discovered that eight months before his death, Mussadiq received a letter from Diedre Higglesworth of the International Tribunal on War Crimes in London WC2, United Kingdom, informing him of the hearings in Paris on the war in Vietnam. It lay next to a sheet from the

Ettilaat (Information) newspaper dated 26 Tir (fourth month) 1338 Iranian Year / 1959 AD.

Although Tukrosta was only twelve when Mussadiq died, she seemed to know a great deal about him. "He did not eat much himself, only bread and yogurt," she said. "During his lifetime Mussadiq distributed all his land to the tenants, very little was left in his own name. [Mussadiq had inherited the whole village and vast tracts of surrounding agricultural land.] He was very kind and generous; he gave every child in the village clothes and a copy of the Quran. He once gave me small, white homeopathic pills."

Then she quoted Mussadiq's line that summarized his whole political career: "When I turned off the oil valve of the British company, I signed my death decree." He wanted to be buried in Tehran, she added, "But the Shah did not allow it as he feared that his mausoleum would become a place of pilgrimage."

The idea of reburying him in Tehran revived briefly after the 1979 revolution, but his survivors were not too keen as they were unsure of which way the wind would blow in a few years—well aware that Mussadiq's currently high stock might fall precipitously, requiring his corpse to be removed from the capital.

Thus, the first Iranian leader in modern times who established rapport with common folk, despite his aristocratic origins, and came to epitomize Iranian aspirations for achieving economic and political independence and ending oligarchic rule at home, lies unsung under the floor of his unprepossessing home.

Known initially as Muhammad Mussadiq al Saltane, he was a son of Mirza Hidayatollah Vazir-e Daftar, the finance minister of Nasser al Din Shah, and a Qajar princess: their pictures adorn one of the rooms at Qala Ahamadabad. Mirza Hidayatollah died when Muhammad was in his early teens, by which time he was known as a child prodigy. By sixteen he became the chief tax auditor for the Khurasan Province. He was also elected to the

First Majlis in 1906 but was prevented from taking his seat as he was below the required minimum age of thirty. A staunch constitutionalist, he left Iran three years later in protest at the storming of the Majlis by Muhammad Ali Shah, and enrolled at l'Ecole de Sciences Politiques in Paris. He returned home in 1910 to recover from an illness.

He then enrolled at the university in Neuchatel, Switzerland, and obtained his doctorate of law in 1914. He returned to Iran to finish his research for a book on the Sharia, Islamic law. Due to the outbreak of World War I in September 1914, he stayed on, and began teaching at the Tehran School of Law and Political Science. In his book *Iran and the Capitulation Agreements*, he argued that as a preamble to Iran developing a modern legal system, it must impose the existing law equally on everyone, including foreigners, and desist from granting special privileges to any person or organization, local, or alien.

When he was appointed Deputy Finance Minister in 1917, he demanded punishment for all those who were involved in corruption. His insistence on this issue, and his refusal to indulge in nepotism, led to his dismissal two years later. Angered by this, he departed for Neuchatel. But when he learned of the infamous 1919 Anglo-Persian Agreement, he rushed home by ship and landed at Bandar Abbas. Here the dignitaries of Fars Province persuaded him to become the provincial Governor-General.

After serving in the national government—following a coup by Reza Khan in 1921—in three different jobs, Mussadiq quit the executive. He won a seat in the Fifth Majlis (1924–26). Here he distinguished himself not merely by his erudition and eloquence at the podium, which were punctuated by his theatrical gestures, but also by his appearance. Tall, with slumped shoulders and sad, droopy eyes and a very long nose in a thin, long, pale face with a high forehead, he was instantly recognizable, a plus for any ambitious politician. He was prone to periodic attacks of severe stomach upsets, ulcers, and hemorrhaging—and allied symptoms such as nervous fits and breakdowns. His frailty came to symbolize the state of Iran, enfeebled and embattled as it was.

There were times when emotion overpowered him to the extent that genuine tears trickled down his elongated cheeks. Other times, such emotional outpouring combined with physical exhaustion made him faint, much to the embarrassment of those present. Later, the Anglo-American media would focus on his tendency to weep and to wear his favorite pink pajamas, sometimes covered by a fawn-colored jacket, during his cabinet sessions while he rested on a heap of pillows. Overlooked, of course, was the principled shrewdness that informed his political conduct at home and abroad, and the Shia tradition of expressing one's emotions dramatically in public to commemorate the suffering that the martyred Imam Hussein endured in 681 A.D. and expiate the guilt felt by the faithful due to their failure to aid him in his hour of need.[2] His wry sense of humor went unnoticed in the West, unfamiliar with the subtleties of the Persian language.

Mussadiq was one of the five deputies who opposed the motion to depose Ahmad Shah in 1925 and appoint Reza Khan as Regent. Yet, so high was Mussadiq's standing, that Reza Shah instructed Prime Minister Muhammad Ali Furuqi to offer the Foreign Ministry to Mussadiq. Firmly opposed to monarchical dictatorship, Mussadiq rejected the offer.

He won a seat in the Sixth Majlis (1926–28). Even though he refused to take the oath of office, which included a pledge to respect the authority of the Shah, he was permitted to take his seat. This enhanced his already high prestige.

Reza Shah rigged the subsequent Majlis poll so thoroughly that all his opponents, including Mussadiq, lost. That ended the parliamentary career of forty-five-year-old Mussadiq. He retired to his Ahmadabad estate and busied himself with farm management and reading while maintaining keen interest in national affairs. He regarded the deal Reza Shah made with Anglo-Iranian Oil Company (AIOC) in 1933 as harmful to Iran's interests. The growth of Iranian economy, fueled by its oil revenues, had resulted in an accelerated growth of a modern middle class and the emergence of an industrial proletariat who, lacking any economic or filial links with feudal landlords, aristocrats, or rich bazaar merchants, were keen to create a political space outside the patronage of the Royal Court. But Reza Shah suppressed this development.

Three years later, Mussadiq went to Germany for medical treatment only to discover that there was nothing seriously wrong with him. That encouraged Reza Shah to imprison him without charge on his return home in 1940. He was released once Reza Shah was forced to abdicate in 1941.

In the wake of Reza's abdication, political parties and groups, including the social democratic Iran Party, the liberal nationalist Democrat Party, and the leftist *Tudeh* (Masses) Party, started to mushroom. This encouraged Mussadiq to resume public life. He won a seat in the Fourteenth Majlis (1944–46). He was a prime mover of the legislation banning any further granting of oil concessions. His uncompromising speech, lambasting Reza Shah's dictatorship—summarized in his memorable one-liner, "No nation goes anywhere under the shadow of dictatorship"—and welcoming the political reform since his abdication, won Mussadiq many admirers inside and outside the Majlis. However, his proposed electoral reform bill in 1947 in the Fifteenth Majlis failed to pass. Angered and dispirited, he once again retired to his Qala Ahamdabad.

But his retirement proved short-lived. Working with fellow democrats, he forged together a coalition of the Democrat Party, the Iran Party, and the leftist Toilers Party, which had a base among industrial workers, and many middle-class independents, under the banner of the National Front in October 1949. He was unanimously elected its leader. It aimed to end the Iranian oligarchy's political hegemony at home and its alliance with imperialist Britain, especially the Anglo-American Oil Company (AIOC), and build a democratic, independent, and economically vibrant Iran.

The next four years would prove to be the most tumultuous in the life of Mussadiq as well as Iran.

Oil Nationalization

The campaign for the elections to the Sixteenth Majlis (1950–52), held during July 1949–February 1950, centered around nationalizing the British-owned Anglo-Iranian Oil Company. A majority of the new deputies backed the AIOC's nationalization. Anti-British feeling was so rampant that Iranians publicly applauded the assassination of pro-British Premier Gen. Ali Razmara by an Islamic militant in early March 1951. By the end of April, both Majlis and the Senate had passed the oil nationalization bill and spelled out the details of the takeover of the AIOC, including its oil concession covering a large area of Iran, by the newly established National Iranian Oil Company (NIOC). On May 1, these bills became law, and Mussadiq formed the next government.

Britain combined its vehement protest and boycott of Iranian oil with covert moves to undermine Mussadiq by deploying the extensive intelligence network it had built up before and during World War II when it occupied most of Iran. To implement Britain's anti-Mussadiq plan, Christopher Montague (Monty) Woodhouse, a balding, sharp-featured, middle-aged senior official of the British Secret Intelligence Service MI6, arrived as "information officer" at the British embassy in Tehran from the Royal Air Force base at Habbaniya, Iraq, armed with weapons and gold sovereigns worth millions of Iranian rials. He turned over most of the cash to the Rashidian brothers, who were involved in the ship-ping, banking, and real-estate business—Assadollah (organizer), Qodratollah (entrepreneur), and Saifollah (strategist)—and who had worked for London during World War II to undermine German influence.[3] This money was to be used to suborn military officers, parliamentarians, senior clerics, politicians, newspaper editors, and gang leaders in Tehran. Woodhouse also liaised with his CIA counterpart, Roger Goiran, in Tehran.

Equally vital to Woodhouse was Gen. Senator Fazlollah Zahedi, a handsome, extroverted military officer turned politi-cian with a weakness for beautiful women and gambling, who had set out to band together royalist military and gendarmerie officers under the aegis of the clandestine Committee to Save the Fatherland. The fifty-six-year-old Zahedi was fanatically loyal to the Pahlavis, having served under Col. Reza Khan in the Cossack Brigade, who, after promoting him to brigadier general at twenty-five, appointed him governor of oil-rich Khuzistan Province, and then commander of the garrison in Isfahan, the country's second largest city. Following Reza Shah's deposition in 1941, he was interned like many other pro-German officers for the rest of World War II. On his release, Muhammad Reza Shah appointed him Governor-General of Fars Province and then made him police chief in Tehran. In 1950, after having nominated Zahedi as a senator, the Shah persuaded Prime Minister Mussadiq to appoint him Interior Minister. After a few months, Mussadiq dis-missed Zahedi when he ordered the Tehran police to fire at peaceful protestors during a visit by an American envoy. Zahedi succeeded in recruiting many of the two hundred military and police officers who were retired or cashiered by the Mussadiq government in 1952 by getting them to enroll into the innocuous sounding Retired Officers Club.

Britain's call for a boycott of Iran's oil was heeded by most Western nations. Consequently, Tehran's earning from oil exports in 1951 fell by half from $45 million in the previous year, when they accounted for seven-tenths of its total exports revenue.

In the spring of 1952 Iranian politicians were focused on the elections to Seventeenth Majlis (1952–54), unaware that agents recruited by the Rashidian brothers had bribed many candidates and were funding their campaigns, especially in the provincial cities. In Tehran, where voting took place under the watchful eyes of the agents of the contesting candidates, Mussadiq's National Front won all the seats.

In the provinces, however, monitoring of the poll was slack. This afforded opportunities to the richly funded pro-British candidates to swing the vote in their favor, some of whom managed to win. But, in the absence of strict monitoring of the poll in the provinces, the results were mixed. So, after the declaration of the results from seventy-nine seats (in a house of 136) in early June, the government decided to halt the count—"the destabilization of Iran," as Mussadiq's supporters described it—until the return of its delegation from The Hague to submit its argument for oil nationalization at the International Court of Justice (ICJ) where Britain had taken its case.[4]

On July 13, 1952, Mussadiq's demand that he should appoint his Minister of War was rejected by the Shah, who had exercised that privilege so far. Mussadiq resigned four days later. When the Shah named Ahmad Qavam al Saltane (who happened to be a second cousin of Mussadiq) as the Prime Minister, there were instant demonstrations, strikes, and riots. These continued until Saltane resigned on July 21. The Shah had underestimated the popularity that Mussadiq had gained by abolishing the landlords' practice of extracting free labor from their peasants, spending part of the landlords' rental income on rural housing and public baths, and introducing unemployment and sick benefits to industrial workers, thereby garnering support among peasants and urban working class. Now, reluctantly, the Shah recalled Mussadiq, who won an overwhelming vote in the Majlis. On July 23, the ICJ refused to be drawn into the oil dispute because it was not between two governments. This further boosted Mussadiq's popularity.

On August 3, he approached the Majlis for emergency powers, allowing him to rule by decree (instead of laws passed by the Majlis), for six months to tackle the worsening economic situation due to a sharp drop in foreign earnings. It obliged. In this he had the active backing of Majlis Speaker Ayatollah Abol Qasim Kashani. To maintain the support of Kashani and other senior clerics, Mussadiq released twenty-eight members of the *Fedaiyan-e Islam* (Self-sacrificers for Islam), a militant Islamic group, including the assassin of Prime Minister Razmara, banned the sale of alcohol, and dropped his plans for enfranchising women.

The Mussadiq-Kashani combine represented an alliance of modern and traditional middle classes, both of whom wanted to rid Iran of foreign domination. During the next few months, however, as the Western boycott of Iranian oil began to squeeze Iran further, and Mussadiq's appeals to U.S. President Harry Truman for aid fell on deaf ears, this alliance became strained. An open split came when, in order to lower food prices, the Minister of Economy prepared to open state-run bakeries. Kashani successfully mobilized the guilds of Tehran's Grand Bazaar to protest on the ground that the government was interfering with a free-market system.

The erosion of support among the traditional middle classes made the Mussadiq government increasingly dependent on the following that the Tudeh Party could muster in the street, the oil industry, and the civil service. This further alienated clerical leaders from the Mussadiq government. Ironically, until mid-1952, the Tudeh had regarded Mussadiq as an ally of America—an assessment based in the Iranian leader's refusal to recognize that Washington and London were bound together by special relationship, and his naive belief that unlike Britain, America was in essence an anti-imperialist nation nursing benign feelings toward Iran. It was only later that the Tudeh changed its view of Mussadiq and began cooperating with his National Front.

Meanwhile, the subversion from the British Embassy in Tehran continued. On October 13, 1952, the Iranian authorities arrested a general and a few businessmen for plotting against it with "a foreign embassy."[5] Nine days later, Mussadiq cut off diplomatic ties with Britain. Even though all diplomats departed, Monty Woodhouse left behind a working group under dapper Assadollah Rashidian, the plump, chubby-faced, organizing genius among the Rashidian brothers.

In mid-November, the British government dispatched Woodhouse to Washington after the victory of the Republican Gen. Dwight Eisenhower in the presidential poll, in which he had emphasized his anti-Communist credentials, for meetings with senior U.S. officials. Following his superiors' instructions, Woodhouse refrained from arguing that Mussadiq must be overthrown because he had nationalized the foremost British oil corporation, and instead stressed that the Iranian demagogue must be toppled because he was paving the way for a Communist takeover in Iran. He disclosed MI6 plans for a coup, involving the Rashidian brothers and the clandestine Committee to Save the Fatherland, consisting of disenchanted retired and serving army and police officers, under cover of the Retired Officers Club, which was actively co-opting parliamentarians, clerics, newspaper editors, urban mobsters, and tribal leaders.

In Tehran, faced with a paltry income from oil exports and failure to secure loans from the World Bank due to Washington's opposition, Mussadiq returned to the Majlis in mid-January 1953 with a request for a yearlong extension of his emergency powers. This was opposed by, among others, Speaker Kashani.

Mussadiq, in the end, succeeded in getting the extension, but the break between him and Kashani became irreparable. Thus, the alliance between the traditional and modern middle classes, forged earlier, broke down even before the much-anticipated showdown between the Shah and the government. Something similar would happen twenty-six years later, in the post-Shah era.

Mussadiq used his extraordinary authority to order the return of Reza Shah's illegally acquired lands to the state, cut the Court budget, and forbade communication between the Shah and foreign diplomats. He then appointed himself acting War Minister. To dramatize his disapproval of Mussadiq's actions, the Shah threatened to leave the country. That, in turn, led to the incident (described earlier in this chapter) when Mussadiq had to flee in his pajamas to escape the wrath of the crowd stage-managed by British agents. To resolve the dispute between the Shah and the Prime Minister, the Majlis appointed a committee. It ruled that since the constitution put the military under the government's jurisdiction, the Shah should cede his active command of the military. He refused. So on May 24, 1953, all but three of the fifty-seven deputies present voted to implement the committee's recommendation and reduce the Shah's powers.

Meanwhile, having embraced the CIA's Operation Ajax (TPAJAX, in the CIA lexicon, where the Shah appeared as KGSAVOY) in April, Britain's MI6 advised its agents to work for the American agency. The CIA lost no time in flying the Rashidian brothers to Washington to check out their veracity and reliability. They had already succeeded in getting Kashani, as well as Muzaffar Baqai, the left-leaning nationalist leader of the Toilers Party, a constituent of the National Front, prone to shifting his political position dramatically, to defect from the Mussadiq camp. With this, the CIA's psychological campaign against Mussadiq took off, with covertly funded Iranian opinion makers, journalists, and politicians denigrating the Prime Minister. Being an ardent liberal and constitutionalist who believed in the freedom of expression, Mussadiq was loath to use the coercive tools of the state against his opponents, and steadfastly refrained from muzzling the press.

In late May, the CIA finalized a detailed plan for the coup— allocating $150,000 for secret agents to discredit Mussadiq and his government as "corrupt, pro-Communist, hostile to Islam, and bent on destroying the morale and readiness of the armed forces"; allocating Zahedi $135,000 to win "additional friends" and influence "key people" in addition to over $100,000 given to him earlier; budgeting $11,000 a week to buy up Majlis deputies; engaging hoodlums to launch assaults on clerics and their properties and make it appear they were ordered by Mussadiq or his followers; and assemble thousands of paid demonstrators for an anti-Mussadiq rally on the day of the coup.[6] By now, Zahedi had bribed and armed dissident tribes, and co-opted anti-Mussadiq mullahs, including Kashani, as well as mobsters from Tehran's Grand Bazaar.

On June 14, President Eisenhower gave his approval to Operation Ajax after CIA director Allen Dulles had briefed him. Kermit Roosevelt was to be the field officer to implement Operation Ajax. A grandson of President Theodore Roosevelt, Kermit—born to a businessman father and his wife in Buenos Aires, Argentina—was raised near his grandfather's estate in Long Island, and educated at Harvard University, where he majored in history. After a stint as a lecturer at Harvard's history department, he joined the Office for Strategic Services, the predecessor of the CIA. His bespectacled face, with a prematurely receding hairline, and winsome smile gave him the air of a perpetual academic. His courteous, soft-spoken, unassuming manner masked a steely disposition. After field assignments in Egypt and Italy, he was promoted to the CIA's area chief for the Middle East when he was barely thirty-three. He took keen interest in the events in Iran. On the U.S. presidential polling date in November 1952, soon after Mussadiq had closed the UK embassy, he was in Tehran, working actively with the CIA station chief, Roger Goiran.

In early July 1953, when Kashani, who had been meeting Zahedi over the past several months, failed to get reelected Speaker, he became a vociferous member of the anti-Mussadiq camp.

From then on, events moved fast.

Mid-July to August 22, 1953

July 19: Kermit Roosevelt arrived in Iran as "James Lockridge" by car from Iraq, and stayed in a north Tehran villa rented by a local CIA agent.

July 27: Mussadiq ordered a referendum on the dissolution of both houses. Since the opposition boycotted it, he won almost all the votes. He then formally dissolved the Majlis and the Senate.

August 1: Brig. Gen. H. Norman Schwarzkopf Senior—who, as Col. Schwarzkopf, had served as an adviser to the Iranian Interior Ministry from 1942 to 1948 in charge of the gendarmerie affairs—arrived in Tehran on a diplomatic passport as part of his "worldwide tour," with a couple of large bags containing a lot of cash. After conferring with Roosevelt, he met the chief Iranian players in Operation TPAJAX and handed them generous amounts of cash.

When he called on the Shah at his Saadabad Palace, he found the monarch prevaricating about sacking Mussadiq, arguing—rightly—that he lacked the constitutional power to dismiss Mussadiq, who, despite the ailing economy and CIA-inspired attacks on him in the press, remained immensely popular.

By early August, the anti-Mussadiq press propaganda had

painted Mussadiq as a power-hungry crypto-Communist with Jewish parentage bent on ending the Pahlavi dynasty. The bulk of these articles were penned by CIA scribes in Washington and telexed to the U.S. Embassy in Tehran. "Any article I would write . . . would appear almost instantly, the next day, in the Iranian press," Richard Cottam, working for Operation Ajax in Washington, would reveal decades later. "They were designed to show Mussadiq as a Communist collaborator and as a fanatic."[7]

August 2: During his audience with the Shah, Assadollah Rashidian told the monarch that America and Britain were so intent on mounting a coup that nothing would change their minds. Later that day, a U.S. agent at the court told the Shah that an American envoy speaking for Eisenhower and British Prime Minister Winston Churchill wished a clandestine audience. The Shah agreed to send a car to Roosevelt's villa at midnight.

August 2–3, night: Dressed in a dark turtleneck shirt, Oxford-gray slacks, and Persian footware, Roosevelt sat in the car's backseat. As the vehicle ascended a foothill of Elborz Mountains to Saadabad, he lay down on the car floor and covered himself with a blanket. After the car was given a perfunctory wave at the steel gate, it halted short of the Saadaabad Palace. The Shah, a small, slight figure, approached it, opened a back door, and sat next to Roosevelt as the driver left the vehicle. Roosevelt told the Shah he had U.S. $1 million cash in Iranian rials.

August 3: It was the first day of the weeklong referendum on dissolving the Seventeenth Majlis.

August 3–4, night to August 7–8: At their nightly meetings, Roosevelt and the Shah finalized a four-part plan: an alliance with the clergy coupled with organizing anti-Mussadiq publications and crowds, monitoring the opposition through paid agents, consolidating the support of royalist military officers, and an overall coordination of the operations with Zahedi and his allies.

August 8–9: The last Roosevelt-Shah confabulation continued until the small hours. They decided that after signing the royal decrees drafted by Roosevelt—one dismissing Mussadiq, and the other appointing Gen. Zahedi (who had gone underground in July to avoid arrest on treason charges) as Prime Minister—the Shah and his wife Sorya Isfandiari would fly to their hunting lodge on the Caspian near Ramsar, which had a landing strip. Then the coup was to be launched in four stages—an orchestrated campaign in mosques, newspapers, and streets to damage Mussadiq's popularity was to be followed by royalist military officers handing him the Shah's decree dismissing him, and the mobs seizing the streets, leading to the emergence of Zahedi to accept the monarch's nomination as Prime Minister.

August 10: It was the last day of the referendum on the dissolution of the Majlis. Given the boycott by the opposition, it resulted in an almost unanimous "Yes." That morning, by the time a CIA messenger arrived late at the Saadabad Palace with the royal decrees for the Shah to sign, he and his wife had already left for Ramsar in their twin-engine Beechcraft.

August 11: Col. Nematollah Nasseri, the narrow-eyed, round-headed, plump-faced commander of the Imperial Guards, flew to Ramsar with the decrees and got the royal signatures. Due to bad weather he sent them to Tehran by car.

August 12: The signed decrees reached Roosevelt. On the other side, Mussadiq declared his intention to dissolve the Majlis and order fresh elections.

August 13 and 14 (Thursday and Friday): Due to the Iranian weekend, Roosevelt moved the coup date to Saturday night, as advised by his local aides. He shifted his command post from the north Tehran villa to a basement in the U.S. Embassy compound in central Tehran. Summarizing the situation, a CIA document (now declassified) reported: "At this time the psychological campaign against Mussadiq was reaching its climax. The controllable press was going all out against Mussadiq . . . CIA agents gave serious attention to alarming the religious leaders at Tehran by issuing propaganda in the name of the Tudeh Party, threatening these leaders with savage punishment if they opposed Mussadiq. Threatening phone calls were also made to them, in the name of the Tudeh, and one of several sham bombings of the houses of these leaders was carried out."[8]

August 15–16, night: After reaching the house of Mussadiq loyalist Gen. Taqi Riahi, the military Chief of Staff, to serve an arrest warrant on him, and finding it abandoned, Col. Nasseri led an armored column to Mussadiq's house at the corner of Kakh and Heshmat Dowla Streets, only to find his forces surrounded by the troops of Gen. Riahi, who had been tipped off earlier by a seemingly royalist officer. Nasseri was arrested, and his forces disarmed.

August 16: At 7 A.M., speaking on Tehran Radio, Mussadiq declared victory over a coup attempt by the Shah and "foreign elements." The Shah and his wife fled to Baghdad. Several leading conspirators were arrested, and the rest went underground. Given an option by the CIA headquarters to leave or stay, a depressed Roosevelt decided to hang on.

Jubilant Mussadiq partisans poured into the streets in Tehran and elsewhere. But the government failed to act with resolve, partly because the radicals in the National Front demanded proclamation of a republic while the moderates proposed a referendum to turn the Shah into a nominal head of state. Meanwhile, the Tudeh Party urged an immediate break with America.

Roosevelt met Zahedi, who was in hiding. Accepting his advice, Roosevelt rushed to get photocopies of the royal decrees, and dispatched CIA agents to distribute them, especially in the poor districts of south Tehran, a source of easily assembled mobs. He handed out generous funds to the Rashidian brothers to arrange pro-Shah demonstrators. At his behest, the U.S. military attaché Gen. Robert McClure tried to bribe several military commanders and succeeded in a few cases in Tehran. Roosevelt's general strategy was to engender an atmosphere of chaos for the next two days and then unleash pro-Shah military officers to seize Tehran Radio and other vital public buildings as a prelude to arresting Mussadiq. U.S. Ambassador Loy Henderson, who had decided earlier to linger on in Beirut, returned to Tehran.

By the end of the day some mobs chanting pro-Tudeh and pro-Mussadiq slogans and destroying property found themselves confronting others shouting pro-Shah slogans. Mussadiq, a liberal democrat to the last, had ordered the police not to interfere with the citizens' right to demonstrate.

August 16–18: Three days of rioting and demonstrations, coupled with increasingly radical demands by the demonstrators unnerved Mussadiq. They also caused an open rift between the National Front's moderate wing and the Tudeh.

August 17: With several newspapers publishing the royal decrees and the CIA-inspired rumor that Mussadiq's attempt to capture the throne had been foiled by patriotic military officers, and only a few dailies reporting the truth that Mussadiq was the target of the coup, the tempo of demonstrations and rioting rose, with a section of the demonstrators toppling the statues of Reza Shah and Muhammad Reza Shah. The Shah and his wife left Baghdad for Rome. Roosevelt persuaded Ambassador Henderson to meet Mussadiq to complain about the harassment reportedly suffered by the Americans in Tehran.

August 18: Henderson complained to Mussadiq that his compatriots were being harassed, and threatened to evacuate the Americans if their maltreatment continued. He promised U.S. aid if law and order was restored. Mussadiq was shocked to hear the complaint, and genuinely concerned at the prospect of the Americans departing. He immediately ordered the police chief to curb the demonstrators, a large majority of whom were his staunch supporters. Worse, he ordered Gen. Muhammad Daftary, a royalist officer close to Zahedi, to assist the police. He prohibited further demonstrations, urged all pro-government leaders to restrain their followers, and rejected the offer of active help from the Tudeh leadership. In short, Mussadiq unilaterally disarmed his camp, a fatal mistake.

"Policemen and soldiers swung into action last night against rioting Tudeh (Communist) partisans and Nationalist extremists," reported Kennett Love in the *New York Times*. "The troops appeared to be in a frenzy as they smashed into rioters with clubs, rifles, and night sticks and hurled tear gas bombs."

This provided a cover to the royalist officers and Zahedi's Committee to Save the Fatherland to mount an anti-Mussadiq coup. It also gave an opportunity to CIA-funded American and British agents to entice certain groups from south Tehran to turn themselves into vocal, pro-Shah elements to provide a veneer of populism to what was a military operation.

To ensure a large pro-Shah crowd the next day, Assadollah Rashidian advised Roosevelt to co-opt senior clerics, especially Kashani, since they could mobilize men quickly.

August 19: Early in the morning, Roosevelt rushed $10,000 to Ahmad Aramesh, a pro-British confidante of Kashani, with a message to pass on the sum to Kashani. (What actually happened remains unclear and unverified so far.) The day started with some two hundred weightlifters from local gymnasiums, led among others by mobster Shaaban Jaafari Bemukh, marching through the Grand Bazaar, chanting "Long live the Shah!", toward central Tehran, with the marchers on the margins handing out 500-rial notes to the onlookers to swell the procession.[9] On its way northward, the mob ransacked three pro-Mussadiq newspaper offices and eight public buildings, including the Central Police Station and the General Staff Headquarters. It encountered armed resistance by Mussadiq partisans, who also faced pro-Shah troops that arrived from the Hamadan garrison 200 miles (320 km) to the west.

Around 1 P.M., the mob seized the Tehran Radio station. Immediately, the royalist announcer declared that the Shah's decree appointing Gen. Zahedi as Prime Minster had been implemented. This was a lie. Just then Zahedi was battling to capture Prime Minister Mussadiq at his residence, which was being fiercely defended by pro-Mussadiq troops. It took Zahedi thirty-five Sherman tanks and nine hours to overpower his adversaries.[10] Mussadiq escaped by climbing over the back garden wall. That day, 164 soldiers and civilians, some of them carrying 500-rial notes in their pockets, were killed.[11]

August 20: Mussadiq surrendered. He would be sentenced to three years solitary imprisonment.

August 22: The Shah and his wife returned to Tehran to much acclaim. Among those who welcomed them were not only Zahedi, Nasseri, and Henderson but also Kashani and Jaafari Bemukh.

The CIA-MI6-engineered coup of August 19, 1953, which left

three hundred people dead and a few thousands injured, gave a new lease of life to the Shah's reign.

In a sense, the events of March 1951 to August 1953 were a rerun of the Constitutional Revolution. Then the Anglo-Russian Entente of 1907 had prepared the ground for the subsequent end of the revolution through Russian pressure and British complicity. Now America—a power that most secular nationalists had initially considered to be benevolently neutral to Iran in its dispute with the British—had clandestinely allied with Britain to overthrow a government that represented popular nationalist interests. This reprehensible act of the United States left a deep scar on the minds of Iranians, implanting most of them with abiding animosity toward America. Little wonder that, since the severing of diplomatic relations between Tehran and Washington in 1979, the leaders of the Islamic Republic have insisted on a public apology from the U.S. for this monumental violation of Iran's sovereignty and gross interference in its domestic affairs as a precondition for government-to-government talks. But it was not until 2000 that Madeleine Albright, the then U.S. Secretary of State, got around to offering a convoluted regret on an issue of paramount interest to Iranians of all political hues—a subject that is covered at length in Chapter Nine.

At the same time, events were different from that of 1905 to 1911. Whereas the traditional middle classes, led by the clergy, played a leading role in the constitutional movement, they were only junior partners in the oil nationalization movement, which was led by the representatives of the modern middle classes, whether in the National Front or the Tudeh Party. This happened because of Reza Shah's suppression of the clergy and because of the unprecedented growth in the size of the modern middle classes during his reign. A quarter of a century later, for different reasons, the roles of these sections of society would reverse once again.

The Pahlavis:
Modernizing Dictators

◆ CHAPTER 4 ◆

As you go past the black, unornamented steel-bar gates of the century-old Niavaran Palace in the affluent suburban village of that name on a foothill of the Elborz Mountains in north Tehran, the first object that catches your eye is a gigantic statue of a majestically robed and capped Amir Kabir (a.k.a. Mirza Taqi Khan) in white plaster, his haughtiness emphasized by his defiant posture next to a closed, nondescript building. A very able man, Amir Kabir, son of a steward in the royal household, rose to become the Chief Minister of Nasser al Din Shah, a Qajar king, who ruled Iran almost throughout the latter half of the nineteenth century.

Amir Kabir was the first top official to attempt to modernize Iran in the mid-nineteenth century, starting with the reorganization of the armed forces along European lines by establishing a military college that combined martial training with technical-scientific education. His pioneering effort left a deep mark on a succession of graduating military officers. Among them was the father of Reza Khan, an aspiring semiliterate soldier from a village in the Caspian province of Mazandaran, who would rise to become the *Shah-en-shah* (King of kings) of Iran and the founder of the Pahlavi dynasty. Amir Kabir is also highly regarded by today's clerical rulers because he suppressed Babis—a heterodox sect of the followers of Ali Muhammad Shirazi, who declared himself a *bab* (door) to the Hidden Imam of Shias—in 1848–50. As a result, a university and a main road in Tehran continue to carry his name.

The grounds of the Niavaran complex consist of impressively well-maintained pathways, memorable for the green-painted streetlights that illuminated late nineteenth-century Paris, and meticulously manicured lawns with flower beds. To reach the residence that Muhammad Reza Shah built for his family in 1957 you have to go past the one constructed by his father, a tall, mustached man with stern looks, and a dignified bearing despite his thin legs. The two-story palace with a basement is scarcely awe-inspiring or even mildly attractive. It is indeed permeated with melancholy that lifts only when you come across the turquoise and yellow tiling in a part that was once used as an imperial living quarter. The gloom disappears altogether when you enter rooms with walls that are decorated with mirror mosaics—thousands of small mirror fragments set at angles to one another to reflect light and distort images simultaneously—often found at religious shrines in Iran.

The basement is remarkable for the red, green, gold, and white upholstered chairs that surround a large dining table, reflecting the haphazard way the Shah and his second wife Sorya Isfandiari had chosen the furniture, mixing the period pieces of France's Second Empire with the latest French fashion. A painting of Napoleon retreating from Moscow confirms the couple's Francophilia.

Another place that drew my immediate attention was Muhammad Reza Shah's modest bedroom in a basement alcove. It was furnished with his daily diary written on large golden paper in Persian and English, and a small collection of books where the titles *Marathon* and *The Vantage Point* stood out. However, I had to cover my nose with a handkerchief to block the nauseating smell of phenol tablets scattered around the room to protect the books and fabrics from moths and other insects.

After the stink of the Shah's bedroom at the Niavaran Palace, a tour of the Saadabad Palace Complex in another part of north Tehran—scattered over a vast area of towering cedars, pines, cypresses, white birches and plane trees, manicured lawns, half-tended greenery, and gentle brooks—was life-enhancing. Bird song filled the air sweetened by musk roses and honeysuckle. The sprawling complex, now containing several museums, is served by an internal bus service. In fact, the Saadabad Palace Complex is now a popular spot for picnicking, especially in the sweltering months of summer, when the pressure of gridlocked streets, combined with the unchanging, architectural ugliness of the metropolis, becomes almost unbearable for many Tehranis.

What immediately caught my eye after passing the gated entrance was a pair of boots of bronze, a little higher than me at six-feet (1.83 meters), near the entrance of a building with broad limestone steps—a remnant of the mammoth statute of Reza Shah that was toppled by the revolutionaries in 1979.

Ironically, the other image that attracted me, with my eyes lingering long and lasciviously on it, was a marble frieze of naked women at the top of the columns of the entrance to the Green House, the palace of Reza Shah. Having seen virtually nothing more than a monolithic, monotonous image of women covered in black chadors for days on end, here I felt like a parched traveler in a desert arriving at an oasis. With that as the hors d'oeuvre, I was not surprised to see Reza Shah's bedroom furnished with a collection of French miniatures, with European beauties, green-eyed, rosy-cheeked, their enormous breasts covered tantalizingly.

The other centerpiece of the complex is the palace built by his son, Muhammad Reza, both as an office and a residence for use during summer. Instead of attempting to incorporate the world-renowned elements of the Persian-Islamic architecture, that reached its apotheosis in the Taj Mahal in India, the last Shah settled for a bland concrete box. Its waiting hall is furnished in the style of Louis XVI with gold-flecked wallpaper and crystal chandeliers crafted in Italy, and decorated with paintings by Henry Hadfield Cubley, a mediocre Scottish landscape artist of the late nineteenth and early twentieth centuries.

While the bedroom of Farah Diba, the Shah's third and last wife, a reedy, emaciated-looking woman, furnished with a cream and blue bed and a large television set, boasts an extraordinarily intricate silk carpet of over 273 sq. meters (435 sq. feet), the largest ever made, her husband's bed in gold satin is a replica of the one used by Napoleon.

What was truly remarkable about these palaces was the total absence of any Islamic image. There was no picture of the Kaaba, the centerpiece of the Grand Mosque in Mecca, which an affording Muslim is enjoined to visit once in his/her lifetime, or of the shrine of Imam Ali in Najaf or Imam Hussein in Karbala. Nor was there even a calligraphic rendition of the word "Allah" or "Ali" in Arabic or Persian. Equally remarkable was the absence of a small mosque in these palace complexes, or even a modest room in the royal residence set aside for prayers.

It was Reza Shah who had shifted the court and the royal household almost completely from the more modest royal buildings in south Tehran—the Gulistan and Marmar (lit., Marble) Palaces. He did so after April 1926 when, dressed in military uniform and royal jewels, he crowned himself.

This was the climax of the process triggered by his bloodless coup against the government of Fathollah Gilani on the night of February 21, 1921, followed immediately by his assurance to Ahmad Shah that he had acted to safeguard the monarchy from revolution. In reality, Col. Reza Khan, then commander of the elite Cossack Brigade, had led a force of three thousand from Qazvin, the British headquarters in the north, to Tehran at the secret instigation of Britain. Having despaired of the ineffective administration of the ruling Qajar elite, allied to feudal aristocracy, which inhibited its plans to fully exploit Iran's oil resources, the British government had decided to supplant the Qajar power with a new and stronger force.

When Reza Khan proposed Zia al Din Tabtabai, a pro-London journalist, as Premier, the Shah complied. Reza Khan joined the cabinet as War Minister. To show their independence from Britain, Tabtabai and Reza Khan signed a treaty with Bolshevik

Russia and submitted it to the Majlis for ratification. Three months later, Reza Khan eased out Tabtabai.

His successor, Ahmad Qavam al Saltane, a rich plantation owner in the Caspian province of Gilan, appointed Arthur Millspaugh, an American economist, the treasure-general to increase the government's revenue to maintain an enlarged armed force of forty thousand, created by merging seven thousand Cossacks and twelve thousand-strong gendarmerie with the existing army. In 1922–23, Reza Khan conducted a series of successful campaigns against the tribal and nontribal revolts in the provinces. In October 1923, he returned triumphantly to Tehran only to discover a plot against his life. He decided to lead the government while retaining the War Ministry. His ambition only grew.

He realized, however, that he could not confront the Shah until and unless he had the backing of Shia religious leaders in Qom and Najaf. So he allowed Sayyid Abol Hassan Isfahani and Shaikh Muhammad Hussein Naini, then the marja-e taqlid (source of emulation) of most Iranians—based in Qom after their expulsion from Najaf by the British Mandate—to tour Iran and propagate their views.

He also toyed with the idea of avoiding confrontation with the Shah by transforming Iran into a republic just as Kemal Ataturk had done in Turkey. This displeased senior clerics in Qom, who regarded Kemalism as un-Islamic. So, when Isfahani and Naini were allowed to return to Najaf, Iraq, by the British in April 1924, Reza Khan traveled to Qom and disowned republicanism. In return, Isfahani and Naini published a manifesto that said that the people of Iran should not deviate from "this Muslim circle [of Reza Khan's government] which gives currency to Islam. Those who oppose this command will be considered infidel."[1]

Thus fortified, Reza Khan marched with twenty-two thousand troops to the oil-rich Khuzistan province where the semi-independent Shaikh Muhammad Khazal had refused to pay taxes. Khazal surrendered unconditionally. This enabled Reza Khan to consolidate his power.

In January 1925, while Ahmad Shah was on a European tour, Reza Khan made a pilgrimage to Najaf where he sought the backing of Isfahani and Naini in his bid for the Peacock Throne by promising that as Iran's ruler he would implement the provision of the 1906–07 constitution that required vetting of all legislation by senior clerics. Unconvinced of Reza Khan's sincerity, Isfahani and Naini refused to be part of his plan to block the Shah's return. So next month he secured emergency powers from the Fifth Majlis (1924–26), including the title of the Commander in Chief of the military.

Among his early decrees was one that required all citizens to acquire a birth certificate and a surname. He chose for his family the name of the ancient Iranian language, Pahlavi. He orchestrated propaganda against the ruling Qajar dynasty. It reached a peak in October when the Shah was in Paris. By an overwhelming vote, the Majlis decided to depose him and appoint Reza Khan as Regent. His first act was to ban gambling and sale of alcohol, slash bread prices, and to promise to enforce moral conduct and the true laws of sacred Islam, thus propitiating senior Shia clerics.

Reza Shah (r. 1925–41)

On reaching the pinnacle of power, Reza Pahlavi Shah began centralizing and modernizing the state. He created a national civil service and police force. He quickened the pace of economic development, fueled by oil revenues, engendering a rising class of commercial and industrial bourgeoisie, and enlarging the size of the modern middle classes: secular teachers, lawyers, doctors, engineers, technicians, civil servants, and journalists. He considered the clergy to be ill-equipped to deal with the problems of modern times, and found it irksome having to work with the

Sixth Majlis (1926–28) where two-fifths of the deputies were clerics. He steadily curtailed clerics' power in their traditional fields of law, education, and religious endowments.

Reza Shah adroitly combined universally popular measures with socioeconomic reform that ran contrary to clerical interests. In 1927, he dismissed Millspaugh and unilaterally cancelled the economic privileges, often in terms of exploitation of Iran's natural resources or collection of customs duties for cash paid upfront by the privileged country—called capitulations—accorded European nations, particularly Russia and Britain, over the past century, thus implementing a proposal Mussadiq had made in his book *Iran and the Capitulation Agreements.* He increased tariffs on imports. These moves pleased merchants who had welcomed the Commercial Code of 1925 which, by legalizing joint stock companies, had opened the way for rapid economic advancement.

He subordinated the Sharia courts to the state and increased the government's control of the *waqf* (religious endowments) department. By tightly controlling theological schools, he presided over a decline in the number of religious students. While he lost ground among clerics and theological students, he gained popularity among civil servants, merchants, and the commercial bourgeoisie because of his aggressively nationalist economic policies. To create a national Iranian identity out of many ethnic ones at the popular level, a law passed at his behest in 1928 required all males to wear Western-style dress and a round, peaked cap.

To insulate Iran from the ill-effects of the Great Depression, he nationalized the import-export trade in 1931. Dissatisfied with low oil royalties, he unilaterally cancelled the concessions to the British-owned Anglo-Persian Oil Company (APOC) in November 1932—a step that was greeted with rejoicing in the streets. After APOC had taken its case to the League of Nations, the Shah signed a new agreement with it under the League's aegis in 1933. It offered better terms to Iran, including the reduction of the concession area of 500,000 sq. miles to 100,000.[2]

Inspired by the improved status of women he noticed during a trip to Turkey in 1934, he took several steps in that direction. He ordered all public places and educational institutions to admit women. He outlawed the veil—particularly chador, an all-embracing shroud. He banned military officers appearing in public in the company of veiled women. To set an example, he arrived at a degree-awarding function at a Tehran teachers' training college along with his wife and two teenage daughters wearing skirts and blouses, an unprecedented step. Clerics opposed Reza Shah's moves, arguing that the veil is enjoined by the Quran, but he ignored their protest.

He decreed that all men replace their peaked caps that he had prescribed earlier with European felt hats. He reduced the powers and scope of the Islamic Law courts and strengthened the secular, state courts. In 1939, he banned self-flagellation in public on the anniversary of Imam Hussein's death on the tenth day of Muharram, the first month in the Islamic calendar. He also actively discouraged the public performance of Shia passion plays performed before the mournful day of Ashura, Tenth Muharram, to commemorate the heroic tragedy of Imam Hussein in 681 AD, and prohibited the pilgrimage to Mecca. By blatantly manipulating elections, he reduced the share of clerics in parliament from 40 percent in the Sixth Majlis (1926–28) to none in a decade.

The building of fourteen thousand miles of roads and Trans-Iranian Railway by August 1938 boosted industrialization.

To counterbalance the traditional commercial and political dominance of London and Moscow, Reza Shah cultivated strong ties with Berlin—especially after the rise in 1933 of Adolf Hitler whose autocracy and ultranationalism appealed to him. Political and economic ties between Tehran and Berlin grew stronger. Encouraged by the Persian ambassador in Berlin, the Shah changed the name of his country from Persia to Iran, a variant of the word "Aryan," meaning "noble." APOC's management followed suit and renamed the corporation Anglo-Iranian Oil Company (AIOC).

By the time World War II broke out in September 1939, Germany accounted for nearly half of Iran's foreign trade. German experts were then engaged in building Iranian roads, railways, and docks—as well as the organizing of the Youth Corps. Reza Shah declared Iran to be neutral in the conflict. In the winter of 1940–41, as the war seemed to swing in favor of the Axis Powers, the British protested against the presence of German agents in Iran, which was host to an estimated two thousand Germans.[3]

The German invasion of the Soviet Union in June 1941 was seen by the British as part of a pincer movement, its other arm being the German thrust into North Africa to crush the British resistance there. The Allies deliberately played up the issue of German spies. Their real fear was the possibility of Reza Shah upgrading his strong sympathies with Germany into a military alliance. This had to be aborted at all costs, they decided, and Iran had to be converted into a corridor for supplying Allied war materials to the Soviet Union, which was invaded by Germany in June 1941.

On August 25, 1941, Soviet and British troops invaded Iran at five points. Iranian resistance collapsed after two days, and a ceasefire was signed. The Soviet forces occupied the northern part of Iran, and the British the southern. On September 16, fearing that Soviet troops were marching down from Qazvin to Tehran to depose him, Reza Shah abdicated in favor of his eldest son, Muhammad Reza, who was educated at a Swiss private school and the Tehran Military Academy. He left for the British-ruled island of Mauritius, and then for South Africa where he would die three years later.

"Reza Shah's work for rapid modernization from above, along with his militantly secularist cultural and education program, helped to create the situation of 'two cultures' in Iran," notes Niki R. Keddie, an American specialist on Iran. "The upper- and new-middle classes became increasingly westernized and scarcely understood the traditional or religious culture of most of their compatriots. On the other hand, peasants and urban bazaar classes continued to follow the ulema [clerics], however politically cowed the ulema were. These classes associated 'the way things should be' more with Islam than with west."[4] This was to have an important bearing on the rise of a revolutionary movement in the late 1970s.

Muhammad Reza Shah (r. 1941–79)

The twenty-two-year-old Muhammad Reza Pahlavi—a small, unprepossessing figure, noted merely for his sharp-featured face— found his kingdom occupied by foreign powers, his army reduced to safeguarding internal security, and his regime beset with dislocated transport system, falling production, shortage of food and other necessities, hoarding and profiteering, and soaring inflation, with prices rising sevenfold in three years. Feeling vulnerable, he yielded to clerical pressures, and annulled his father's bans on Shia passion plays and pilgrimage to Mecca. He even instructed government offices to observe the Islamic prohibitions during the fasting month of Ramadan, a small but highly visible step.

When World War II ended in August 1945, it did not lead to the immediate pullout of all foreign soldiers from Iran. It was only after the Soviet troops had withdrawn in May 1946, and the Iranian forces had quelled autonomous governments in Kurdistan and Azerbaijan in December, that he was able to exercise authority over all of Iran.

In 1947, he felt confident enough to dismiss Prime Minister Ahmad Qawam al-Saltane, who had been instrumental in reimposing the Shah's authority in Azerbaijan. However, Ibrahim Hakimi, the ruler's choice for Premier, faced stiff opposition from Muhammad Mussadiq, and scraped through by one vote in the Majlis.

On February 4, 1949, there was an unsuccessful attempt on the Shah's life by a press photographer. The attacker was killed on the spot. But his identity papers showed him to be working for the *Parcham-e Islam* (Flag of Islam), a religious publication, and belonging to the journalists' union, affiliated to the pro-Tudeh labor federation. So the Shah repressed both religious and secular leftist groups. He imposed martial law, requiring martial law administrators to report to him direct. He banned the Tudeh Party which, though established in 1942, traced its roots to the Communist Party of Iran set up twenty-two years earlier (a brief chronicle of the two parties appears in Chapter Seven).

At his behest, the Majlis passed a law that restricted political activity, thus reversing the growth of political parties and groups that had followed his father's deposition. Moderate clerical leaders rallied round him. But that did not deter many senior clergy from issuing religious decrees in favor of the nationalization of the Anglo-Iranian Oil Company, a subject that engaged most Iranians during the election campaign for the Sixteenth Majlis (1950–52).

The nationalization of the AIOC and the subsequent crisis dominated Iranian life until the CIA-MI6-sponsored coup against the Mussadiq government on August 19, 1953. It destroyed any chance Iran had of evolving into a Western-style democracy under the leadership of Mussadiq. The Shah set up military tribunals to punish all those who had participated in anti-royalist activities. These tribunals would become a permanent feature of his regime. The persecution of the Shah's adversaries continued unabated for two years, and resulted in the deaths of five thousand Iranians and the self-exile of fifty thousand.[5]

The Shah's Second Coming

Returning to the throne, the Shah was generous with praise and patronage to all those who worked for his comeback. At the same time he was not indiscriminate. For instance, he kept Ayatollah Abol Qasim Kashani at bay, considering him unreliable and essentially rebellious.

Senior religious leaders publicly approved the repression the Shah unleashed on the Tudeh in 1954–55. In contrast, they acquiesced discreetly when the ruler meted out similar treatment to the Fedaiyan-e Islam, a militant, underground organization, in late 1955 after it had condemned the inequitable oil agreement the Shah signed with the Western consortium in August 1954 which was ratified by the Majlis two months later. The Shah tried to project himself as a savior of Islam. He and his wife Sorya Isfandiari visited the Shia holy shrines in Qom, Mashhad, and Karbala, and made a pilgrimage to Mecca.

In the aftermath of the CIA-sponsored coup against Mussadiq, the influence of the U.S. in Iran rose sharply.

Between August 1953 and December 1956, Washington provided Iran with military and economic aid of $414 million.[6] With it, came thousands of Americans, a development much resented by nationalist Iranians, secular and religious.

Iran's oil income jumped from $34 million in 1954–55 to $181 million two years later. With the state receiving such vast sums, corruption increased, so also the Shah's self-confidence. His dismissal of Gen. Fazollah Zahedi, a linchpin in the CIA-engineered coup, in April 1955 showed his increasing ambition to arrogate all power. To improve his popularity, the Shah instructed the newly appointed Prime Minister Hussein Ala, his former Court Minister, to eradicate endemic corruption.

In 1955, the Shah formed a political police force under military officers to gather intelligence and repress opposition, a prelude to the establishment of Savak—an acronym for *Sazman-e Aminyat Va Ettilaat-e Keshavar* (Organization of National Security and Intelligence). The law of March 1957 formalized the ad hoc arrangement, with a clause in it describing Savak's main function as "the gathering of information necessary to protect national security; to prevent the activity of groups whose ideology is contrary to the constitution; to prevent plots against national security."[7] Savak maintained strong ties not only with the CIA, which trained its operatives, but also Israel's foreign intelligence agency, Mossad. Savak was attached to the Prime Minister's office, and its head had the status of a Deputy Premier.

By 1957, the Shah had smashed the Tudeh Party as well as all the constituents of the National Front. But the overthrow in July 1958 of Iraqi King Faisal II by nationalist, republican officers, resulting in the end of pro-West monarchy in Iraq, rattled him. He invited U.S. President Dwight Eisenhower to enter into a mutual defense pact. Eisenhower agreed to sign a more limited executive arrangement to assist the Shah in countering "overt armed aggression from any nation controlled by international Communism" if he pledged to spend U.S. nonmilitary aid on economic development rather than imports of consumer goods, and to liberalize the political system.[8] This set the scene for the emergence of state-controlled party politics in 1959: Premier Manuchehr Eqbal heading the ruling Melliyun (Nationalist) Party, and Assadollah Alam, a boyhood friend of the ruler, leading the opposition Mardom (People's) Party.

In short, by the late 1950s, the Shah had laid the necessary political-economic infrastructure for rapid economic development under state-dominated capitalism: a process set to expand the size of the modern middle and upper classes—white-collar professionals, and mercantile and industrial bourgeoisie—and reduce the size of the traditional upper and middle classes: feudal lords, tribal chiefs, mullahs, bazaar merchants, and craftsmen.

To facilitate rapid capitalistic growth, the Shah needed to break the shackles of feudalism, the strong feudal elements embedded in the landed gentry who had a stake in maintaining the skewed ownership of agricultural land. Half of the cultivated land of 4.5 million hectares (11.1 million acres) belonged to absentee landlords. Among them were the religious endowments managed by clerics. By contrast, 40 percent of all rural households were landless, and only 5 percent of peasants were owner-occupiers, the rest being tenant farmers.[9] Redistribution of land was overdue, but the halfhearted land reform bill that the Majlis passed in May 1960 fell into disuse almost immediately.

The Shah's rigging of the subsequent Majlis polls and frequent changes of Prime Ministers delayed the process. An amended Land Reform Act emerged in 1962. The Shah promoted Assadollah Alam, his Court Minister, to Prime Minister to implement the new law and establish local councils as part of a theoretically multilayered democracy, urged on him by U.S. President John Kennedy.

Finally, on January 6, 1963, the Shah launched a six-point White Revolution: agrarian reform, forest nationalization, sale of public-sector factories to compensate landlords, votes for women, profit-sharing in industry, and eradication of illiteracy. The state-run media lumped together the secular National Front—which, while favoring reform, attacked the unconstitutional manner in which it had been decreed—and religious opposition, labeling them "reactionary." The followers of the National Front and militant clerics resorted to street protest and backed their leaders' call for a boycott of the referendum on January 25. The Shah responded by arresting the National Front leaders and prominent opposition clerics.

According to his government, 91 percent of the 6.2 million eligible voters cast their ballots, with 99.9 percent saying "Yes."

None of this discouraged the regime's opponents who prepared to demonstrate their strength on March 21, the Iranian New Year, Nawruz. A fortnight earlier, the pro-regime *Ettilaat* (Information) published a series of editorials, arguing that the reforms were in conformity with the Sharia, Islamic law. Describing Islam and other monotheistic religions as "eternal," it declared: "By the same token, religion is a matter apart from politics. Politics is an everyday term, religion an eternal one." Such statements were anathema to radical clergy, particularly Ayatollah Ruhollah Khomeini.

Ignoring dire warnings, anti-Shah demonstrators took to the streets on Nawruz in major cities. In Qom, the protest was led by theological students who had been agitating against the scheduled opening of liquor shops in the holy city. Paratroopers and Savak agents attacked seminaries in Qom and Tabriz, and, according to unofficial estimates, killed "hundreds."[10]

Khomeini was arrested but released shortly after. Sporadic demonstrations continued throughout April. To punish the theological students, the government suspended their exemption from conscription. This only raised tempers.

Tension rose sharply in late May as the grieving month of Muharram approached. On June 3, the tenth of Muharram, the mournful day of Ashura, Khomeini referred to the Shah in an incendiary speech, while addressing the faithful in Qom. "You miserable wretch, isn't it time for you to think and reflect a little, to ponder where all this is leading you?" he asked of the Shah rhetorically. "Religious scholars and Islam are some form of Black Reaction! And you have carried out a White Revolution in the midst of all this Black Reaction." He then referred to clerics in Tehran being taken to Savak offices and ordered "not to say anything bad about the Shah, not to attack Israel, and not to say that Islam is endangered." He explained that the clerics' differences with the government comprised exactly these three points. "Mr. Shah, do you want me to say that you don't believe in Islam, and kick you out of Iran? Do you know that when one day something changes, none of these people who surround you today will be your friends?"[11] The speech electrified the audience, and turned the Ashura procession into a mammoth anti-Shah demonstration.

Next day copies of Khomeini's speech appeared on the walls of Fatima Massoumeh's shrine and the adjoining Faiziya Seminary. Thousands gathered to read and discuss it. Khomeini was arrested in the early hours of June 5/(Iranian) Khordad 15.

The news spread instantly, and led to anti-government demonstration in Qom and other cities. The accompanying rioting was so severe that the twin events were later collectively called the Khordad 15 Uprising. The scale and severity of popular anger against his regime unnerved the Shah. He took personal control of the government and riot-control operations. He declared martial law in riot-torn cities, and pressed tanks and troops into action with orders to shoot to kill. Among the thousands of Iranians arrested were twenty-eight ayatollahs.

It took the troops two days to crush the uprising. According to the government, sixty-eight people were killed, and another 150 wounded. But, Marvin Zonis, an American academic, who witnessed the army firing outside Tehran's Grand Bazaar, put the number of dead and injured at "many thousands."[12] Dr. A. R. Azimi, writing in the Tehran-based *Payam-e Emruz* (Today's Message) on June 10, estimated the number of dead at ten thousand.

By unleashing the firepower of modern military on unarmed civilians, the Shah cowed the populace. The clergy's call for a national strike on June 11 drew a poor response. This signaled the Shah's success in crushing religious opposition, having earlier smashed its secular counterpart, the Tudeh and the National Front.

Having established his supremacy, the Shah relaxed his iron grip, slightly. He released Khomeini on August 3, and put him under house arrest in a north Tehran suburb. But when Khomeini called on the electorate to boycott the parliamentary poll in September, he was reimprisoned. In the Twenty-second Majlis (1963–67), the freshly formed New Iran Party claimed the loyalty of 140 deputies, and its leader Ali Mansur became the Prime Minister.

In April 1964, following a Savak statement that Khomeini had promised not to act "contrary to the interest, and law and order, of the state," he was freed. On his release, Khomeini denied that he had given such an undertaking.

In late October, the Shah managed to get the Majlis to pass a law by a narrow majority that gave diplomatic immunity to all Americans working on military projects in Iran to fulfill Washington's precondition for giving $200 million credit to Tehran to buy U.S.-made weapons. "American cooks, mechanics, technical and administrative officials, together with their families, are to enjoy legal immunity, but the ulema [clergy] of Islam, the preachers and servants of Islam, are to live banished or imprisoned," Khomeini told a gathering outside his home in Qom. "Today, when colonial territories are bravely freeing the bonds that have chained them, the so-called progressive Majlis . . . votes for the most shameful and offending decrees of the ill-reputed government."[13]

On November 4, 1964, Khomeini was arrested and put on a plane bound for Turkey. After living in Bursa for a year, he moved to Najaf, Iraq, where many decades earlier his grandfather Sayyid Ahmad Mousavi al Hindi had met Yusuf Khan Kamaraei, a notable from Khomein, whose daughter he would marry.[14]

In April 1965, there was another failed attempt to assassinate the Shah. His attacker, a conscript in the Imperial Guard, was killed instantly by royal bodyguards. Following the death of

Mansur, the Shah promoted Amir Abbas Hoveida, Finance Minister and Deputy Leader of the New Iran Party, who was popular with businessmen, to Prime Minister.

As the Commander in Chief, the Shah kept a close watch on the military leadership, personally vetting all promotions above the rank of major. He kept senior officers under the surveillance of the military intelligence's J2 Department, originally established by his father on the lines of the French Deuxieme Bureau, and rewarded them with generous salaries and fringe benefits during service, and lucrative jobs in public-sector undertakings after retirement. Though nominally attached to the Prime Minister's office, Savak operated under military protection, and thus came within the Shah's direct jurisdiction.

Following the June 1967 Arab-Israeli War, which underscored the explosive instability of the Middle East, Washington's interest in Iran, already high, rose further. American military and civilian presence in the country increased perceptibly, a development resented by most urban Iranians. They found ways of expressing dissent—mildly—when an opportunity arose. For instance, in the 1968 local elections, 90 percent of Tehran's voters abstained, a record.[15]

Yet Prime Minister Hoveida managed to collect "voluntary" contributions from bazaar merchants and others to the tune of $200 million to match the sum contributed by the government treasury for the belated coronation of Muhammad Reza Pahlavi Shah on October 26, 1967, his forty-eighth birthday.

This extravaganza was dwarfed on October 15, 1971, on the eve of his fiftieth birthday by the lavishness with which he celebrated two thousand five hundred years of "unbroken" monarchy in Iran—a blatantly false claim due to the absence of kingship in Iran from 640 to 1501—at Persepolis, once the capital of the ancient Achemenian dynasty.

Among those who attended the celebration were sixty-eight kings, queens, princes, princesses, and heads of states, including

Emperor Haile Selassie of Ethiopia, King Constantine of Greece, and Vice President Spiro Agnew of the U.S. They and their retinues were accommodated in luxury tents, made of inflammable fabric in beige and royal blue and spread over 2.5 sq. miles (6.5 sq. km)—with special roads built to the site—and were plied with the finest French wines and cuisine prepared by Maxim's of Paris. The peak of their entertainment came with the parading of more than six thousand Iranian soldiers, wearing makeup and false beards, and dressed in the uniforms of every period of Persian history from Cyrus I of the Achemenian dynasty to the present. Missing from this historical reenactment was the epoch starting with 636, when Muslim Arabs defeated Sassanian monarch Yazdegard III at Qadasiya (now in Iraq), bringing Islam to Persia, and ending with the overthrow of the Timurid rulers in 1500, unveiling the reign of the Safavids and a steady conversion of Persians to Shia Islam.

Oddly, while establishing the Department of Religious Corps and Religious Affairs, the Shah's Religious Endowment Department had cited Article 39 of the 1906–07 Constitution, requiring the monarch to promote Jaafari Shiaism. After initiating a program of training religious propagandists for posting in rural areas, it formed the Religious Corps in August 1971 with thirty-nine graduates of theology faculties of the Universities of Tehran and Mashhad. The regime hailed them as "the mullahs of modernization." This was part of the Shah's multipronged strategy of weakening the traditional clergy, which included using bribes to co-opt fence-sitters and punishing those who refused to cooperate.

Having usurped all temporal power in Iran, the Shah started visualizing himself as an agent of God. "I believe in God, and that I have been chosen by God to perform a task," he told Oriana Fallaci, an Italian journalist, in September 1973. "My visions are miracles that saved the country. My reign saved the country, and it had done so because God is on my side."[16]

The megalomania of the Shah, who in March 1973 nationalized the two-decades-old Western oil consortium operating in Iran, rose further as petroleum price jumped in late 1973 to early 1974, following the October 1973 Arab-Israeli War. Iran's oil export income rose two-and-half times in a year—to $11.65 billion in 1974—with the output remaining steady at 2.2 million barrels per day (bpd). He now frequently mentioned his aim to make Iran the fifth most powerful nation on earth—after America, the Soviet Union, Japan, and West Germany.

But the inflated Five Year Plan of 1973–77, which included a massive boost in arms expenditure, overheated the economy, causing rapid migration of rural workers to cities, high inflation, and widespread corruption. Rapid capitalist growth had the combustible effect of segmenting Iran's urban dwellers into six classes. At the top were sixty-odd families directly related to the Shah or one of his brothers, sisters, or cousins. Then came about one thousand aristocratic families: some of them invested in urban projects before the 1963 agrarian reform and others after. Next followed some two hundred elderly politicians, and retired civil and military officers, who won government contracts for the companies they directed. They thrived as the military budget shot up from $225 million in 1966 to $9,500 million a decade later, and the size of the armed forces rose to four hundred thousand, a tenfold increase in half a century.[17] The last in the upper-class category were the nonaristocratic entrepreneurs who had emerged mostly during and after World War II.

Of the one million families belonging to the traditional middle classes, half of them originated in the bazaar. The rest were traders and entrepreneurs who, functioning apart from the bazaar, owned 420,000 rural workshops, often weaving carpets, and 440,000 medium-sized commercial farms, and shops outside the bazaar.[18] Both groups were related to clerics.

At 650,000, the modern middle classes had doubled over the past generation. Consisting of three hundred thousand civil servants, two hundred thousand teachers, and sixty-one thousand white-collar professionals and managers, they formed nearly 7 percent of the total labor force of 10 million.[19]

At the bottom of the social pyramid were some 2.5 million families of the urban working class, industrial and nonindustrial, which had grown fivefold in a little over a decade. Among the nine hundred thousand industrial workers, two-thirds worked in factories employing less than ten persons. A quarter of the non-industrial working class was engaged in distribution and other services, and the rest were construction laborers, peddlers, hawkers, and menials.[20]

Many of the nonindustrial workers were recent arrivals from villages where, as landless peasants or former nomads, they had worked as agrarian laborers, construction workers, shepherds, or workshop employees. Their kinsmen in rural areas, still per-forming these tasks, amounted to 1.1 million families. So the nonindustrial working class as a whole accounted for almost a quarter of the national workforce. Together with the industrial working class, it formed more than a third of the total workforce.

It was against this socioeconomic backdrop that the Shah tried to solve the problems created by an overheated economy—with the annual growth rate rising to 42 percent in 1975—and 35 percent inflation, and simultaneously confront the alienated traditional middle classes in his quest for power and glory.

As described earlier (in Chapter One), the official anti-profiteering campaign took a heavy toll in the bazaar. On top of that the government encouraged the rise of supermarkets by pro-viding them with cheap bank credit. Also, by controlling food prices, the government reduced farm incomes, which drove tens of thousands of marginal farmers to cities. As devout Muslims, the rural poor had always looked to the clergy for guidance and succor. They continued the tradition when they migrated to urban centers, thus enhancing clerical power.

Rapid influx into urban centers overstretched the existing

facilities: housing, electricity, water supply, and cooking gas. Rents exploded, rising threefold in five years, often consuming nearly half of the earnings of many middle-class families. Discontent was rife in the modern middle classes too, but they lacked any outlet for expression. All newspapers and journalists were affiliated to the Rastakhiz Party. Its nominees also controlled radio and television as well as the Ministries of Information and Arts and Culture.

Only the anti-Shah clerics were able to offer a semblance of open opposition through periodic statements and demonstrations. Khomeini's exile in Najaf helped them particularly after the accord that the Shah signed with Iraq in March 1975, which eased border crossings and led the Iraqi government to allow 130,000 Iranian pilgrims annually to visit the Shia holy cities of Karbala and Najaf, where Khomeini was based.

Most clerics were upset when the Shah tried to project himself not only as the Political Leader but also the Spiritual Leader. To make the latter point dramatically, he introduced a Royalist calendar, dating back to the pre-Islamic Achemenian dynasty, on the completion of half a century of the Pahlavi rule on April 24, 1976. Since the new calendar deviated from the Islamic heritage, Hojatalislam Abol Hassan Shamsabadi of Isfahan attacked it. A few days later he was found murdered.

The demonstration by Qom's theology students to commemorate the June 5, 1963, uprising was the largest such gathering since the fateful events of thirteen years earlier, giving a lie to the Shah's claim that the anti-regime opposition was limited to "a handful of nihilists, anarchists, and Communists."

Abroad, especially in the U.S., where the national mood had turned introspective in the wake of America's defeat in Vietnam in 1975, there was growing unease at the dictatorial policies of the Shah. During his election campaign for U.S. President, Democrat candidate Jimmy Carter named Iran as one of the countries where

America should do more to protect civil and human liberties. Once in the White House, Carter stressed that the states violating human rights might be denied U.S. weapons or aid, or both.

This was why the Shah changed course. Political liberalization, which began in February 1977 with the release of 357 political prisoners, gathered pace in the summer. Each concession by the regime brought further demands from the opposition. Both modern and traditional classes became active, albeit in different ways. Writers, academics, politicians, lawyers, and even judges resorted to addressing open letters to the ruler whereas bazaar merchants and religious students staged demonstrations and clashed with the police. Being close to the urban poor, both politically and geographically, the traditional middle class provided leadership to the urban underclass, which eventually adopted the revolutionary slogan "Death to the Shah," and stuck to it. To be sure, popular demands, orchestrated by Khomeini from Najaf, rose incrementally.

The revolutionary process went through seven rising stages before reaching its goal of the Shah's overthrow, with the earliest ones—from February to October 1977 and November to December—dominated by secular forces, giving way steadily to Islamic elements during the remaining phases of January to June 1978; July to September 8 (Black Friday); September 9 to November 5; November 6, 1978 to January 16, 1979 (when the Shah left Iran); and January 16 to February 11, 1979.

In March, a critical letter addressed to the Shah by Ali Asghar Javadi, a former editor of the *Kayhan* (World) newspaper and an essayist on Islam and socialism, tested the waters. The absence of any official action against him encouraged Javadi to publish a two-hundred-page essay in May, criticizing the state of contemporary Iran. Again the Shah, who gave an unprecedented audience to Amnesty International, a London-based human rights organization, left Javadi alone.

This emboldened fifty-three lawyers to address a letter to the ruler alleging government interference in the judicial system. In June, forty writers sent a letter to Premier Hoveida to lift censorship. Later that month, in an open letter, three National Front leaders called on the Shah to respect the constitution, "abandon the single party system, permit the freedom of the press and association . . . and establish a government based on a majority which has been elected and which considers itself answerable to the constitution."[21]

To appease the rising tide of discontent, the Shah replaced Prime Minister Hoveida in August with Jamshed Amouzgar, a fifty-one-year-old technocrat who led the "liberal" wing of the Rastakhiz Party. He immediately opened all trials, including the ones before military tribunals, to the public, and required the security authorities to produce a detainee before a magistrate within twenty-four hours. Considering this move inadequate, 120 lawyers met in October to set up the Association of Iranian Jurists (AIJ), which, in turn, appointed a working group to publicize torture by Savak and monitor prison conditions. Many professors and teachers demanded academic freedom.

By then the National Front had revived, and so had the Liberation Movement of Iran, dating back to 1961, and the Tudeh Party. They had all started publishing semiclandestine literature.

On November 15, while Iranian students in America were demonstrating against the Shah's visit to the White House, their colleagues in Tehran took to the streets in sympathy. Those arrested in Tehran sought lawyers from the AIJ. Tried by civilian courts, they were either released or given light sentences. This dispelled the long-held fear among Iranians that opposing the Shah meant torture and stiff prison sentences by military tribunals meeting in secret.

Alarmed by this, the Shah tried to regain the initiative by mounting an offensive against the clergy in general and

Khomeini in particular since they, in his view, lacked support among the modern middle classes. On January 7, the Women's Day in Iran, the *Ettilaat* published an unsigned article, entitled "Iran, and the Black and Red Reactionaries."[22] After a few general remarks about the White Revolution and the Black Reaction of the clergy, the article described "a religious leader chosen to direct the Black Reaction" as "adventurer, without faith . . . with a questionable past, linked to the more superficial and reactionary colonialists." He was Ruhollah Khomeini, better known as "the Indian Sayyid." While his links with India had never been exposed before, it was obvious he had contacts with the British. In his youth, he wrote romantic poetry signed "Al Hindi" (The Indian). Now he opposed the Shah's reforms. He received a lot of money from the English, through an Arab, to carry on fighting the Shah.[23]

By sponsoring this attack on Khomeini, the Shah committed a blunder. It enraged Qom in the way Khomeini's arrest in 1963 had. The bazaar and seminaries closed in protest. On January 9, more than forty thousand theological students, demanding restoration of freedom to the faithful in mosques, faced the police armed with loaded guns. Many of them offered themselves fearlessly to the security forces, setting a pattern that would be repeated many times by tens of thousands of protestors during the next turbulent year. In Qom on that day, between ten and seventy-two demonstrators lost their lives.

Feeling threatened, the Shah mobilized his base. On January 26, between one hundred thousand and three hundred thousand people, gathered in Tehran to celebrate the fifteenth anniversary of the White Revolution. This would prove to be the first and last show of strength by the Shah's partisans.

By calling on the faithful to demonstrate on the fortieth day memorial of the Qom martyrs, Khomeini snatched the initiative from the Shah and kept it until he had toppled the Pahlavi dynasty.

The Shah's failing health partly explained why he did not reverse his liberalization policy at its incipient stage. In early 1978, his French doctors told him that his cancer had reached an advanced state. As his son, Reza Cyrus, was then a minor, he decided to groom his wife Farah Diba as the future ruler. Since she could not be as autocratic as her husband, he decided to continue the liberalization process. Out of this consideration arose his decision in late August to appoint Jaafar Sharif-Emami as Premier to conciliate the regime's most powerful adversary, the clergy. Washington backed this move.

In the past, the Shah had acted resolutely only when he had the unequivocal backing of the military at home and the U.S. government abroad. This time military leaders were unhesitatingly behind him. But the Carter administration was divided, with the faction led by Zbigniew Brzezinsky, the National Security Adviser, urging tough action against the opposition, and Cyrus Vance, Secretary of State, advising compromise.

The Shah showed poor judgment while taking some vital decisions. He thought that getting Khomeini away from Iraq would lessen his impact on Iranians. So he gave a tactical nod to French President Valery Giscard d'Estaing before the latter admitted Khomeini to France in October. Judging by the international publicity Khomeini received during his stay in France, the Shah realized that he had blundered. But by then it was too late. His fate was finally sealed when oil workers went on an indefinite strike and his army began to disintegrate.

His desperate, last-minute ploy to appoint Shahpur Bakhtiar, who once served as deputy labor minister under Mussadiq, failed to impress Iranians, religious and secular, who were by now unanimous in their demand for him to step down. On January 16, 1979, he left Iran, ostensibly for a holiday in Aswan, Egypt, never to return, dying of cancer eighteen months later in America.

This marked the end not just of the Pahlavi dynasty but also monarchy with an unbroken history dating back to the Safavids, who adopted Twelver Shiaism as state religion in 1501.

Khomeini, the Pioneer, and Khamanei

◆ CHAPTER 5 ◆

"Welcome to the hometown of Khomeini." So runs the greeting to a visitor to Khomein in white Persian and English letters against a green background on a concrete arch. These plain words refer to a man who, at the age of seventy-six, led the world's last great revolutionary movement in the twentieth century to victory by uniting the disparate anti-status quo forces on a maximalist platform: the end of the Pahlavi dynasty.

Half a mile down Khomein's main thoroughfare, lined with bustling stores, repair shops, tea stalls and restaurants, at a road junction, on a vast multicolored billboard, the nature of that revolution is spelled out in Persian and English next to the portrait of Ayatollah Ruhollah Khomeini—the all-too-familiar sharp features, gray beard, stern eyes looking at middle distance, capped by a neat black turban, a headgear indicating descent from Prophet Muhammad[1]: "IMAM KHOMEINI (PBUH)[2] WAS THE REVIVER OF RELIGIOUS GOVERNMENT IN CONTEMPORARY WORLD."

At the junction, if you turn sharp right into Saheli Street (formerly Al Hindi Street), you see a sprawling mansion on the right-hand side and a sign, posted *Beit al Nour* (House of Light).

A complex occupying 46,270 sq. feet (4,326 sq. meters), it consists of four adjoining houses, each with a courtyard with a small pool and flower bed in the middle and a few trees on the perimeter, and a three-story watchtower. In the past, the complex served not only to accommodate the family of Ahmad Mousavi al Hindi, who sired only one son, Mustafa, but also Mustafa's three sons and three daughters, Ruhollah being the youngest—but also the theological school that Ayatollah Mustafa al Hindi, being the town's chief cleric, established after completing his religious

114

studies in Najaf. It was there that Ahmad al Hindi, who had arrived there for further theological studies from the Oudh province in northern India, had met Yusuf Khan Kamaraei, a notable of Khomein, and agreed to marry his daughter. And it was with Kamaraei's financial support that Ahmad acquired this real estate.

Arriving at the House of Light in July 2004, I was struck by the overall transformation that the place had undergone since my last visit there a quarter century earlier. Then it stood in an unpaved alleyway, called Al Hindi Street, off an equally unprepossessing main road in a town that had the depressing hallmarks of a back-water provincial settlement. A nondescript entrance near the tower led to a courtyard with a dried-up pond in the middle (it was December) surrounded by assorted rooms on two sides and a wall on the third. Today Khomein is a thriving town of 130,000, served by clean paved roads with tree-covered islands in the middle, flower beds, and rows of streetlights, each encased in large twin globes resting on tubular arms extending from a slender green shaft.

As part of the general uplift of the town, 180 miles (290 km) southwest of Tehran, a once unremarkable real estate of the Khomeinis has been transformed into an attractive, even vibrant, place of pilgrimage, with the mansion enclosed by a low brick fence studded with square steel bars facing the street, and the new entrance emblazoned with a banner saying in Persian, "House of Revered Imam Khomeini." Inside, each of the four courtyards has its own ambience, the smallest one used as a pri-vate quarter by Mustafa al Hindi, and later inherited to his eldest son, Murtaza. A larger courtyard with a circular pond at its center, and surrounded by rooms that once served as classrooms for the-ological students, is now surrounded by large portraits of Khomeini and his two sons, Mustafa (who died in mysterious circumstances in 1977) and Ahmad, who survived his father.

As you walk through the well-preserved rooms, you come across a tribute to Khomeini in Persian and English that reads, "Imam Khomeini first opened his eyes to the world and illuminated the Islamic world with his radiance and splendor in 1902 (1320 Iranian year) coinciding with the auspicious birthday anniversary of the Noble Lady of Islam, Fatima al Zahra (PBUH), 20 Janadi al Thaniya." Equally eye-catching is the framed copy of the Identity Document issued to Khomeini by the interior Ministry of the Islamic Republic of Iran: "Number A/12/514514. Sayyid Ruhallah Mustafavi born in 1279 (Iranian year) . . . Issued by Ali Akbar Rahmani on 20.11.1358."

Across the street, an airy, well-stocked shop sells pictures, audiotapes, and videotapes of Khomeini. The glass walls of the store are decorated with color pictures of Khomeini and Ayatollah Ali Khamanei, with his long, silvery white beard and uncommonly thick-rimmed glasses, flanked by the portraits of Imam Ali, the founder of Shia Islam. Mahdi Rahimi, a slim, clean-shaven young man, wearing designer glasses, offered me a pack of Khomeini's pictures that showed him wearing merely a skull cap, cuddling his grandchildren, and sauntering around a lawn in a lush garden.

The images took me back to the time in April 1983 when Iran was in the thick of war with Iraq. Along with other foreign journalists, I visited the administrative residence-mosque of Khomeini in the north Tehran suburb of Jamran, which was ringed by computerized, semiautomatic Soviet-made anti-aircraft guns programmed to shoot any aircraft sighted in the area by the early warning radar screens. Revolutionary Guards, in charge of Khomeini's security, strictly controlled the access to his place. Within these constraints, Khomeini addressed select groups of Iranians—employees of the National Iranian Oil Company (NIOC), relatives of the war dead, cadres of the Reconstruction Crusade, leaders of bazaar merchants, or Majlis deputies—during his weekly public appearance.

Security checks started at the junction of Martyr Husseinkiya Street and Yasser Road, where I was frisked by Revolutionary Guards and made to surrender all my possessions—rings, a camera, a watch, and even my notebook—at a check post. I underwent two more body searches as I walked along a cobbled alleyway. There I gave up my shoes before I could enter the mosque, a bare concrete building with a mural on the wall, painted in red and black carried the slogan, "Every place is Karbala [where Imam Hussein was killed], Every day is Ashura [the day Imam Hussein was killed]," with a balcony that led to Khomeini's offices.

It was in Karbala, Iraq, that Imam Hussein, a grandson of Prophet Muhammad, died more than thirteen centuries ago along with seventy-two ill-equipped followers while fighting a well-armed enemy force of four thousand. The event is reenacted as a passion play every year by Shias in a ten-day ceremony, which culminates into an *Ashura* (*lit.*, Tenth) ceremony when Shia men, marching in a mourning procession, flagellate themselves, often drawing blood.

After an interminably long wait—during which two preachers, called *rowzeh-khanis* (*lit.*, readers of the *Garden [of martyrdom]*; see further Chapter Six, p. 155), alternatively recited graphic tales of the suffering of Imam Hussein that induced tears, even sobbing, from the five-hundred-strong audience of men (sitting on the carpeted floor) and women (in the gallery) related to the war dead—Khomeini appeared, unaided. Erect, composed, a patriarch in the biblical mold, he slowly raised his right arm to bless the gathering. The electrified audience, men and women alike, greeted him with clenched fists, shouting, "*Allahu Akbar, Khomeini Rahbar* (Allah is great, Khomeini is Leader)"; and "Death to America, Death to Russia, Death to Israel." He moved slowly to sit down in a chair, and said nothing while the chanting continued. The state-run television crew recorded the event for broadcasting nationwide. After a while, an aging head of the Martyrs Foundation in a long robe and white turban read out a brief report saying how the foundation was helping the survivors of those martyred in the war. When he finished, Khomeini rose and raised his hands in blessing. Excitement gripped the audience again and loud chants followed as Khomeini disappeared behind an open door at the back of the balcony.

I retailed my visit to Rahimi. "I was only two when the revolution happened and twelve when Khomeini died," he said. "He was incredibly brave and the Shah wanted to kill him." He paused to serve a customer. "I am proud to be born in Khomein, a famous place, which draws people from all over Iran and even abroad to see Khomeini's home. After our twelve Imams, Khomeini is the most important." (Indeed, to distinguish Khomeini from other ayatollahs and grand ayatollahs, the Iranian government and people refer to him as Imam Khomeini.) Three-quarter mile (1 km) away, at Venus Restaurant, its tall, dark owner, Muhammad Reza, with a prominent Adam's apple, was equally admiring. "All the people in Khomein love Khomeini," he said. "He was important in the world of all Muslims, not just Iranian Muslims."

Ruhollah's childhood was unusual. He was only five months old when his father was murdered in February 1903. As a member of a deeply religious family, his instruction in the Quran started when he was six. After finishing his Persian education at fifteen, he was tutored in Islam for four years by his elder brother Murtaza Pasandida. He then joined the seminary in Arak run by Ayatollah Abdul Karim Haeri-Yazdi. When Haeri-Yazdi moved to Qom in 1922 to revive the seminaries there, Khomeini went with him. Three years later, Khomeini graduated in the Sharia, ethics, and spiritual philosophy. In 1929, he wrote a thesis on ethics and spiritual philosophy in Arabic, entitled *The Lamp of Guidance*, which impressed his teachers. He established himself as a learned teacher of ethics and philosophy as well as an uncommonly disciplined person. He applied his specialist knowledge to contemporary issues, and taught his students to regard the addressing of current social problems as part of their religious duty.

As mentioned earlier (in Chapter One), Khomeini's first book, *The Secrets Revealed*, was published anonymously in 1942. It upheld private enterprise and attacked secularism. "We say that the government must be run in accordance with God's law [i.e., Sharia], for the welfare of the country; and the people demand it," he wrote. "This is not feasible except with the supervision of the religious leaders. In fact, this principle has been approved and ratified in the [Iranian] constitution, and in no way conflicts with public order, the stability of the government, or the interests of the country."[3]

Three years later, he graduated to the rank of hojatalislam (*lit.*, proof of Islam), which allowed him to collect his own circle of disciples, who would accept his interpretations of the Sharia. This happened at a time when the most senior cleric of Iran, Ayatollah Muhammad Hussein Borujerdi, belonging to the quietist school, urged the clergy to shun politics. Borujerdi's stance went down well with Muhammad Reza Shah. Following a failed assassination attempt on his life in 1949, the Shah pressured Borujerdi to stop Khomeini's classes at the prestigious Faiziya Seminary. Khomeini then delivered lectures first at Salmasi Mosque and then at Mahmoudi Mosque in the main street of Qom.

During the early stages of the oil nationalization movement, Khomeini stood on the sidelines. In its latter phase, he was critical of Muhammad Mussadiq who, in his view, was falling under the influence of the Tudeh Party, which he detested. He was equally opposed to the American influence that rose sharply after the August 1953 coup. He decried the deal the Shah made with the Western oil consortium a year later, and deplored the government's overdependence on foreign investments. Later he openly condemned "the plundering of the nation's wealth" by "traitors" in the government allied to "imperialists."[4]

After Borujerdi's death in 1961, his disciples urged Khomeini to publish his interpretations of the Islamic law. The result was his book entitled *Clarification of Points of the Sharia*. In the words of Marvin Zonis, an Iran specialist, it contained "a rigorous, minute, specific codification of the way to behave in every conceivable circumstance, from defecation to urination to sexual intercourse to eating to cleaning the teeth."[5] It led to his promotion to ayatollah.

The death of Ayatollah Abol Qasim Kashani in 1962 left the radical clergy leaderless. Given the status that sixty-year-old Khomeni had by now acquired, he stepped into the shoes of Kashani with ease. In a series of sermons at the Faiziya Seminary in early 1963, he attacked the Shah's White Revolution as phony. As described earlier (Chapter Four), he went on to challenge the Shah and lost.

From his exile in Najaf in 1965, he kept up his campaign against the Shah—an enterprise that the leftist Baathists, who seized power in Iraq in 1968, found convenient since they too were opposed to the pro-Western Shah.

Khomeini used the Perespolis celebrations in 1971—when hundreds of thousands of protesting students and bazaaris undertook a token fast on the day the Shah and his guests feasted on fine food and wines—to attack the institution of monarchy openly and vehemently. "[Islamic] Tradition relates that the Prophet said that the title of King of Kings, which is [today] borne by the monarchs of Iran, is the most hated of all titles in the sight of God," Khomeini declared. "Islam is on the whole opposed to the whole notion of monarchy . . . Monarchy is one of the most shameful and disgraceful reactionary manifestations."[6]

Monarchy was one of the subjects he tackled in his series of lectures published in 1971 as *Hukumat-e Islam: Vilayat-e Faqih*

(Islamic Government: Rule of the Faqih). In it, he argued that instead of prescribing do's and don'ts for believers, supervising welfare for widows and orphans, and waiting passively for the return of the Hidden (Twelfth) Imam, Shia clerics must strive to oust corrupt officials and repressive regimes and replace them with ones led by just Islamic jurists.

Unhappy at the Iraqi Baathist regime's mistreatment of the Shia clergy, Khomeini sought permission in 1972 to leave for Lebanon, but was denied it.

In 1975, Khomeini attacked the founding of the Rastakhiz as the sole ruling party in Iran. His call was taken up by many clerics and theological students. Among other things, it led to the closure of the Faiziya Seminary in Qom. As a result of a rapprochement between Iraq and Iran in the wake of the Algiers Accord in that year, the number of Iranian pilgrims to Najaf and Karbala rose sharply, to 2,500 a week. This made it easier for Khomeini to guide his followers in their anti-Shah campaign through smuggled tape recordings. These audiotapes became all the more important as the revolutionary process, consisting of massive and repeated demonstrations and strikes, gathered momentum through several stages over a two-year period, from February 1977 onward, in seven stages.

The turning point in the movement came in January 1978— heralding the third stage of the anti-Shah movement—when a scurrilous attack on him in the pro-government *Ettilaat* newspaper inflamed popular feelings and placed the initiative firmly with Khomeini. He made astute use of Shia history and Iranian nationalism to engender and sharpen anti-royalist militancy among a rapidly growing circle of Iranians.

On the eve of the fortieth-day memorial to the Qom martyrs, numbering ten to seventy-two, on February 18, the three Qom-based grand ayatollahs urged the faithful to join the mourning processions. They did. There were peaceful demonstrations in eleven cities where main bazaars and universities closed down. In the rioting in Tabriz, where the protestors raised the daring slogan "Death to the Shah!" for the first time, some policemen quickly changed to civilian clothes to avoid shooting the rioters as ordered. This set a pattern to be followed later by not only policemen but also army troops. Khomeini congratulated Tabriz's "upright men and honorable youths" who cried, "Death to the Shah!", and called for demonstrations on the fortieth-day memorial of the Tabriz martyrs.

This time violence erupted in Yazd in central Iran, and more protestors were killed by the police. Another round of the fortieth-day mourning demonstrations and more violence followed. The Shah himself commanded the armored troops used in Tehran to quell the rioters. It was not until May 12 that order was restored. Three days later, a 25 percent rise in gasoline prices set off another bout of rioting.

To avoid another round of the fortieth-day mourning protest, the Shah promised to reopen Qom's Faiziya Seminary, increase the quota for pilgrims to Mecca, ban pornographic movies, call off the anti-inflation campaign by disbanding price-control inspectors and releasing the imprisoned merchants, and removing the much-despised Gen. Nematollah Nasseri as head of Savak, the hated and feared secret police and intelligence agency. But Khomeini urged his followers to keep up the pressure until "the evil regime" was overthrown. In the event, the June 19 protest passed off peacefully.

But by now, unluckily for the Shah, the recessionary policies of the past ten months pursued by Jamshed Amouzgar's government had created a fertile ground for the rise of protest on economic grounds. This drew the industrial and non-industrial working classes into the anti-Shah agitation, thereby escalating the struggle and transforming it into an unambiguously revolutionary movement.

To reduce excessive inflation and deficit financing, Amouzgar curtailed or axed many industrial and construction projects. This transformed a labor market short of workers into one with four hundred thousand jobless. While inflation fell by four-fifths in a year from 35 percent in 1977, growth declined from 14 percent in 1977 to a mere two percent in the first half of 1978. This was the end of continued prosperity during 1963 to 1977, when real per capita income rose fivefold, from \$200 to \$1,000.[7]

The cancellation of the annual bonus for factory and office workers came at a time when Savak's control over their unions was slackening. Beginning mildly in June, the working-class protest gathered steam in September, expressing itself in strikes and participation in demonstrations. On July 22, tens of thousands of workers joined a funeral procession for a cleric killed in Mashhad in a car accident. In the clashes with the police that followed, at least forty people were killed. Most cities staged seventh-day mourning processions for the Mashhad dead.

This provided a prelude to the fasting month of Ramadan that started on August 5, with the faithful breaking their fast in mosques and listening to sermons, sometimes accompanied by Khomeini's tapes. "Ramadan sermons provided a perfect and powerful vehicle for spreading a basically political message, urging men to rise and act against tyranny," wrote the editors of *The Dawn of the Islamic Revolution, Volume I*. "Preachers drew on the Shia themes of struggle and martyrdom . . . It was not difficult to draw a parallel between the hated figures of the Yazid and Muawiya and the Shah, or between the Umayyad dynasty, with its bent for luxury and pomp, and the Pahlavi dynasty."[8]

There was a series of riots in several major cities between August 7 and 17, when demonstrators took control of Isfahan and held it for two days. The army firings claimed one hundred lives. On August 19, a fire inside a cinema in Abadan killed 410 men, women, and children, when doors were deliberately closed and the fire stations responded tepidly, raising popular suspicions of Savak's involvement. The nightly rioting by the mourners reached a peak on the seventh day.

"By mid-summer 1978," noted Michael M. J. Fischer, author of *Iran: From Religious Dispute to Revolution*, "all sectors of society had joined in: the students, intellectuals and bazaaris who began things; the construction workers hurt by the economic slow down; the factory workers, incensed by embezzlement of pension funds and demanding higher wages; the civil servants who had suffered wage freeze for three years under soaring inflation; the urban slum dwellers, many of them squeezed off the land; and the bazaaris who had been the objective of punitive price campaigns."[9]

To defuse the deepening crisis, the Shah replaced Amouzgar with Jaafar Sharif-Emami, Chairman of the Senate and a grandson of a reputed ayatollah, Sharif-Emami released many leading clerics, abolished the royalist calendar, shut down casinos, ended subsidies to the Rastakhiz Party, and lifted censorship.

Khomeini warned against complacency. "Pay no attention to the deceptive words of the Shah, its government and its supporters," he warned on September 6. "The Shah and his government . . . are . . . traitors, and to obey them is to obey the *taghut* [personification of evil] . . . Inform the whole world of their barbarous deeds with strikes and demonstrations." He then addressed the troops with a clear aim of dividing a wedge between them and the Shah. Extending his hand to "all those in the army, air force, and navy, who are faithful to Islam and the homeland," Khomeini called on them "to renew your bonds with the beloved people and refuse to go on slaughtering your children and brothers for the sake of the whims of this [Pahlavi] family of bandits."[10]

The next day, half a million people marched from north Tehran to the Majlis in the south, shouting "Khomeini is our leader" and "We want an Islamic republic," with thousands of marchers wearing white shrouds of martyrs, signifying their willingness to die.

The Shah responded with martial law and daylight curfew which was enforced at 6 A.M. the next day, September 8, a Friday, the weekly holiday of communal prayers. Many of the protestors gathering in the streets of south Tehran were unaware of the curfew. So too were the fifteen thousand people who had crowded into the Jaleh (renamed Martyrs') Square in east Tehran, a residential district of bazaaris. At 8 A.M., tanks, troops, and helicopter gunships began firing to kill. By the time the military had cleared the area by noon, some 1,600 people lay dead. September 8, 1978 went down in Iranian history as the Black Friday.

With this, the Shah crossed the Rubicon. His action confirmed Khomeini's perception that the monarch was quite capable of massacring thousands to maintain his absolutist power. But while most Iranians were disgusted and outraged, they were not cowed. If anything, the anti-Shah forces resolved to take an uncompromising stance, which unveiled the next phase of their revolutionary struggle which lasted for about two months.

On his part, the Shah arrested opposition leaders, persuaded the Iraqi authorities to place Khomeini under house arrest in Najaf, extended martial law to more cities, and reintroduced censorship. But, when government censors arrived at the leading Tehran newspapers on September 12, all the four thousand employees walked out. Three days later, Sharif-Emami lifted censorship.

He lost all credibility when, on September 18, the employees of the Central Bank released a statement showing that he had recently transferred $31 million abroad. He was one of the 177 super-rich Iranians who together had transferred a total of $2,000 million. The fact that thirteen top military officers had together exported $253 million abroad had a debilitating effect on the moral of conscripts who, forming half of the infantry, received a daily stipend of $1. Drawn from all sections of society, the young draftees were more receptive to Khomeini's ideas than professional soldiers or officers.[11]

In early October, workers closed down fifty major manufacturing and service establishments. Postal workers, bank employees, hospital staff, journalists, miners, and customs officers combined their demands for wage rises of 50 to 100 percent with calls for the dissolution of Savak, the ending of the martial law, and the return of Khomeini.

Instead, at the Shah's behest, Khomeini was expelled from Iraq. After an unsuccessful attempt to cross into Kuwait, he flew to France on October 6. Three days of strikes and demonstrations followed in Iran. To de-escalate the situation before the fortieth-day memorial of the Black Friday's martyrs on October 17, the Shah dissolved the Rastakhiz Party, and initiated a series of amnesties.

Settled in Neuphle-le-Chateau, a Paris suburb, Khomeini gave four to five interviews to the international media daily. He appealed to Iranians to join in the mourning procession on October 17. Addressing the army, he stressed the Islamic nature of the ongoing struggle aimed at overthrowing the corrupt Pahlavi regime and liberating "the destiny and resources of our country from foreign control."[12]

The bloody demonstrations of October 17 and 18 produced their share of martyrs. For the first time *all* workers went on a two-day strike. The trend continued. By the third week of October, the country was paralyzed by a general strike. The Shah was rattled. He floated the idea of constitutional monarchy through Sharif-Emami. At the latter's initiative, Mahdi Bazargan, leader of the Liberation Movement of Iran, and Karim Sanjabi of the National Front flew to Paris for talks with Khomeini. He rejected the idea.

Instead, Khomeini called on the oil employees to stop working. They went on an indefinite strike on October 31. The loss of $74 million a day sealed the fate of the Shah's regime.

It received a penultimate blow on November 4, when, defying martial law, protesting students at Tehran University tried to demolish the Shah's statue at the main entrance. In the subsequent firing by the army troops, thirty to sixty students were killed. The next day, the bazaar closed as student protestors from affluent north Tehran and working-class protestors from south Tehran met along Reza Shah Avenue (later renamed Inqilab-e Islami, Islamic Revolution)—the dividing line between the two Tehrans—to form a chanting mass of two hundred thousand people. Then rioting started. Despite the comparative restraint by the troops, sixty-five persons lay dead. This unveiled the next phase in the escalating revolutionary struggle.

Worried by the large-scale unrest in the capital, despite martial law, the Shah replaced Sharif-Emami with Gen. Gholam Reza Azhari, Commander of the elite Imperial Guard, on November 6, and instructed him to form a military government to stop violence and rioting while he himself projected a conciliatory image.

"I have read the revolutionary message of you, the people, the Iranian nation," the Shah said in a television address on November 6. "I guarantee that in the future the Iranian government will be divorced from tyranny and oppression, and will be run on the basis of the constitution and social justice."[13]

If the Shah had really heard "the revolutionary message" of the people, Khomeini retorted, he would abdicate and offer himself for an Islamic trial. In Paris, Sanjabi called for a referendum to establish a national government based on the principles of "Islam, democracy, and national sovereignty." But before he could repeat this demand on his return to Tehran on November 11, he was arrested. This set off a general strike in Tehran and the oil cities in Khuzistan.

Yielding to military pressures, 60 percent of the oil employees resumed work on November 16 to produce just enough to meet domestic demand and pay for essential imports. This meant an output of 1.1 million barrels per day (bpd) instead of the 5.3 million bpd before the strike.

Tensions rose sharply as the month of Muharram, due on December 2, approached. National Front leaders called for a general strike on the first and tenth days of Muharram. On the first three nights of Muharram, thousands of men, wearing white shrouds, defied night curfew. The consequent army firings killed seven hundred men in various cities. This led to an indefinite strike by oil workers on December 5.

As a compromise, Azhari agreed to allow marches on Ashura, Muharram 10, if opposition leaders promised to lead them personally along prescribed routes. He released Sanjabi and 471 other political prisoners.

On Muharram 9, a march of three hundred thousand to one million people in the capital, led by Sanjabi and sixty-eight-year-old Ayatollah Mahmoud Taleqani, a white-bearded, bespectacled, black-turbaned, left-of-center cleric of high standing, took six hours to pass the city center on its way to the Martyrs' (former Jaleh) Square. It ended peacefully as did most such marches in other cities. For the first time they drew large numbers from surrounding villages. With this, the revolutionary movement became all-encompassing.

Ashura, Muharram 10 (December 11), witnessed nearly two million people in Tehran, led again by Taleqani and Sanjabi, pass through the city center for eight hours to reach the Martyrs' Square. There, the rally ratified a seventeen-point charter by acclamation. The charter included an end to monarchy, acceptance of Khomeini as the Leader, and the establishment of an Islamic government. This event conferred legitimacy on the anti-Shah opposition—an alliance of religious and secular forces—as a genuinely representative, future government of the Iranian people.

Khomeini's call for a general strike was taken up by National Front leaders who settled for December 18. The success of the strike strengthened civil servants' resolve to continue their weeks-long stoppage. Furthermore, that day more than five hundred soldiers in Tabriz, equipped with a dozen tanks, defected to the opposition. Due to the hundreds of desertions in the army garrisons of Qom and Mashhad, the army's morale was waning. More disturbingly for the Shah, intelligence reports said that in Kermanshah and Hamadan, the soldiers had begun passing on arms clandestinely to the local mosque-based Revolutionary Komitehs.

This signified the end of the road for the military government. So the Shah decided to co-opt a National Front Leader as the next Prime Minister. On December 29, sixty-two-year-old Shahpur Bakhtiar, who had served as a Deputy Labor Minister under Mussadiq, agreed to form the next government on the (unwritten) conditions that the Shah would immediately go on holiday and that he would act as a constitutional monarch in the future. This led to Bakhtiar's instant expulsion from the National Front.

On January 1, the Shah said that he would like to take a vacation "if the situation permitted." Two days later, Bakhtiar received the endorsement of the Majlis, with 140 of the 165 members present voting for him, and the Senate.

Khomeini now focused on isolating the Bakhtiar government while pressing on with his aim of overthrowing the Shah. Aware of the hardship being caused by paucity of heating oil in the middle of winter, Khomeini instructed oil workers to produce enough to meet domestic needs—about 700,000 bpd.

Bakhtiar combined the release of the remaining political prisoners with a pledge to disband Savak. He cancelled foreign weapons purchase contracts worth $7 billion. He supported *two* days of mourning for the Qom martyrs of the past year. But strikes continued. The strikers were waiting for the Shah to leave. Sensing the growing popular impatience, Bakhtiar announced on January 11 that the Shah would leave for America the following week. The next day he announced the formation of a nine-member Regency Council.

Khomeini had his own plans. "In accordance with the rights conferred by the laws of Islam and on the basis of the vote of confidence given to me by the overwhelming majority of the Iranian people," he announced the establishment of the council of the Islamic Revolution on January 13. Its task was to study conditions for the formation of a provisional government charged with convening a constituent assembly to produce a constitution for the Islamic Republic, holding elections, and transferring power to the elected representatives.[14]

On January 16, the Shah finally left for Aswan in Egypt, ruled by pro-American President Anwar Sadat. Expecting to be recalled after a military coup for which he had made secret arrangements, he decided to stay in the region, and not to fly to the U.S.[15]

Khomeini knew that he was on a winning streak, but he was equally aware that the Shah was too cunning and powerful to give up the Peacock Throne forever. The only way to ensure final victory was to continue strikes and marches.

To discourage precipitate action by the royalist generals, Taleqani warned on January 22 that the people would launch a jihad against the army if it attempted a pro-Shah coup. Bakhtiar tried to reach a compromise with Khomeini, but to no avail. When he refused to reopen the Mehrabad Airport in Tehran in order to block Khomeini's return, air force technicians seized it on January 30 and compelled Bakhtiar to reopen it.

Khomeini and his entourage, accompanied by many journalists, arrived in Tehran on February 1. Three million people lined up the streets to greet him. "It was an occasion of unbridled rejoicing, for which there has probably been no parallel in modern world," wrote Mohamed Heikal, a veteran Egyptian author and journalist, in *Return of the Ayatollah*. "If the Hidden Imam had reappeared after eleven hundred years, the fervor could hardly have been greater. People were shouting, 'The soul of Imam Hussein is coming back!' 'Now is the hour of martyrdom,' and similar cries of ecstasy."[16]

On February 5, Khomeini announced the appointment of Mahdi Bazargan as the Prime Minister of the Provisional Islamic Government. Iran thus entered a period of dual power with two parallel governments.

From February 10 to 11, armed revolutionaries, and thousands of army and air force deserters, went about systematically destroying what remained of the Shah's once formidable war machine. They first captured an arms factory and nine police armories. All told, they distributed some three hundred thousand weapons, including seventy-five thousand submachine guns to their unarmed comrades. Thus armed, the revolutionaries fought the thirty thousand-strong Imperial Guard, consisting of two armored divisions. In the street battles that ensued, the Guards were unable to make use of their heavy tanks and armored vehicles. They were defeated and their headquarters in Lavizan overrun. The military apparatus in Tehran was destroyed—with commanders dispersed, arrested or killed, and ranks abandoning their weapons and uniforms and melting into the population.

At 2 P.M. on February 11, 1979, the Military Supreme Council, led by Gen. Abbas Karim Gharabaghi, announced its "neutrality" and ordered the troops to return to their garrisons. What Gharabaghi now commanded was a pale shadow of the Shah's 414,000-strong military machine. The next day, as the revolutionary forces announced the capture of the Shah's Niavaran Palace, Bakhtiar went underground.

With this, the revolutionary movement, which according to the Islamic regime claimed forty thousand lives, achieved its goal. It marked the end of a remarkable era in Iran and the region.

Khomeini, the Islamic Ruler

Once the revolutionary forces had expelled the Shah and neutralized the remnants of his military, their unity began to crack. Each of the coalescing groups had a different vision of the post-Shah Iran. Militant clergymen and their nonclerical allies loyal to Khomeini wanted an Islamic regime of an orthodox mold led by clerics. Lay Islamic radicals, headed by Provisional Premier Bazargan of the Liberation Movement of Iran favored a less-rigid model than Khomeini loyalists. Liberal, secular forces, represented by the National Front, aspired to create social democracy. The leftist, Islamic strand of the revolutionary movement, dominated by the Mujahedin-e Khalq Organization (MKO), led by Masoud Rajavi, wanted to create an egalitarian Islamic society by blending Shia Islam and Marxism. Such Marxist-Leninist groups as Tudeh and Fedai Khalq visualized the current revolution as an intermediate step toward a Socialist revolution.

Except Khomeini loyalists, who had the most extensive network based in mosques throughout the country, they would all be disappointed.

On March 30 and 31, the provisional government held a referendum on the question, "Should Iran be an Islamic republic?" By lowering the voting age from eighteen to sixteen, it enfranchised hundreds of thousands of young demonstrators of the past year. (The voting age would later be reduced to fifteen, the lowest in the world.) The authorities claimed 89 percent turnout, with 98 percent saying, "Yes."

By the time elections were held for the Assembly of Experts to draft a constitution in August, Khomeinists had formed their own Islamic Republican Party (IRP) and consolidated control over society through Revolutionary Komitehs formed secretly during the revolutionary struggle.

The constitution, based on the doctrine of the Rule of the Jurisprudent, was ratified in a referendum in December. It described Khomeini as a marja-e taqlid (source of emulation), the highest religious title in Shia Islam, and the Leader of the Islamic Republic.

Convinced that Iran could never be truly independent until it had excised U.S. influence from all walks of Iranian life, Khomeini kept up his campaign against the U.S., the prime source to him of moral corruption and imperialist domination, describing it routinely as the "Great Satan." He was pleased when, following the storming of the U.S. Embassy in Tehran in November 1979, Washington cut off its diplomatic links with Iran.

In the election for President in late January 1980, victory went to Abol Hassan Bani-Sadr primarily because of the (informal) endorsement he got from Khomeini. Keen to maintain a balance between clerics and pious nonclerics, Khomeini favored Bani-Sadr, who became part of the small coterie of exiled Iranians who advised him during his stay in the Parisian suburb of Neuphle-le-Chateau. A son of an ayatollah, Bani-Sadr met Khomeini in 1972 in Najaf. A longtime exile in Paris first as a student and then as an academic, Bani-Sadr had traveled to Najaf for his father's funeral. In the elections to the Majlis, the IRP did well. This did not augur well for Bani-Sadr, who did not belong to the IRP, and who, driven by his intellectual snobbery, made no effort to reach a modus vivendi with the senior clerics who set up the IRP with the blessing of Khomeini. Instead, he tried to create a diffuse constituency of his own through his newspaper *Inqilab-e Islami* (Islamic Revolution, circulation, thirty thousand), a feeble strategy.

Bani-Sadr's problems multiplied when the Majlis foisted on him Muhammad Ali Rajai, a highly religious bricklayer from a provincial town who was jailed and tortured by Savak, as the Prime Minister in August 1980. Poles apart, socially and politically, Bani-Sadr and Rajai clashed often.

However, the differences between Bani-Sadr on one side and Rajai and the IRP-dominated Majlis on the other got submerged into the national emergency triggered by Iraq's invasion of Iran in September 1980, when Khomeini appointed Bani-Sadr the Commander in Chief. To cool tempers, Khomeini advised that the speakers addressing the Ashura congregation on November 19 should limit themselves to strictly religious topics. IRP leaders complied, but Bani-Sadr attacked "the party" (meaning the IRP) for being "repressive and dictatorial." This revived the earlier conflict.

Soon a correlation developed between war-front developments and domestic politics. Improvement on the battlefront encouraged dissent at home. In the spring of 1981, Khomeini imposed a truce between Bani-Sadr and the IRP. However, this did not apply to the MKO, which IRP leaders detested. The MKO had been particularly popular with sons and daughters of traditional middle classes, the mainstay of the IRP. Its history of armed resistance to the Shah since the early 1970s in which its guerrillas suffered many deaths appealed to young Shias. Khomeini was also hostile to the MKO because it had intervened directly into his regime's power politics, and subscribed to a hybrid ideology incorporating Marxism.

Khomeini's attitude toward Bani-Sadr hardened once he was presented with information in April 1981 of the CIA's contacts with him in Paris and later in Tehran.[17] He backed the Majlis's decision to strengthen the powers of Prime Minister Rajai at the expense of Bani-Sadr. Unbowed, speaking in his hometown of Hamadan on June 6, Bani-Sadr called on the youth to resist "all violators of law" and "tendencies toward dictatorship." Addressing Bani-Sadr on state-run radio, Khomeini said, "You saw what I did to Muhammad Reza Pahlavi. I will do the same to you if you do not obey the Islamic Majlis, the Islamic prosecutor-general, and the Supreme Defense Council."[18]

On the eve of the Majlis vote on June 20, 1981, the MKO and other smaller groups mustered two hundred thousand people in central Tehran. In the pitched battles that erupted between them and the Islamic Revolutionary Guards, thirty people, including fourteen guards, were killed. Once the Majlis impeached Bani-Sadr by 177 votes to one, he went underground, and a few days later flew incommunicado to Paris along with Rajavi, the MKO leader.

Bani-Sadr's presidency had made less-committed citizens believe that the clerics were willing to share power with others. In reality, however, the comparatively moderate leaders were of temporary value to Khomeinists, who wanted to use them to buy time to build up their organizations and consolidate their hold over the state apparatus and religious network.

From then on, Khomeini only endorsed those politicians for presidency who were his proven acolytes, the prime examples being Rajai and Hojatalislam Ali Khamanei.

In June 1982, after Iran's military had expelled Iraq from most of the Iranian territory it had occupied, Khomeini had the option of accepting a truce with Baghdad or continue fighting. He chose the latter course because he reckoned that if peace returned, his argumentative followers would start quarrelling again.

Iran's path to victory was blocked in November 1983 when the U.S. administration of President Ronald Reagan concluded that Iraq's defeat would amount to an unacceptable setback for America, and began assisting Baghdad materially.

By the mid-1980s, however, Khomeini had succeeded in maintaining his popularity and holding presidential and Majlis elections on time despite the war with Iraq. His regime linked state machinery with the country's religious network that extended to the remotest hamlet in the form of Islamic Associations that, while raising religious consciousness of citizens, provided local clerics with a means to monitor public opinion. It tried to win the backing of the inhabitants of villages and small towns, forming half of Iran's population of forty-five million, by extending such public services as roads, schools, health clinics, telephones, and communal baths through its generously funded Ministry of Reconstruction Crusade. It directly controlled the broadcasting media and the Islamic Republic News Agency (IRNA) while the privately owned newspapers exercised self-censorship.

Khomeini's regime turned the Friday prayer sermon delivered in Tehran for nationwide broadcasting into a means to educate and inform the public about the nation's problems and achievements. The daily involvement of hundreds of thousands of ordinary Iranians in the running of the revolutionary institutions that mushroomed before and after February 1979 broadened the Islamic regime's popular base.

Khomeini succeeded in intertwining war and revolution. To the extent that mobilization for war was easier and more dramatic than for revolution, hostilities with Iraq served a valuable purpose for his regime. He managed to maintain popular support for the war, in which two-thirds of the fighting force was voluntary, and which was increasingly funded by the general public through contributions in cash and kind.[19]

Despite Washington's increasingly overt assistance to Baghdad, in early 1987, the Iranian forces came close to reaching the boundaries of Basra, the second largest city of Iraq. The Iraqis pushed them back, however.

Khomeini's failing health made him focus on his succession and finding means to ensure the survival of the Islamic Republic.

For this purpose he fell back on the Islamic tenet of *maslehat* (expediency). In January 1988, he ruled that the imperative of maintaining the Islamic order in Iran was paramount and super- seded all other consideration, including strict adherence to the Sharia, and such pillars of Islam as daily prayers, fasting during Ramadan and pilgrimage to Mecca. His popular and religious standing was such that there was no overt or covert dissent on his *fatwa* (religious decree). The following month, he established a thirteen-member Expediency Consultation Council System— popularly called the Expediency Council—to determine the interests of the Islamic state and resolve differences between the President, the Majlis, and the Guardians Council. (This ad-hoc council would be incorporated in the revised constitution the following year.) By housing the Expediency Council at the former Marmar (*lit.*, Marble) Palace in south Tehran—almost equidistant from the Majlis building and the complex accom- modating the President and the Guardians Council near the Pas- teur (misspelled "Pastor") Square—Khomeini emphasized the mediatory role of the council.[20]

In spring 1988, Iran's military setbacks in its war with Iraq led Khomeini to put Ali Akbar Hashemi Rafsanjani, then Majlis Speaker and a member of the Supreme Defense Council, in overall charge of the war effort. Following Rafsanjani's downbeat reports, Khomeini realized that if he did not stop fighting, the Islamic Republic would disintegrate, and that led him to accept the United Nations-brokered ceasefire in July. "I had promised to fight to the last drop of my blood and to my last breadth," he said. "Taking this decision was more deadly than drinking hem- lock. I submitted myself to God's will and drank this drink to His satisfaction. To me, it would have been more bearable to accept death and martyrdom. Today's decision is based only on the interests of the Islamic Republic."[21]

Within a year, Khomeini was dead. His demise marked the

end of a remarkable period in recent history—eleven years of revolutionary turmoil and war, filled with dramatic events; the birth of an unprecedented sociopolitical system; and the upsetting of the balance of power in the world's most strategic region that had prevailed since World War II, with America finding its longtime ally turning into a vehement adversary.

During those extraordinarily turbulent times, exercising his acumen and authority stemming from his popularity and charisma, he managed to hold together a vast country of 636,300 sq. miles (1,648 million sq. km), populated by ethnic Persians, Azeri Turks, Kurds, Arabs, Baluchis, and Armenians. He also succeeded in maintaining amity among his squabbling followers who kept on pulling in opposite directions despite the pressures of war.

In the midst of the overwhelming grief that seized the nation, the Assembly of Experts, made up of clerics, met. During an eight-hour session, the assembly elected Khamanei the Leader by sixty votes to twelve, after hearing testimony from Rafsanjani and Ahmad Khomeini, the surviving son of the ayatollah, that Khomeini had twice recommended Khamanei as the future Leader. The assembly also elevated his religious status from hojatalislam to ayatollah.

Contrary to the dire predictions of many Western specialists that, with the charismatic figure of Khomeini gone, a debilitating power struggle would ensue, the transition of the supreme power to Khamanei, a comparatively junior cleric, was smooth.

Khamanei inherited an all-pervasive network that functioned in parallel to the state administration. In running his own secretariat, he had the assistance of four advisers, two of them military officers, with its main function being collecting and collating information domestically and internationally. He appointed personal representatives, who reported to him directly, to twenty-three state and religious agencies, from the

Supreme Defense Council (later Supreme National Security Council), the military, the Islamic Revolutionary Guards Corps, and the Baseej volunteer force to the Islamic Propagation Organization, Directorate of Mosque Affairs, the state-run media, and many foundations with enormous economic assets. In addition, he nominated the Executive Committee and Secretariat of the Central Council of Friday Prayer Leaders. And his twenty-six provincial representatives reported to him direct. This was part of a unique social system in the world that combined citizens' secular and spiritual spheres of life.

Ali Khamanei as Leader of the Islamic Republic

Born into a religious family in Mashhad in 1939, Ali Husseini Khamanei pursued his theological studies at first in his hometown. As a teenager, he became a disciple of Ayatollah Ruhollah Khatami, whom he visited in the oasis town of Ardakan in central Iran, and whose son Muhammad would later become President of Iran. After pursuing further Islamic studies in Najaf, he ended up in Qom, where he became a student of Khomeini. He participated in the June 1963 anti-government protest. After Khomeini's deportation to Turkey, he returned to Mashhad, where he taught at the local theological college.

During the next decade he was arrested six times for his anti-Shah activities, and spent three years in prison, where he suffered torture and humiliation, including the removal of his turban and shaving off of his beard. His release from jail in 1975 was followed by an internal exile in Iranshahr in the distant Baluchistan-Sistan province. This ended during the revolutionary upsurge of 1977–78, and enabled him to return to Mashhad and participate in the escalating movement.

Khamanei was one of Khomeini's first appointees to the Islamic Revolutionary Council (IRC), which assumed supreme power after the revolution. He was a cofounder of the Islamic

Republican Party, which became the ruling party. Later the IRC appointed him its representative at the Defense Ministry, where he headed the political-ideological bureau, which was charged with inculcating service personnel with Islamic ideology and keeping a watchful eye on the officer corps. He was elected to the Assembly of Experts, which drafted the constitution. Following the death in September of Ayatollah Mahmoud Taleqani, Khomeini appointed him the Friday Prayer Leader of Tehran, a highly prestigious position.

Elected to the Majlis in early 1980, he was active in the IRP's parliamentary wing. In May, he became Khomeini's personal representative on the Supreme Defense Council. During his sermon at the Abu Zar Mosque near Tehran's Grand Bazaar on June 27, 1981, a bomb, hidden in a tape recorder placed near him by an MKO activist, exploded, injuring his arm, lungs, and vocal chords.

Following the death the next day of the IRP's Secretary-General, Ayatollah Muhammad Beheshti, along with seventy-three other IRP leaders—caused by a bomb planted by the MKO—Khamanei was elected the party's Secretary-General. And after the assassination of President Muhammad Ali Rajai on August 30, again due to a bomb explosion triggered by the MKO, he was chosen the IRP's candidate for the presidency. He gained 95 percent of the vote.

In 1982, he was elected to the Assembly of Experts. He won 89 percent of the ballots cast in the August 1985 presidential poll. But when he tried to replace his left-of-center Prime Minister Mir Hussein Mousavi, he met stiff resistance from Majlis deputies. He and Mousavi belonged to the opposing factions within the IRP and could not reconcile their differences. This led to Khomeini ordering the dissolution of the IRP in July 1987. A year later, instructed by Khomeini, Khamanei accepted the United Nations Security Council Resolution 598 for a ceasefire in the Iran-Iraq War.

Following Khomeini's death on June 3, 1989, the hastily assembled Assembly of Experts elected him Leader of the Revolution by sixty votes to twelve.

The Constitution Review Panel, appointed by Khomeini five weeks before his death, made forty-two changes to the document, including lowering the religious requirement of the Leader, and enhancing his powers by authorizing him to formulate general policies in consultation with the Expediency Council and supervise the execution of these policies.

While maintaining Khomeini's pattern of periodically issuing radical statements, Khamanei encouraged President Rafsanjani to implement economic reform—even at the expense of bringing about social justice that Khomeini had considered paramount.

In the political sphere, Rafsanjani took a step that would have important consequences later. He established the Center for Strategic Research, an independent think tank, under Hojatal-islm Muhammad Mousavi Khoeiniha, a leftist theologian, to come up with fresh ideas and perceptions on sociopolitical trends. Its membership included Abbas Abdi, a prominent journalist, Saeed Hajjarian, a former Deputy Intelligence Minister, Muhsin Kadivar, a theologian, and Ataollah Mohajerani: they would emerge as leaders of the reform movement during the next decade. Their papers covered such subjects as civil society and political freedoms within an Islamic framework, independent political parties, fostering and sustaining peaceful political rivalry, and the rule of law. They also initiated public-opinion polls.

Meanwhile, Khamanei tried to consolidate his authority. Guided by him, the Guardians Council's Competence and Qualification Committee rejected 60 of the 169 candidates for the election to the Assembly of Experts in October 1990, ostensibly for their "dubious behavior in the past" or for their lack of experience in jurisprudence, or for their refusal to take the theological test proposed by Khamanei, which many with the rank of hojatalislam and above found too demeaning.

The use of the Guardians Council as a means to control national politics occurred again in 1992. At the behest of Khamanei and Rafsanjani, the council disqualified most leftists, including prominent clerics, from contesting Majlis seats. So the Fourth Majlis (1992–96) ended up with conservatives and independents forming a large majority. The leaders of this Majlis prevailed upon Rafsanjani to purge the Center for Strategic Research of its "undesirable" elements, who included its chairman, Khoeiniha.

Rafsanjani's weakened status, following his reelection in 1993 with a much reduced popular vote, allowed Khamanei to enhance his power further. This encouraged his acolytes to lobby for his elevation to a marja-e taqlid in Iran after the death of Grand Ayatollah Muhammad Ali Araki in November 1994 at the age of 102—or 105, according to the Islamic calendar[22]—who had acquired this title following the demise of Khomeini. Most of the leading senior theologians regarded Khamanei as lacking the degree of piety and learning as well as teaching experience that the title required.

Calling on the government not to interfere in the selection of the marja, the Association of the Qom Teachers produced a list of seven ayatollahs, including Khamanei, Hussein Ali Montazeri, a dissident cleric, Muhammad Qomi Tabtabai, and Muhammad Rouhani, a one-time opponent of Khomeini. After studying the list, 150 Majlis deputies declared Khamanei "to be the most informed person concerning Islam and the Islamic world and the most qualified authority for the leadership of the Muslim society." They reached this conclusion on the basis that political experience was as important as theological learning. On December 9, the Judiciary Chief, Ayatollah Muhammad Yazdi declared Khamanei as Iran's marja, and warned the clergy not to challenge his decision.

Senior theologians in Qom took offense, and conveyed it to Ahmad Khomeini, the surviving son of the Republic's founder, who acted as an intermediary between the competing sides. A compromise was devised in private. Five days later, Khamanei declined the post of the marja inside Iran due to the already high volume of work, but added that he was willing to be a marja for the Shias outside Iran. However, most Shias outside Iran were the followers of Grand Ayatollah Ali Sistani, based in Najaf.[23]

By 1996, the reformist intellectuals sacked from the Center for Strategic Research had formed an informal circle, which included Muhammad Khatami and his younger brother Muhammad Reza Khatami. They sensed the wide chasm that had developed between the people and the conservative establishment in the wake of the postwar reconstruction and economic liberalization that had led to widespread black market activity, tax evasion, corruption, and rampant inflation.

But before agreeing to run for President, Muhammad Khatami, then head of the National Library, insisted on explaining his ideas and program to Khamanei, a onetime acolyte of his father Ruhollah. During his theological studies in Qom, Khatami had become a close friend of Ahmad Khomeini whose wife's cousin, Zohreh Sadiqi, would marry Khatami. And, being a sayyid, a descendant of Prophet Muhammad, Khatami wore a black turban as did Khamanei.

In his meeting with Khamanei, Khatami reportedly argued that action was required to adapt Islam to modern times and to reverse the trend toward disenchantment among Iranian voters, especially the young, who were turning up in dwindling numbers to exercise their right to vote. Since clerics had become an integral part of the state, a steady delegitimization of the state would have negative impact on them and the Islamic order they represented. That in turn could lead the Leader to resort to coercion to suppress rising dissent in order to hold the state together.[24]

Given his intellectual and religious standing, Khatami probably received a sympathetic hearing, not concurrence with his views.

When, on the eve of the 1997 presidential poll, rumors spread that wide-scale rigging of the election was in the offing, Khamanei intervened. "I shall not allow anyone to give himself the right to cheat in the election, which is contrary to religion and contrary to political and social ethics," he told a meeting in Tehran. Describing the elections as "a divine test," he said that "Islamic Iran must not be found wanting."[25]

On Khatami's landslide victory in a poll in which seven out of eight Iranians participated, Khamanei immediately confirmed his election as President—as required by the constitution.

However, Khamanei had no intention of loosening his grip on the clerical body to which he owed his office: the Assembly of Experts. He once again used the Guardians Council to achieve his aim. It disqualified more than half of the four hundred candidates for the eighty-six-member assembly to be elected on October 23, 1998. Some of them were rejected because they refused to take the obligatory examination to prove their theological expertise, and others because they failed the test. However, as before, the council offered no official explanation. What was different this time was that heeding the calls for liberalization from different quarters, including Qom-based Grand Ayatollah Yusuf Saanei, the council ruled that nonclerics, male or female, could be candidates if they met the high standards of religious expertise. Unsurprisingly, all thirty-seven male and nine female nonclerical candidates failed the theological test. And so did most of the pro-reform ones. The Islamic Left refused to endorse any list after its candidates were disqualified. The centrists produced a skeleton list of their own. The voter turnout was only 50 percent. So the sociopolitical composition of the new assembly—fifty-four conservatives, sixteen reformists, and sixteen independents—came as no surprise.[26]

The first test of the Khamanei-Khatami relationship came in July 1999 when university students protested against fresh restrictions on the press. When the initial peaceful protest escalated into anti-regime rioting, Khatami had no choice but to condemn the unrest as harshly as Khamanei did. On July 14, the followers of both leaders joined hands to display popular support in the street, which resulted in some three-quarter million people marching peacefully in the capital. Both Khamanei and Hassan Rouhani, Secretary-General of the Supreme National Security Council, described students as much valued members of the nation.

However, the conservative judiciary applied the amended Press Law rigorously. Its important victim was the six-month-old *Neshat* (Vitality) newspaper with the third highest circulation in the country. Its suspension came in September after it published an article questioning the legitimacy of capital punishment, thus challenging the "eye-for-an-eye" principle enshrined in the Sharia. The appropriate verse in the Quran (5:49) reads: "A life for a life, an eye for an eye / a nose for a nose, an ear for an ear / a tooth for a tooth, and for wounds / retaliation; but whosoever foregoes it / as a freewill offering, that shall be for him / an expiation."[27] The Press Court found the newspaper's managing director, Latif Safari, guilty of insulting the basic tenets of the Quran, and sentenced him to thirty months in jail.

While disagreeing with the Press Court, the Culture and Islamic Guidance Minister Ataollah Mohajerani called on reformist publications to restrain themselves so as not to give conservatives pretexts for actions against them. This was seen as a conciliatory move that was soon reciprocated at the highest level. On October 1, delivering a sermon on the one hundredth birthday of Ayatollah Khomeini (according to the Islamic calendar), Khamanei said in the presence of Khatami, "The authorities today are pious. The President is a cleric, he is pious, he loves the Household of the Prophet [Muhammad], and he is working for the rebirth of Islam."[28]

The next issue to test Khamanei's relationship with Khatami came during the interregnum between the first and the second rounds of the Majlis elections during February to May 2000.

Reformists' capture of two-thirds of the seats declared in the first run on February 19 was a tonic to them and their supporters—a much relished vengeance against conservatives whose maneuvers had succeeded in virtually keeping them out of the previous Majlis poll. Reflecting the bullish mood, the pro-reform press went into an overdrive in publishing stories about corruption and political violence in the recent past. These proved hugely popular with the reading public, to the dismay of the conservative camp, and that in turn encouraged the pro-reform newspapers to push the boundaries even further and come dangerously close to questioning the very foundations on which the Islamic Republic rested. "This radicalization of the press had the hallmarks of a classic Iranian rebellion, in which the absence of a supportive political institution soon leaves the initiative in the hands of even more radical elements and, ultimately, threatens chaos," noted Saeed Barzin, an astute student of Iranian history, in the *Middle East International*.[29] It was incumbent upon Khamanei that Iran did not reach that brink, he opined.

On March 12, there was a failed assassination attempt on Saeed Hajjarian. A brilliant tactician, he was the main brain behind Khatami's stunning victory in 1997. His tenure as a Deputy Minister of Intelligence during 1984 to 1989 gave him an insider's view of how this and other ministries functioned. After spending the next four years at the Center for Strategic Research, he turned to journalism. In a series of articles in the *Sobh-e Emruz* (Daily Morning), he exposed the Intelligence Ministry's involvement in political killings over the years. Now, as a victim of a botched assassination attempt, he became a living martyr of the reformist camp. Its newspapers had a field day, and put conservatives even more on the defensive.

Khamanei was quick to condemn the attack and promised swift action. He was, however, disturbed about the general drift of the events. What snapped his patience was the "Iran after the parliamentary elections" conference in Berlin, sponsored by Heinrich Boll Foundation, on April 7–9. The twenty-one Iranian participants included leading reformists. The subjects included violation of human rights, the treatment of religious and ethnic minorities, the role of women, and political and social freedoms.

Some reformist speakers questioned whether Iran should have a religious regime and whether women should be obliged by law to wear a veil. The state-run Iranian television inflamed feelings in Iran by airing certain provocative parts of the proceedings. Right-wingers at home presented the event as part of a plan to build bridges between the pro-reform camp in Iran and the foreign-based, leftist, secular Iranian opposition, despite the fact that the conference was held with the knowledge and acquiescence of the Tehran government, which had not barred anyone from attending.[30] However, this interpretation of the event was accepted by Khamanei and his close aides, who were already under pressure from the clerical establishment to curb the reformist movement.

The about-to-be-dissolved Fifth Majlis stiffened the Press Law on April 17 by outlawing criticism of the Leader or the constitution. Three days later, Khamanei addressed the subject before one hundred thousand young people at Tehran's Grand Mosque. "There are ten to fifteen newspapers which undermine Islamic principles, insult state bodies and create social discord," he said. "Unfortunately, some of the newspapers have become the bases of the enemy. They are performing the same task as the BBC Radio and the Voice of America, as well as the British, American and Zionist television broadcasts intend to perform."[31] The audience responded with chants of "Death to mercenary writers" and "Shame on you hypocrites, leave the press."

Between then and April 26, the judiciary closed down fourteen reformist publications with a total circulation of one million. "The general shutdown of the moderate press, approved by Khamanei, was in the hope of calling a time-out in the increasingly vicious battle between the two sides being waged after the first round of the Majlis elections through the newspapers," reported Susan Sachs in the *New York Times*.[32]

Conservatives, urged by Khamanei to speak up, criticized Khatami for ignoring the clerical establishment in his vision of civil society he wished to create, and failing to condemn blatant violation of the law by the pro-reform press. This infuriated many in the reformist camp, especially the young, who wanted to demonstrate in the streets. But Khatami advised caution, saying, "We have to move through this sensitive period with calm, tranquility and composure." He was helped by Khamanei who held out an olive branch to the reformist camp when, despite the shutdown of most of its press, it did well in the second round of the Majlis election on May 5.

Khamanei reversed his earlier assertions that there were no factions within the political-religious establishment. In a Friday sermon in mid-May he said, "The two factions, the progressive and the faithful, are as necessary as the two wings of a bird." Pointing out that some of the progressives had joined forces with the factions outside the Islamic establishment, even those who believed in secularism, he demanded that progressives must sever their ties with secularists and de-escalate their rhetoric.[33] Later, addressing a meeting of judges, Khamanei tried to establish his neutrality by accusing reformists of trying to hobble courts, and conservatives of trying to exploit them for their own aims. He urged the judges to shun politics and function strictly in accordance with the law. Mohajerani, the reformist Minister of

Culture and Islamic Guidance, addressed a letter to all newspapers urging them to stick strictly to the Press Law.

But then, before the new Majlis could meet, the Expediency Council declared that the Majlis had no authority to investigate any institution or foundation under the purview of the Leader.

What was worse, the reformist deputies discovered that their hands were tied even in matters they had taken to be the province of the Majlis. They were all set to liberalize the stiffened Press Law on August 6, but were barred from doing so by Khamanei's ruling that the bill was illegitimate and "not in the interest of the system and the revolution." That was the end of the matter. Even Khomeini at the peak of his popularity had never squashed a bill at its first reading.

However, that did not mean that Khamanei would always have the last word.

That is what happened in January 2004. When he urged the Guardians Council to reconsider especially the rejections of the sitting parliamentarians as candidates for the next Majlis, the council went on to *raise* the number of such rejections, rather then reduce them. It thus defied the Leader publicly and underlined its own independence.

Nonetheless, the role and status of the Leader remains one of the two unresolved core problems of the Republic, the other being social and political freedoms. Is the Leader empowered by a popular mandate or by God? Many traditional clerics argue that the divine right to govern—implicit in the vilayat-e faqih doctrine—makes public accountability unnecessary. But this interpretation conflicts with the amended 1989 Constitution, especially Article 107, which states that "the Leader is equal with the rest of the people of the country in the eyes of the law." Nor is it in line with the practices of the Assembly of Experts: it appoints a committee to judge whether or not the Leader's performance is within the constitutional limits, and whether or not it is generally "satisfactory."

During its six monthly sessions, held mostly in Qom and closed to the public, the assembly discusses the committee's report and forms an opinion.

But neither the names of the committee members nor the contents of their reports are published. It is vaguely assumed by the insiders that only if the committee was to find the Leader's performance unsatisfactory would it be expected to issue a statement to that effect. It is this total lack of transparency that a growing body of politically aware Iranians find unacceptable.[34]

The issue of where sovereignty lies in a society of Muslims has baffled religious scholars for many generations at the prime learning centers of Shia Islam in Najaf, and in Qom.

Qom:
The Religious Capital of Islamic Iran

◆ CHAPTER 6 ◆

I n between my first trip to Qom in 1979, the year of the revolution, and my most recent, a quarter century later, much
had changed. Gone was the old, congested, potholed road to
the holy city from Tehran, which slowed our progress. Instead,
our car now covered the 90 miles (145 km) distance in a little
over an hour along a smooth six-lane highway crisscrossed by
electric cables, held up by towering pylons, with an occasional
red plastic sphere attached to a cable.

All around us lay a bleak, dun-colored terrain, potted with scrub
and low hills. Viewing the desolate landscape, I understood—as I
had never before—the primacy of blue domes in Islamic architecture, the iridescent blue conveying a life-enhancing reference to
water to the parched traveler as well as paying homage to the
heavens above.

Toward the end of the journey, the landscape opened to salt
flats, the source of brackish water with which Qom—perched on
the edge of the Great Salt Desert—is associated. Dialectically, the
other thing that Qom is associated with is a sweet meat, called
sohan (a caramel and pistachio brittle) that one Western writer
found "sinfully delicious."

The first radical change that struck me at a traffic roundabout
on entering Qom's dusty outskirts was a mammoth rendering in
steel of the word "Allah" in Arabic tailored as a pair of swords in
brackets, which is the official logo of the Islamic Republic.
Another departure from the past was the drying up of the Khanshor River, bisecting the city, to the extent that its bed has been
concreted and used as a car park, a market, and a playground.
Along part of the old riverbank runs the city's only broad avenue.
All the significant sites are within a walking distance from this
road: the gold-domed shrine of Fatima Massoumeh (One Who

Shuns Sin; Innocent), major mosques, world-renowned seminaries, state-of-the-art Islamic computer centers where Quranic teachings and interpretations have been placed in cyberspace, and the teeming bazaar, noted for its pistachio-caramel brittle, blue pottery, silk carpets, prayer rugs, small tablets of the compressed earth (of holy Qom) used in Muslim prayers, and gaudy calendars of the Grand Mosque in Mecca, with the Holy Kaaba (Black Stone) at its center, and pithy inscriptions from the Quran.

Qom's skyline, though, has remained essentially as it has been for several centuries—blue, green, and, yellow domes and minarets emerging from buildings made of reddish bricks, except the recent Qom International Hotel built with distinctive yellow bricks.

The centerpiece of Qom, a city of a million souls, is the vast shrine that contains the tomb of Fatima Massoumeh. It is a revered place of pilgrimage, attracting thousands daily, fronted by a neat, open square, surrounded by shops selling linen shrouds for pilgrims to be blessed. The main gate to the shrine bars photography and non-Muslims. Nonetheless, I had entered the vast forecourt in December 1979, accompanied by my translator, Farhad Ganji,[1] to gaze at the tombs of the past rulers of Iran, their gravestones shining in the weak winter sun. A swarm of pigeons came fluttering in while kites wheeled in the sky and white doves clung to the towering minarets whose green lights, lit up at night, add luster to the golden dome—a sight visible for miles around the city.

Together Farhad and I had entered the inner sanctum past the dazzling silver and crystal furnishing of the outer chamber over which a stern Khomeini gazed from a large portrait of his. It reminded me very much of the inner sanctum of Imam Hussein's shrine in Karbala, Iraq. Just as in Karbala, here all was gold, silver, light, glitter. I was dazzled by the walls and the ceiling, covered with tiny, angular mirrors, bouncing off the glow from chandeliers.

The hall was crammed with people, men as well as veiled women, gravitating toward or drifting away while circumambulating the tomb. Smelling of sandalwood, the tomb sheltering the sarcophagus of Fatima Massoumeh was encased by a compartment made of silver grilles, its crisscross bars, having been rubbed endlessly by human hands and lips, shining brilliantly. Following the pious pilgrims, I touched the silver grille, and then rubbed the palms of my hands over my face, as if to imbibe the piety gained by the holy touch—a gesture common among Hindus as well, who, having held their hands momentarily over a sacred oil lamp or candle lighting up an image of a deity, gently rub their faces with them.

Parallels with Imam Hussein and Karbala were appropriate. After the death in early 681 AD of Muwaiya ibn Abu Sufian—the Umayyad governor of Syria who had challenged Ali ibn Abu Talib, a cousin and son-in-law of Prophet Muhammad, for the caliphate—his son, Yazid, became the caliph. Hussein, the oldest surviving son of Ali, then living in Medina, staked his claim to the caliphate on the grounds that it belonged to the House of Prophet Muhammad, of which he was the most senior member, and that Yazid was a usurper. His stance won him swift and fervent messages of support from the Iraqi town of Kufa, a stronghold of Ali's partisans. This news reached Yazid who rushed a trusted aide, Ubaidullah ibn Ziyad, to Kufa, where he neutralized the anti-Yazid forces through coercion and bribery.

By then the unsuspecting Hussein, accompanied by his family and seventy-two retainers, was well on his way to Kufa. On Muharram 1, 61 AH, After Hijra, Migration [of Prophet Muhammad from Mecca to Medina][2] (May 8, 681 AD), Hussein's entourage was intercepted near Karbala, some 30 miles (48 km) from Kufa, by Yazid's soldiers. For the next eight days their commander tried to obtain Hussein's unconditional surrender. But Hussein, believing in his right to the caliphate, resolved to do battle and perish rather than surrender or retreat. He also reck-oned that his martyrdom would revitalize the claim of the House of the Prophet to the caliphate. On the morning of Muharram 10, Hussein led his small band of partisans to confront Yazid's four thousand heavily armed troops. His warriors fell one by one; and he was the last to die. He was decapitated and his head was pre-sented to Yazid. This heroic tragedy of a man of charisma and piety tells the faithful that the true believer should not shirk from challenging the established order if it has become unjust and oppressive, despite slender chances of overthrowing it.

Eight centuries later, the Safavid rulers of Iran would publish the bloody, graphic descriptions of the heart-wrenching suffer-ings of Hussein and other martyrs as a book, entitled *The Garden of the Martyrs*. Those preachers who started using it as their text became known as *rowzekhani* (*lit.*, readers of the *Garden*). In the holy Shia places, it is common for pilgrims to hire them to render the story in highly emotive terms, setting off a raucous competition between different preachers.

Qom developed as a refuge for the opponents of the Umayyad dynasty (r. 661–750 AD), starting in 685 AD, soon to be called Shia Ali, partisans of Ali—set apart from Sunnis, the People of the Sunna, custom of Prophet Muhammad followed by his three successors, Caliphs Abu Bakr, Omar, and Othman—whom Shias did not recognize as legitimate caliphs since they did not belong to Prophet Muhammad's family.[3] These Arab inhabitants of Qom succeeded in either expelling local Zoroastrian inhabitants or converting them to Islam while at the same time adopting Per-sian as their mother tongue.

The settlement thus became a symbol of resistance to the Sunni governors and their tax demands. In 816 AD, Fatima, sister of Imam Ali Reza, the Eighth Imam of Twelver Shias, was on her way to see her brother in Mashhad when she fell ill in Saveh, 60 miles (100 km) from Qom. The residents of Qom invited her to their town. She arrived, only to die soon after. Over the years, her grave turned into a most important religious site in Iran. During the Tenth century, as home to 266 Shia clerics and only fourteen Sunni clerics, Qom became a place of Shia learning before Najaf. After the first dome was erected over Fatima Massoumeh's grave in 1151, the shrine began attracting pilgrims. The Mongol invaders destroyed Qom in 1224. It remained moribund until the rule of the Safavids in 1501, which lasted 235 years.

Among the major differences that arose between Shias and Sunnis was the practice of *ijtihad* (interpretative reasoning). Having accepted the Quran and the Prophet Muhammad's Sayings and Doings as the Sharia (*lit.,* Path), Islamic Law, it became necessary for Muslims and their rulers to interpret the Sharia to address unprecedented situations. During the early Islamic era, ijtihad was freely practiced by the learned to interpret the Sharia, the interpretation being either arbitrary or based on analogy. Its practitioners were called *mujtahids.* By the mid-ninth century AD, four major schools of Islamic law had emerged within Sunni Islam: Hanafi, Maliki, Shafii, and Hanbali. In order not to upset the consensus thus gained with some new radical innovation, the Sunni clergy from the tenth century onward declared that the gates of ijtihad had been shut. In Shia Islam, however, ijtihad did not remain dormant for long. The destruction in 1258 of the (Sunni) Abbasid Caliphate by the Mongol ruler Hulagu Khan created a political-ideological vacuum in which Shiaism thrived. Jamal al-Din al Hilli (1250–1325), a Shia thinker, rehabilitated ijtihad.

In the early sixteenth century, the Safavids, claiming descent from the Sixth Shia Imam, Jaafar al Sadiq, adopted Twelver Shiaism as state religion at a time when a majority of Persians were Sunni. It was not until the eighteenth century that Shiaism became the predominant sect among Persian speakers. There was correlation between this phenomenon and the importance of Qom, the winter capital of the Safavids, where Shah Tahmasp I (r. 1524–1576) rebuilt the dome over Fatima's grave in 1547. In their rivalry with the Sunni Ottoman Turks, the Safavids stressed their Shiaism. So the significance of Qom rose. Shah Abbas I (r. 1587–1629) constructed an extensive complex around Fatima's grave. His successor turned two of the shrine's courtyards into the Faiziya Seminary, which would become the largest theological college in Iran.

After the capture of Mesopotamia—containing the leading Shia holy cities of Najaf and Karbala—by the Ottomans in 1638, the Safavids tried to build up Qom as an alternative place of Shia pilgrimage and learning.

The Qajars, who succeeded the Safavids after a chaotic inter-regnum of five-and-a-half decades in 1790, continued the Safavid tradition of placing royal and noble mausoleums in Fatima's shrine complex. By this time, the conflict between traditionalists who, believing in the literal acceptance of the scriptures, argued that practicing Shias could interpret the Sharia for themselves, and mujtahidis or *usulis* (those believing in principles), who reasoned that mujtahids were needed to interpret the principles of the faith, was settled in favor of the latter. Usuli jurists ruled that mujtahids could collect *khums* (*lit.*, one-fifth)—one fifth of the income of a Twelver Shia—on behalf of the Hidden (Twelfth) Imam Muhammad al Qasim,and spend it on the social welfare of the community.

In the mid-eighteenth century, the leading mujtahid ruled that a Shia must select one of the several living mujtahids to follow as a marja-e taqlid, (source of emulation)—a practice that continues.

Through his scholarship, a mujtahid or mara-e taqlid tried to know the infallible will of the Hidden Twelfth Imam. So, compared to the temporal ruler, he was less fallible. He reached judgments on political matters impinging on Islamic principles independently of the temporal ruler. Since, unlike the Safavids, the Qajars did not claim descent from a Shia Imam, mujtahids became a power center in their own right, apart from the state. Among them two schools developed: interventionists, who offered cooperation with or opposition to the state, and quietists, who shunned politics.

Often, acting on behalf of their followers, mujtahids interceded with the government, and let their mosques and offices be used as havens for those avoiding state action against them. It was thus that Shia clerics became channels for the expression of popular disaffection.

Meanwhile, the Qajars' commitment to Shia Islam remained solid. After the puritanical Wahhabi warriors had ransacked the embellished golden-domed shrines of Imams Ali and Hussein in Mesopotamia in 1802, Fath Ali Shah (r. 1797–1834) embellished the cupola of Fatima Massoumeh's shrine with golden leaf to turn Qom into a leading place of pilgrimage. In 1883, Nasser al Din Shah reconstructed some parts of the complex, including the new courtyard.

The uncertain conditions in Iraq that followed the Ottoman Empire's collapse in 1918 encouraged the leading Shia clerics of Najaf and Karbala—expelled from Iraq by the British mandate following a national uprising in 1920—to resurrect Qom as a leading place of learning. This led to the arrival of Ayatollah Abdul Karim Haeri-Yazdi from Arak, along with one of his students, Ruhollah Khomeini, and the revival of the Faiziya Seminary. With this, Qom once again became a preeminent Shia center of religious learning, *hawza-e ilimiya*.

In his drive to gain legitimacy for his rule, Reza Khan Pahlavi successfully canvassed support among the clerical leaders of Qom. But after installing himself as monarch, he severely curtailed clerical authority in education, law, religious endowments, and Islamic propaganda. However, out of the khums (the religious tithe) they received from their followers, the ayatollahs continued to build hospitals, libraries, and flood walls, and maintain welfare systems.

As described earlier (in Chapter Four), Qom emerged as the main center of resistance and confrontation with Muhammad Reza Shah at a time when most of the fifteen thousand theology students in Iran were concentrated in Qom.[4]

Soon after his triumphant return to Tehran from a Paris suburb in 1979, Khomeini returned to his home in Qom. Government ministers traveled frequently to the holy city to consult him. The next year he left it for Tehran, mainly to avail himself of better medical facilities after suffering a heart ailment.

The Islamic Republic and After

Today, Qom is the undisputed religious capital and ballast of the regime. Here piety rules. When I asked Muhammad Javad Islami, an old caretaker at the Faiziya Seminary wearing a white knitted skull cap, how long it took a student enrolling at eighteen, to get his degree, he replied, "Students study only for God, not for a degree." For every ten men in shirt and trousers you see one in tunic and cloak of an existing or prospective Shia cleric. On the other hand, the sight of a man or woman walking on a pavement with a mobile phone glued to his/her ear—a regular feature of all Iranian cities—is rare in Qom.

It abounds in ayatollahs. It also has a large share of the country's grand ayatollahs—a status accorded only to those ayatollahs who have shown exceptional piety and scholarship and also possess long teaching experience. They are all based near the center of the city, in the labyrinthine back streets, asphalted for vehicular traffic, which alert drivers keep surprisingly safe.

What is common between ayatollahs and their superiors is their right to practice ijtihad (interpretative reasoning). Since this inevitably leads to different interpretations, Shiaism is not monolithic. For instance, Khomeini's doctrine of vilayat-e faqih

(Rule of the Jurisprudent), was disputed by Grand Ayatollah Muhammad Shariatmadari, an ethnic Azeri, who was opposed to the idea of clerics getting involved in the day-to-day administration of a country. Following the revolution in February 1979, Khomeini found his leadership balanced by Ayatollah Mahmoud Taleqani on the Left, and Shariatmadari on the Right. With Taleqani's death in September, the Islamic establishment became bipolar, with Shariatmadari leading the quietist clerics who advocated nonintervention in day-to-day running of the government, in opposition to the interventionist school led by Khomeini.

Shariatmadari abstained in the referendum on the Islamic constitution in December 1979, objecting to the excessive powers given to the Leader, Khomeini, and condemned the seizure of American diplomats as hostages. The differences between him and Khomeini became irreconcilable, and were taken up by their respective followers in the streets of Tabriz, an Azeri stronghold, and Qom in January 1980.

Shariatmadari lost and was placed under house arrest. Secret documents retrieved from the U.S. Embassy showed that he had accepted funds for promoting nonalcoholic American drinks—such as Pepsi Cola—in Iran, and that the Central Intelligence Agency station there had maintained contacts with him. After the arrest of his son-in-law, Ahmad Abbasi, in April 1982 for coplotting a coup, the government raided his house and seminary, and publicized his clandestine contacts with the CIA. The Association of the Qom Teachers annulled his religious status. Four years later he died of natural causes.

The next leading cleric to fall out with Khomeini was Ayatollah Hussein Ali Montazeri who was groomed to be his successor. A student of Khomeini in Qom, he became his personal representative in Iran after Khomeini's expulsion from the country in 1964. Arrested during the anti-Rastakhiz Party protest in March 1975, he was tortured in jail, and released in November 1978. After the revolution, Khomeini appointed him the Friday Prayer Leader of Qom, a highly prestigious position, and gave him a seat on the governing Islamic Revolutionary Council. He was elected Chairman of the Assembly of Experts which drafted the constitution. In 1980 Khomeini put him in charge of the secretariat of the Friday Prayer Leaders, based in Qom.

The official campaign to bolster Montazeri's standing gathered pace in the spring of 1983, when in all government offices Khomeini's portrait was accompanied by a smaller picture of Montazeri—a white-turbaned face with a trimmed white beard laced with black hair, his thick eyebrows covered by even thicker plastic frame of his spectacles. Born into a poor peasant family in a provincial town, he was genuinely modest, and had suffered jail and torture due to his active anti-Shah activities. But he lacked charisma and, more seriously, political cunning and sound judgment.

After a brief session of the Assembly of Experts in November 1985, one of its members, Ahmad Barkbin, revealed that the assembly had chosen Monatzeri as Khomeini's successor. This was done in order to give Montazeri a chance to develop his leadership potential while Khomeini was alive. In a doctrinally oriented regime, that had moderates, centrists, and radicals in its ruling establishment, it was axiomatic that the Leader must not alienate any specific group. He could best do this by supporting now one faction and then another: an astutely balanced act. This was what Khomeini did. "For the sake of maintaining balance among various factions, I have always issued bitter and sweet instructions because I consider all of them as my dear ones," Khomeini said toward the end of his life.

But Montazeri failed to emulate the style of his former theological teacher. His statements and guidelines on specific issues were invariably moderate, advocating leniency in the application of Islam and its principles. By favoring liberalization of the economy and allowing a fair degree of opposition, he alienated centrists and radicals. He therefore came to be perceived as a partisan of one faction—a liability for a man being groomed to become the Leader. Also, instead of presenting a balanced assessment of the Islamic revolution by listing both its achievements and failings, he repeatedly stressed its failure to deliver its promises. So Khomeini changed his mind about him in March 1989, and he fell out of favor.

Montazeri then immersed himself in teaching. After Khomeini's death, he publicly questioned the religious learning and standing of Leader Ayatollah Ali Khamanei. He was put under house arrest. In 1994, when a move was afoot to raise the religious status of Khamanei, the Association of the Qom Teachers prepared a list of clerics worthy of promotion, and it included Montazeri. By so doing, religious scholars showed their independence from the state, thus underscoring their long and worthy tradition.[5]

It continues. Indeed, since Khamanei lacks the religious credentials of Khomeini, and since his acolytes are increasingly stressing political grounds as the main source for his legitimacy, differences intensified between reformist clerics, who think that the Republic has become too much of a theocracy, and the conservative, hard-line mullahs surrounding Khamanei.

Preeminent among the grand ayatollahs, who keep challenging state policies by issuing dissident *fatwas* (religious decrees), is Yusuf Saanei, who has served in such august bodies as the Guardians Council and the Assembly of Experts. A small, cheery man of Mongoloid origin, sporting a threadbare white beard below his chin, Saanei operates from a modest room equipped with a bookcase, a carpet, and a single electric bulb.[6]

He was born to a trained cleric and a religious mother in 1931 in Yangabad-e Jarquye village, an hour's drive from

Isfahan. He arrived in Qom in 1955 for further religious studies, and became a theology teacher there six years later. He was arrested in 1978 for political activities. After the revolution, he was elected to the Assembly of Experts which drafted the constitution. Khomeini appointed him to the Guardians Council in 1980; and he also served as Prosecutor General during 1983 to 1985. Khomeini appointed him to the newly established Expediency Council in 1988.

Within a decade of Khomeini's death, Saanei had established himself as the leading liberal grand ayatollah by issuing a string of fatwas that were at variance with the official policies. He ruled, for instance, that all music was legitimate except the lyrics that were un-Islamic or depraved at a time when most music was banned and female singers were not allowed to perform in public.

Saanei's most controversial fatwa pertained to citizens' rights. "It is my interpretation from the Quran that all people have equal rights," he told Robin Wright of the *Los Angeles Times* in the summer of 2000, repeating a statement he had made many times before in his lectures to the theological students in Qom. "That means men and women, Muslims and non-Muslims too. And in a society where all people have equal rights, all people should make decisions—equally." [7]

It therefore seemed logical for him to declare (a) that any discrimination based on gender, race, or ethnicity was illegitimate, and (b) that no one was more equal than others. Out of (b) emerged his fatwa that since no one was infallible the Leader's right to assume the supreme office and his actions required endorsement by the citizenry. "Humans can always make mistakes," he said. "And no one leader or group of people is above the law or 'more equal' than anyone else. So power must lie with the people, the majority, not individuals or institutions." [8] Since Article 107 of the 1989 constitution equates the Leader with "the rest of the people of the country in the eyes of the law," Saanei's fatwa did not clash with the existing constitution.

Earlier, Saanei told Geneive Abdo, a Tehran-based American journalist, that the Islamic system must adapt to the changing times if it is to survive the coming-of-age of the postrevolution generation. "When human ideas have changed, we must look at our fiqh [jurisprudence] and our interpretations [to see if they] will provide the answers to these [contemporary] problems," he said. "We have obtained Islamic laws from the books we had before now, and if they [mujtahids] waned to write down those penal codes or laws today, they might have different interpretations of the material upon which they were based."[9]

The rationale that Saanei offered was the same as advanced by Abdul Karim Soroush, a dissident, nonclerical Islamic thinker. But they had reached the same conclusion through different routes. Soroush had followed the thinking of the Indian-born Muhammad Iqbal, a pious layperson, whereas Saanei had remained firmly rooted in his traditional theological upbringing and study. "I have reached these ideas with the same methods of study and thought taught in the seminaries throughout the ages," he told Wright. "Only my interpretation of what I have found in the sacred texts is different. But my conclusions are just as purely Islamic. And whatever I'm telling you is what I'm saying in the seminaries."[10]

On the opposite side of the spectrum was Ayatollah Muhammad Taqi Mesbah-Yazdi, head of the conservative Haqqani Seminary in Qom and a member of the Assembly of Experts. He has been preeminent in speaking and writing about the role and legitimacy of violence in political affairs, sanctifying use of force by individuals against anyone who dared to seek or articulate interpretations of the Sharia that were at variance with the official version. "When people are convinced that the plots against the Islamic state are endangering it, they must act because this is a case where the use of force is necessary even if thousands get killed . . . Not using force against those who commit offenses will lead to more violence and chaos. Islam says mohareb (those who wage war [against the Islamic order]) should be executed or their hands cut off, or be deported."[11] His views were widely and vehemently disputed by clerics and nonclerics, who challenged him to debate the issue on television. He refused.

Mesbah-Yazdi's views inspired Ansar-e Hizbollah vigilantes whose ranks in Tehran were filled partly by the students of the Marvi Seminary near the Grand Bazaar. They were equally inspired by the thoughts of Hojatalislam Ruhoallah Husseinian, a bearded, stocky intellectual with florid cheeks, in charge of a think tank in north Tehran. "Our republic is an Islamic republic, which means it is not a liberal republic," he explained to Abdo. "The Guardians Council is authorized to maintain our country's Islamic nature. Just as democrats in the West come up with various qualifications, such as Christian Democrats [or Social Democrats], so the world republic has the same flexibility. Iran is a guided Republic . . . You should not compare the Islamic Republic with Western republics. The Islamic nature of our system necessitates a kind of supervision so it does not deviate from the Islamic framework."[12]

The roots of Ansar-e Hizbollah went back to the Hizbollah, which was established soon after the revolution.

Led by Hojatalislam Hadi Ghaffari, it was found to have surreptitious links with the ruling Islamic Republic Party. One of the Hizbollah's virtues to its political masters was that it was loosely structured. It played an important role in the street at crucial moments in the history of the revolution in confronting and intimidating those the regime regarded as counterrevolutionaries. It started with harassing all "un-Islamic groups" that had established offices on university campuses. After Khomeini had denounced in particular the Mujahedin-e Khalq Organization

(MKO) in March 1980, it targeted the MKO, which led to many bloody skirmishes.

Once political challenges to the Islamic regime had subsided, Hizbollahis concentrated on social matters such as the observance of women's Islamic dress and the ban on alcohol. They were unhappy at the promulgation in December 1982 of Khomeini's Eight-Point Decree on civil liberties and the transfer of moral offenses from Revolutionary Courts to Public Courts. "To spy and search is contrary to Islam," stated Khomeini's decree. "We should not engage in oppression. We should not investigate what is going on in people's homes."[13] In February 1983 they demonstrated in the predominantly working-class south Tehran demanding strict adherence to Islamic morals and warning those who might be tempted to transgress them due to the recent liberalization.

Later, their self-assigned functions were taken over by the uniformed members of the Baseej militia, an auxiliary of the Islamic Revolutionary Guard Corps (IRGC). In the late 1980s, the Hizbollah's ranks were swollen by many veterans of the Iran-Iraq War. Following Khomeini's death, the party's leaders vowed to defend what they regarded as his legacy, and opposed pragmatic changes, economic and cultural, that were introduced in the postwar period. They also decided to set up an associate organization called the *Ansar-e Hizbollah* (Helpers of Hizbollah). It was led by Hussein Panah and Masoud Dehnamaki.

Ansars resorted to tearing down advertisements for luxury Western products, damaging fashionable boutiques, and harassing young, unmarried couples trysting in parks.

They cropped up during the election campaign for President in 1997. By disturbing an election rally of Muhammad Khatami in Mashhad on April 19, they grabbed media headlines. When, following his electoral victory, reformers assumed a high profile, Ansars began attacking secular intellectuals, reformist and leftist newspapers, and liberal-minded university students. With the Law Enforcement Forces and judiciary turning a blind eye, they assaulted several progressive clerics, including Hojatalislam Abdullah Nouri, then a cabinet minister. He and his reformist cabinet colleague, Ataollah Mohajerani, were attacked by the Ansars after Friday prayers in Tehran in early September 1998.

The outrage caused by this event was so severe that it could not be ignored by the office of Leader Khamanei. It seemed that a word went out from there to the Ansar leaders to control their followers. At the same time the investigation in the assault case was intensified. It led to the arrest of three Ansars in January, who were sentenced to six to eighteen months in jail and twenty to forty lashes.[14]

Yet six months later, Ansars were the ones to attack the peaceful student protesters as the LEF stood by idly, triggering five days of street rioting. Their intellectual guru, Mesbah-Yazdi, was foremost in the calls for tough action—even outside the law—against protesting students.

Soon after, Intelligence Minister Ali Yunusi publicly referred to "pressure groups"—meaning primarily the Ansar-e Hizbollah, and secondarily the small Fedayin-e Islam, which dated back to prerevolution times. Describing their members as "war veterans with elevated religious principles," he said, "Legal political factions do not support these groups officially. But that does not mean that no one in the military or Intelligence Ministry supports them . . . Many files have been opened on these groups, but officials are either frightened of pursuing these cases or are doubtful about the guilt of the accused."[15] This was an undisguised admission by a powerful Cabinet Minister of his helplessness to curb illegal activity.

Moreover, when actionable information on the workings of the Ansars and their funding emerged in a videotaped testimony, the judiciary moved in to protect them. The existence of the videotape became public when, in mid-July 2000, court officials charged two lawyers, human rights specialist Shirin Ebadi, and Hojatalislam Muhsin Rahami, with "disrupting the political situation in Iran" by conspiring with Ilah-e Sharifpour Hicks, a representative of the New York-based Human Rights Watch, during her visit to Tehran in May, to produce and distribute the videotape. The Iranian lawyers and Hicks were also charged with coercing Amir Farshad Ibrahimi, a former member of the Ansar-e Hizbollah, to make the confession he did on tape. According to him, Ansars had been given a go-ahead on disrupting public meetings, assaulting reformist activists, and assassinating Abdullah Nouri. He alleged that powerful conservatives, including senior ayatollahs and politicians, approved their plans. He also revealed that the organization was funded by bazaar merchants, who supported the conservative clerical establishment.[16]

What is noteworthy is that all these widely varying, even mutually hostile, factions, parties, and individual religious leaders derive their stances and actions from a single source: Shia Islam. As the above survey of this Islamic sect shows, such differences have coexisted for many centuries—primarily because, unlike in Sunni Islam, the doors of *ijtihad* (interpretative reasoning), were not closed shut by leading Shia clerics. This tradition helped Khomeini. As a popular ruler of a state like no other in modern times, he improvised as he went along driven by a sole motive: consolidation of the revolution and the Republic.

In the early days of the Islamic Republic he considered it sagacious to have a directly elected President who did not wear clerical robes. Both Bani-Sadr and his successor Muhammad Ali Rajai were laymen. Had Rajai not been assassinated by an MKO mole inside the government two months after being elected President in 1981, he would have served his full four-year term. But he was. Those who followed him were all mullahs.

Clerics as Elected Presidents

Of the three clerics to be elected president, Khamanei was conservative, Ali Akbar Hashemi Rafsanjani centrist, and Khatami reformist.

Under the 1979 constitution, Khamanei had to work along with the Prime Minister who had the confidence of the Majlis. His conservative, free-market views on the economy clashed with those of Premier Mir Hussein Mousavi, who believed in a strong public sector. When the state's legislative and executive organs reached an impasse, Khomeini acted as the final arbiter. In 1988, he established the Expediency Council to resolve differences between the President, the Majlis, and the Guardians Council, an arrangement that was incorporated in the revised constitution of 1989. It also abolished the post of the Prime Minister, thus giving a freer hand to the next popularly elected President: Rafsanjani.

Born into a religious family in Behraman in 1933, Rafsanjani went to Qom for his theological studies. During the power struggle between Premier Muhammad Mussadiq and the Shah during 1951 to 1953, he sided with Mussadiq. Later, he became a student of Khomeini. After Khomeini's deportation in 1964, he handled Islamic charities on the exiled leader's behalf and consulted him on political affairs. He was arrested and tortured in the mid-1970s. One of the cofounders of the Tehran branch of the Association of Combatant Clergy (ACC), Rafsanjani was actively involved in the 1977–78 revolutionary movement, particularly the formation of the Revolutionary Komitehs. He was one of the members of the Islamic Revolutionary Council and a cofounder of the Islamic Republican Party. He was an active member of the 1979 Assembly of Experts which drafted the constitution.

After his election as a Majlis deputy from Tehran, he was voted Speaker of the House in July 1980, a post to which he was reelected every year until the legislature's dissolution in 1984. As Speaker he played a pivotal role in the impeachment of President Bani-Sadr in mid-1981. In 1982, after his election to the Assembly of Experts, he was chosen its Vice President. He acted as Khomeini's personal representative on the Supreme Defense Council.

In mid-1982, when during the Iran-Iraq War Iran recovered the area lost earlier to its foe, Rafsanjani advocated advancing into Iraq if the latter did not meet Iran's demands, including a compensation payment of $100 billion for war damages. After his election to the Majlis in 1984 he was reelected Speaker, a position confirmed annually for the next four years.

Following Iran's military setbacks in the spring of 1988, Khomeini put him in overall charge of the war effort. Having realistically assessed the deteriorating situation, in mid-July 1988 he persuaded the Assembly of Experts to recommend to Khomeini a truce called earlier by the United Nations Security Council. Khomeini accepted the recommendation.

When President Khamanei was promoted to succeed Khomeini as Leader in June 1989, Rafsanjani ran for the presidency, and secured an almost unanimous vote. He excluded radicals from his government and introduced economic liberalization. He pursued a pragmatic foreign policy, improving relations with Germany, France, Japan, and the Soviet Union (later Russia). But due to a drop in oil prices, the economy suffered and inflation rose. So his popular vote in the 1993 presidential poll fell by almost a third on a low turnout.

As a result, he lacked the political clout he possessed during his first term. The conservative-dominated Majlis blocked his ambitious plans for political and economic reform. The internal balance of power shifted in favor of Khamanei who consolidated his authority at the expense of the popularly elected President who became a political prisoner of the conservatives in the Majlis.

Even though the oppressive, demanding environment of the war years was gone, Rafsanjani's government pursued repressive policies toward dissidents, which were implemented by the Ministry of Intelligence, euphemistically called Ministry of Information. Following their unpublicized arrest, the dissidents were often put on government-run television to recant their anti-regime activities. After 134 members of the Writers Association had signed a letter calling for an end to censorship in 1994, several of them were assassinated or died in suspicious circumstances. In the late 1990s, several courageous journalists would publish detailed stories of how some eighty writers, poets, translators, political activists, and ordinary citizens died or disappeared over the past decade.[17]

Postwar reconstruction had both positive and negative effects. It resulted in the improvement of neglected towns and cities, a boost to the hitherto weak private sector, the mushrooming of large infrastructure projects, and a dramatic expansion in higher education. On the negative side, it fostered a robber baron attitude that led to an explosion in black market activities, tax evasion, and administrative corruption, as well as high inflation.

So a wide gap developed between large sections of society and the alliance that Rafsanjani forged with conservatives. At the same time, electors in general wanted the government to tone down its ideological rhetoric and focus more on tackling such problems as inflation, joblessness, drug addiction, and pollution in cities. This was the sociopolitical background to the 1997 presidential contest that Khatami decided to enter.

Born in 1943 to Sakine Ziyai and Ayatollah Ruhollah Khatami in the oasis town of Ardakan in central Iran, Muhammad grew up in a well-to-do household, where his father was a compulsive reader and listener to foreign radio broadcasts. While Ruhollah wanted Muhammad to follow his example and become a cleric, the latter was keen to study philosophy. As a compromise, the father let Muhammad study philosophy after his religious studies in Qom.

Arriving in Qom in 1961, he became a student of Khomeini and a friend of his son, Ahmad. Then, instead of seeking exemption accorded to theological students, he did his compulsory two-year national service in the army as a junior lieutenant, an experience that brought him into contact with all segments of Iranian society, a useful political asset.

After graduating in philosophy from Isfahan University in 1968, he obtained a master's degree in educational sciences at Tehran University three years later. During his university years, he was politically active against the Shah's regime. His studies at secular universities exposed him to the works of not only Plato, Aristotle, Niccolo Machiavelli, Thomas Hobbes, John Locke, and Jean Jacques Rousseau but also of Frantz Fanon, a radical Algerian nationalist, Aime Cesaire, a West African radical, and Che Guevara, an Argentinean involved in the Cuban revolution. Consequently, he acquired a perspective and sensibilities that were way beyond the enclosed world of the traditional Shia seminaries.

He was active in the Association of Combatant Clergy formed clandestinely in the mid-1970s in Tehran. It sent him to Hamburg, West Germany, in 1978 to run the Islamic Center that administered a Shia mosque. There he learned English and German.

After the revolution, he was elected to the First Majlis from Ardakan in 1980. The same year, Khomeini appointed him head of the giant, state-owned Kayhan Publishing Company, which published newspapers and books. In 1982, he became Minister of Culture and Islamic Guidance, a position he held for a decade. In that capacity he enforced strict censorship, and oversaw the passage of the Press Law in the Majlis in 1985. It was only after the end of the Iran-Iraq War in 1988 that he began to relax restrictions on literature, cinema, music, and art. He reinstated awards for the best books and set up a Press Arbitration Council to help mediate accusations against journalists and writers. As a member of the Society of Combatant Clerics, founded by radical and leftist clerics in 1988, he earned the opprobrium of conservatives. Little wonder that the conservative-led Fourth Majlis (1992–96) found his policies too liberal and forced him to resign.

Immediately, Rafsanjani appointed him an adviser to the presidential office. He also became head of the National Library. He published a collection of essays, entitled *Fear of Waves*, in which he argued that even though Islam was superior to Western thought, it was no longer responsive to modern life, especially when it came to freedom, which he described as "one of the basic needs of human beings." As the upholder and practitioner of human freedom, the West had acquired more economic, political, military, scientific, and technical power than the Muslim world, he argued.

Khatami's political break came after Khamanei had informally overruled Mir Hussein Mousavi as a presidential candidate in early 1997, and Ayatollah Muhammad Khoeiniha, the managing director of the influential *Salaam* newspaper, and a leading member of the radical Society of Combatant Clerics with its decade-old clerical and seminary network, persuaded Khatami to run. Once he had cleared his views with Khamanei whose parents had been close to his, he was in the race as a serious contender.

Yet, it was not until May 7, about a fortnight before the election, that the Guardians Council released the list of approved candidates.[18] His main contender was forty-four-year-old Hojatalislam Ali Akbar Nateq-Nouri, a favorite of the clerical establishment who had been the Majlis Speaker since 1989—a fact stressed by the slavish manner in which the state-run broadcasting media reported his every activity.

Several factors, religious and secular, favored Khatami. In religious terms, being a sayyid, a descendent of Prophet Muhammad and therefore entitled to wearing a black turban, he was superior to Nateq-Nouri, who donned a white turban. Besides being a son of a renowned ayatollah, Khatami had family ties with the Khomeini household. While Nateq-Nouri traveled by a chauffeur-driven Mercedes, Khatami either used a battered bus or a locally made Paykan car.

Despite his professorial looks—neatly trimmed salt-and-pepper beard on an oval face donning designer glasses—Khatami came through as an accessible, candid man, who smiled readily, and delighted in talking about Ping-Pong, swimming, and wishing his wife, Zohreh Sadiqi, could drive. His genuine modesty contrasted with the arrogance of Nateq-Nouri who had taken his victory for granted.

Khoeiniha turned his newspaper offices into the headquarters of Khatami's election campaign, which was masterminded by Saeed Hajjarian. When the centrist Servants of Construction (SOC) could not find a suitable candidate of its own, it endorsed Khatami. Thus the Khatami camp secured the financial and administrative resources of the SOC available through the office of Tehran's mayor, Gholam Karbaschi, expert in modern management practices, who also controlled the capital's billboards. To this alliance was added the energy and extensive network of the university student movement, formally called *Daftar-e Tahkim-e Vahadat-e Howze va Daneshgah* (University-Seminary Unity Consolidation Bureau)—or Unity Consolidation Bureau (UCB), for short.

While backing the revolution and the constitution, including the office of the Leader, and the Islamic dress for women, Khatami advocated making the Islamic system relevant to the public at large by creating an open civil society that would harmoniously blend sacred and secular aspects of life. His platform of promoting the rule of law, countering fanaticism and superstition, ending the political monopoly of conservatives, and generating more jobs and better educational opportunities appealed especially to young people, women, and intellectuals. The nation's youth perceived in him a mild, tolerant personality, ready to pay attention to their grievances, both social (such as strict segregation of sexes) and economic (namely, dearth of jobs). He advocated freedom and equality for women within an Islamic context. Khatami's emphasis on the rule of law appealed especially to the modern middle class, the mainstay of the centrist SOC. Finally, by having the courage to discuss publicly the role of ethnic and religious minorities—Christian, Jews, Zoroastrians, Azeris, and Baluchis—he won their vote.

A series of televised debates on the eve of the poll finally clinched the election for Khatami. The viewers were impressed by his candid, informal style, combined with his shining intellect, which put the pompous, stodgy Nateq-Nouri in an unfavorable light.

On the polling day, May 23 (Khordad 2 in the Iranian calendar), almost nine-tenths of the thirty-three million electors participated. Nearly 69 percent—amounting to twenty million—favored Khatami, and only 25 percent Nateq-Nouri. Surprisingly, Khatami performed well even in villages and small towns where inhabitants follow the guidelines offered by local clerics.

Khatami's victory created an environment in which reformists could popularize their ideas mainly through the print media. They seized the opportunity. In January 1998 came the start of the *Jame* (Association), edited by Mashaallah Shams al Vazien—a small, balding, bearded, chubby man—and published by Hamid Reza Jalaipour, who was also its chief columnist. Both of them had impressive credentials. A bitter opponent of the Shah, Shams al Vazien had lived in exile in Lebanon during the 1970s. On his return to Iran after the revolution, he was appointed to the editorial board of *Kayhan*, a staunch supporter of the Islamic regime. Jalaipour, a heavy-set man with a permanent five days' stubble, who faced imprisonment for his anti-Shah activities, went on to secure a doctoral degree in political science from London University. His sister was among those who seized the American Embassy in Tehran. After his return to Iran, he was appointed Mayor of Mahabad and then Deputy Governor of Kurdistan province.

In June 1998, the *Jame* published criticism by General Rahim Safavi, commander of the IRGC, at a closed-door meeting of the Supreme National Security Council in Qom, concerning those clerics "whose promotion of democracy threatened the cult of martyrdom." He warned that "a new case of [religious] hypocrisy is taking shape with the use of mullahs' costumes. We must root out counterrevolutionaries wherever they are. We must use the sword to chop off the heads of some and cut out the tongues of some others." Safavi and his allies accused the paper and the journalists of "having infringed the general's privacy and free speech," thereby conceding implicitly that there is such a concept as right to free speech. In his reply, Jalaipour declared that "it was no longer possible to manipulate the memory of war martyrs in politics."[19] As a person who had lost two brothers in the Iran-Iraq War, he was eminently qualified to offer this rebuff to Safavi.

By then, the *Jame* had covered other subjects that the regime regarded as taboo. These included torture in jails, relations with America, exploitation of religion for political ends, and weaknesses of the late Khomeini's leadership.

Pro-reform publications demanded more accountability and

transparency in the Islamic regime whereas their conservative opponents asserted that excessive accountability and transparency would dilute Islamic and revolutionary values, and undermine clerics' role to guide the Iranian republic which is Islamic, and would lead to instability. In response, reformists argued that the key to stability lies with democracy and open access to reliable information for the general public. "We [reformers] are in favor of making government responsive, institutionalizing the sovereignty of law, and not undermining it in the name of religion, revolution, and war," said Jalaipour.[20] The debate remained inconclusive, with the judiciary firmly on the conservative side.

In July, the Press Court ruled that the news item on Rahim Safavi was "distorted and reckless," and added that the publications of the pictures of the young men and women dancing in the streets of Tehran following Iran's victory over America in the World Cup soccer on June 20 violated Islamic principles. It revoked the newspaper's license.

Within a few weeks, Jalaipour and Shams al Vazien launched the *Tous* (Peacock). It lasted about a month. They responded by starting the *Sobhe-e Emruz* (Daily Morning). Taking note of the events, Khatami invited their families to his home. "You have my sympathy but my hands are tied," he reportedly told them. "It is unfortunate that Mr. Jalaipour and Mr. Shams al Vazien went so fast that they didn't see the yellow light. They think they're living in Switzerland."[21]

But Khatami's advice lost its force when, despite popular demands, backed by the pro-reform press, the Guardians Council barred many moderate clerics from contesting the elections to the Assembly of Experts in October.

What shocked the middle classes was the assassination of several writers and dissident politicians in late 1998. In November, three authors, who were in the process of founding a secular

Writers Association, were kidnapped and killed, and their corpses thrown in the streets of Tehran. The next month, seventy-year-old Dariush Foruhar, a leader of the (now banned) National Front who served as Labor Minister in the provisional government after the revolution, and his wife, Parvane, a writer and poet, were fatally stabbed at home by someone who had made an appointment to see him.

Leader Khamanei strongly condemned the murders and instructed the intelligence agencies to apprehend the culprits. Declaring that "Islam is a religion of compassion," he alleged that unrest was being promoted by "Islam's enemies," and "foreign elements,"[22] without offering any evidence. Khatami appointed a three-member committee, consisting of the Intelligence and Interior Ministers and a representative of Khamanei.

In mid-January 1999, the committee announced the arrest of ten suspects, some of them Intelligence Ministry agents. Six of them were later released. The remaining four worked for the Intelligence Ministry, and included a Deputy Minister, Said Emami, who had held this job since 1990 despite the purported disapproval of Presidents Rafsanjani and Khatami. They were alleged to have a death list. Intelligence Minister Qorban Ali Najafabadi said that "evil and deviant agents" within his ministry were responsible for "the monstrous crimes which have brought the Islamic system into disrepute."

In the chorus of condemnation that followed, conservative politicians joined in. Reformists claimed that conservative Najafabadi had been "imposed" on Khatami, and that it was high time the ministry was restructured. Khatami acted. In late February he replaced Najafabadi with Ali Yunusi, who won the endorsement of nearly two hundred Majlis deputies. The pro-reform press was rife with rumors and revelations. And, in mid-June, the plot thickened when the Chief Judicial Investigator revealed on television that Emami had hanged himself in his cell.

"Iranians are not used to such transparency about matters of this kind and the revelations have left them perplexed and confused," reported Saeed Barzin in the *Middle East International*. "Until recently the Intelligence Ministry was spoken of only in hushed voices, in dark corners or in private places. Now newspapers—which are becoming more investigative and independent in their newly found and jealously guarded freedom—have pounced on the story like hungry beasts. They are cornering the Ministry of Intelligence and clawing for more information and explanations . . . A former Intelligence Minister, Ali Fallahian, is already being implicated in the press."[23] This case and Emami's alleged actions would hang over Iranian politics like a cloud for almost a year.

Meanwhile, ignoring Khatami's advice, Jalaipour and Shams al Vazien started *Neshat* (Vitality) in March 1999 after the closure of the *Sobhe-e Emruz*. At that time, the most popular newspaper was the *Khordad* (named after the month in which Khatami had his landslide victory), run by forty-year-old Hojatalislam Abdullah Nouri, a small, heavy-set cleric with a trimmed beard and an impressive background. A confidante of Khomeini, who appointed him as his personal representative to the Islamic Revolutionary Guards Corps, he became Interior Minister in President Rafsanjani's government in 1989, a job he held for four years. He got the same post under President Khatami, but was forced to resign in June 1998 when the conservative-dominated Majlis found his policies too liberal. He then launched his newspaper whose runaway popularity made him the prime target of conservatives. To them he became the archetypical "hypocritical cleric," the term used earlier by Gen. Safavi of the IRGC.

In the February 1999 local elections, the first to be held in the Islamic Republic, the "Islam of Love" list headed by Nouri won all the fifteen seats in Tehran. In most of the major twenty-five cities, the reformist-led coalitions won handsomely. This gave much impetus to the pro-reform press.

The conservative-dominated Majlis responded by tightening up the Press Law, which triggered the student protest in July.

Armed with the amended Press Law, the judiciary moved against the leading pro-reform publications.

After shutting down the *Neshat* in September, the Special Court for Clergy (SCC) issued a forty-four-page indictment against Nouri, accusing him inter alia of challenging the absolute authority of the Leader and opposing Khomeini's teachings.

During a two-week open trial, starting on October 30, 1999, Nouri defended himself for three days. He cited Article 107, which describes the Leader being at a par with all Iranians "in the eyes of the law." Therefore, like any other individual, the Leader had to obey the law and he possessed no powers above those granted to him by the constitution. He stressed that Islam was not monolithic, and that he favored the version that recognized the people's right to choose their own destiny and that used state authority to serve the people rather than rule them. His long, written defense statement proved so popular that the pro-reform press published it as a series of articles, and the authorities refrained from interfering. On November 11, the clerical jury found him guilty on fifteen counts; and the judge sentenced him to five years in jail, which would later be reduced to two years. Khatami publicly deplored the action against Nouri. Addressing the minority pro-reform deputies at the Majlis complex, he said, "It is to the detriment of the revolution, system and society if an impression is created than an individual's views are confronted in any other way than a satisfying analytical approach."[24]

Soon after came the case of Shams al Vazien, the former editor of *Neshat*, now editing the *Asr-e Azadegan* (Age of the Free), his fourth newspaper in two years—all funded by members of a rising business class that backed political reform, and popular with adult, educated, middle-class Iranians, estimated to be five million strong. The charges pertained specifically to the article questioning the legitimacy of capital punishment, and generally to stoking student protest by giving it excessive prominence.

After being found guilty by the Press Court, he appealed. He lost and, finally, in April 2000, like his managing director, Latif Safari, he was handed a thirty-month jail sentence.

It was during the second half of April that Khamanei mounted a frontal attack on the pro-reform publications. He condemned "domestic hypocrites" for doing America's bidding in the cause of globalization. "I am not against press freedom. But some newspapers have been created with the aim of inciting public opinion and creating differences and mistrust between the people and the system." [25]

A few days later, the judiciary suspended more than a dozen reformist newspapers.

Despite this, the reformist candidates did well in the second run of the Majlis poll in early May, garnering more than two-thirds of the seats in the chamber.

But when Khamanei overruled their move to liberalize the Press Law in August, they lost their initial confidence to advance social and political freedoms. Khatami repeatedly expressed his inability to enforce the constitution, one of his major functions.

"Personally, I would prefer to be somewhere else," he said, announcing his bid for reelection in the spring of 2001, wiping away his tears. His campaign lacked the conviction and enthusiasm of the earlier bid for presidency. In his speeches, he admitted that he lacked the authority to carry out his principal responsibility—implementing the constitution.

In the June 2001 presidential election, Khatami won nearly four-fifths of the vote on a turnout of 67 percent, with his nearest rival getting a mere 16 percent of the ballots. Nonetheless, after his election, he declared that the aim of his second term would be to blend "independence, freedom and progress," with Iran's

"Islamic identity"—a bland, overarching sentiment with which few Iranians could disagree.

Given the continued resistance by the conservative judiciary, the pace of political reform slowed. Popular mood among the modern middle classes and the young turned increasingly apathetic, with interest in politics declining sharply. Instead, they became more interested in improving their living standards. In this they were aided by firm oil prices that boosted the Iranian economy.

Contrary to the calculations of the U.S. President George W. Bush's administration that—following the invasion of Iraq in March 2003 and the overthrow of President Saddam Hussein—petroleum prices would fall to $20 a barrel due to the spurt in the Iraqi oil output caused by the application of the American expertise to Iraq's long-neglected oil industry, actual prices of the commodity shot up to $55 a barrel in October 2004.

These price movements were of deep interest to the residents of Iranian cities in general, and Qom in particular: it is an important junction for the petroleum and gas pipelines that run between the oil fields of oil-rich Khuzistan and Tehran. Moreover, the discovery of an oil field near the city in 1956 bolstered its economy—hitherto dependent on agriculture, carpet weaving, carpentry, brick-making, herding, and catering to the needs of hundreds of thousands of pilgrims and fifty thousand seminarians. Little wonder that Qom houses an impressively large office of the National Iranian Oil Company along Imam Khomeini Avenue.

Oil:
Life Blood of Modern Iran

♦ CHAPTER 7 ♦

The locally assembled French Peugeot was new, and the asphalted road smooth. I sat comfortably in a backseat, confident that my driver, Nemat Ali, though young, was reassuringly cautious. Yet my journey felt hazardous. It was the terrain—more like a moonscape rather than anything on Earth.

The landscape had changed abruptly as we drove east from Shuster—an ancient settlement, with its Shadorvan and Band-e Qaisar bridges on the Karun River dating back to the pre-Islamic Sassanian era—toward the ubiquitous Zagros Mountain range, with strips of its rugged exterior fashioned into asphalted hairpin bends and steep slopes, hugging stomach-churning sheers.

Crisscrossing the Zagros during my 3,000-mile (4,500 km) journey in the summer of 2004 proved to be an open-air lesson in geology, with the mountain range's surface changing from dusty, yellow particles to dun-colored rocks peppered with scrub, to soil carpeted with pine trees, to sedentary rock—slate—laid out layer upon layer like vast pieces of hard cheese. Near Shuster, the mountainous slate was often gray, sometimes reddish. "It is the red cheese time," I said to Nemat. He replied with a semi-audible grunt, focused as he was on maneuvering expertly the narrow, winding road on our way to Masjid-e Suleiman, the Mosque of Suleiman, a famous holy man who once lived there— a town of 150,000 people, with a military airport nearby.

While the car rolled forward, my thoughts rolled back a century, and zeroed in on James B. Reynolds, a British geologist and petroleum engineer. A tall, robust figure, with a fleshy face, Reynolds was seldom seen in public without his pipe and solar hat, or his little dog. I mulled over the way he managed to transport equipment weighing 40 tons (41 tonnes) from Chia Surkh near the Iranian-Iraqi border in 1904 to this mountainous region of Maiden-e Naft (*lit.*, Field of Oil), some 330 miles (540 km) apart. He did it in a circuitous way, by shipping it first to Baghdad by road, deploying nine hundred mules, then to Basra by boat, next to Khorramshahr (then named Mohammara) in Iran, on to the penultimate leg of the journey to Shardin. It took his men a whole year to fashion a road to Maiden-e Naft, which he had visited earlier to discover its rocks "saturated with petroleum." And one more year lapsed before Reynolds and his men reached the sites near Masjid-e Suleiman.

Reynolds was a man of many talents, who had explored for oil earlier in Sumatra, Indonesia. He started out with generous funding by London-based William Knox D'Arcy, who won the oil concession for all of Iran, except the five northern provinces, for sixty years from Muzaffar al Din Shah in 1901 for £20,000, "an equal amount in the shares of his company, and 16 percent of the profit." The Shah had taken his cue from his predecessor, Nasser al Din Shah, who in 1872 gave Baron Paul Julius de Reuter, a British businessman of German origin (now immortalized in Reuters News Agency), exclusive rights in Iran for railways, tramways, roads, telegraph lines, irrigation works, all the minerals except gold and silver, customs collection, and a state bank for an advance of £40,000 and 60 percent of the profits from the customs concession.[1]

Over time, D'Arcy, a prematurely bald, heavily built and puffy-faced Englishman, with long sideburns that merged with his abundant mustache, would win the epithet of "a capitalist of the highest order." He had a knack for betting on the right horse at race courses. In another context, he chose Reynolds, an India-born Englishman, who turned out, after long, nerve-racking months, to be a winner.

A graduate of the Royal Indian Engineering College, Reynolds started his career with the Indian Public Works Department. He had a gift for rigging machines and picking up foreign languages while maintaining his taciturnity. During his years in Sumatra he turned into an anthropologist. He was as demanding of himself as of others. Above all else, Reynolds was tenacious. He had started on his latest venture in 1902 in the 1,000 sq. mile (2,590 sq. km) area of the Chia Surkh sector by having all machine parts shipped to Basra, then transported upstream to Baghdad, and finally transported by mules and porters over the rocky Iraq-Iran border. There, assisted by drillers from Azerbaijan—which had a long established oil industry of its own—Canada, and Poland, he assembled the machinery, and got to work in abominable conditions, frequently hobbled by lack of spare parts and edible food, and enduring extremes of baking heat and freezing cold.

His success came in January 1904 when he struck oil. The discovery raised the spirits of D'Arcy, an equally colorful character albeit in a different mold. Born in 1848 in Newton Abbot, England, to a solicitor, he went to a private school in London. At seventeen, he migrated along with his father to Rockhampton in Queensland, Australia. There he became a successful lawyer as well as an addict of horse racing. His gambling instinct led him to organize a syndicate to revive the old Mount Morgan gold mine. It yielded far more of the much coveted metal than anybody had dreamt of. So when he returned to England in 1889 he did so as a very affluent businessman. In London he established himself as a speculator and organizer of syndicates. Following the death of his wife, he married Nina Boucicault, a glamorous actress, famous for her dinner parties. His lifelong interest in horse racing secured him a private box at the Epsom racing track adjacent to the royal box.

When Edouard Cotte, an agent of the recently deceased Baron de Reuter, approached D'Arcy in 1900 to invest in petroleum exploration in Iran, which had experienced oil seepage for centuries and whose inhabitants used it for binding bricks and caulking boats, the enterprising D'Arcy showed instant interest. He dispatched two geologists to visit the areas around Chia Surkh and Shuster. They submitted favorable reports, and that in turn led to the agreement D'Arcy made with Muzaffar al Din Shah.

Unfortunately, his high hopes, aroused by the discovery of oil in the Chia Surkh region, crashed when the two wet wells ran dry after a few months. Having sunk more than £300,000 into the venture, he was unwilling to invest any more.

Luckily for D'Arcy, at this point the Burmah Oil Company (BOC) showed interest in his rights. A spin-off of a network of trading houses in the Far East, BOC was established by Scottish merchants in 1886 in Glasgow. It had succeeded in upgrading primitive oil collection by villagers in Burma into a commercially viable enterprise with a refinery in Rangoon and sales outlets in British India, of which Burma was then a part. In 1904, BOC reached an agreement to supply oil to the British Admiralty, only to realize that its Burmese output was insufficient to meet the admiralty's demand. So its directors turned to D'Arcy. Out of this emerged the Concession Syndicate in 1905.

It was the Concession Syndicate that funded Reynolds's move to the Maidan-e Naft region, the last throw of the dice by the British venture capitalists. Reynolds arrived there with his equipment in 1906. So rough was the terrain that it took many months to build a road to the sites in and around Masjid-e Suleiman. It was not until January 1908 that drilling started. Working conditions were as grueling here as they had been in the Chia Surkh area. Procuring drinking water was a Herculean task.

Another major problem was security. Within months of Britain and Russia signing a convention in August 1907, dividing Iran into the Russian-influenced zone in the north, the British-influenced zone in the south (See Iranian map, pp. viii–ix), and a neutral zone in between, the British Indian government rushed a small detachment of soldiers of the 18th Bengal Lancers under

Lt. Arnold Wilson to protect Reynolds's workforce while pretending to provide a guard for the British consulate in Ahvaz—a clear violation of Iran's sovereignty.

But these problems dwarfed in relation to the fast deteriorating financial situation in Britain. The project had so far cost D'Arcy and BOC £500,000, a monumental sum—today's £200 million. Nervous BOC directors called on D'Arcy to provide £20,000 cash by April 30, 1908. An equally distraught D'Arcy ignored the deadline. On May 14, the directors sent a short cable to Reynolds telling him to expect a letter of instructions. In it they ordered him to go no deeper than 1,600 feet (488 meters) for the two wells being drilled. If he failed to strike oil by then, he should stop drilling, shut down the operation, and take as much of the machinery as possible to Mohammara/Khorramshahr.

While the BOC letter meandered its way eastward across Europe, hopeful smells began emanating from one of the two wells. Then a disaster struck. A drill bit got unscrewed and got lost in the bore hole. It took several days to recover the drill bit and resume drilling through the hardest stratum yet encountered. Now the vapors of the released natural gas began rising so abundantly that the crew could only not smell them but also see them.

It was so hot that both Reynolds and Lt. Wilson slept outside their tents at the base camp some distance away from the noisy work sites where drilling continued round the clock. As usual they went to bed on the night of May 25. Around 4 A.M. on May 26, a sudden, dramatic outburst of human shouting mixed with earth's rumbles and sprouting of gushing oil—rising 50 feet (15 meters) above the top of one of the derricks—woke them up. Reynolds jumped up, saw the sight, dressed, and rushed to the scene to savor every moment of it. The drill hole was less than 1,200 feet (366 meters) deep, barely three-quarters of the depth mandated by BOC directors.

Almost a century later, looking at a badly printed picture of this historical scene on page 493 of *History of Masjid-e Suleiman: History of the Beginning of the Oil Industry* (in Persian)—given to me by the author, Danish Abbas Shahani, a slender man of sixty, with a gaunt face and a balding head—I recognized Reynolds by the solar hat he was wearing, a trademark of the British in tropical and subtropical countries. Unknown to him, at 100 sq. miles (259 sq. km), Reynolds had tapped into the largest oil field discovered so far in the world.

Such turning points in history inevitably get transmuted into myths and legends. A legend attributes more to Lt. Wilson than he actually did or said. One such tale has him send a cryptic cable to BOC, "See Psalm 104 verse 15 third sentence." It reads, "that he may bring forth out of the earth oil to make a cheerful countenance."[2]

In any event, following the lucky strike at Masjid-e Suleiman, the Concession Syndicate morphed into Anglo-Persian Oil Company (APOC) in 1909, a corporation that would dominate the economic and political life of Iran for more than four decades.

Today both the oil well and the original 75-foot (23 meter) drilling rig along with its accompanying steam engine and boiler, all freshly painted in navy blue, and resting on a raised platform, surrounded by a high fence wall—with a large signpost above the entrance in Persian and English "MASJID-I SULAIMAN WELL NUMBER 1 THE FIRST OIL WELL IN MIDDLE EAST"—remain the prized possession of Masjid-e Suleiman. They are overseen by the National Iranian South Oil Company, a subsidiary of the National Iranian Oil Company (NIOC), with a caretaker living on the site.

The Company's public relations director, Mirza Javad Ahmadi, a broad-shouldered man of medium height sporting a few days' dark stubble, took me to the historic site, a short drive from the company's spacious headquarters. Past a low, grilled steel gate, a large signboard by the steps to the drilling rig's platform provided the essential information in blue and red lettering in Persian and English:

WELL NO.1 MASJID-I-SULAIMAN
COMMENCED JANUARY 23TH 1908
STRUCK OIL AND WELL COMPLETED MAY 26TH 1908
DEPTH 1,179 FEET/360 METERS
PRODUCTION 36,000 LITRES/8,000 GALLONS PER DAY

"In 1908, Masjid-e Suleiman was a small hamlet," Ahmadi told me. "The inhabitants made a living by farming and tending cattle. During summer it was so hot that most of them would migrate to Shiraz. Even though we are situated among high hills, the last time we had some snow was five years ago." Pointing to the bare hill surrounding the site, he said, "This was a hill forest here. The forest was so thick that bears roamed and the area was called the Bears' Valley. When Reynolds' workmen arrived here, they cut trees and used them as fuel for the boiler which powered the drilling rig." I looked around 360 degrees, and saw nothing but bald, brown mountains.

The oil field that Reynolds struck now runs from Izeh to the east, Dezful to the north, and Haftkul to the south, and covers 150 sq. miles (440 sq. km). One of the eighty active oil fields in Iran, it has 440 production units. Keen to take pictures of donkey pumps at work, I asked Ahmadi if he could take me to the nearest working oil well. "There are no donkey pumps," he said with a touch of pride. "The gas pressure is so high we don't need pumps to extract oil. All we have to do is to control the pressure, and thus the oil flow." The nearest production unit was 3 miles (5 km) away near an ancient fire temple of Zoroastrians, he told me—one among nearly ten thousand oil and gas wells nationwide.

Oil: A Blessing and a Curse

With the British Admiralty's decision in March 1913 to switch from coal to oil in order to make its battleships more powerful and speedy, the importance of petroleum increased. To ensure adequate supplies to the admiralty, the British government decided to acquire 51 percent interest in APOC.

Britain's success in striking oil in Iran aroused the interest and envy of Russia and the United States. To the chagrin of the Russian and American oil corporations, by then the oil concessions were available only in the five northern provinces of Iran. In 1916, Georgian entrepreneur Akady Khoshtaria reestablished his claim to a concession in the north granted to him two decades earlier.

With the Bolshevik Revolution in Tsarist Russia in 1917, the political situation changed radically in the region. Determined to turn a new leaf, the Soviet government in Moscow signed a treaty with Tehran in February 1921 that declared all treaties between Iran and Tsarist Russia null and void.

The attempts by the Standard Oil Company of New Jersey (now Exxon) from 1920 to 1921 and by Sinclair Oil in 1923 to secure petroleum concessions in the north failed. The British were keen to keep the Americans out, so also were the Soviets.

On assuming supreme power in 1925, Reza Shah formed Kavir-e Khorian (*lit.*, Desert of Khorian) Company, which bought 25 percent of the rights of the oil concessionaires in the Semnan-Damghan-Gorgan region of the vast, ill-defined northeastern province of Khurasan. Soon Khoshtaria turned up to buy 65 percent interest, and through him the Soviet government acquired this equity. Its half-hearted exploration for oil proved sterile.

As described earlier (Chapter Four), Reza Shah got tough with APOC, and signed a new agreement with it under the aegis of the League of Nations, which stipulated a reduction of 80 percent in APOC's concession area in two stages. APOC, renamed

Anglo-Iranian Oil Company (AIOC) in 1935, would fail to honor its pledges to improve the wages and promotion prospects of its Iranian employees and provide them with roads and educational and health services.

Like the Soviet-owned oil companies, the attempts of American-Iranian Oil, a subsidiary of Seaboard Oil Company in 1937, and Standard-Vacuum (Mobil), to gain concessions in the north failed.

Soon after the Soviet troops had entered Iran's Azerbaijan and Khurasan provinces in August 1941, Moscow requested Tehran for help in developing the Kavir-e Khorian Company's oil concessions. Tehran refused. The Soviets drilled in the region, but again found nothing.

In September 1944, the Soviet Union pressed Iran for oil exploitation rights in all the five northern provinces for five years. Tehran replied that no concession would be granted until after the war. In early December, the Majlis passed a resolution, introduced by Muhammad Mussadiq, which barred (on pain of three to eight years imprisonment) any government official from discussing oil concessions with any official or unofficial representative of a country or company, or signing any agreement concerning petroleum.

Following the Shah's signing of an agreement with Moscow on April 8, 1946, conceding oil concessions to the Soviet Union, Premier Ahmad Qavam al Saltane concluded a deal with Moscow to form a joint Soviet-Iranian oil company with 51 percent Soviet interest in order to encourage the Soviets to withdraw from Azerbaijan. They did so in May on the understanding that the final agreement would be ratified by the Majlis by late October. But due to the deliberately staggered elections to the Fifteenth Majlis, the document came up for ratification in October 1947. The deputies rejected it by 102 votes to two, arguing that it violated the 1944 oil law.[3]

As it was, rebuffing the Soviet Union was only part of the

five-clause law. The last clause instructed the government to undertake necessary measures to secure "the national rights . . . in respect of the natural wealth of the country, including the southern oil."[4] It would prove to be the seed that would mature into a full-blown oil nationalization movement and bring Mussadiq to power.

Public opinion in Iran was inflamed further against AIOC when it announced a profit of £40 million ($112 million) in 1947 with Iran receiving a paltry £7 million in royalties. In addition, AIOC sold Iranian oil at a substantial discount to the navy of the British government, which was also the majority owner of AIOC.[5]

The contrast between the living conditions of the Iranians in Abadan, the site of the AIOC oil refinery, and their British superiors in 1949 was stark, as highlighted by Manuchehr Farmanfarmaian, an Iranian oil expert.

"Wages were 50 cents a day," he reported. "There was no vacation pay, no sick leave, no disability compensation. The workers lived in a shantytown called Kaghazabad, or Paper City, without running water or electricity . . . In winter the earth flooded and became a flat, perspiring lake. The mud in town was knee-deep, and canoes ran alongside the roadways for transport. When the rains subsided, clouds of nipping, small-winged flies rose from the stagnant waters to fill the nostrils, collecting in black mounds along the rims of cooking pots and jamming the fans at the refinery with unctuous glue . . . [In summer] The heat was torrid . . . sticky and unrelenting—while the wind and sandstorms whipped off the desert hot as a blower. The dwellings of Kaghazabad, cobbled from rusted oil drums hammered flat, turned into sweltering ovens . . . In every crevice hung the foul, sulfurous stench of burning oil—a pungent reminder that every day 20,000 barrels or one million tons a year, were being consumed indiscriminately for the functioning of the refinery, and AIOC never paid the government a cent for it. To the management of AIOC in their pressed ecru shirts and air-conditioned offices, the workers were faceless drones." While "in the British section of Abadan there were lawns, rose beds, tennis courts, swimming pools and clubs"; in Kaghazabad, "there was nothing—not a tea shop, not a [public] bath. Not a single tree. The tiled reflecting pool and shaded central square that were part of every Iranian town, no matter how poor or dry, were missing here. The unpaved alleyways were emporiums for rats."[6]

This was the case *after* strikes by oil workers in 1946 who were organized into trade unions by the Tudeh Party of Iran: Party of Iranian Working Class. Formed in January 1942, it evolved out of the Communist Party of Iran, established in June 1920, which had helped found the short-lived Soviet Republic of Gilan along the Caspian Sea. After it was crushed by the Tehran government in November 1921, the remnants of the Communist movement survived under the guise of local cultural and sports clubs. This lasted until 1931 when the government outlawed the formation of groups advocating Communist ideology. In 1937, it convicted fifty-eight members of the Marxist Circle in Tehran. Following the deposition of Reza Shah in 1941, all political prisoners were released, and the Communist movement revived. But to respect the law and make the new organization more attractive to peasants, workers, and artisans, former Marxist Circle members decided to form a democratic front, naming it the Tudeh (*lit.*, Masses) Party. It grew dramatically. By staging a series of strikes in the oil industry in the mid-1940s, the pro-Tudeh trade union won concessions from AIOC. In 1946, the party had twenty-five thousand members and seventy-five thousand sympathizers; and its trade union federation had four hundred thousand members. In the Majlis it had eight members and twenty-four sympathizers. Its stress on modernism and its progressive views on sociocultural issues appealed especially to women and young people.

On becoming Prime Minister, Mussadiq applied the doctrine of "negative equilibrium" to Iran's foreign affairs, including oil. The leftists interpreted his breaking of the British oil monopoly in the south, exercised by the Anglo-Iranian Oil Company, as a pre-amble to giving concessions to the Soviets in the north. The centrists saw it as being strictly neutral between the Soviet Union and Britain with a view to eliminating their interference in Iranian affairs. The pro-West nationalists considered Mussadiq's policy as a new variant of the old "three power game" played by Reza Shah—the third power this time being America, replacing Germany—using the U.S. as a counterpoint to Britain and the Soviet Union. Mussadiq's actions put him firmly in the last category.

On its part, Moscow moved fast to assist Mussadiq. Once he had expelled the last British employee of the AIOC in October 1952, Moscow contracted to buy petroleum from the nationalized oil industry. It also signed a commercial agreement with Iran. Its lead was followed by Czechoslovakia and Hungary. But Mussadiq, a staunch anti-Communist, refrained from strengthening economic ties with the Soviet bloc. He feared that such a move would destroy any chance of economic and military aid from Washington, something he badly needed. He remained naïvely hopeful to the last of separating the U.S. from Britain, and achieving the objective of destroying British economic domination of Iran with American help.

As described earlier (in Chapters Three and Four), oil nationalization was at the core of the conflict between Mussadiq and Muhammad Reza Shah: it led to the Shah's flight from Iran in mid-August 1953, followed by his return on the heels of the CIA-engineered coup against Mussadiq's government.

On Washington's advice, the Shah retained the oil nationalization law on the statute books, but downgraded the NIOC's role. The NIOC leased the rights to, and management of, Iranian oil, including marketing, in 1954 for the next twenty-five years to a Western consortium, consisting of AIOC, 40 percent; Royal Dutch Shell, 14 percent; five major U.S. oil companies (Exxon, Gulf, Mobil, Socal, and Texaco) 8 percent each; and Compagnie Francaise des Petroles (later Total SA, and then TotalFinaElf) 6 percent. It was not until 1967 that NIOC managed to sell 100,000 bpd on its own.

Meanwhile, Iran became one of the six founder-members of the Organization of Petroleum Exporting Countries (OPEC), an international body to coordinate the hydrocarbon policies of its constituents, at its founding meeting in Baghdad in September 1960. The other members were Iraq, Kuwait, Saudi Arabia, and Venezuela. At the same time, to persuade the Western oil consortium to increase its output, the Shah gave further concessions to it.

Later, encouraged by the self-reliant policies advocated by OPEC, the Shah pressed the consortium to renegotiate the leasing agreement. On the tenth anniversary of the White Revolution in January 1973, he announced the nationalization of the Western oil consortium. This happened in July when the NIOC took over all the operations of the consortium as well as its ownership. Following the quadrupling of petroleum prices from 1973 to 1974, the Shah increased output sharply. It reached 6 million bpd in 1974, and was achieved by overexploiting oil wells. In 1977, the oil revenue of $19.5 billion provided three-quarters of the government's annual income. During the revolutionary turmoil in 1978 the production declined to 5.3 million bpd, with 4.5 million bpd sold abroad.

The strike of oil workers in October 1978, which dramatically dried up the government coffers, played a key role in the overthrow of the Pahlavi dynasty.

Whereas the economic boom, generated by the dramatic oil price rise combined with the doubling of output, followed by a recession, created general conditions for the revolutionary overthrow of the autocratic monarchy, encouraging the industrial working class to cripple the economy, the indefinite strike by oil workers, still under the influence of the underground Tudeh Party, delivered the coup de grâce.

Oil and the Islamic Republic

Muslim scholars, whether Shia or Sunni, are unanimous that mineral resources are the property of the community at large. Petroleum and natural gas deposits are therefore the property of the government in an Islamic state, be it Sunni Saudi Arabia or Shia Iran—making the public sector in these countries predominant in the economy. It was that interpretation about the ownership of minerals that drove Ayatollah Abol Qasim Kashani to back the oil nationalization movement in the late 1940s and early 1950s. Though Muhammad Reza Shah did not denationalize oil in 1953, he contracted the extraction and sales of the commodity to a Western consortium—a move that was condemned by such senior clerics as Ayatollah Ruhollah Khomeini. The ayatollah was also against the overexploitation of oil fields that the Shah undertook from the mid-1970s to fulfill his grandiose dreams of unprecedented power. Khomeini therefore promised to reverse this trend as well as end Iran's overdependence on petroleum exports to earn much-needed foreign currencies.

But such dramatic political events as the seizure of the American Embassy in Tehran within nine months of the revolution, which led to economic sanctions by the West, followed by an invasion by Iraq in September 1980, spiked whatever ideas Khomeini had about the oil industry before the revolution.

The loss of Iran's supplies to the international oil market, caused by the revolutionary turmoil, pushed the price from $13 to $20 a barrel. So, with the resumption of exports at 3.2 million bpd in the spring of 1979, Iran earned more than it did with much larger exports before the revolution of February 1979.

The Western economic boycott of Iran, following the takeover of the U.S. Embassy in Tehran in November 1979, disrupted the Iranian input into the international market and led to another price rise. Thus, Iran continued to earn more than before while producing less.

The outbreak of the Iran-Iraq War in September 1980, primarily in the Iranian oil province of Khuzistan, destabilized the market further, pushing the dollar price into the upper 30s in the spring of 1981. In 1982, oil provided 98 percent of Iran's foreign earnings, indicating a greater dependence on petroleum exports than ever before. In the mid-1980s, Iran's output fell to 1.4 million bpd, and then stagnated at 2.5 million bpd during the war.

During the stalemate in the war from April 1984 to January 1986, Iraq escalated its attacks on Iranian oil tankers, using French-made Exocet air-to-ship (surface-skimmer) missiles, and intensified its air raids on the Kharg oil terminal, which handled most of Iran's petroleum exports. Iran retaliated by hitting ships serving the ports of Kuwait and Saudi Arabia, which were aiding Iraq, in the Lower Gulf. In May 1985, Iraq intensified its tanker war and strikes on Kharg, reaching a peak in mid-August. All told, Iraq hit thirty-three ships in the Gulf in 1985, and Iran fourteen.

Iran survived by pumping oil at Kharg into its own tankers, which delivered the commodity to its customers at its offshore islands in the Lower Gulf outside the range of the Iraqi bombers.

The steep decline in the oil price from $28 to below $10 a barrel—caused by Saudi Arabia and Kuwait flooding the market during the spring of 1986—reduced Iran's oil income from $13.1 billion in 1985 to $7.2 billion, with its average exports at 1.6 million bpd. This severely damaged its ability to conduct the war. It never recovered from this loss, which in essence paved the way for its acceptance of a United Nations-brokered ceasefire.

So, both in war and peace, oil determined the main course of Iran's modern history.

From mid-1986, using covert official U.S. military expertise, Iraq began using its air force more aggressively than before, hitting Iran's economic and infrastructural targets and extending its air strikes to the Iranian oil terminals in the Lower Gulf. During 1986, Iraq struck eighty-six ships in the Gulf, and Iran forty-one.

In its intervention in the war in October 1987, the American Navy destroyed two Iranian offshore oil platforms in the Lower Gulf allegedly in retaliation for an Iranian missile attack on a U.S.-flagged supertanker docked in Kuwaiti waters.

After the war Iran increased its output steadily from 2.87 million bpd in 1989 to 3.62 million bpd in 1993, with exports around 2.5 million bpd and oil revenue at $14.5 billion. But falling oil prices, fluctuating around midteens, worsened the budget deficit. They led to the rise of Iran's foreign loans to a staggering $30 billion by the end of 1993, due largely to the excess of imports over exports, which from 1991 to 1992 was $10 billion on a two-way trade of $47 billion. The Iranian rial's value fell from Rls 1,500 to US$1 to Rls 2,000. The government imposed import quotas and limited export of foreign currencies.[7]

Overall, the petroleum industry had suffered due to the 1980s war that had raged in the oil-bearing region, chronic under-investment, a ban on oil and gas concessions to foreign companies, and the American economic sanctions.

There was acute need for foreign investment in the industry. But it had to be balanced by Article 43 (8) of its constitution specifying "prevention of foreign economic domination of the country's economy." That precluded equity or production-sharing rights for foreigners. On the other hand, the 1987 Complementary Law to the Establishment of Oil Ministry (1979) allowed contracts between the Oil Ministry, state companies, and local and foreign persons and legal entities. Within this framework, the Oil Ministry devised a buy-back formula that allowed it to pay the "guest company" in oil and gas to the point of enabling it a rate of return of 15–18 percent on its investment within four to five years.

In 1991, the Majlis opened Iran's offshore fields to foreigners on a buy-back basis. The reasons were technical and sociopolitical. Offshore fields required complex technology. Also the foreigners stayed out, at sea, which suited both sides. The foreign oil company (often already operating in one of the six Gulf monarchies) moved its equipment by ship from a nearby location, and its personnel were not subject to such restrictions as a ban on alcohol and the compulsory use of veil for women.[8]

But it would take four years before a $650 million contract with Conoco, a unit of DuPont, an American corporation, to develop Iran's offshore fields would be ready for signature.

Meanwhile, the disaffection caused by reduced oil revenue and economic liberalization, which reached a peak with the devaluation of the Iranian rial by 95.6 percent in March 1993, burst into wide-scale rioting in Shiraz, Shushter, and Arak, culminating in three days of bloody rioting in Mashhad in which six people were killed in police firings. The pattern of violence was the same everywhere. The security forces would tear down illegally built shantytowns near cities, the squatters would fight back, march to the city center and attack public offices, loot shops, and burn cars and buses.

Underlying the apparently insignificant grievances that triggered the riots was the impoverishment of the populace caused by high inflation and static earnings, resulting from a drop in oil prices, from an average of $30 a barrel to about $20. To reduce high inflation—one of the rioters' major grievances—by increasing the supply of goods, the government allowed virtually unrestricted imports of goods. In the process it incurred high foreign debts, which in a year soared to $13 billion.[9]

The March 1995–February 2000 Five-Year Plan called for an investment of $30 billion in oil and gas, with $9 billion to come from abroad. By mid-1998, Iran claimed to have signed up $4 billion in foreign investment.

A setback to the Iranian plans came in March 1995 when, in order to contain and isolate Iran, U.S. President Bill Clinton issued an executive order barring American individuals or companies from working in Iran's oil and gas industry.[10] He thereby blocked the Conoco deal to develop Iran's Sirri A and E offshore oil fields. Under the U.S. law then in force, the oil contracts signed by American companies with Iran were not illegal provided the commodity did not enter the United States.

Tehran turned this contract over to Total SA of France, formerly Campaigne Petroles de France. As with Conoco, the NIOC did not give Total SA any rights on the reserves and the project had to be completed in five years, when Total was required to hand over operational control to the NIOC.

On April 30, 1995, Clinton announced that he was banning trade with Iran forthwith. That stopped U.S. oil corporations buying $4 billion worth of Iranian crude annually, and American companies exporting $326 million worth of goods—mainly corn, rice, and oil industry equipment—to Iran.

In August came the Iran-Libya Sanctions Act (ILSA). It gave the U.S. President discretionary power to impose two of the six sanctions against any individual or company anywhere in the world that invested $40 million or more in an Iranian or Libyan oil or gas project: a ban on imports of the goods or services of the offending entity; a federal government ban on the purchases from the sanctioned entity; a ban on all American financial institutions to lend it $10 million or more; prohibiting the sanctioned entity from acting as a primary dealer of U.S. Treasury Bonds, or as an agent of the U.S. government or as a repository for U.S. government funds; a ban on U.S. Export-Import Bank assistance; and a denial of licenses for the export of controlled technology to the sanctioned entity.[11]

Washington's pressure on the European Union to toe its line on Iran failed. The EU argued that severing trade ties would have to be done within a United Nations context, and that was not in the offing. The commercial links between Iran and the EU, involving vital oil trade, were too tight to be loosened or cut. Overall, the EU imported 10 percent of its crude oil from Iran, with France, Italy, and Germany being major buyers. On its part, in 1996, Iran sold one-third of its $17 billion worth petroleum exports to the EU, and imported goods worth $11.5 billion.[12]

Declining oil prices, combined with the U.S. Iran-Libya Sanctions Act which—in the estimation of Ali Shams Ardekani, Secretary-General of Iran's Chamber of Commerce, Industries, and Mines—cut Tehran's normal annual oil income by 6 to 12 percent, had made even the economic nationalists in the conservative camp realize that the only way to cope with the escalating demographic and economic pressures was to open up the oil industry to foreign investment. In March 1997, the Majlis authorized the Oil Ministry to sign $5.4 billion worth of contracts with foreign companies during the financial year ending next March.

In September 1998, an oil consortium, led by Total SA (later TotalFinaElf) of France, and including Gazprom of Russia and Petronas of Malaysia, with 40:30:30 shares in the equity, signed a $2 billion contract with the NIOC to develop its vast offshore South Pars gas field (phases two and three), after an NIOC subsidiary, Iranian Offshore Engineering and Construction Company, had finished the first phase. The plan was to extract 20 billion cubic meters of natural gas annually by 2001, enough to satisfy two-thirds of France's demand.

Total SA was the favorite because it was already developing the adjacent part of the Pars gas field under the Qatari jurisdiction. The full exploitation of this vast field with total reserves of 300,000 billion cubic meters of gas and condensates was to be carried out in eight phases. Though Total's president, Thierry Desmarest, had told the Paris-based *Le Monde* (The World) that "the French law prohibits French companies submitting to U.S. extra-territorial legislation," he took no chances. Before signing the contract with the NIOC, Total SA sold whatever minor holdings it had in the U.S.[13] Washington declared that Total, Gazprom, and Petronas had violated its Iran-Libya Sanctions Act, and that it would penalize them. But it never did—because that would have meant applying an American legislation extraterritorially, thus violating international law.

Another major power that valued its oil trade with Tehran was China, which was Iran's second most important supplier of weapons, including speed patrol boats, gunboats, anti-ship missiles and cruise missiles.[14] With Beijing turning into a net importer of oil in 1993, it became more interested in strengthening ties with Tehran than before, with the latter supplying China with some 100,000 bpd in 1996, a figure that would rise steadily in the coming years. During his visit to Tehran in late 2004, Chinese Foreign Minister Li Xhaoxing would sign an oil and natural gas deal with Iran. In the same week, the Indian Oil Corporation would agree to invest $3 billion in an Iranian gas field with Petropars of Iran.[15]

In 1998, because of falling oil prices—at their lowest in four years—caused by a severe economic downturn in Southeast Asia in the summer of 1997, and compounded by OPEC's decision in November, to raise output by 10 percent to 27.5 million bpd, Iran's economy suffered. At $9.9 billion, Iran's oil income in March 21, 1998 to March 20, 1999—the Iranian calendar year—was almost half the figure for 1996 to 1997. Economic growth fell while inflation rate rose sharply. This continued until March 1999.

It was against this backdrop that in 1998 the Majlis passed a law entitled, "Utmost Capacity of Local Technical and Engineering and Industry, and How to Materialize Projects and Facilities in Order to Export." That is, it approved the Khatami government's plan to open much of the oil and gas sector, including onshore fields, to foreign companies.

Clinton's failure to apply ILSA sanctions against to the Total-led oil consortium in May 1998 helped Iran. It removed a major hurdle to large-scale foreign investment in its oil sector, and encouraged interest from European companies, especially British—BG (British Gas), Enterprise, Lasmo, and Monument. In Iran it helped break down resistance to a more ambitious foreign investment program. In August, the Iranian Oil Ministry unveiled forty-three projects worth $8 billion before seventy foreign companies in London. Of the U.S. companies, Mobil and Arco officially informed Iran that they were interested in the projects. Others expressing interest were Chevron, Conoco, Kerr-McGee, and Unocal.

In March 1999, at the behest of Iran, now the second largest producer in OPEC, the cartel cut 1.7 million bpd from its current output of 23 million bpd, with four cooperating non-OPEC countries—Mexico, Norway, Oman, and Russia—reducing their production by nearly half a million bpd. The subsequent improvement in oil price lifted Iran's oil revenue from 1999 to 2000 to $13 billion at an average output of 3.52 million bpd.

Six months later, the NIOC announced the discovery of the biggest oil field in thirty years at Azadegan in the Khuzistan province, estimated to contain five to 6 billion barrels. This led to its decision to add 1 million bpd new capacity every five years, reaching 5 million bpd in 2005.[16]

The NIOC announcement came on the heels of major deals signed by Royal Dutch-Shell, Elf, Agip of Italy, and Bow Valley of Canada to develop offshore oil and gas fields. These and other corporations were only too aware of vast oil and gas reserves that Iran possessed.[17]

On their part, Iranian officials tried to get the best possible contracts for their country. Explaining the procedure for selecting the winner of a bid, an NIOC official in Tehran told me that the Oil Ministry made a short list of four to six bidders after it had examined their overall track record, financial state, and capacity to raise loans. Then it talked to each company separately. Next, its Technical Committee examined the track record of each company in a specific area—augmenting the present capacity, exploring, developing a virgin field, etc.—and how advanced its technology was in that field. Finally, it estimated what the chances were for NIOC employees to pick up the new technology during the project period, which was often four to five years. Then its Economic Committee examined the price that the bidder was demanding for its services. Then the Oil Ministry reduced the list to two, and tried to play off one bidder against the other. "Just as in a football match, at the eighty-ninth minute nobody knows the winner, so also here," said the NIOC official. "The winner comes up at the last minute."[18]

On the advice of the NIOC, the Oil Minister made his recommendation to the ten-member Supreme Economic Council (SEC), chaired by the President, since it was the SEC that handled contracts of international importance impinging on foreign policy. The SEC's decision was then endorsed by Leader Khamanei. Because of the highly technical nature of the oil and gas industry, the SEC invariably endorsed the Oil Minister's recommendation.

Due to successive cutbacks in OPEC output in 1999, the petroleum price rose from $13 a barrel in the previous year to $18. The subsequent increase of $2.5 billion in its oil revenue enabled Iran to reduce its foreign debts by about a quarter, to $11.6 billion. At home, though, the workforce was rising by 4 percent annually whereas the economic growth was only half as much. The privatization program was faltering due to lack of private capital. And the government had failed to reduce the cost of subsidizing food and gasoline by targeting them at underprivileged groups. The $10 billion spent annually on state subsidies continued to drain the public exchequer and had a deleterious effect on the economy.

But continued petroleum price hikes since 1999, with a barrel selling for $55 in November 2004, kept Iran's oil receipts running at $35 billion a year, twice the budgeted figure.[19] By then Iran had set up an Oil Stabilization Fund where it deposited its oil revenue above the budgeted amount to cover any future deficit due to a fall in petroleum prices. Also, its policy makers were buoyed by the discovery of new major oil and gas fields. These factors boosted manufacturing and retail trade in the private sector, with the car output heading for one million in 2004, registering elevenfold increase in a decade, in a nation of seventy million.

Reflecting the improved economy, the Tehran stock market rose 130 percent during March 2003 to March 2004.

It came as no surprise then that during my July 2004 visit to Iran I saw more and newer cars on roads. The old, polluting vehicles had almost disappeared. Another feature that stood out in the towns and cities I passed through were recently planted trees along wide avenues divided by middle islands covered with trees and shrubs. All these settlements invariably displayed gaudily painted portraits of "martyrs"—those who died in the Iran-Iraq War of 1980 to 1988. The nearer I got to the Iraqi border the more prominent became this feature.

The inhabitants of the urban centers that suffered heavily due to the Iraqi bombardment and/or ground fighting still harbored deep feelings against Iraqis. One such place was Bushehr, a port with a long history as the base of the British Political Resident for the Persian Gulf, which was occupied by Britain during World War I. Recalling the damage done to the city by the Iraqis, Khosrow Warrast, a mild-mannered, middle-aged headwaiter at Malvan Hotel and Restaurant told me, "America is doing to Iraq what Iraq did to Iran during the eight-year war."

Khorramshahr, a leading oil city along the Iraqi border, suffered more than Bushehr. Here I encountered Sayyid Mahmoud, a small, dark, bespectacled man, fishing along the esplanade on the Karun River a few hundred yards from its confluence with the Shatt al Arab (Arvand Rud, to Iranians), the disputed fluvial border between Iran and Iraq that triggered the conflict.

Describing himself as a retired shepherd, Mahmoud pointed to the many damaged or destroyed houses across the road, which included his old residence. "It was good that the Americans came and threw out Saddam who was killing people," he said. "Now they alone should stay in Iraq and not allow others like France to join them because that will change the American plan."

Iran and Iraq:
Neighbors, Not Friends

◆ CHAPTER 8 ◆

Though the Battle for Hill 270 near the Iranian border town of Mehran in September 1986 was just a snapshot in the album of the Iran-Iraq War, it reflected fairly accurately the big picture in the ongoing conflict.

Soon after Iraq invaded Iran in 1980, it captured Mehran—a settlement of twenty-five thousand people—and destroyed or damaged 2,500 houses, 550 shops, and 14 mosques. The Iraqi occupation of the town and its surrounding hills, extending many miles (km) into Iran, ended in July 1982. Then, following the Iranian success in seizing Iraq's Fao Peninsula in February 1986, the Iraqis recaptured Mehran and its hilly environs on May 17.

Iraq proposed exchanging Mehran for Fao. Tehran rejected the offer. Its forces retook Mehran on July 30. But to consolidate their gains, they had to retake the surrounding hills. On September 26–27 night, using surprise guerrilla tactics against the heavily fortified Hill 270, they did so.

Arriving on the scene soon after on a sunny morning, several foreign reporters and I witnessed the signs of the recently expelled Iraqis—empty cans of French-made milk powder and Austrian-processed beef with potatoes, and Iraqi newspapers.

What instantly grabbed our attention, though, were the boxes of mortars marked: "CN 1860101 GHQ Jordan Armed Forces, Dir of Plng N Org, Amman, Jordan," and Egyptian bombs with yellow casing. Another intriguing article was a gray plastic casing with the inscription: "N5 Anti-personnel Mine, Mod. Valemarra 69. Contract N 1654/ A.S. /84 Lot N 004/85," with no indication of the country of origin. A few of these deadly weapons were still in place, as were several conventional mines. There were many more spent grenades and conventional mines scattered all over the terrain. The extensive barbed-wire rolls, reinforced with steel spikes testified to the hurdles that the Iranian forces had to overcome to seize their target.

From the trench on top of the hill, we could see the Iraqi bunkers barely 500 yards (457.2 meters) away. The fresh autumnal air cracked with periodic machine-gun fire as each side directed bursts at the other.

The visit to Hill 270 was arranged by the authorities at the Iranian military unit headquarters near Salehabad, a forty-five-minute flight by a helicopter. A spokesman there claimed that when their troops attacked the Iraqis at Hill 270 in the dead of the night, the Iraqis were asleep. "This was also the case in Fao," he added. He was referring to the peninsula in the deep south of Iraq that the Iranians had captured seven months earlier.

When some eighty soldiers and civilians gathered for the evening prayers, they were led by Hajji Mujtaba Namdar, a small, bearded, square-shouldered cleric, wearing a brown cloak and a white turban. After the prayers, Namdar delivered a sermon. "If we make peace with Saddam [President of Iraq], he will grow strong and attack us again. After six years of war, what are we to say to the relatives of those who have been martyred or disabled? The Iranian people are shouting 'War, war until victory.' Even if it takes twenty years to secure victory, we will go on. Dying for Islam is as sweet to us as honey."

The next day we saw the thirty-two-year-old cleric at Zaloo Aab command post near Hill 270. He had changed his tunic and cloak for a soldier's khaki pants and shirt. He was part of the political-ideological department in the military, which educated officers and ranks in Islamic history and ideology.

The importance of clerics at the battlefront was underscored by Ali Akbar Hashemi Rafsanjani, the spokesman for the Supreme Defense Council and Speaker of the Majlis. "Your presence on the war front can be more effective than sending a million videocassettes there," he told a contingent of clerics departing recently for the battlefield. "Showing a cleric carrying an RPG-7 (rocket-propelled grenade) or riding a motorcycle along the front can boost the morale of millions of people, and encourage them to enlist for the war."[1]

That explained why, at the Salehabad army headquarters, the mosque, housed in a 135 feet (41 meters) by 30 feet (9 meters) shelter, was the hub of activity. A large full-length picture of Ayatollah Ruhollah Khomeini, with his hand raised in blessing, dominated a wall. A green arrow near the podium at the far end of the hall pointed toward Mecca to which the faithful must bow during prayers. Verses from the Quran, printed on broadcloths, covered the walls. To this had been added black flags, signifying the current month of Muharram, when Imam Hussein, especially revered by Shias, was killed at Karbala some thirteen centuries before.

The Baseej volunteers units marching off to the war fronts from the Iranian hinterland were called "caravans to Karbala," and the war communiqués frequently described the Iranian forces as "marchers to Karbala"—a place in southern Iraq then ruled by "infidel" Saddam Hussein.

As it was, competition and rivalry between Iran and Iraq dated back to the days of the Ottoman Turkish Empire (1517–1918) and the Persian Empire under the Safavids (1501–1732). Iraq, then called Mesopotamia, was the easternmost province of the Ottomans and Iran was the nucleus of the Safavid realm.

After Shah Ismail Safavid (1501–24) had consolidated his newly won territories, he adopted Twelver Shiaism as the official religion in order to appeal to the heterodox sentiments of his subjects, and differentiate himself sharply from the competing Sunni Ottoman Turks, who were keen to incorporate Iran into their empire. Because Safavids considered themselves guardians of Shiaism, they wanted free access to the Shia holy shrines in Najaf and Karbala. When this was denied, they attacked and occupied Iraq in 1623. Their occupation lasted just fifteen years. Following Iraq's recapture by the Ottomans, the two sides signed a treaty whereby the Safavids accepted Iraq as part of the Ottoman Empire, and the signatories promised to refrain from interfering in each other's affairs.

After a period of two centuries of peaceful coexistence, however, the two neighbors returned to their old ways. Between 1834 and 1840, the Ottomans attacked the port of Mohammara (later called Khorramshahr) in Iran, then ruled by the Qajar dynasty, and persecuted the Iranian Shias living in Iraq. Russia and Britain intervened to resolve the conflict. The Second Treaty of Erzerum of 1847 signed by the Ottomans and the Qajars moved the fluvial borders between Iraq and Iran from the western bank of the Bahmanshir River to the eastern bank of Shatt al Arab for about one-third of its length of 120 miles (200 km).

A new factor was added to the Iran-Iraq equation when in 1908 a British company, the Concession Syndicate, discovered oil in commercial quantities at Masjid-e Suleiman in Khuzistan province, paving the way for the British government's involvement in Iran's oil industry. Following the 1913 Constantinople Protocol, a definitive map of the Iranian-Iraqi border was produced by the time World War I erupted the following year.

As a result of that conflagration, the 1917 Bolshevik Revolution, and the dissolution of the Ottoman Empire, Iraq emerged as a quasi-independent state under the British Mandate. Once Iraq acquired independence in 1932, the two neighbors faced each other as independent states for the first time.

One of their major disputes concerned demarcating the Shatt al Arab as an international border. Iraq demanded complete sovereignty over the waterway whereas Iran proposed dividing it up along its deepest channel—the thalweg principle. Urged by the League of Nations to negotiate directly, the two neighbors complied. During the talks, however, a military coup in Iraq ushered in a government that was feeble and confused. Under growing pressure from Iran, bolstered by the British oil interests and government, Iraq conceded the thalweg principle for 4 miles (6.4 km) opposite Abadan, the seat of a vast oil refinery of the Anglo-Iranian Oil Company (AIOC). The result was the Iran-Iraq Frontier Treaty signed in July 1937.

Following the signing of the Treaty of Good Neighborly Relations twelve years later, mutual ties were raised to the ambassadorial level. In January 1957, both countries endorsed the doctrine of U.S. President Dwight Eisenhower, which promised support to any Middle Eastern government against "overt armed aggression from any nation controlled by international Communism."

But, with the overthrow of the pro-Western Iraqi monarchy in July 1958 by nationalist military officers, who adopted a non-aligned foreign policy, the peaceful coexistence between Iran and Iraq ended. Encouraged by Washington, Muhammad Reza Shah revived the earlier Iranian demand that the thalweg principle be applied to the whole of the Shatt al Arab frontier. Iraq rejected it. As before, Iraq's strategically weak position was further compromised by three coups in a decade, the last one by the Baathist military officers in July 1968.

In February, the Shah unilaterally abrogated the 1937 treaty and started using Iranians to pilot Iran's ships plying in the Shatt al Arab as Iranian gunboats steamed up the waterway along the middle channel. He also tried to engineer a coup against the Baathist regime, which was foiled in January 1970.

Once Britain, the dominant foreign power in the Persian Gulf for many generations, decided to quit the region by December 1971, it coordinated its policy with America to make the Shah of Iran a bulwark against any revolutionary changes in the oil-rich area. In response, Baathist Iraq signed a fifteen-year Treaty of Friendship and Cooperation with the Soviet Union in 1972.

Flush with funds acquired due to the dramatic rise in oil prices from 1973 to 1974, the Shah vastly increased his military and weapons arsenals. He tried to destabilize the Baghdad regime by arming Kurdish nationalists in Iraq. At its peak, the resulting conflict involved forty-five thousand Kurdish guerrillas who pinned down four-fifths of Iraq's one hundred thousand troops and half of its 1,390 tanks.[2] By then the Iranian forces were covering the Kurdish insurgents with artillery fire and anti-aircraft missiles. In January 1975, the Shah posted two regiments of his uniformed army into the "liberated" Kurdish areas in Iraq.

Soon tension between Iran and Iraq reached such a pitch that it threatened to escalate into a full-scale war between them. Both sides realized the danger, and encouraged mediation, first by Turkey and then Algeria.

This was the background to the conclusion of an accord on March 6, 1975, in Algiers by the Shah of Iran and Saddam Hussein, then Vice President of Iraq, during a summit conference of the Organization of Petroleum Exporting Countries (OPEC). The signatories agreed to delimit their river boundaries "according to the thalweg line" and "to end all infiltrations of a subversive nature."[3] The subsequent treaty between Iran and Iraq was signed in Baghdad on June 13 and ratified by both parties on September 17.

The Algiers Accord signified victory for Iran. And, just as in 1937, the weakness of its government had led Iraq to yield to Iran. Harassed and exhausted by the Iranian-backed Kurdish insurgency to the point where it was left with only three bombs for its air force, Baghdad swallowed a bitter pill by agreeing to extend the thalweg formula to the rest of its fluvial border with Iran. In the event, this agreement would last only five years.

Soon after the overthrow of the Shah in Iran in early 1979, Khomeini tried to export his revolution into Iraq. Three factors made Iraq his prime target: secularism of the Baathist regime; oppression of the Shia majority by the Sunni-dominated ruling

Baath Socialist Party; and the existence of six Shia holy shrines in Iraq.[4] The Baathists, having consolidated their hold on state and society over the past decade, were determined to meet the challenge from Iran head on.

It was ironic that a hitherto pro-Western, conservative, secular regime in Tehran had been transformed into a revolutionary proselytizer, threatening the status quo in the region that the erstwhile radical, pro-Soviet Iraq was now keen to preserve.

The escalation of tension, which culminated in the outbreak of war in September 1980, came in three stages: the formal assumption of Iraq's presidency by Saddam Hussein in July 1979; the failed attempt to assassinate Iraq's Christian Deputy Premier Tariq Aziz (born Mikhail Yahunna), followed soon by the execution of Ayatollah Muhammad Baqir al Sadr, a popular Shia cleric and a friend of Khomeini, in April 1980, against the background of rising Shia opposition to the Baathist rule; and the foiling of an attempted military coup by Iranian monarchists—working in conjunction with Saddam—in Iran on July 9–10. Finally, the Shah, who retained the loyalty of many Iranian politicians and former generals, died of cancer on July 27.

The Shah's demise deprived Saddam of his surrogate to overthrow Khomeini, thus leaving him no option but to undertake the task himself by attacking the Iranian regime. He had several internal and external reasons for invading Iran. He feared that any recurrence of recent Shia rioting would encourage Kurdish secessionists to revive their armed struggle and reignite civil war. In his view the only certain way to abort such a possibility lay in destroying the source, moral and material, of Shia inspiration: the Khomeini regime.

As for the timing, he decided to act before the U.S. presidential poll in early November 1980, calculating that a newly elected American President would probably settle the nine-month-old American hostage crisis and normalize relations with Tehran, thus strengthening his adversary.

Once Saddam had finalized his plans and secured the Saudi and Kuwaiti rulers' active backing in August, events moved fast. There were a series of border clashes especially in the central Qasr-e Shirin and the Zain al Qaus sector in the first half of September.

In a televised speech to the recently elected National Assembly on September 17, after accusing Iran of violating the Algiers Accord by "intervening in Iraq's domestic affairs by backing and financing ... the leaders of the mutiny [by Kurdish guerrillas] ... and by refusing to return the Iraqi territory," Saddam said, "We consider the Accord as abrogated from our side, also." He then tore up Iraq's copies of the Algiers Accord and the subsequent Iran-Iraq Treaty of International Boundaries and Good Neighborliness.[5] With this, according to Saddam, Iraq regained full sovereignty over the Shatt al Arab, and demanded that henceforth the Iranian ships using the waterway must engage Iraqi pilots and fly the Iraqi flag. Tehran refused. Heavy fighting erupted along the waterway.

On September 22, 1980, Iraq invaded Iran at eight points on their 730-mile (1,200 km) common border with a third of its 240,000 troops, and bombed its military installations and economic targets.

Saddam thus started what would turn out to be the longest conventional war of the twentieth century. It went through nine distinct phases before ending on August 20, 1988, with a United Nations-mediated truce.

Nine Phases of the Eight-Year War

PHASE 1: September 1980 to March 1981

Iraq advanced into Iran. On September 28, the UN Security Council Resolution 479, treating the invader and the victim as equals, urged a truce. Iraq announced its readiness to cease fire if Iran accepted its claimed rights over the Shatt al Arab. Though Iran had only one hundred thousand men in its military, a quarter of the prerevolution size run by officers with a low morale, and depleted arms arsenals, it rejected the resolution as unfair.

Khomeini argued that, by attacking "Government of God" in Iran, Saddam had assaulted Islam, and therefore it was a religious duty of every Muslim to fight Saddam's regime and die, if need be, and become a martyr. In Shia Islam, martyrdom is a highly revered concept: Imam Hussein is regarded as the Great Martyr. The appropriate verse in the Quran (3:163) reads, "Count not those who are slain God's way as dead, / but rather living with their Lord, by Him provided, / rejoicing in the bounty that God has given them, / and joyful in those who remain behind and have not joined them."[6]

While even the Islamic Conference Organization (ICO) failed to condemn Iraq for its aggression and side with Iran, at home Khomeini succeeded in sublimating war with Islam. This was aptly captured by the slogan, "War can be as holy as prayer when it is fought for the sake of Islam" displayed frequently in offices and on street walls.

Khomeini's appeals and the rallying of Iranians of all classes to defend their country, and the government's decision to turn the Baseej volunteer force into an auxiliary of the Islamic Revolutionary Guard Corps (IRGC), could not mask the weakness of the Iranian military, which had been shattered by the events culminating in the Shah's overthrow. By mid-November it had ceded Khorramshahr to the Iraqis who had besieged the nearby Abadan. Iraq now occupied 10,000 sq. miles (25,900 sq. km) of Iran in the southern and central sectors.

Soon, however, weather, geography, and Saddam's poor generalship came to Iran's rescue.

Of the four strategic urban centers near the border, the contiguous Abadan-Khorramshahr were oil cities with large ethnic Arab populations, and Ahvaz and Dezful to the north were part of the vital oil pipeline linking Khuzistan's oil fields with Tehran, with Dezful-Andimeshk also forming a strategic road junction west of the Zagros Mountains. Near Dezful were the vast Vahidyeh air base and a hydroelectric dam. Early on, Saddam had to choose between Khorramshahr-Abadan and Ahvaz-Dezful. He opted for the former on the false hope, fed by the faulty intelligence of his spying agencies that ethnic Arabs there would welcome the "liberating" Iraqi troops. They did not. And capturing Khorramshahr and besieging Abadan proved so arduous for his troops that Saddam lost any chance he had of seizing Ahvaz and Dezful.

The result was a military stand-off.

By now Washington was routinely passing on satellite and high resolution reconnaissance pictures of Iranian troops to Riyadh, knowing that the Saudi kingdom was transferring these to Iraq. The same applied to the information collected by four American-manned Airborne Warning and Control Systems (AWACS), leased by the U.S. to Saudi Arabia in September 1980, for round-the-clock surveillance of the Persian Gulf, a fact later confirmed by Saddam.[7]

PHASE 2: April 1981 to March 1982

The stalemate continued. The Iranian military, much enlarged by a surge of patriotism among Iranians, blocked further Iraqi advance. In September, it lifted the siege of Abadan. Various efforts by the UN and the ICO to end the conflict foundered. Iran refused to negotiate so long as Iraq occupied its land.

Unable to capture either Dezful or Ahvaz, Iraq began hitting these cities with Soviet-made Frog-7 surface-to-surface missiles with 75-mile (120 km) range.

PHASE 3: March 1982 to June 1982

In March–April 1982, the Iranians amassed forces in the Dezful-Shush area to retake territory from the Iraqis. They succeeded. On May 24, Iran retook Khorramshahr, then broke the Abadan siege, and drove the Iraqis back to the international frontier.

This caused a severe crisis in Baghdad. On June 9, Iraq announced its readiness for a truce. In return, Iran demanded the removal of Saddam from power. This was out of the question. On June 20, Saddam declared that Iraq's voluntary withdrawal from Iran would be completed within ten days. But on June 30, the Iranian leaders found that contrary to Saddam's claim of total Iraqi withdrawal, his forces had evacuated some indefensible positions to regroup elsewhere. In any case, Khomeini reckoned—rightly—that if he accepted a ceasefire the clerical and nonclerical politicians in Iran would resume their quarrelling and escalate it to the point of seriously weakening the still fledgling Republic he had founded.

After some hesitation, Iran decided to enter the Iraqi territory. That changed the situation diplomatically. As a signatory of its Friendship and Cooperation Treaty with Iraq, the Soviet Union reversed its position on arms supplies, which it had stopped after Iraq's invasion of Iran. Its fresh shipments would include Scud-B surface-to-surface missiles with 185-mile (300 km) range.

PHASE 4: July 1982 to March 1984

Iran's troops marched into Iraq after recapturing Mehran in the central sector. Its government gave the Baseej auxiliary force a mission to "liberate Karbala," thereby encouraging the Baseej personnel to go to the war front wearing red bands with the inscription of "Lovers of Karbala." Soon every large mosque and workplace would house a Baseej unit.

Having rejected the UN Security Council's call for a truce and withdrawal of the belligerents to the international border, Iran tried to conquer Basra in mid-July. With nine divisions locked in the largest infantry combat since World War II, fierce battles raged for a fortnight. Finally, Iran managed to hold only 32 sq. miles (83 sq. km) of Iraqi land. Yet it stuck to its earlier conditions for withdrawal from Iraq: removal of Saddam from the presidency, the appointment of an international tribunal to determine and punish the aggressor, and an acceptance of its claim of $150 billion as compensation for war damages.

In October, Iran reclaimed some territory in the northern sector. Iraq's air strikes on Iran's Nawruz offshore oil field in March 1983 caused the largest oil spill in the history of the Persian Gulf. In April Iran's major offensive to reach the strategic Basra-Baghdad highway failed.

On the 20th of that month, I visited Dezful, a city of two hundred thousand, along the Karun River, after it had been hit by three Soviet-made surface-to-surface Iraqi missiles. Instead of reaching their intended destination—the nearby Vahidyeh air base—the missiles had devastated dozens of residential buildings in the city, killing 15 and injuring 105. The sight of demolished homes, with household goods destroyed, and children's toys and tricycles crushed, was depressing.

To my surprise, the next afternoon I witnessed half of Dezful's adult population, male and female, on the march, bearing the coffins of the dead to the local cemetery, carrying banners and chanting defiant slogans. A few weeks later, assisted by government funds, the residents would busily start rebuilding their houses and shops.

There were several reasons for the high morale locally and nationally. The regime had succeeded in presenting the conflict as one between believers and the infidel Baathist regime, which, by its own admission, was secular. There were as yet no palpable signs of war at least in Greater Tehran, accounting for one-fifth of the national population, such as blackouts, long lines for food or cloth, gasoline rationing, sand bags, or air-raid shelters. Most shops were full and streets choked with cars.

On the other hand, young soldiers and Revolutionary Guards ambling about in streets were a common sight. This was so because the Iranian army was now 320,000 strong, the air force

70,000, and the navy 23,000—the total reaching the prerevolution figure; and the size of the IRGC had risen to 150,000. This led to lower unemployment, particularly among educated young people, a plus for the government. At major squares in Tehran there were vans from the Blood Transfusion Organization of Iran. State-controlled radio and television bulletins invariably led with dispatches from the fronts, and newspapers displayed war stories prominently on front pages. Martial songs and uplifting snatches of Beethoven's Fifth Symphony regularly punctuated radio and television programs.

Also, excepting the heavily subsidized and freely available flat bread at 12 cents a loaf, foodstuffs, washing powder, and heating fuel were rationed. Per capita weekly ration for rice was one pound, and for meat three-quarter pound. For those who needed more there was the free market, where rice sold at two to three times the official rate of $1 (£0.70) a pound, and meat sold at three times the official rate of $2 (£1.40) a pound. The average weekly wage was $86 (£60). The system worked smoothly because most of the goods were bought directly by the Commerce Ministry or the Government Trading Corporation.

Since rationing imposed equality in consumption, it helped the government to portray itself as egalitarian. The working and lower middle classes were pleased to know that the upper classes were entitled to only as much food and fuel at official prices as they were, and no more.

As in all wars, this one made many of Iran's industries self-sufficient. For its spare parts for the U.S.-made weapons, Iran turned to Vietnam with its vast stores of leftover U.S. weapons and spare parts. Later it approached private firms in Amsterdam, Athens, Madrid, Seoul, and Singapore for these items. The Reagan administration covertly encouraged these sales to let the war drag on and make the conservative Arab monarchies, fearful of Iran's Islamic republicanism, more dependent on Washington for security.

This changed after America included Iran in its list of countries that support international terrorism in January 1984.

Iran faced a severe problem regarding warplanes all along. Before the revolution, it had 430 combat aircraft, all of them U.S.-made. It lost eighty in three years. Of the rest, only about a third were airworthy. By contrast, Iraq possessed about four hundred Soviet- and French-made warplanes. So Iran could use its planes only for defensive purposes such as protecting airfields, refineries, oil fields and installations, and large cities. After spring of 1982, it lacked warplanes to provide air cover to its troops. And, because its offensives in the later period were launched without air cover, it suffered heavy loss of life—especially when Iraq began using chemical weapons on the battlefield from October 1983 onward.

Yet, buoyed by its record annual oil income of $23 billion in 1983, Iran persisted with periodic offensives. In mid-February 1984, it made a second attempt to cut off the strategic Baghdad-Basra highway, but again failed. Following an offensive in the Haur al Hawizeh marshes in late February, it seized Iraq's oil-rich Majnoon Islands.

PHASE 5: April 1984 to January 1986

There was renewed stalemate. However, Baghdad made diplomatic gains when the Reagan administration, having removed Iraq from the list of nations that support international terrorism in November 1984, restored diplomatic ties with it two months later after a break of eighteen years.

Iraq escalated its attacks on Iranian oil tankers, using French-made Exocet air-to-ship (surface-skimmer) missiles, and intensified its air raids on the Kharg oil terminal, which handled 85 percent of Iran's petroleum exports, thus initiating a war of the tankers. Iran retaliated by hitting ships serving the ports of Kuwait and Saudi Arabia, which were aiding Iraq financially, logistically, and intelligence-wise, in the Lower Gulf. For the Iranian year ending in March 1984, its oil income at $14.7 billion was well below the budgeted $21.1 billion.

That month, an Iranian brigade reached the Baghdad-Basra highway, but was unable to withstand the Iraqi counterattacks. In May, Iraq intensified its tanker war and strikes on Kharg, reaching a peak in mid-August. Due to these attacks, followed by a similar onslaught in November, Iran's oil exports declined sharply. Later, Iran would recover to sell 1.2 million bpd to 1.6 million bpd, just enough to pay for the war.

By then, however, public disaffection began to rise perceptibly. A middle-ranking civil servant in Tehran with a take-home monthly pay of $650, paid $350 on rent for a two-bedroom apartment and had to moonlight as a taxi driver or sales assistant. Some government bureaucrats resumed taking bribes, a practice that had disappeared in the wake of the revolution.

Murmurs of popular discontent reached Khomeini, who read five Tehran-based newspapers every morning, and listened to the reports from the grassroots as well as Majlis proceedings broadcast live on radio. He instructed the government to provide safety valves for popular discontent. So it encouraged citizens to complain by writing to semiofficial newspapers or phoning the complaints line on the state-run radio, which launched a half-hour phone-in program each morning for this purpose. Prime Minister Mir Hussein Mousavi publicly bemoaned self-censorship by the newspapers now regulated by the 1985 Press Law.

On March 5, 1985, Iraq bombed a steel factory in Ahvaz and an unfinished nuclear power plant at Haleyle near Bushehr. By so doing, Iran argued, Baghdad had breached the June 1984 UN-sponsored agreement to refrain from hitting civilian targets. From this ensued the "War of Cities," with Iran targeting Basra and Baghdad, and Iraq hitting sixteen Iranian towns and cities, including Isfahan. It ended on June 14, the last Friday in Ramadan—celebrated in Iran as the Jerusalem Liberation Day—when, defying the Iraqi threats of air raids on Tehran, one to five million Iranians gathered at the Tehran University for Friday prayers and sermon.

It was at this point that the Iranian leadership seems to have decided to explore the option of embarking on a program to produce a nuclear weapon.

PHASE 6: February to December 1986

The war of attrition continued. Washington began to intervene actively on the Iraqi side. The Iranian assault in February 1986 in the south, which resulted in the capture of 310 sq. miles (800 sq. km) in the Fao Peninsula, broke the stalemate. A determined effort by Iraq, which mounted 18,648 air missions between February 9 and March 25, 1986—compared with 20,011 missions in the whole of 1985—to regain Fao met with failure.[8] The Iranians claimed that during the whole of the Fao operations, which included several unsuccessful Iraqi counteroffensives, they destroyed 141 Iraqi tanks and 86 Iraqi planes and helicopters. They put the number of Iraqi casualties at thirty-five thousand.[9]

In March 1986, following a report by UN experts on Iraq's use of poison gases, the UN Security Council combined its condemnation of Iraq for deploying chemical weapons with its disapproval of the prolongation of the conflict by Iran.

The next month, flooding of the oil market by Kuwait and Saudi Arabia caused the price of petroleum to plunge below $10 a barrel, down from $27 the previous December. This sharply reduced the oil income of Iran and Iraq, but the latter was cushioned by the $12 billion a year it received in aid from its Gulf allies, the West, and the Soviet Union.

By contrast, the isolated Iran felt the pain. As it curtailed food imports, the free-market price of foods rose sharply, and the public grumbling became more explicit and persistent. But, instead of promising to ease the economic burden, Khomeini called on Iranians to participate in the war. "Khomeini felt that once people had been to the front and experienced the conditions under which combatants operate, they would complain less about shortages of certain foods and services," Irfan Parvez, a senior editor at the *Kayhan International*, explained to me in Tehran.

Officials encouraged volunteers to go to the front. I saw President Ali Khamanei on the marble steps of the Majlis building in south Tehran address thousands of Iranians gathered to give an upbeat send off to the Baseej volunteers on their way to the front chanting, "Pilgrims, be prepared; Karbala is ready." "The enemies of the Islamic revolution had hoped that the Iranian people would become tired as the war with Iraq went on, but five years later the people continue to demonstrate their support," he said bravely. The stark fact was that by then the conflict had claimed 500,000 Iranian casualties—180,000 killed and 350,000 injured.[10]

On the other hand, the authorities were generous in compensating the war veterans' families. The wife or parents of the dead fighter were assured of a monthly income of $280 plus $56 allowance for each child by the Martyrs Foundation. For every child the foundation deposited $112 a month until he/she was eighteen.

The Martyrs Foundation was funded by the profits of the properties of rich exiled Iranians and grants from the affluent religious trusts and the government. In the case of a dead military soldier, the family also received $32,000 in compensation. It also got preference in the allotment of such scarce goods and services as cars, motorcycles, refrigerators, housing, and university placements.[11]

Iran's total fighting force was now 1.2 million strong, with half of them belonging to the IRGC. Yet the proportion of war and war-related expenditure remained about 30 percent of the total budget of $42 to $46 billion over the past few years. The government achieved this by gradually shifting the war burden to the voluntary sector. The Baseej militia, serving without pay, now contributed about a quarter of the total manpower at the fronts. And more and more materials and cash came from the public.

For example, during my visit to the Saadi Tile Company's factory at Islamshahr, eight miles south of Tehran, in December 1985, I found that half of the 1,440 workers donated one day's wages every month to the war fund. It maintained an office for a Baseej unit in a room covered with portraits of Khoemini and inspiring war posters. Two-fifths of the Baseej volunteers had served at the front for a minimum period of three months at least once. The commander, Daud Arab Karamane, a thirty-two-year-old, craggy-faced time clerk, had been to the front three times since 1982 when the practice started.[12] So far six Baseej volunteers had been killed. Those with six months' war experience or more received preference for promotion at work. This applied as much to factories as it did to offices, private or public.

A list of war contributions in the *Kayhan International* in early February 1986 read: "Semirom: 8,394 kilograms of wheat and wheat flour; 847 bars of soap and boxes of detergent. Roodehen: 17 trucks, 19 gas stoves; 10 air conditioners; one truck load of apples." Cash contributions ranged from Iranian rials 90,000 to 6,930,000 (U.S. $1,500 to U.S. $115,500/£750 to £57,750). The next day, according to a government communiqué, 920 trucks filled with contributions from the inhabitants of Mazandaran, Kurdistan, and Isfahan provinces left for the battlefronts.

The campaign to blend war with Islam continued unabated. On a typical Friday, a multicolored sea of people assembled in a vast enclosure near the mosque at Tehran University for midday prayers. The colors were those of the uniforms worn by the armed forces, each segregated in a contiguous section of the prayer grounds—Iranian military men in khaki, Islamic Revolutionary

Guards in olive green fatigues, Iraqi prisoners of war in blue. Then there were women in black chador, covered from head to toe. The size of the congregation, including government and religious leaders, varied from 50,000 to 250,000.

From an enclosed podium protected by sandbags, the prayer leader, usually President Khamanei, spoke with one hand resting firmly on the barrel of a gun, a symbol of Iran's resolve to fight for victory in its long war with Iraq. In general, he or another senior leader usually delivered a sermon that explained official policies on anything from gasoline rationing to the latest development in the war. These proceedings were broadcast on radio and television nationally while similar meetings were held throughout Iran's cities and towns by prayer leaders who were appointed by Khomeini and who reported to him. In a country where privations of war and a sluggish economy were a fertile ground for political discontent, Friday prayers were one of the main mechanisms Iran's theocratic rulers deployed to explain their policies to the public at large.

On the eve of the weeklong sixth anniversary of the war on September 22, 1986 [13] Khamanei and Speaker Rafsanjani fielded uncommonly sharp questions from their interviewers who reflected the views of the anti-war dissidents. This was done to rebut the arguments of the articulate "end-the-war" minority. [14]

The authorities built an artificial lake in Tehran to represent the Shatt al Arab waterway—complete with the Fao peninsula. There the battle was replayed daily for audiences of up to one hundred thousand, using audiotapes of the actual communications that took place on the night of February 8, 1986, between the war room and the Iranian reconnaissance teams sent out across the river. The successful battle plan involved surrounding the town of Fao by landing troops in the rear by helicopter, capturing the rocket-launcher sites, and reaching the local salt factory. Then, at the right moment, when the proper offensive got going, sound effects were used to simulate air strikes and artillery and machine-gun fire. The effect was quite electrifying—for the victors and their spectators. The next day, the foreign defense attachés present at Iran's military parade counted weapons on display from eleven different countries.

The overall message was that Iran continued to show innovation both in military tactics and in procuring weapons from abroad to be able to prosecute the war even after six years.

Aided by direct, albeit covert, assistance of U.S. Air Force officers, Iraq began hitting Iran's economic and infrastructural targets accurately, and extended its air strikes to the Iranian oil terminals in the Lower Gulf.

During 1986, Iraq struck sixty-six Iranian ships while Iran's score was forty-one.

The Iranian Oil Ministry began constructing twelve floating jetties near and outside the Persian Gulf out of the range of Iraqi bombers to be completed by March 1987—as well as a string of well protected fixed oil terminals south of Kharg.

In early November 1986, the expose of the clandestine U.S. arms-for-hostages deal with Iran by *Al Shira* (The Sail), a Beirut-based magazine, proved a diplomatic boon for Iran. The magazine disclosed that America had secretly sold weapons to Iran. Aware of Iran's geostrategic importance, Washington wanted to end the hostility that Tehran had shown toward it since the 1979 revolution. It also wanted to gain the freedom of the American captives taken by the pro-Iranian groups in Lebanon, then in the midst of a long civil war. This arms sale was contrary to the declared policies of President Reagan: it had imposed an arms embargo on Tehran, and it had repeatedly vowed not to deal with terrorists and hostage-takers.

The scam had a devastating impact on the public opinion in America and abroad. In a televised address to the nation on November 13, Reagan justified his action in order to secure an end to the Gulf War and the release of American hostages. He added,

"The Iranian revolution is a fact of history; [and] between American and Iranian basic national interests, there needs be no permanent conflict."[15] The Iranian public and politicians interpreted this statement as a victory for them. A week later, Khomeini described the episode as "an issue greater than all our [previous] victories." He added, "Those who broke relations with Iran came back, presenting themselves meekly and humbly at the door of the [Iranian] nation to establish relations and making apologies."[16]

But the triumphal mood of Iranians would evaporate as Washington resorted to aiding more actively and openly Iraq as it escalated its air campaign against Iran.

PHASE 7: January 1987 to January 1988

Nineteen eighty-seven proved to be the make or break year in the Iran-Iraq War.

Having failed to expel Iran from its soil, especially the Fao Peninsula, Iraq targeted Tehran, Qom, and Isfahan for aerial bombardment and long-range missiles in early January 1987, thus initiating a war of the cities. It did so to weaken Iranian leaders' political will. They responded by hitting Baghdad with long-range missiles, and turning Basra into a besieged city.

During the visit of Iranian Foreign Minister Ali Akbar Velayati to Moscow in mid-February, the Soviet Union tried to mediate between the two combatants. Saddam Hussein agreed to "suspend" the war of the cities if Moscow agreed to replace Iraq's lost warplanes with advanced Soviet combat aircraft. The Soviets agreed.

By the time the war of the cities was suspended on February 18, it had affected thirty-five Iranian urban centers and killed three thousand. By contrast, the missile attacks and the besieging of Basra had cost only three hundred Iraqi lives.[17]

Iran mounted a massive offensive in the south that brought its forces within 7 miles of Basra, but failed to capture it when the Iraqis used chemical weapons on a large scale.

During the spring the Iranians and their Iraqi Kurdish allies captured territory in Iraqi Kurdistan.

On July 20, the UN Security Council unanimously passed Resolution 598, calling for a ceasefire and the withdrawal of warring forces. The ten-article text included a clause for an impartial commission to determine war responsibility, one of the major demands of Iran. Iraq said it would accept the resolution on condition that Iran did the same. Tehran refused to do so.

Four days later a Kuwaiti supertanker on the first Gulf convoy escorted by U.S. warships hit a mine, believed to have been planted by Iran. The subsequent naval buildup by the United States, Britain, and France brought sixty Western warships in the region.

On the seventh anniversary of the war on September 22, 1987, Iraq had nearly four hundred combat aircraft, six times the number of Iran's airworthy warplanes. Baghdad possessed 4,500 tanks, 3,200 armored fighting vehicles, and 2,800 artillery pieces versus Tehran's respective totals of 1,570, 1,800, and 1,750. Iraq had 955,000 regular troops as against Iran's 655,000; and, at 650,000, Iraq's Popular Army was slightly larger than Iran's Revolutionary Guards Corps at 625,000.[18]

In October 1987, the U.S. Navy sank three Iranian patrol boats near Farsi Island, claiming that Iran had fired on a U.S. patrol helicopter; and U.S. warships destroyed two Iranian offshore oil platforms in the Lower Gulf in retaliation for an Iranian missile attack on a U.S.-flagged supertanker docked in Kuwaiti waters. Tehran's capacity to mount major offensives was much reduced due to its shortage of foreign exchange, needed for essential military purchases, and professionally trained soldiery, and the damage done to its bridges, factories, and power plants by ceaseless Iraqi bombing.

Nonetheless, before the year ended, Iran had managed to strike eighty-seven ships in the Gulf, more than twice the previous year's figure, ahead of Iraq at seventy-six.

PHASE 8: February to June 1988

Iraq renewed the war of the cities by targeting Saqqez in northern Iran. The Iranians responded with missile attacks on Baghdad. On February 27, 1988, Iraq retaliated by hitting Tehran with long-range missiles—named, ironically, Al Hussein, a modified version of the Soviet-made Scud-B, with reduced payload which doubled its range to 370 miles (600 km). This demoralized the residents of Tehran, causing a minor exodus of people to outlying areas or cities farther away from the international border. Iran retaliated by targeting Baghdad, much nearer the international border than Tehran, with its surface-to-surface missiles.

By the time the revived war of the cities ended on April 20, at least a third of Tehran's residents had decamped. Their fear was enhanced by what happened in Halabja in Iraqi Kurdistan, and the wide publicity that the Iranian and international media gave to the event.

On March 13, Iran and its Iraqi Kurdish allies captured Halabja, a town of seventy-five thousand, situated 15 miles (24 km) from the Iranian border. Three days later the Iraqi air force attacked it with poison gas bombs, killing between 3,200 and 6,800 people, mainly civilians, and injuring another 10,000. The pictures of men, women, and children frozen in instant death, relayed by the Iranian media, shocked the world. In killing its own unarmed citizens with chemical weapons, the Saddam Hussein regime did something unprecedentedly abhorrent.[19]

This was a propaganda boost to Iran's leaders. But, by overexploiting the episode, they demoralized their own people, especially in Tehran, where residents feared that Iraqi missiles carrying warheads filled with poison gases would hit the city.

Between April 16 and 18, Iraq recaptured the Fao Peninsula, using chemical weapons, while U.S. warships blew up two Iranian oil rigs, destroyed one Iranian frigate and immobilized another, and sank an Iranian missile boat. From May 23 to 25,

Iraq, using poison gases, staged offensive strikes in the northern and central sectors, and then in the south, regaining Shalamche. Between June 19 and 25, Iraq recaptured Mehran in the central zone and then the Majnoon Islands in the south—using chemical weapons in both cases.

PHASE 9: July to 20 August 1988

Iraq tried to seize Iranian territory but failed. On July 3, the USS *Vincennes*, an American cruiser, shot down an Iran Air airbus carrying 290 people over the Lower Gulf. While the Pentagon explained that the cruiser's commanding officer had mistaken the aircraft as a warplane, the Iranian leaders, including Khomeini, were not convinced. Indeed, this incident confirmed Khomeini's unpublicized perception, dating back to the spring, that America was preparing to enter the war formally on Iraq's side. Though the U.S. would agree in principle to compensate Iran and the families of those killed in the Iran airplane, its high officials reckoned privately that the Iranian government would avenge these deaths by staging terrorist attacks on American targets sooner or later.

Following hurried consultations in Tehran among top leaders, on July 18, Iran unconditionally accepted UN Security Council Resolution 598. Two days later Khomeini stated that acceptance of a truce was "in the interest of the revolution and the system at this juncture."

From July 22 to 29, Iraq mounted offensives in the northern, central, and southern sectors to capture Iranian land. It failed in the north but succeeded elsewhere. However within a week Iran had regained its lost territory. On August 20, a truce came into effect under UN supervision.

At 194,931, Iran's official figure for the war dead was believed to be about two-thirds of the actual figure. While Iraq did not publish any figures officially, the estimates of its war fatalities were put at 160,000 to 240,000. According to the

Stockholm International Peace Research Institute, Iran spent $74–91 billion on the war and its military imports amounted to $11.26 billion. The corresponding figures for Iraq were $94–112 billion and military imports of $41.94 billion.[20] It also kept its economy running by employing 1.5 to 2 million foreign workers. That is how it managed to achieve an unrivaled force ratio—regular military personnel per one thousand inhabitants—of 63.3, nearly five times the figure for Iran whose Islamic regime was routinely described in the West as run by fanatical mullahs.[21]

In the end, neither combatant lost much territory either on land or the Shatt al Arab bed; nor was there a change of regime in either country. But the war enabled Khomeini to mobilize Iranians, religious and secular, on a patriotic platform, and have his own often fractious followers sink their differences on how to run the country, especially the economy. Conscious of the cementing effect of the war, he repeatedly rejected offers of mediation and a ceasefire. Had Saddam not invaded Iran, it was likely that the fledgling Islamic Republic would have slipped into civil war. The Iraqi President could therefore be perceived, rightly, as an inadvertent contributor to the consolidation of the Islamic revolution in Iran.

However, it could also be argued that by getting Khomeini's regime entangled in a long, expensive war, Saddam succeeded in containing Islamic fundamentalism—a task that the Gulf monarchs and the West, particularly the U.S., too wanted him to perform. The downside of this for the West and the Gulf rulers was that, having expanded its military from less than 250,000 men to more than one million during the war, Iraq under Saddam emerged as the most powerful nation in the Middle East, outstripping Turkey and Egypt.

In short, the Iran-Iraq War sowed the seeds for Saddam's invasion of Kuwait which came in August 1990.

After the Longest War

Following Khoemini's death in June 1989, Saddam halted all anti-Iranian activities, including radio broadcasts of the Mujahedin-e Khalq Organization (MKO). The goodwill thus generated did not last long. A fortnight later at his instigation, Egypt, Jordan, and North Yemen (the constituents along with Iraq of the newly formed Arab Cooperation Council) backed Baghdad's claim to both banks of Shatt al Arab.

In the summer of 1990, Iran and Iraq had a common interest to reverse the oil price fall in the summer of 1990, caused by overproduction by Kuwait and the United Arab Emirates. So at the fateful OPEC conference on July 25 they joined hands to push the reference price from $18 to $21 a barrel, and succeeded.

President Rafsanjani condemned Iraq's invasion of Kuwait on August 2, 1990. To secure his eastern front, however, Saddam addressed a letter to Rafsanjani in which he agreed to abide by the 1975 Algiers Accord, withdraw troops from the occupied Iranian territory, and undertake an immediate exchange of prisoners of war. (During the conflict, Iran took some seventy thousand Iraqi prisoners of war, and Iraq forty thousand-plus.) Rafsanjani accepted the offer, thus putting a final seal on the demarcation of the fluvial boundary of the two countries that had dogged their relations since 1932. Iraq vacated all of the 920 sq. miles (2,380 sq. km) of the Iranian territory it had been occupying. This allowed Saddam to withdraw three hundred thousand troops facing Iran and deploy them elsewhere.

Welcoming the new development, Rafsanjani repeated Iran's call that Iraq must vacate Kuwait. While declaring that Iran would abide by the UN resolutions on Iraq, he demanded that all foreign forces that had assembled in the region to punish the aggressor must leave once the crisis was over. He also ruled out any use of Iranian airspace or territory by the U.S.-led coalition to attack Iraq or Kuwait.

Within a week of the start of the 1991 Gulf War on January 16, Iran protested that the Allied attacks on Iraq far exceeded the UN mandate to liberate Kuwait. Between January 26 and 28, 135 Iraqi aircraft sought refuge in Iran. Much to the Pentagon's chagrin, the fleeing Iraqi planes could not be intercepted and destroyed by the Allied air force because most of them made only short trips across the border from small airfields in northern Iraq. To keep up the pretense of neutrality in the war, Tehran officially protested to Baghdad about its planes arriving in Iran without prior authorization.[22]

As relentless Allied bombing of Iraq continued, Tehran Radio said on February 9, "Iran cannot be indifferent to the massacre of innocent Muslims and the destruction being inflicted on Iraq."

Iran became a key player in the diplomatic field, with Iraqi leaders using Tehran as a staging post for their important trips to Moscow to end the war. It coordinated its peace moves with the Soviet Union, but these failed.

When the U.S.-led Allies mounted ground campaign on February 24, Rafsanjani said, "The U.S. and its allies proved that they are after something beyond a mere Iraqi pullout from Kuwait."[23] When the war ended, Iran called on the Allies to withdraw their troops from the Persian Gulf region "as soon as possible." They did—except from Kuwait and Saudi Arabia.

When Shia uprisings erupted in southern Iraq in early March, Rafsanjani weighed in. Addressing Saddam Hussein, he said, "You know well that you are undesirable in your country as well as in the region. So, don't further stain your bloodied hands by killing more innocent Iraqis. Yield to the people's will, and step down."[24]

Rafsanjani's intervention, and the participation of Iran's Islamic Revolutionary Guards and the armed partisans of the Tehran-based Supreme Council of Islamic Revolution in Iraq (SCIRI), who arrived from Iran with green banners of Islam and portraits of Khomeini, proved counterproductive. These moves alienated the bulk of the Iraqi Shias who until a few years ago were engaged in a deadly struggle with the Iranians, and alarmed Saudi Arabia, Kuwait, and America. Inimical though these states were to Saddam, they did not wish to see his regime replaced by one modeled on theocratic Iran, thus enabling Tehran to emerge as the uncontested Leader of the Gulf.

When finally Saddam's forces regained control of the south by March 16, all the Iranian government could do was to declare March 18 as the day of mourning for those Iranians who fell in Baghdad's military onslaught in the south and the desecration of the Shia holy shrines in Najaf and Karbala.[25]

Once Saddam had reestablished control over all of Iraq, the regimes in Iran and Iraq settled for a peaceful coexistence while nurturing dissident groups of the other side—the MKO in Baghdad and SCIRI in Tehran. Every time the U.S. bombed Iraq for its alleged violations of the UN Security Council resolutions, Iran condemned the action and expressed sympathy for the Iraqi people suffering the consequences of the most comprehensive UN sanctions.

Frosty relations between the two neighbors began to thaw after Muhammad Khatami's election as President in May 1997. Iranian Foreign Minister Kamal Kharrazi met his Iraqi counterpart, Muhammad al Sahhaf, at the UN headquarters in September in New York, the first meeting of its kind.

In December, Khatami used the hosting of the Islamic Conference Organization summit in Tehran to improve relations with Iraq by publicly welcoming Iraqi Vice President Taha Yassin Ramadan. The following year, Iraq inaugurated a program to receive three thousand Iranian Shia pilgrims a week after a break of nearly two decades. The two governments reached an accord to expand trade, with Tehran agreeing to increase its food and medicine exports to Iraq under the UN oil-for-food scheme.

During his visit to Tehran in January 2000, Abdul Ghafour Yunus, chairman of the Iraqi Chambers of Commerce, said, "U.S. efforts to tighten the embargo on Iraq will only be neutralized through collaboration between Iranian and Iraqi officials, and especially their private sectors."[26] Already the public sectors of the two states were cooperating in helping Iraq smuggle its petroleum by using the territorial waters of Iran for hefty fees, thus enabling its government to earn foreign exchange outside the UN oil-for-food program. This trade started in 1997 when the oil-for-food scheme for Iraq was implemented. After loading oil at Iraq's terminal, the tankers used the protected sea lanes within the 12-mile (19 km) wide territorial waters of Iran to navigate the Gulf, and then sailed out to the high seas. American sources put the value of this trade at $1 billion a year.

Aware of the popular sympathy that Iranians had developed for the suffering Muslim people of Iraq, Khatami ensured that Iran participated in the air flight busting that started in late summer 2000. By having Kharrazi lead the Iranian delegation, Khatami underscored the significance of the first Iran Air flight in October 2000. After meeting Saddam Hussein, Kharrazi said that the Iraqi President had expressed his "willingness and determination to normalize relations with Iran." More significantly, Kharazi added, "We have decided to activate the 1975 [Algiers] agreement in order to set up balanced and good-neighborly relations."[27]

So twenty years after Saddam invaded Iran after tearing up the Algiers Accord during a television address, the two neighbors were—as it were—returning to square one.

With U.S. President George W. Bush labeling Iran and Iraq as part of the "axis of evil" in his State of the Union speech in January 2002, relations between the two neighbors warmed further.

During the run-up to the Anglo-American invasion of Iraq in March 2003, however, the Iranian government followed a schizophrenic policy: it gave a green light to SCIRI to participate in

Washington's preinvasion plans while it reiterated that any armed action against Iraq had to be sanctioned by the UN Security Council.

Once Saddam Hussein's regime was overthrown in April, there was quiet satisfaction among the Iranian people and politicians. After all, they had been the first victims of Saddam's aggression. Now Iran's leaders demanded that the U.S.-led troops should leave Iraq and hand over peacekeeping and holding of elections to the UN. Washington had no such intention.

Indeed, in the first flush of the Pentagon's quick victory in Iraq, reports began emanating out of Washington that Iran was to be the next member of the "axis of evil" to undergo a "regime change." The first stage of the operation was to destabilize the regime at home by making use of the anti-regime Iranians settled in America who operate many Persian-language satellite radio and television channels as well as run Web sites.

In a concerted move, they named June 10 night as the opening shot in a movement to destabilize the "mullahocracy" in Iran. Disturbances broke out in Tehran and continued for the next ten days with declining support. "The number of protestors was never more than a few thousand," reported Jim Muir, the BBC's correspondent in Tehran. "Indeed, the overt incitement from U.S.-based exile media and open encouragement by U.S. officials from President Bush played nicely into the hands of the system's hard-liners, allowing right-wing vigilantes to club and stab protestors savagely and with impunity on the grounds that they were traitors acting out of the orders of the country's foreign enemies."[28] Washington's blatant encouragement for street demonstrations was self-defeating. It made protestors in particular and reformists in general appear as stooges of America, a recipe for political suicide.

This meant that the Bush administration's options to undermine the regime in Iran were limited. Iran, on the other hand, continued to play both sides of the fence in Iraq. SCIRI leaders participated first in the U.S.-appointed Iraqi Governing Council in July 2003, and then again in the interim Iraqi government set up—in essence by the Bush administration—in June 2004 to take over some authority on the eve of the departure of American Pro-consul Paul Bremer.

By contrast, following the call by Hojatalislam Muqtada al Sadr to his Mahdi Army volunteers to mount an armed uprising against the Anglo-American occupiers in early April 2004, Iran's leaders praised his action. Addressing the Friday prayer congregation in Tehran on April 9, Rafsanjani, who had met al Sadr in June 2003 at the annual memorial service of Khomeini near Tehran, described Saddam's supporters as terrorists. "Contrary to these terrorist groups in Iraq, there are powerful bodies which contribute to the security of that nation," he said. "Among them is the Mahdi Army, made up of enthusiastic, heroic young people."[29]

Later, President Khatami aired his views. "I regret the mistaken U.S. policies have made these [Iranian] efforts [to settle the Iraq crisis] fail," he said. "There is only one solution to the crisis, the withdrawal of the occupying forces from Iraq, letting the UN play a stronger role and transferring power to the Iraqis."[30]

Following the much-trumpeted transfer of power to the interim Iraqi government by Washington in June, the security situation in Iraq did not improve. Indeed it got worse. "The United States has reached a dead end in Iraq like a trapped wolf, and it is trying to frighten people by roaring and clawing," Khamanei told an assembly of clerics in Tehran in early August 2004. "But the people of Iraq will not allow it to swallow their country."[31]

Though the context had altered somewhat, the basic message of Khamanei and his mentor, Ayatollah Khomeini, regarding America had remained unaltered for a quarter century.

*Iran and America:
Allies Turned Adversaries*

◆ CHAPTER 9 ◆

The size of the sprawling diplomatic complex matched its importance. So too did its location in central Tehran—at the junction of Takht-e Jamshid (Throne of Jamshid) Avenue and Roosevelt Avenue. Housed inside a high brick wall compound—a quarter mile each way—the old U.S. Embassy included not only the main administrative building, a chancery, the ambassador's mansion, several houses for the senior diplomats, but also a warehouse, an electric power plant, tennis courts, a football field, a swimming pool, a parking lot, and a spacious garden. Following the election of a leftist government in Greece after the overthrow of its military junta in 1974, the U.S. transferred its regional espionage center from Athens to Tehran where Muhammad Reza Pahlavi Shah, holding aloft the national flag bearing a lion, sat firmly on the Peacock Throne. With that the significance of the American Embassy in Tehran rose sharply.

Nowadays, the 30-acre complex houses Imam Hussein University and the Organization of the Islamic Revolutionary Guard Vocational School, with the former chancery transformed into classrooms for computer courses. Since admission to the site is denied to foreign journalists and writers, the only way a visitor can get some idea of the enormity of the place is to take a seat by the French windows of the third-floor restaurant of Mashhad Hotel across Taleqani (formerly Takht-e Jamshid) Avenue.

That is what I did during my visit to Tehran some weeks before the twentieth anniversary of the U.S. Embassy takeover in November 1979. I broached the subject of Iranian-American relations with the headwaiter, Shahriyar Isfahani, a tall, gangling man with sunken cheeks. "If relations with America were restored, then there will be less economic pressure on us," he said. "But America should promise not to dominate us." He remembered the many demonstrations outside the embassy when it was seized by militant students.

So did fifty-five-year-old Amir Zarkesh, a plump man with graying stubble and unkempt hair, who makes tea in the kitchen. "There were demonstrations for several weeks," he said, reminiscing without any emotion. "I saw them from the kitchen. Some demonstrators slept in the street even though it was quite cold. The local shops were closed for several days due to these demonstrations."

Although I was there too, covering the event for the *Sunday Times*, I lacked the vantage point of Zarkesh. I could only watch and listen at street level—as did several American and European television camera crews camped out in front of the main entrance that was then at the middle of the wall facing Taleqani Avenue, and not at the corner—at the intersection of Taleqani Avenue and Martyr Moffateh (old Roosevelt) Avenue, as it is now.

All through the early weeks of the embassy occupation there was enough in the air to make a foreign visitor feel that the nation was going through a "second revolution"—focused on purging American influence that had permeated all facets of life in Iran, except the mosque. It was signaled by the fall of the laymen-dominated provisional government of Mahdi Bazargan on November 6, with the thirteen-member Islamic Revolutionary Council, containing six clerics, becoming the sole repository of power.

The occupied American Embassy became a rallying point and a place of pilgrimage. Its perimeter of black-painted steel bars and the buildings behind it, facing Taleqani Avenue, were bedecked with a huge portrait of Khomeini and many banners in English, Persian, and Arabic, the most prominent being "*Allahu Akbar* [God is Great]," "NO NEGOTIATION, JUST DELIVERING SHAH," and "Khomeini's Leadership Brings Unity [in Persian]." The whole area was a beehive of activity round the clock, with the arch lights of the several Western camera crews banishing the darkness of the night.

During daylight, it was almost like London's famed Speakers' Corner—without the speakers holding forth on top of soap-boxes, interrupted by occasional, good-natured heckling from the audience—but with people hanging around in knots, talking politics, debating, distributing leaflets with information about the activities of respective parties or factions, or selling political literature. Every so often they would stop to watch columns of demonstrators march past the embassy carrying placards and shouting slogans. One day it was factory workers marching, the next bazaar merchants and sales assistants; then it was the turn of students of secondary schools, boys or girls, followed by hospital staff, civil servants, journalists, employees of the National Iranian Oil Company, and so on.

My weeklong straw poll conducted in different parts of Tehran in late November for the *Sunday Times* showed that a large majority of adult Tehranis had visited the U.S. Embassy at least once, either individually, or as part of a marching, shouting column. The most frequent slogans that I heard were: "Give us the Evil Shah [then in an American hospital]," "*Allahu Akbar, Khomeini Rahbar*" ("God is Great; Khomeini is Leader"), and "*Marg bar America*" ("Death to America").

According to Hidayat Hadavi, an unshaven, bespectacled office clerk of thirty-five from south Tehran, and a frequent anti-Shah demonstrator, the occupation of the American Embassy had helped Khomeini regain his declining popularity after the revolution. "Let us hope Khomeini keeps going in the anti-imperialist direction of the past weeks," he told me.

Nearly two decades later at Mashhad Hotel, Amir Zarkesh went further down his memory lane. "I remember the days when Americans visited Tehran and stayed at our hotel—during the Shah's time," he said. "Then you'd see half-naked American women at the swimming pool here. They used to be very noisy, those Americans. Some guests couldn't sleep due to the noise they made."

The moment Zarkesh still savored was when, from his kitchen, he saw the students "jump over the wall and go inside quickly."

Actually, what Zarkesh witnessed was the second seizure of the embassy, the first having occurred on February 14, 1979, in the immediate aftermath of the final battles that established the supremacy of the armed revolutionary forces over the Shah's military. Some 150 armed members of the leftist *Fedai Khalq* (*lit.*, Popular Self-sacrificers) attacked the U.S. diplomatic mission. The Marine guard resisted the assault for an hour before surrendering. The Fedai occupation ended a few hours later when Deputy Prime Minister Ibrahim Yazdi intervened.

In the U.S., the media turned steadily against the revolution, a process aided by the summary executions meted out to many pro-American generals and politicians by the Revolutionary Courts. On May 17, the U.S. Senate voiced its "abhorrence" at "the summary executions without due legal process" Tehran Radio retorted that the same Senate had said nothing against the massacre of hundreds of Iranian revolutionaries in the streets some months before. Widespread demonstrations against the Senate resolution followed. On August 10, Iran cancelled three-quarters of its pending $12 billion worth of orders for U.S. weapons.

The situation deteriorated dramatically after October 22, when the U.S. administration of President Jimmy Carter allowed the deposed Shah, suffering from advanced cancer, to enter America, thus violating the promise it had given to Iran. On November 1, three million people marched in Iran to demand the former Shah's extradition from the U.S. This precipitated the seizure of the U.S. Embassy on November 4.

The well-planned operation had its roots in the immediate

aftermath of the revolution. Before his execution on February 15, 1979, Gen. Nematollah Nasseri—head of the Savak intelligence agency, who had been arrested eight months earlier by the Shah's government for illegal detentions and torture—made several confessions. In one, he told his interrogators that Savak had an agent, code-named "Hafiz," inside the U.S. Embassy. The Iranian authorities contacted him. Since he was neither American nor Iranian, Hafiz felt vulnerable. Before he was allowed to leave Iran in early September, he passed on two sets of documents to Ali Akbar Hashemi Rafsanjani, then Deputy Minister of Interior. They showed that contrary to its public statements, the Carter administration was actively considering admitting the Shah into America. It also revealed that the embassy was courting dissident officers in the military as well as Kurdish and Azerbaijani leaders.[1]

This led to a decision, taken at the highest political level in Tehran, to take over the embassy and seize all its documents. The task was assigned to Ayatollah Ruhollah Khomeini's son, Ahmad. He in turn chose Hojatalislam Muhammad Mousavi Khoeiniha, head of the Tehran University Revolutionary Komiteh, to implement the task. Khoeiniha enlisted trusted activists from the Islamic Associations at Tehran's major universities as well as a few young, nonstudent militant leaders. Together they assembled a well-trained force of between forty and fifty, who then studied the detailed layout and plans of the embassy.

With Carter's decision to let the Shah into the U.S., the public mood in Iran turned virulently anti-American. On November 2, Ayatollah Ruhollah Khomeini urged students to intensify their campaign against America to secure the Shah's return to Iran to face criminal and other charges in an Iranian court. He declared November 4 as the Students' Day. At the planned student rally at the Tehran University campus, some 450 activists of the Islamic Associations at local universities never arrived. Instead, they seized the U.S. Embassy within three hours.

The embassy staff tried to destroy as many secret papers as they could by using shredders and incinerators. But the forty to fifty hard-core assailants, who entered the main embassy building with stunning speed and precision, captured most of the documents intact. They also preserved the shreds that would later be painstakingly reconstituted.[2] During the following months, these documents proved to be a treasure trove to Islamic leaders while their description of the embassy as the "nest of spies" caught on. They used the seized papers to discredit and eliminate most of its opponents, and even some of its lukewarm supporters.

After taking sixty-six U.S. diplomats hostage, the militants—calling themselves *Khat-e Imam* (Khomeini), Partisans of Imam—declared that they would exchange their hostages for the Shah to be tried for his alleged crimes against the Iranian nation. Such a deal was out of the question, said the Carter administration. "We are not the least bit surprised that Uncle Sam is trying to protect the Shah," said Masoud Manuchehri, a thirty-year-old soft-spoken carpet seller, in Tahran's Grand Bazaar. "After all, in the past our country was run as a colony of America, and the Shah was an American puppet." His assistant Jamal Taqavi who, as part-time Revolutionary Guard, took up night watch outside the embassy, described it as "a nest of spies," and its occupation by militant students as part of "continual political education of the Iranian masses."

No wonder the resulting crisis lasted 444 days.

The fact that the month of Muharram started a few weeks after the embassy takeover helped the Islamic regime. In a television address on the eve of Muharram (beginning November 20), Khomeini said that whereas last Muharram the Iranian people had faced the Shah, "a Child of the Mother of Corruption, America," today they faced "the Mother herself." The next day, Muharram 1, marking the first day of the ten-day mourning for

Imam Hussein, millions of people marched against U.S. imperialism all over Iran.

While playing up the perfidiousness of U.S. President Jimmy Carter, who had broken his promise of not letting the former Shah into America, the Iranian TV highlighted Khomeini's magnanimity when he ordered the release of five women and eight African-American hostages, reducing the total to fifty-three. The news that the Shah wanted to leave America but was failing to find a country whose leader would let him in—leading Henry Kissinger, former U.S. Secretary of State, to describe the Shah as "a flying Dutchman without a port of call"—delighted Iranians.

By focusing Iranians' attention on the American misdeeds in Iran, the embassy siege united the nation and strengthened radicals at the expense of moderates. It proved to young Iranians that Khomeini and his followers were as anti-imperialist as the competing Mujahedin-e Khalq Organization (MKO) and Fedai Khalq, thus draining away support for secular leftists. It enabled the regime to engage the masses politically, rally popular support for the Islamic constitution, which was approved in a referendum on December 1.

Meanwhile, following the publication of some of the seized documents in Iranian newspapers, revealing "U.S.-British plots in Iran," Khomeini called Carter "an enemy of humanity." Carter responded by banning imports of Iranian oil and freezing Iran's estimated assets of $12 billion in U.S. banks.

As American and British warships began joint naval exercises in the Arabian Sea, the hostage-takers warned that all American hostages would be "destroyed" if Washington used force against Iran. With the release of thirteen diplomats (on Khomeini's orders), the hostage total dropped by about a fifth.[3]

When its diplomatic moves to get the hostages freed failed, the Carter administration considered attacking Iran's Kharg oil terminal, imposing a naval blockade, and mounting air raids against Iran. But the Soviet intervention in Afghanistan in late December 1979 caused a rethink. The U.S. calculated, rightly, that the ensuing military chaos in Iran would provide the Soviets with an opportunity to advance through Iran to the Persian Gulf. On the other hand, the fear of an American attack on Iran was one of the main reasons for the Soviet march into Afghanistan.[4]

Washington therefore opted for a clandestine rescue mission under the command of Col. William Boykin of the Delta Special Force—who, a generation later, would be appointed Deputy Undersecretary of Defense for Intelligence in charge of capturing or killing Osama bin Laden and Saddam Hussein, despite his repeated assertions, as a rabid Evangelical Christian speaker, that Satan was the mastermind of the terrorists because "he wants to destroy us at a Christian army"—from the U.S. aircraft carrier *Nimitz* in the Arabian Sea on April 24 and 25. The plan was to sneak in six to eight helicopters to a disused air strip near Tabas, 380 miles (600 km) southeast of Tehran, and fly in a large contingent of specially trained American commandos by six C-130 transport planes from the Quna air base in Egypt. The commandos would fly to Damavand, 30 miles (50 km) east of Tehran, where most of the four hundred Iranian agents had already gathered along with a fleet of trucks. The commandos and Iranian agents would drive to the U.S. Embassy in Tehran, which would have by then been infiltrated by still more American agents. Once the commandos had secured the embassy by incapacitating the Iranian guards, they would radio the helicopters at Damavand. They would then transport the hostages to Manzariyeh airport 70 miles (110 km) south of Tehran. There, all would be transferred to the waiting C-130s and fly out of Iran as other U.S. aircraft, equipped with sophisticated devices, jammed Iran's radar systems.

Things didn't quite go to plan. One of the helicopters at the Tabas airstrip broke down. Then one of the arriving C-130s collided with a stationary helicopter, causing an explosion and the death of eight troops. Finally, the secrecy of the mission was compromised by the unexpected arrival of a bus with fifty passengers aboard, and its interception by the American officers at the site. Carter had to abort the mission. Among the incriminating material abandoned at the airstrip was $1 million in Iranian currency. It was earmarked for the American agents in Iran who were getting restive at not having been paid after the seizure of the U.S. Embassy. The debacle led to the resignation of Cyrus Vance, Secretary of State, who was not even told of the rescue mission.

In Tehran, a government investigation discovered the following very suspicious facts: Iranian radar systems failed to detect U.S. helicopters and aircraft; all anti-aircraft batteries had been transferred from Tehran to Kurdistan a few days before the American mission; and a deliberate destruction of the abandoned U.S. helicopters at the Tabas airstrip in the wake of the aborted mission. The Americans obviously had people working inside the Iranian military. The suspicion fell on Gen. Amir Bahman Bagheri, commander of the air force. He was arrested in June.

That month the Iranian government held an international conference on U.S. intervention in Iran, which was attended by three hundred delegates from fifty-seven countries and organizations. Among the documents it released was a secret memorandum by Zbigniew Brzezinsky, the U.S. National Security Adviser, to Vance, which recommended "destabilization" of Khomeini's regime through Iran's neighbors with the immediate goal of imposing "a moderate" government on Iran.

By late spring Carter had managed to integrate the hostage issue into American domestic politics, a grave mistake, as it turned out, which would come to haunt him. Whereas at the beginning of the crisis, 66 percent of voters supported his handling of the hostage issue, the figure fell to 12 percent in July 1980.[5] From then on, this subject remained as important to the electorate as the economy.

Following the Shah's death in late July, 187 U.S. House Representatives sent a letter to the Iranian Majlis to consider the hostage issue. Its four-point response was formalized by Khomeini on September 11: return of the Shah's assets to Iran; cancellation of U.S. financial claims against Iran; unfreezing of Iranian assets; and Washington's promise of noninterference in Iran's affairs. Ronald Reagan, the Republican challenger to Carter, said that he would accept three of these conditions, and leave the question of the Shah's assets to U.S. courts to decide.

Enter Saddam Hussein

On September 22, Iraq attacked Iran. According to Iranian President Abol Hassan Bani-Sadr, Washington had an inkling of Iraq's plans. The Carter administration may even have, through Saudi Arabia, encouraged Iraq to attack—seeing in the move a solution to the hostage crisis. Since U.S. intelligence had predicted Iran exhausting its spare parts of its predominantly U.S.-made arsenal in three weeks, Carter's senior advisers visualized Tehran growing desperate to obtain them from the Pentagon, a situation tailor-made for a swap: American spares for hostages.

But, as stated earlier (Chapter Eight), Iran turned to Vietnam, which was flush with huge stocks of abandoned American spare parts and weapons. That gave special significance to a popular slogan, "Vietnam shows America is nothing."

In desperation, Carter authorized behind-the-scene talks between his officials and their Iranian counterparts at the United Nations in New York. They struck a secret deal. Referring to the Iran-Iraq War, Carter said on October 18 that the U.S. would like to see "any invading forces withdrawn." On October 26, the Iranian Majlis decided to consider the recommendations of its committee on the hostages. Two days later Carter promised that if the hostages were released his administration would airlift the arms and spares that Iran had already paid for. He was desperate to parade the freed hostages on television to bolster his chance of winning the presidential poll on November 4. Due to the eight-hour time difference between Washington and Tehran, a day was lost. The next day, twenty radical Majlis deputies stayed away and deprived the chamber of a quorum. Then Friday, the weekly Islamic holiday, intervened.

By the time the Majlis reassembled on November 2, Carter's camp was in despair. By an overwhelming majority, the 185 deputies in the chamber accepted the Majlis committee's recommendation to release the hostages subject to Washington accepting Khomeini's demands. The next day Carter called the decision "a positive basis" on which to end the crisis. The student captors handed over the hostages to the government. But this was much too close to the polling day to help Carter. He lost to Reagan.

Most Iranians regarded Carter's defeat as a case of poetic justice. America had imposed Muhammad Reza Shah Pahlavi on them in August 1953, and made them suffer his repressive, autocratic rule for a quarter century. Now they had been able to determine the outcome of an American presidential election. They had gotten even with Carter, who had been fulsome in his praise of the Shah and had backed him during the revolutionary crisis, and had finally let him enter the U.S. Furthermore, contrary to the promises of noninterference in the internal affairs of the Islamic regime, his administration had actively tried to destabilize it and impose a government congenial to American interests.

Though Carter managed to implement the deal with Iran before formally handing over power to Reagan on January 21, 1981, the Iranian government denied him the pleasure of receiving the freed hostages as U.S. President.

Royal Lion and Republican Eagle

As international relations go, Iranian-American ties have a comparatively short history. Though the first contacts between the U.S. and Iran date back to 1835, when American missionaries established contacts with the Nestorian Christians in Iran's Azeri-speaking area, Washington established diplomatic relations with Iran only in 1883. Efforts by American petroleum corporations in the 1920s and 1930s to gain oil concessions in the five northern provinces proved fruitless partly because both the British and the Soviets were determined to keep them out.

But after Muhammad Reza Pahlavi was placed on the Peacock Throne in 1941, he courted the U.S. in order to neutralize the traditional influence of London and Moscow. Washington obliged. In March 1942, President Franklin Roosevelt ruled that Iran was eligible for lend-lease aid. "The U.S. alone is in a position to build up Iran to the point at which it would need neither British nor Soviet assistance to maintain order in its house," said a State Department memorandum in January 1943. Seven months later, Secretary of State Cordell Hull said, "It is to our interest that no great power be established on the Persian Gulf opposite the important American petroleum development in Saudi Arabia."[6] Over the next few years, Washington seconded several American officers, including H. Norman Schwarzkopf Sr., to train the Iranian police and gendarmerie. Also both the military and civilian intelligence (in the form of the Office of Strategic Services, the CIA's antecedent) units became active in Iran.

In 1953, the CIA turned Iran into a test case for overthrowing legitimate governments, an enterprise that would be repeated many times in other countries in the coming decades. With this, America replaced Britain as the dominant Western power in Iran. U.S. companies were preeminent in the Western oil consortium, which was given a contract to run Iran's petroleum industry on behalf of the National Iranian Oil Company (NIOC). In 1955, the Shah took his country into the Western-sponsored Baghdad Pact, and two years later he subscribed to the Eisenhower Doctrine.

U.S. Under Republican Presidents (1981–1993)

Nearly a quarter century after the CIA-engineered coup in Tehran, another Republican U.S. President, Ronald Reagan, found himself having to deal with Iran as the first item on his foreign agenda. He conceded that there was nothing America could do to take revenge on Iran for keeping American diplomats hostage for one year and seventy-nine days. Reiterating that he would honor the terms agreed by Carter, he lifted American economic sanctions on Iran.

Reagan also maintained formal neutrality in the Iran-Iraq War. But from mid-1982 onward, as Iran gained superiority on the battlefield, his administration leaned more and more toward Iraq. It started with providing direct financial aid to Baghdad in the form of credits to buy American agricultural produce. It then undertook a major policy reassessment in the wake of the killing of 241 U.S. Marines stationed at Beirut airport in a truck-bombing by militant Lebanese Shias in October, a terrorist attack in which it saw Iran's hand.

In November 1983, Reagan signed a secret National Security Presidential Directive, stating that Iraq's defeat would be "contrary to U.S. interests."[7] The State Department removed Iraq from the list of nations that supported international terrorism. Reagan conveyed the gist of his directive to Saddam Hussein in a letter delivered to him by Donald Rumsfeld, a top corporate executive then temporarily serving as a presidential envoy to the Middle East, during their meeting in Baghdad in December. Six weeks earlier, Saddam's troops had used poison gases against the Iranians, a subject Rumsfeld conveniently failed to mention.

To further the objective of helping Iraq, and to punish Iran for its suspected involvement in the Beirut truck-bombing, in January 1984 the Reagan administration put Iran on the list of nations that supported international terrorism, thus subjecting it to rigid export controls. In March, Washington launched its "Operation Staunch" to pressure its allies not to sell arms or spare parts to Tehran.

As soon as Reagan was reelected in November, he announced

the restoration of diplomatic ties with Baghdad. From then on, the U.S. made its intelligence in the Gulf available to Iraq on a regular basis by establishing direct links between the CIA headquarters in Langley, Virginia, and the American Embassy in Baghdad. In July, a U.S. spokesman said that being neutral in the Iran-Iraq War did not mean that "We don't have sympathies."[8] Washington then concluded an agreement with Iraq concerning trade, industry, agriculture, energy, health, and telecommunications. Such a policy stemmed from the "zero-sum" concept—based on a close study of the interrelated histories of the two neighbors—strengthening Iraq meant weakening Iran, and vice versa.

But while the State Department was vigorously pursuing "Operation Staunch" against Iran, the CIA, the National Security Council (NSC), and the White House were engaged in secret deals with Tehran regarding the exchange of American hostages in Lebanon for the sale of U.S.-made arms and ammunition. The American officials involved in the clandestine deals passed on the moneys obtained from Iran to the Contra guerrillas fighting the leftist government in Nicaragua, thus contravening the ban that U.S. Congress had imposed on financially assisting the ultra right-wing Nicaraguan insurgents. The subsequent exposure of these shenanigans, called the Iran-Contra Affair, in November 1986 put Iran at an advantage, at least diplomatically.

At the policy level, the scam arose out of the U.S. decision makers' schizophrenia about supplying arms and ammunition to Iran. On one hand, they wanted to keep the Iranian air force small and crippled to deny Tehran victory. On the other hand, they did not want the Iranians to stop using U.S.-made planes, tanks, and electronic systems altogether, because that made them dependent on the Pentagon. The continued supplies of U.S.-made arms and ammunition were also meant to bolster the power of certain Iranian military officers, expected to become powerful in the post-Khomeini era.

Starting with the abduction of William Buckley, the CIA sta-tion chief in Beirut, in March 1984, the number of American hostages taken by the pro-Iranian Lebanese groups rose to five in a year. The abductors wanted America to end its arms embargo against Iran in exchange for freeing the hostages.

In July 1985, Khomeini said that if Reagan accepted Islamic rev-olution as reality, then that would be enough to start talking to each other. That month Reagan allowed his National Security Adviser, Robert "Bud" McFarlane, to propose that Tehran should influence the pro-Iranian Lebanese groups to free their American hostages in exchange for the sale of U.S.-made weapons to Iran. In September, in exchange for the sale of 508 U.S.-made anti-tank missiles, one American hostage (Rev. Benjamin Weir) was released. But the second swap of 120 anti-aircraft missiles and 4,000 anti-tank missiles for the remaining captives (excluding Buckley, who had died in captivity) proved problematic.

When in March 1985, Iran broke Iraqi defense lines near Qurna and cut Baghdad-Basra road without any air support, the Pentagon was impressed. With the help of Iran's former Deputy Prime Minister Ibrahim Yazdi then visiting Washington, McFar-lane set up a back channel with Tehran. Further impetus came when Speaker Ali Akbar Hashemi Rafsanjani intervened to get the release of the last four TWA passengers who had been hijacked and taken to Damascus. Reagan wrote a personal note of thanks to Rafsanjani. The release of a further captive came after five hundred anti-tank missiles had been delivered to Iran in late October.

When George Shultz and Caspar Weinberger, respective State and Defense Secretaries, learned of the deal, they protested. Reagan put the process on ice, but not for long.

On May 28, 1986, McFarlane, traveled to Tehran with a plane-load of U.S.-made weapons and spares. His four days of talks with low-level officials were fruitless. However, more weapons were delivered, and on July 26 Reverend Lawrence Jenco was released in Lebanon. More weapons and spares came from the Clark airbase in the Philippines with spares for F-4, F-5, and F-14 warplanes. On November 2, David Jacobsen of the American University of Beirut was released.

Once the scam was exposed in November it cut Reagan's approval rating at home from 67 percent to 46 percent, and paralyzed his administration for several months. Washington's Arab allies were shocked and incensed. This was particularly true of Iraq, which had been assured clandestinely three years earlier the U.S. would ensure that it was not defeated in its war with Iran.

As stated earlier (in Introduction) in his television address to the nation on November 13, Reagan highlighted the extraordinary importance of Iran's geography and oil reserves. The euphoria that Reagan's speech created in Iran, however, proved short-lived. In early 1987, while Iran was engaged in a massive offensive to capture Basra, the second city of Iraq, Reagan, committed to preventing Iraq's defeat at any cost, banned the import of Iranian oil. Baghdad was quick to fill the gap. In mid-May, even after Iraq had "accidentally" fired two Exocet missiles at USS frigate *Stark* 85 miles (135 km) northeast of Bahrain, killing thirty-seven crewmen, U.S. Assistant Defense Secretary Richard Armitage, went on to reiterate, "We can't stand to see Iraq defeated."[9]

As the war entered its seventh year on September 22, 1987, Iran found itself facing the combined strength of the Iraqi air force with nearly four hundred warplanes and the U.S. naval force of some forty warships. In October, U.S. Congress voted to impose an embargo on all imports from Iran, thus reverting Washington to the position it held in the wake of the American hostage-taking eight years earlier.

Since the Iran-Iraq War ended in a draw in August 1988, the U.S. felt satisfied.

The scene seemed set for the reinforcement of U.S.-Iraq ties, Saddam Hussein reckoned, especially when Washington rushed to blame Iran for the midair bomb that destroyed a Pan Am civilian aircraft killing 278 people over the Scottish town of Lockerbie in December 1988. (More than a decade later, Libya would accept responsibility for the explosion, and pay compensation to the families of those killed.)

The need for closer Washington-Baghdad ties sharpened when any designs that the American policy makers had of molding Iranian politics to their satisfaction following Khomeini's death in June 1989 came to nothing: the transition of power to lackluster Ayatollah Ali Khamanei was surprisingly smooth, providing no opportunity for manipulation by America.

Indeed Saddam Hussein's perception that U.S. President George Herbert Walker Bush was eager to reinforce Washington's links with Iraq was a major factor in his aggressive policy toward Kuwait. His brutal invasion of a small, weak neighbor in August 1990 impacted on the Tehran-Washington relationship.

In the immediate aftermath of the Iraqi attack, Iran found itself in the same column as the U.S. administration of President George Herbert Walker Bush. But soon its leaders tried to distance themselves from it. They became highly suspicious of the motives of Washington as it swung swiftly into action to assemble an extraordinarily large force in the Persian Gulf region.

In a public speech on September 12, Khamanei expressed strong opposition to the presence of the U.S. troops in the area and to "America's demanding, bullying, and shameless attitude." Addressing Washington, he said, "What has the security of the region to do with you? It is the business of the nations of this region." He then condemned those "nations and governments who allow the aggressor America to come here to plan in accordance with its own interests and to set up a security system in the Persian Gulf." He added, "We shall not permit the Americans to establish a foothold for themselves in the region, where we are present . . . and to turn it into a sphere of the American power, and to acquire the power to administer the affairs of Muslims, and especially the affairs of the sacred regions of Muslims and their two holy shrines [in Mecca and Medina]."[10] Thus Khamanei condemned America as much as Saudi Arabia whose ruler had invited the infidel American troops to his country.

The Bush Sr. administration reacted to Khamanei's attack more in sorrow than in anger, insisting that Tehran had "misunderstood" its position, and reassured Tehran through the Swiss Embassy (which had been looking after U.S. interests there since 1979) that the Pentagon had no intention of staying on in the Gulf, militarily, once the Iraqis had been expelled from Kuwait. On their part, the Iranian leaders did not translate Khamanei's fatwa into action against the U.S. presence in the Gulf. Indeed, despite repeated calls by radical Islamist politicians to side with Iraq to confront the infidel, imperialist America, President Rafsanjani refused to do so. As President of the country that had been the first victim of Saddam's aggression, Rafsanjani was in tune with popular feelings on the subject.

Iran declared that it would abide by UN sanctions on Iraq while making clear that the Muslim people of Iraq must not be deprived of food and medicine. Throughout the crisis, Iran maintained its opposition to the overwhelming military presence of the U.S. in the Persian Gulf while condemning the Iraqi action and insisting on the return of Kuwait to the ruling al Sabah family. This policy seemed to have overwhelming support among Iranian people and politicians.[11]

While there was some flexibility in the Bush Sr.'s White House regarding Iran for tactical reasons, the U.S. Congress—heavily influenced by the long-established, powerful, pro-Israeli American-Israeli Public Affairs Committee (AIPAC), and the Mujahedin-e Khalq Organization (MKO), and its political arm, the National Council of Resistance in Iran (NCRI), richly funded by anti-clerical Iranian exiles in the U.S., as well as memories of the 444-day siege—remained resolutely hostile to the Islamic Republic. In 1992, it passed the Iran-Iraq Non-Proliferation Act, which authorized the President to impose sanctions at his discretion on any individual or company assisting Iran or Iraq in developing non-conventional weapons or missiles.

The defeat of Bush Sr. by the Democrat candidate, Bill Clinton, did not alter the frosty American-Iranian relations.

Clinton's "Dual Containment" Policy and After

Indeed, President Clinton's appointment of Warren Christopher as Secretary of State in January 1993 meant that U.S.-Iran relations would remain solidly frozen. As Deputy Secretary of State under President Carter, he had been among the top U.S. officials who felt deeply frustrated and humiliated at their failure to free the American diplomats taken hostage by the Iranian students in 1979. He was still nursing the scars of that wretched episode.

In May 1993, Martin Indyk, Special Assistant to President on Near East and South Asian Affairs at the National Security Council, who was a top official of AIPAC before joining the Clinton administration, announced the replacement of the "zero-sum" doctrine applied so far to Iran and Iraq with the "dual containment" doctrine.

"The end of the Cold War and the elimination of the Soviet empire also eliminated a major strategic consideration from our calculus in the Gulf," he said. "We no longer have to worry that our actions would generate Soviet actions in support of our adversaries in the region." Furthermore, he continued, "as a result of the Iran-Iraq War and the [1991] Gulf War, a regional balance of power between both countries has been established at a much lower level of military capability. This makes it easier [for us] to balance the power of both of them."

The new doctrine derived from the administration's assessment that the current Iraqi and Iranian regimes were both hostile to American interests in the region. Accordingly, "we do not accept the argument that we should continue the old balance of power game, building up one to balance the other . . . We reject it because we do not need it . . . As long as we are able to maintain our military presence in the region; [and] as long as we succeed in restricting the military ambitions of both Iraq and Iran . . . we will have the means to counter both the Iraqi and Iranian regimes."[12]

One result of this policy was that in early 1994, at America's behest, the World Bank stopped further loans to Iran and froze the total at $850 million.[13] The World Bank did not reverse its decision even though it issued a favorable report on Iran's economic liberalization program in late 1995.

As described earlier (Chapter Seven), in March 1995 Clinton issued an executive order barring U.S. citizens or corporations from working in Iran's oil and gas industry, which aborted Conoco's impending contract with the National Iranian Oil Company (NIOC). (Interestingly, Dick Cheney, as Chairman of Halliburton, opposed this.) The next month, while addressing a World Jewish Congress meeting in New York, Clinton announced a ban on trade with Iran.

In June 1996, the Voice of America (VOA) began beaming its nonjammable broadcasts into Iran from a powerful 600kW transmitter in Kuwait. Four months later it inaugurated simultaneous radio and television broadcasts in Persian, beaming television transmission of an existing weekly one-hour radio phone-in program via the AsiaSat2 satellite. This magazine program included popular Iranian entertainers based in America, Iranian pop music, and legal advice on how to migrate to the U.S. Despite a ban on satellite dishes since March 1995 as part of a campaign to counter the Western cultural invasion, with fines of up to $1,500, an estimated 250,000 out of 2 million house-holds in Tehran would soon acquire satellite dishes.

The diffuse cultural challenge from America that Iran faced paled in contrast to the provisions of the Iran-Libya Sanctions Act (ILSA)—also called the D'Amato Act, named after Senator Alfonso D'Amato, head of the U.S. Senate Banking Committee—which Clinton signed on August 5, 1996. The act was to remain in force for five years, after which the U.S. Congress could extend it. It gave the U.S. President discretionary power to impose sanctions on any person or company anywhere on the planet that invested $40 million or more in an Iranian or Libyan oil or gas project.

Arguing that this act violated international trading laws, the European Union, based in Brussels, Belgium, threatened retaliation if the U.S. President took action under it. With French oil companies engaged heavily in Iran, France was most vocal in its protest. Germany also expressed its disapproval by renewing its export-credit guarantees to Iran. Japan said it would lodge a complaint with the World Trade Organization (WTO) as ILSA violated WTO rules. The European, Japanese, and Chinese oil corporations were in no mood to kowtow to U.S. legislators: they were convinced that the extraterritorial application of the American law was illegal. Emboldened perhaps by these complaints, during his visit to Tehran in mid-August, Turkish Prime Minister Necmettin Erbakan signed a $20 billion natural gas deal with Iran, scheduled to run until 2020.

Tehran said, with some justice, that Clinton's decision was "lacking international backing." Its confidence stemmed partly from the inauguration of a 90-mile (150 km) rail link between its border town of Sarakhs and Tejan in Turkmenistan in May 1996—the culmination of a five-year project costing $210 million—which was attended by twelve Leaders and Presidents: five Central Asian republics, Iran, Turkey, Azerbaijan, Armenia,

Georgia, Pakistan, and Afghanistan. It underlined once more the unique geostrategic position of Iran.

With this, the old Soviet rail system, covering all eight land-locked Republics of the southern tier of former Soviet Union—Kazakhstan, Kyrgyzstan, Tajikistan, Turkmenistan, and Uzbekistan of Central Asia and Azerbaijan, Armenia, and Georgia of the Caucasus—became linked to the Iranian railway network. The new link provided the landlocked Central Asian states access to the warm water ports of Iran in the Persian Gulf and the Arabian Sea, and thus released them from their dependence on Russia.

None of this discouraged America from pursuing its policy of demonizing Iran. It alleged in August 1996 that Tehran was carrying out a nuclear weapons program at its facilities at Neka, a town near the Caspian coastline, Kelaye, and Karaj, a suburb of Tehran—despite repeated statements by the IAEA in 1995 and 1996 that its inspectors had found no evidence of "suspect, military-related activity" in Iran. Only low enriched uranium unsuitable for weapons was being used to fuel the U.S.-supplied research reactor at Tehran University, according to the IAEA.[14] The U.S. strategy seemed to be to prepare the ground for a military strike against Iran as punishment for its alleged involvement in the earlier blast at the Khobar complex in eastern Saudi Arabia.

An explosion on June 25, 1996, of a 4,500 lb. (2,000 kg) bomb, planted in a fuel tanker, outside the perimeter of the guarded and fortified compound of a residential eight-story block in Khobar, part of a vast complex used by U.S. servicemen stationed at the Dhahran airbase. Creating a 35-foot (11 meter) crater, and sending sound waves that traveled 40 miles (65 km) to Bahrain, it tore into the front of the building, killing nineteen servicemen and injuring four hundred. Two men were seen leaving the fuel truck and speeding off in a car, giving the security men a few minutes to begin an evacuation before the blast.

Washington rushed seventy Federal Bureau of Investigation agents to Saudi Arabia.

One of the two groups claiming responsibility was named after Abdullah al Hudhaif, a cofounder of the opposition Committee for the Defense of Legitimate Rights (CDLR) in Saudi Arabia, who was publicly beheaded for allegedly throwing acid in the face of a police torturer in early 1996. Since it was incredible that somebody detained in a Saudi jail could obtain acid to throw at his interrogator or torturer, the claim of many inside and outside the kingdom was that Hudhaif was tortured to death in detention and that the beheading was a sham, with the head of a corpse being severed in public.[15] The founders of the CDLR—demanding elections and press freedom within the Sharia—included a former chief justice of high court in Saudi Arabia, his U.S.-educated son who was a physics professor, and two lawyers, all of them Wahhabis.

The timing of the blast indicated that there was probably a link between this terrorist act and the explosion on November 13, 1995, of a 220 lb. (100 kg) car bomb in the parking lot of the Saudi National Guard training center in Riyadh run by the U.S., killing seven, including five U.S. military officers, and injuring sixty, a majority of them American. For this too Washington had blamed Iran. But the four suspects arrested in April 1996 and beheaded in early June—Abdul Aziz al Mithan, Khalid al Said, Muslih al Shamrani, and Riyad al Hajja—were Saudi citizens and Wahhabis, puritanical Sunnis who hold Shias in low esteem.[16] Significantly, before their sentence was carried out, the Saudi authorities and the U.S. Embassy in Riyadh had received threats of retribution if they were beheaded.

Washington alleged that the perpetrators of the Khobar explosion, belonging to the Hizbollah group in Saudi Arabia, sponsored by Tehran's Islamic Revolutionary Guards Corps, were trained in Iran. The CIA claimed that it had identified eleven terrorist camps deep inside the Islamic Republic where, it alleged, the Khobar bombers had received their training. However, while the CIA's top managers released satellite and intelligence data to *USA Today*, which published it on August 2, other American officials close to the Saudi investigation said there was no evidence of Iran's involvement.[17]

The same day, in an ominous move, U.S. warplanes violated Iran's airspace near Bushehr, where two nuclear reactors for electricity generation were being built by Russia—which led Tehran to lodge a complaint against America with the UN Security Council. This move by Iran, combined with Clinton's propensity to examine an important international issue from all possible angles—especially including the international law, given his own training and experience as a lawyer (as well as that of his Secretary of State Warren Christopher)—might well have led Clinton to seek the opinion of the White House Counsel on the legality of hitting Iranian targets on the basis primarily of some ill-defined satellite images. The absence of an unqualified legal clearance emanating from the counsel would have dissuaded him from ordering air raids on the suspected Iranian training camps.

The rationale behind the punitive ILSA, advanced by Clinton, was that "Iran and Libya are two of the most dangerous supporters of terrorism in the world." In Iran's case, the terrorism charge pertained chiefly to the assassinations that its intelligence operatives had carried out abroad. It was estimated that in the seventeen years since the revolution, the Islamic regime had assassinated eighty militant opponents in Europe, Turkey, and Iraq.

According to a Beirut-based source well-connected with Iran, and cited by Robert Fisk in the *Independent*, there was a standing order, dating back to the mid-1980s, by the Islamic Revolutionary Guards Corps's intelligence committee to "neutralize all armed opposition to the regime wherever it was."[18]

Its targets fell into two categories: former top officials under the Shah, a fast dwindling number; and those groups that had taken up arms against the Iranian regime, the most prominent being the Baghdad-based Mujahedin-e Khalq Organization (MKO), and the secular, leftist Iranian Kurdish factions, operating from Iraqi Kurdistan then protected by an Anglo-American air umbrella, where the CIA and the British Secret Intelligence Service, MI6, were active.

Following the 1991 Gulf War, the Kurdistan Democratic Party of Iran (KDPI) set up its headquarters in the Iraqi border town of Qala Diza, and the *Komala-e Jian-e Kurdistan (lit.,* Association of Revival of Kurdistan) near Suleimaniya. These groups staged pin-prick raids on Iran, which resulted in the deaths of Revolutionary Guards, charged with safeguarding the national borders; and they were in return attacked by the Iranian forces.

This was the background against which Kazem Darabi, an Iranian intelligence agent, and his three Lebanese cohorts assassinated four Kurdish leaders, including the KDPI chief, Sadiq Sharaf-Kandi, in September 1992 at Mykonos, a Greek restaurant in Berlin, where the Kurds had come to attend a meeting of the Socialist International.

Tension between Iran and its armed opponents rose sharply after the U.S. adopted the dual containment policy. Tehran feared that Washington would use the rebellious Iranians' Iraqi Kurdistan base to undermine the Islamic regime. Iran had made no secret of its policy of retaliating with force against violent rebellious groups, no matter where their activists were based. Israel had been pursuing such a policy since its inception in 1948. More recently, in October 1995, its intelligence operatives assassinated Dr. Fathi Abdul Aziz Shikaki, head of the Islamic Jihad of Palestine, in Malta. But neither America nor any other Western country had considered putting Israel on the list of nations that supported international terrorism.

Tehran's fears were fueled when, following the passage of a

secret directive by the U.S. Congress on December 31, 1995, sanctioning $18 million for a covert action program against Iran, the White House announced that the sum would be spent inter alia to cultivate new enemies of the Islamic regime. (As it was, the CIA was already funding the existing anti-Tehran Kurdish groups.) In retaliation, on January 23, 1996, the Iranian Majlis authorized $20 million to "uncover and neutralize Washington's 'conspiracies and interference in Iranian affairs,' sue the U.S. in international legal bodies, and inform world opinion about America's violation of the UN Charter."

In April 1997, at the end of a three-year trial of Darabi and three coconspirators in a Berlin court, they were found guilty of assassinating four Kurdish leaders. Holland, the then European Union's Chairman, proposed that the member-states should recall their ambassadors from Tehran and put their "critical dialogue" with it on ice. They did so, except Greece. Washington considered the moment propitious to pressure the EU to sever trade ties with Tehran. But an EU diplomatic source said, "Cutting off trade would have to be done within a UN context." That was not on the horizon.

The later American claim that its covert "Operation Sapphire" to expose the Iranian undercover agents in various countries, had debilitated Iran's terrorist activities abroad in 1997 had to be seen against the backdrop of change of leadership at the Intelligence Ministry in Tehran in that year.

Hojatalislam Ali Fallahian, a former Director of the Intelligence College—who had headed this ministry since 1989, and who was alleged to be involved in the Berlin killings as well as assassinations of five Iranian dissidents at home—lost his job to Hojatalislam Qorban Ali Najafabadi, a Majlis deputy.[19]

Enter President Muhammad Khatami

The surprise landslide victory of moderate Muhammad Khatami in May 1997 encouraged the freshly reelected Clinton, and his new Secretary of State Madeleine Albright, to reappraise their policy on Iran. In October, when the U.S. State Department produced a list of thirty terrorist organizations worldwide—as required by the Anti-terrorism and Effective Death Penalty Act, 1996—it included the MKO. That barred it from raising funds in America, its major source of cash. "The MKO qualified for the designation under U.S. law and the move was not made to curry favor with the Khatami government," said James Rubin of the U.S. State Department.[20] Nonetheless it pleased Tehran, even though the MKO's political arm, the National Resistance Council of Iran (NRCI), was spared the ban.

Following an understanding reached surreptitiously by Tehran and Washington, on January 7, 1998, Khatami gave a forty-five-minute interview to the CNN in two parts—an unedited speech, followed by questions by Christiane Amanpour, an American journalist of Iranian origin. Khatami said, "First there must be a crack in this wall of distrust" between the two governments, and that "we must definitely consider the factors that led to severance of relations and try to eliminate them." He then proposed an increase in the exchange of cultural, academic, and sports delegations. Having expressed his views on the CNN, Khatami declared on the Iranian television that, "The revolutionary tradition in foreign policy will continue."[21]

Next day Rubin (who was later to marry Christiane Amanpour) confirmed that top U.S. officials had watched the program. He said, "President Khatami's extensive comments with respect to U.S. civilization and values were interesting . . . We also noted the president's comments that the conduct of relations between nations must be based on mutual respect and dignity; we agree. . . . We noted with interest his regret concerning the hostage-taking [in November 1979]. We welcome his statement that this period in Iranian history is over, and that the rule of law should be respected both domestically and internationally. On terrorism, President

Khatami's rejection and condemnation of all forms of terrorism directed at innocents was noteworthy." Finally he said, "We will look closely at what President Khatami has said regarding people-to-people exchanges and people-to-people dialogue." But, he added, "The best way to address our bilateral differences would be to engage in a government-to-government dialogue."[22]

The three major subjects Washington wanted to discuss were: Iran's support of international terrorism, its program to acquire nuclear weapons, and its opposition to the Middle East peace process. Rubin, of course, made no mention of the subjects Iran wanted to discuss: Washington's efforts to dominate the Persian Gulf region and flood it with its weapons, its strategic alliance with Israel, and the unfreezing of Iran's assets of $10–12 billion in American banks.

Nonetheless, relations between Tehran and Washington began to thaw. Iran gave visas to an American wrestling team in February to participate in the international Takhti tournament in Tehran. The wrestlers were allowed to display an American flag. They received such an enthusiastic welcome from the twelve thousand audience that on the last day American wrestler Zeke Jones, holding up an Iranian flag and Khamanei's portrait, ran round the stadium to the chants of "Jones! Jones!" On that day the tournament's closing ceremony was attended by conservative Speaker Ali Akbar Nateq-Nouri, which implied Leader Ali Khamanei's approval of the Americans' presence in Tehran.

On the Iranian New Year—Spring Equinox, March 21— Clinton sent a message of greetings to Khatami, hoping that "the day will soon come when the United States can once again enjoy good relations with Iran."

Reciprocating the sentiment, Khatami had Clinton's message broadcast on the state-run radio. With this, diplomatic activity picked up during the spring, despite contrary signals emanating from the two capitals.

In May, the annual U.S. State Department report described Iran as "the most active sponsor of state terrorism in 1997," with its agents held responsible for at least thirteen assassinations, mainly the anti-regime activists of the KDPI and the MKO, both based in Iraq. Also, claimed the U.S. document, Iran continued to provide money, training, and weapons to various Middle East terrorist organizations like the (Palestinian) Islamic Jihad and Hamas, and that the leaders of various terrorist organizations had gathered the previous autumn in Tehran to discuss enhanced coordination and seek more funds.[23] On this subject the Iranian leaders argued that since the international law allowed the occupied people to resist the foreign occupiers by "all means necessary," neither the Palestinian groups nor they were doing anything illegal.

The fact that in a statement on May 23, 1998, Saudi Interior Minister Prince Nayif precluded Iran's involvement in the Khobar blast, adding that "Saudi nationals alone were responsible for the bombing in June 1996 at the al Khobar complex near Dhahran airport," made no difference to the Clinton administration's stance on Iran's terrorism.

Its Persian-language trial broadcasts by Radio Free Iran from the studios of Radio Free Europe/Radio Liberty (RFE/RL) in Prague went ahead with a plan to launch a regular program in October. Tehran protested—saying that this was a violation of the 1981 Algiers Accord, signed on the eve of the American hostages' release, whereby Washington agreed not to interfere in Iran's internal affairs—but to no avail.

In its dispute with the EU on ILSA, America lost. Following a meeting in London of Clinton; British Premier Tony Blair, the current Chairman of the EU, and Jacques Santer, President of the European Commission, on May 18, the U.S. yielded to the EU, with Santer repeating his condemnation of the American legislation as "illegal and counter-productive."

Six months earlier, the EU had lodged a complaint against Washington at the WTO in Geneva, challenging ILSA, arguing that it violated the principle of free trade on which the WTO was built, and that any punitive action taken under it against a non-American company or individual would break international law. After initial skirmishes, the two sides told the WTO that they would try to settle the matter bilaterally. They found a solution within the ILSA provision that permitted the U.S. President to waive sanctions for a specific project on the grounds of "national interest" (Section 4c), or for those countries that had taken specific steps to counter state terrorism by Iran or Libya (Section 9c). At first Washington offered to grant a presidential waiver to Total SA, which had signed a contract with the NIOC, on the basis of Section 4c. But the EU insisted on the Section 9c waiver. It succeeded at the London meeting.[24]

On his return to Washington, Clinton issued the waiver to the Total SA-led oil consortium with some trepidation, afraid that the Republican-majority Congress would deprive him of his right to waive sanctions. Nothing of the sort happened. Indeed Senator D'Amato and other Republicans encouraged the State Department to press ahead with its review of the Iran policy, which resulted in Albright's speech on the subject a few weeks later.[25]

On June 17, addressing an Asia Society meeting in New York, Albright called for improved relations between America and Iran, and said that Washington was ready to draw "a road map for normalization of relations." The following day Clinton said the U.S. was seeking "a genuine reconciliation based on mutuality and reconciliation [with an Iran now] changing in a positive way under the reformist influence of President Muhammad Khatami."

These statements basically buried Clinton's own five-year-old "dual containment" policy in the Gulf.

During the 1998 World Cup in France, the match between

Iran and America in Lyons on June 20 ended with a narrow victory by the Iranians of two to one. On its return to Tehran, the Iranian team was received ecstatically by hundreds of thousands of people, men and women alike, in the early hours of the morning, for having beaten the "Great Satan."

Nobody had thought that Khomeini's slogan, "We will make America face a severe defeat"—painted in huge letters in Persian and English—on the compound wall of the former U.S. Embassy in Tehran would be realized even on a soccer pitch.

However, once that happened, the old faded slogan was repainted. And a few new slogans and images were added on the quarter-mile-long perimeter wall along Taleqani Avenue lined on the opposite side with shops displaying expensive, eye-catching carpets and latest electronic gadgetry. By far the most dramatic image was a Statue of Liberty capped not with a female face but a skull.

At Mashhad Hotel, the kitchen worker Amir Zarkesh too remembered 1998. "That is the time American tourists started reappearing," he told me. That was also the year when the annual rally outside the former U.S. mission was held on two different days—November 2 and 4—he recalled.

The first rally was addressed among others by Ibrahim Asgharzadeh, one of the spokesmen of the Khat-e Imam students who had seized the embassy, a bespectacled, middle-aged man with a wide girth. "We are not terrorists, but a people who had been wronged," he declared. "If we had not captured the embassy, we could not have dried up the root of America in Iran." However, bygones were bygones. "Today we invite all [former American] hostages to return to Iran as our guests," he said. "Regarding relations with America, we must look to the future, and not to past . . . We have a new language for the world. We defend human rights. And we will try to make Islam such that it won't contradict democracy." Part of the crowd, consisting of a few dozen young men, did not agree with the conciliatory statements. They set an American flag alight. Their leader, Babak Shahrestani, a tall, slender chemical engineering student in jeans, told Robin Wright, a visiting American journalist, "If Americans come to Iran again, we are afraid they will spy again and make conspiracies against the people or try to topple the government or make the nation dependent [on them] again."[26]

Addressing thousands of Iranian students on the anniversary of the American Embassy takeover, Leader Khamanei said, "Severing of relations between Iran and America has been to the 100 percent benefit of the Iranian people . . . The Americans only want to recover the position they had before the revolution . . . Our importance around the world and in the eyes of other peoples is based on our standing up to America."[27]

Tehran-Washington relations took a nosedive when, commenting on the violent student protests in July 1999, Rubin said, "We have made it clear that we are concerned by the use of violence to put down demonstrations by Iranian students in support of freedom of expression and democratic values, and the rule of law." Iran protested at this intrusion in its domestic affairs. Yet the U.S. Senate passed a resolution in early August "condemning the repressive actions taken by the Iranian government against the democratic movement of Iran."

On August 20, addressing the Friday prayer congregation in Tehran, Ayatollah Ahmad Jannati, head of the powerful Guardians Council, said, "The American support for the [student] agitators is an attempt to overthrow the Islamic regime. The enemy wants to insinuate that [the riots were] the fault of the regime, whereas [in truth] the attack [on the student dormitory] was the work of certain police officers, and there was no link between them and the government."[28]

In September 1999 Clinton addressed a "strongly worded" message through Sultan Qaboos of Oman to Khatami, asking for the extradition of three suspected non-Iranian terrorists living in Iran, allegedly involved in the Khobar bombing. In absence of an extradition treaty between America and Iran, Clinton's demand proved futile.

Another sterile U.S. gesture was made in mid-October when Indyk called for talks between U.S. and Iranian officials to discuss the American agenda without even mentioning the agenda that Iran has mentioned: a fresh American promise of no interference in Iran's internal affairs; releasing of the frozen Iranian assets; lifting of all sanctions, including ILSA and a 1995 law banning trade with Iran; allowing Caspian oil and gas exports to pass through Iran; discontinuing hostile U.S.-sponsored radio broadcasts beamed at Iran from Prague; and ending the Pentagon's heightened military presence in the Persian Gulf—now that Tehran had normalized relations with the Gulf monarchies, a fact highlighted by Iran's hosting of the fifty-four-member Islamic Conference Organization summit in December 1997.

There was no indication that the Clinton administration was in a mood to move on any of these points. Yet there was a continuing debate in the Majlis about relations with Washington. The issue ranged the conservative bloc of 120 deputies against a smaller bloc of reformists, with the former perceiving any contact with the "Great Satan" as undermining all that the Islamic regime stood for, and reckoning that such a move would accelerate consumerism and make ordinary Iranians drift away from Islam, whereas the latter saw merit in exploring normalization of relations with America in a world where it was the sole superpower.

While Clinton and Albright welcomed the reformists' success in the first run of the Majlis elections in February 2000 and called for direct talks between the two countries, later that month, the U.S. Congress, yielding to lobbying by anti-Iran American-Israeli Public Affairs Committee, passed the Iran Non-Proliferation Act by an almost unanimous vote, which required the President to report to Congress twice a year a list of countries that could be subject to sanctions for providing Iran with materials to develop missiles or nonconventional weapons, and impose sanctions at his discretion. Reversing its past declaration to veto such a bill, the White House said that since the new law gave the President sufficient flexibility, he would not veto it. The fresh legislation was aimed primarily at Moscow whose tightening links with Tehran caused great unease at the Capitol Hill and the White House.

Iran's Nuclear Program

Tehran-Moscow relations have a long history. Perched on the periphery of the expanding Tsarist Russia and the recently established British Empire in the Indian subcontinent in the nineteenth century, Iran turned into a buffer between the two competing powers. With the dissolution of Britain's Indian Empire by the mid-twentieth century, Muhammad Reza Shah tried to counterbalance the impact of the neighboring Soviet Union by aligning firmly with the rival superpower, America. The new equilibrium lasted as long he occupied the Peacock Throne. The succeeding Islamic Republic, though opposed vehemently to Washington, remained wary of the atheist Soviet Union. However, that changed with Khomeini's death in mid-1989. Soon after, the Soviet government and Iran signed agreements on commercial, economic, scientific, and technical cooperation in mid-1989.

It was in that context that Russia, the legal successor to the Soviet Union after December 1991, considered the proposal of rehabilitating and finishing a nuclear power plant started before the Islamic revolution. In August 1992, Russia agreed in principle to construct from scratch a nuclear power station plant at Haleyle, 7 miles (12 km) south of Bushehr, and also supply nuclear research units to run on 20 percent enriched uranium fuel to be supplied by Moscow, with Iran participating in the construction.

The work at Haleyle had initially started in 1974—as a result of the successful initiative taken by U.S. President Richard Nixon and Vice President Spiro Agnew two years earlier to convince the Shah to build twenty-two nuclear power plants, an enterprise in which they saw American corporations getting preference and making huge profits. At that time, nuclear power stations were portrayed as a panacea for the world's insatiable need for electricity.[29] But, flush with a bulging exchequer thanks to rising oil prices from 1973 to 1974, the Shah was confident enough to ignore American corporations and award the first contract for a nuclear power plant to Siemens, a West German company. By the time of the 1979 revolution, the plant was partially built. When Khomeini declared the project "anti-Islamic," Siemens packed up and left. During the 1980–88 Iran-Iraq War, Iraqi bombing raids damaged the site.

In December 1994, the Atomic Energy Authority of Iran signed an $800 million contract with Moscow to rebuild two 1,000MW light-water, nuclear-fueled generators, as part of a nuclear power plant, to be finished by May 2003, with Iranian participation in the construction. (Light water is ordinary water, used both for cooling the nuclear chain reaction and for transformation into steam to run the electric generating turbine.) But because progress on the joint venture was slow, Tehran switched to a turnkey arrangement in February 1998. The Russians proposed to use sealed rods, containing hundreds of pellets of 3.5 to 4 percent pure uranium, as fuel. When hit by high-energy neutrons these pellets will undergo controlled chain reaction and heat up the surrounding water, producing steam, which will run the electric generating turbine. Resisting pressure from Washington, Russia confirmed the contract.

In desperate need of foreign exchange, Moscow could not

afford to cancel such a lucrative commercial deal. Nuclear technology was one of its most successful exports, and it had made inroads in several Asian countries, including China and India. It reassured Washington that its reactors could not be used to produce weapons-grade plutonium, and reminded the U.S. that it and South Korea had agreed to supply two similar reactors to North Korea at the cost of $4,600 million. The Clinton administration reasoned that as an oil-and-gas-rich state, Iran did not need nuclear-powered electrical plants. (Nobody had bothered to point out that even though Russia had 6 percent of the global oil deposits and the largest gas reserves in the world, it had developed a thriving nuclear power industry at home and had become a leading exporter of the technology.) If only Nixon and Agnew had made this point to the Shah instead of persuading him to go nuclear in a big way. In any case, the Iranians argued that annual demand for electricity was rising by a staggering 10 percent, and that nuclear power was cheaper and more environmentally friendly than oil or coal; that it was renewable whereas their oil and gas reserves were finite. So it was incumbent on them to plan for the post-oil era for the sake of their future generations.

As it was, Iran possessed uranium ore in the Saqand area northeast of Yazd. All it needed to do was to crush the ore, mix it with water, and put the mixture through a chemical process to purify it and obtain uranium oxide U_3O_8, called yellow cake.[30]

Despite Russia's repeated reassurances, both America and Israel were resolute in their belief that Iran was bent on obtaining nuclear arms, and so they decided to put as many hurdles in Iran's way as they could to gain time to devise, jointly, appropriate response capabilities and doctrines.

On March 13, 2000, Clinton renewed his executive order of 1995 barring trade with Tehran. But then, in the now familiar pattern of a seesaw, came a conciliatory gesture.

Addressing the Princeton-based American-Iranian Council on

March 17, Albright admitted that Washington had created a climate of mistrust with Tehran. "In 1953 the United States played a significant role in orchestrating the overthrow of Iran's popular Prime Minister Muhammad Mussadiq," she said. "The Eisenhower administration believed its actions were justified for strategic reasons. But the coup was clearly a setback for Iran's political development. And it is easy to see now why many Iranians continue to resent this intervention by America in their internal affairs." She also regretted the past "short-sightedness" in U.S. policy, particularly during the Iran-Iraq War, when Washington backed Baghdad. She then held out an olive branch. She promised to "increase efforts" toward "a global settlement" of Iran's claims of its frozen assets in America—a departure from the case-by-case basis used by the Iran-US Claims Tribunal in The Hague since 1981. She announced the immediate lifting of the ban on non-oil imports from Iran. "I call upon Iran to join us in writing a new chapter in our shared history," she concluded.[31]

While welcoming certain elements of Albright's speech, Iranian Foreign Minister Kamal Kharrazi remarked that her initiative was "polluted" by continued American interference in Iran's domestic affairs. "The Americans are presuming that such acknowledgments, which did not even include an apology, will cause us to forget America's acts of treason, hostilities, and injustices," said Khamanei. "America can't do a damn thing"—a slogan coined originally by Khomeini.[32]

Yet, there was forward movement on the unofficial track. On August 30, 2000, the American-Iranian Council and Internews news agency held a reception at the Metropolitan Museum of Art in New York. Among those who attended were five Iranian Majlis deputies, led by Speaker Mahdi Karrubi, and four U.S. lawmakers, including Senator Arlen Specter (Republican, Pennsylvania). The Iranian team—which included Mouris Motamed, the newly elected Jewish deputy, and Elaaheh Kolahi, the only woman parliamentarian who refused to wear a black chador in the chamber, settling instead for a coat and a shoulder-length head covering—was in New York for a summit meeting of the Inter-Parliamentary Union. The American legislators invited their Iranian counterparts to visit the U.S. Congress. The Iranians on their part showed interest in inviting the Americans to Tehran. However, when Karrubi was asked about the meeting later, he described it "an accidental encounter."[33]

Such were Tehran-Washington relations a few months before the U.S. presidential poll when Republican George Walker Bush defeated his Democratic rival Al Gore. At Bush's behest, the American Congress extended ILSA, due to expire in August 2001, by five more years. On September 11 came the terrorist attacks on New York and Washington.

9/11 and Beyond

In the immediate aftermath of 9/11, Iranian-American relations thawed. The Mayor of Tehran sent personal condolences to the Mayor of New York, Rudolph Guiliani. In his sermon to the Friday prayer congregation in Tehran, Khamanei addressed the issue. "Mass killing is a catastrophe wherever it happens and whoever the perpetrators," he said. "And it is condemned without distinction." But, he added, "If God forbid, a similar catastrophe is inflicted on Afghanistan, we will condemn that too."[34]

Admiral Ali Shamkhani, the Defense Minister of Iran, set out the official policy thus: "If strikes against terrorist bases [inside Afghanistan] took place within the framework of the international community, Iran would support it." That is, Tehran would participate in any UN-sponsored action against the perpetrators of the criminal act, well aware that Security Council Resolution 1368 provided the framework within which such action could be mandated by the international community. Iran's position coincided with that of China, one of the Security Council's five permanent members. Its diplomats explained that cooperation needed to be channeled through a multilateral forum like the UN, not through retaliation by America or the North Atlantic Treaty Organization (NATO), and that any U.S. military action should be endorsed by the Security Council.[35]

This was not to be.

As the Pentagon unleashed massive bombing raids on Taliban-controlled Afghanistan, that started on October 7, 2001, Iran's Islamic leaders watched with growing concern. Khamanei condemned the American strikes. "How can you allow innocent civilians to be killed or injured?" he asked. "Terrorism is only an excuse. Why don't they announce their real intention—their motive for grabbing more power, for imperialism? Since when has it become a norm to send troops to another country and hit its cities with missiles and aerial bombardment because of so-called terrorism in that country?"[36] In the Persian media as well as in the Arabic, there was much stress on the fate of Afghan civilians.

While maintaining this stance in public, top Iranian officials chose to ignore any violations of the Iranian airspace that the Pentagon committed in its anti-Taliban campaign. Iran also reportedly supplied intelligence on the Taliban to the U.S.[37] With Tehran's blessings, the pro-Iranian Afghan warlord Ismail Khan, exiled in Mashhad in eastern Iran, coordinated his attack on the Taliban regime with the Pentagon's campaign. But then Iran had been an enemy of the Pakistan- and Saudi Arabia-backed Taliban since its inception in 1994. It had morally and materially helped the anti-Taliban opposition since 1996, and nearly gone to war with the Taliban government in September 1998 when it was urged by Clinton not to do so.

Much to America's annoyance, Iran became the first country to reopen its embassy in Kabul—within ten days of the flight of the Taliban on November 12–13.[38] In early December, however, the Iranian delegation worked closely with its American counterpart in Bonn to install Hamid Karzai, an ethnic Pushtun, as leader of the post-Taliban, interim government in Afghanistan. Tehran pledged $560 million in aid to Afghanistan over the next five years.

So it shocked the Iranian authorities to hear Bush's description of his "axis of evil" in his State of the Union address to the U.S. Congress on January 29, 2002: "Our second goal is to prevent regimes that sponsor terror from threatening America or our friends and allies with weapons of mass destruction . . . North Korea is a regime arming with missiles and weapons of mass destruction, while starving its citizens. Iran aggressively pursues these weapons and exports terror . . . Iraq continues to flaunt its hostility toward America and to support terror . . . States like these, and their terrorist allies, constitute an axis of evil, arming to threaten the peace of the world."[39]

Bush's remarks about an "axis of evil" evoked largely adverse comments not only from Europeans but also many Americans, including Bill Clinton. "They may all be trouble, but they are different," he said. Support for sanctions against Iraq had fallen apart. "Iran has two governments now, progressive elements that the U.S. can work with and hard-liners whose every move must be watched."[40]

As the U.S. began its military buildup in the Gulf region as the year unrolled, Iran's leader urged Saddam to cooperate with the UN in order to deprive Bush of a pretext to invade Iraq. However, such well-meaning advice was superfluous: as early as February 2002, Bush had decided to invade Iraq.

At a press conference in Washington in August, the National Resistance Council of Iran (NCRI) reported that Iran was hiding a massive uranium enrichment facility and other sites from the IAEA. This underground facility turned out to be at Natanz, northeast of Isfahan, which has had a research reactor for many years. This provided the Bush administration with a fresh basis to allege that Tehran was planning clandestinely to produce nuclear weapons. While enriching uranium does not violate the 1970 nuclear Non-Proliferation Treaty (NPT), which Iran had signed, the signatory is required to tell the IAEA about it. But Tehran had not done so. (By January 2002, 188 countries had ratified the nuclear Non-Proliferation Treaty, the exceptions being India, Israel, and Pakistan.)

"The NPT commits the established nuclear-weapons parties (that had manufactured and exploded a nuclear weapon before January 1, 1967)—China, France, Russia, the UK, and the U.S.— not to transfer nuclear weapons and not to assist in their manufacture by the non-nuclear weapons states," writes Frank Barnaby, a British nuclear scientist. "It also commits the non-nuclear weapon states not to receive nuclear weapons or assistance in the manufacture of them. To verify compliance with the treaty, the non-nuclear parties must sign agreements with the IAEA, submitting all their nuclear activities to IAEA safeguards. To encourage the non-nuclear weapon states to join the NPT, the treaty promises cooperation and assistance to these countries in their civil nuclear programs."[41]

In summer 2002, the Bush administration was too focused on planning an invasion of Iraq to ratchet up pressure on Iran. The situation changed once it had overthrown Saddam Hussein's regime in April 2003—especially when the Iranian leaders publicly urged the occupying Anglo-American forces to leave Iraq.

It pressured Iran to open up its nuclear program to greater IAEA scrutiny after the NCRI alleged in May 2003 that a site at Lavizan near Tehran was home to biological weapons research.

While rebuffing Washington's pressure to scuttle the nuclear power plant project, the Russians urged Iran to sign up the IAEA's Additional Protocol, which authorizes the agency to conduct unrestricted inspections of any sites it wished to inspect without warning. The Russians also hinted that they would only start supplying enriched uranium for the Haleyle reactors after Iran has agreed to return the spent fuel rods to Russia for reprocessing to Russia. Iran deliberately dragged out the negotiations on this issue, and advanced the date of commissioning the plant from mid-2004 to early 2006.[42]

Iran felt vulnerable because the IAEA's report of June 16 said that it had failed to meet its nuclear NPT obligations to report the acquisition and processing of nuclear material and the facilities involved by failing to report acquiring some uranium in 1991 and naming the facilities where it processed the material. The report raised questions about Iran's production of uranium metal, and its alleged uranium-enrichment activities. However, it added, Iran was taking steps to rectify the past failures, and concluded that only if Iran signed and implemented the Additional Protocol would the IAEA be able to provide credible assurances about Iran's nuclear intentions.

This was enough to convince the Bush administration that Iran was on its way to producing nuclear weapons, and was therefore a likely candidate as the next target of its "preventive wars." It combined this warning with threats to its allies of additional sanctions on their companies trading with Iran. Submitting to these pressures, Japan postponed signing a $2 billion deal on developing Iran's Azadegan oil field. In response, Iran said that in exchange for its acceptance of a fresh IAEA protocol, the EU and others should lift sanctions that have blocked transfer of peaceful nuclear technology it is entitled to as a signatory to the NPT.

In July 2003, IAEA inspectors arrived in Iran to take samples from the suspected sites. In the same month, the much anticipated talks between the EU and Iran on the Trade and Cooperation Agreement commenced.

France, Germany, and the UK formulated a common policy on Iran's nuclear program. In their letter to Iran's Foreign Minister Kharrazi on August 8, the Foreign Ministers of these EU members—

henceforth EU Troika—indicated that appropriate nuclear technology, including enriched uranium fuel, would be made available to Iran if it complied with the IAEA's requirements. A special IAEA legal team traveled to Tehran to elucidate those provisions of the Additional Protocol that the Iranians found problematic, reassuring them that Iran's sovereignty—as represented by its political, religious, and security sites—would be respected, and that there were very strict practices regarding IAEA requests to inspect the undeclared sites of a country in the Additional Protocol.

Along with this carrot came a stick. During his visit to Tehran on August 30, the EU Foreign Policy Chief, Javier Solane, hinted that if Iran did not adopt the Additional Protocol then its talks with the EU on trade and cooperation would be suspended. In Iran, even die-hard conservatives were agreed that developing cordial relations with the EU was an effective way to counterbalance America's aggressive posture.

While noting, approvingly, Iran's increasing cooperation in providing requested information and allowing access and sampling at its nuclear facilities, the next IAEA report stated that some of the information given now was at variance with an earlier version. The outstanding issues pertained chiefly to uranium enrichment, with the specific example of the inspectors finding particles of highly enriched uranium at the Natanz pilot uranium-enrichment plant.

Washington had banked on using the IAEA report to get the agency's thirty-five-strong Board of Governors to declare that Iran had violated the NPT and refer its case to the UN Security Council. But since the report did not contain convincing evidence of Iran's willful breach of the NPT, the Board of Governors' meeting on September 12, 2003, in Vienna urged Iran to suspend uranium enrichment and clarify all outstanding questions relating to its nuclear activities by October 31.

The deadline created frisson in Iran. Islamic radicals proposed withdrawal from the NPT to preserve national independence and sovereignty that the Islamic revolution had delivered to Iranians. They also condemned the hypocrisy of the U.S.—all set to violate the NPT by testing a new generation of mini atom bombs—and Israel, a nonsignatory to the NPT, which possessed a huge arsenal of nuclear weapons.[43] In contrast, reformists saw the signing of the Additional Protocol a means to garner international confidence in Iran's peaceful nuclear intentions.

To resolve the crisis, Khamanei appointed a committee consisting of the heads of the Government (Khatami), Majlis (Mahdi Karrubi), Judiciary (Muhammad Shahroudi), Supreme National Security Council (Hassan Rouhani), and Expediency Council (Rafsanjani). It decided to cooperate with the IAEA while reiterating Iran's right to (a) generate nuclear power, and (b) process its own uranium for that purpose (which the IAEA asked it to suspend as a confidence-building step until it had secured a clean bill of health), and reiterating that securing a stable fuel cycle was fundamental to its nuclear power program.

A nuclear fuel cycle consists of mining uranium ore (in which only seven out of one thousand uranium atoms are the lighter fissile isotopes U235, the rest being the heavier U238), processing it into uranium oxide (yellow cake), transforming it into uranium tetraflouride (UF4) gas and then uranium hexafluoride (UF6) gas, followed by enriching UF6 to varying degrees of U235 purity: 3.5 to 4 percent for use in nuclear power reactors, 10 to 20 percent for research reactors, and 90 percent-plus pure for nuclear weapons.

In a nuclear power plant, the fuel consists of sealed rods containing hundreds of pellets of 3.5 to 4 percent pure uranium. When hit by high-energy neutrons, these pellets undergo controlled chain reaction, giving off intense heat that transforms the surrounding light (ordinary) water into steam that runs the electricity generating turbines. Once these fuel rods have yielded their energy, they are called spent rods. They can be reprocessed with the aim of extracting from them plutonium (Pu239 or Pu241), which can be used as fissile material. Nuclear fuel thus produces both electric power and more nuclear fuel, and is therefore in principle a renewable source of energy.[44] Altogether this is known as a nuclear fuel cycle.

After several hours of talks with the Foreign Ministers of France (Dominique de Villepin), Germany (Joschka Fischer), and the UK (Jack Straw), Rouhani signed an agreement with them on October 21, 2003, to "address and resolve with full transparency" all the IAEA's remaining questions and to "clarify and correct any possible failures and deficiencies" with the IAEA. While stressing its right to develop peaceful nuclear energy "under safeguards," Iran announced that it had decided "voluntarily to suspend all uranium enrichment and reprocessing activities as defined by the IAEA." This one sentence on suspending enrichment took up two hours of "overtime bargaining" with Rouhani, who repeatedly consulted Khamanei. In return, the three Foreign Ministers said in their letter addressed to Iran that the EU would go along with whatever the IAEA decides, that Iran could expect easier access to modern technology and supplies in a range of areas from the EU, and that the EU and Iran would work for regional security, and (by implication) examine Israel's nuclear program.[45]

The Iranian media were quick to compare—rightly—the collective leadership's decision with the equally momentous act by Khomeini fifteen years earlier to swallow the bitter pill and end the Iran-Iraq War.

Iran's representative at the IAEA, Ali Akbar Salehi, flew to Vienna with a bulky dossier with complete documentation on all outstanding issues, and handed it over on October 24, a week ahead of the deadline.

Noticing Khamanei's silence, hard-liners condemned the

agreement, saying Iran should abandon the NPT and opt for an independent nuclear option—just as Israel had done, and so also Pakistan and India. After the Friday prayers in Tehran on October 25, on the eve of the holy month of Ramadan, they mounted a raucous demonstration, chanting, "Additional protocol is our shame."

In his breaking the *iftar* (fast) speech on November 2, Khamanei announced that the decision to cooperate with the IAEA was taken "widely and carefully" in the interests of the Islamic Republic to "foil an American-Zionist maneuver" to isolate Iran. It did not involve capitulation, he added, and if at any stage the process threatened to damage Iran's interests or values, it would be stopped. That silenced the opposition from hardliners. The conservative *Kayhan* (World) headlined Khamanei's speech as "Final Word," and said "our anxiety had been laid to rest by the Leader's wise and vigilant stance."

Iran-European Union-America Triangle

A natural disaster in Iran provided a brief window of opportunity for a thaw in Tehran-Washington relations. A severe earthquake in the historic town of Bam in central Iran on December 26 led to an estimated deaths of thirty thousand people. Within hours of the tragedy, Richard Armitage, U.S. Deputy Secretary of State, telephoned Javad Zarif, Iran's ambassador to the UN, with an offer of emergency help. Iran accepted the gesture. The U.S. sent an eightystrong team of emergency medics and damage assessment experts in a military cargo plane, and Bush announced a ninety-day suspension of U.S. sanctions, which would have impeded the flow of emergency donations and relief technology for the Bam disaster. At the Friday prayer congregation on January 2, 2004, Ayatollah Ahmad Jannati, the conservative head of the Guardians Council, said, "We slap them [the Americans] in the face and say, for your paltry aid you have sent, we cannot set aside our differences and extend the hand of friendship and relations with you. If you are so full of compassion, why don't you go and help the suffering Palestinians, whose earthquake you created?" Several days after the dispatch of the emergency aid to Bam, Washington offered to send a high-ranking delegation including Senator Elizabeth Dole and a member of the Bush family to Tehran. Iran turned down the offer politely, saying it could be taken up later. Aware of the approaching Majlis elections, the conservatives spurned the American offer.

In February 2004, through an exchange of letters between Iran and the EU in Brussels, Tehran agreed not to test or manufacture parts for centrifuges for enriching uranium or put uranium hexafluoride gas in centrifuges. These centrifuges were based on the P-1 [Pakistan-1] design bought by Iran from Dr. Abdul Qadeer Khan, the "Father of the Pakistani Nuclear Bomb." In return, the EU said it would recommend closing the Iran file to the IAEA if there were no new disclosures and the IAEA Director-General, Muhammad El Baradei, was satisfied with Iran's level of cooperation.

In mid-February the IAEA found evidence that the Iranians had more sophisticated uranium-enrichment design—codenamed "P-2," meaning Pakistan-2—involving steel rotor devices for centrifuges, which spin twice as fast as the aluminum rotors in the earlier P-1 design.[46] So in March the IAEA's Board of Governors passed a resolution deploring Iran's failure to declare "potentially arms-related nuclear activities to the IAEA."

IAEA inspectors found 90 percent enriched uranium at sites other than at Kelaye Electric Company near Karaj, housing a laboratory for testing centrifuges for enriching uranium, and Natanz, the site of the proposed uranium-enrichment plant.[47]

In his talks with Baradei in Tehran in early April, Gholam Reza Aghazadeh, head of the Atomic Energy Authority of Iran (AEAI), explained that the traces of enriched uranium came from contaminated centrifuge components purchased abroad, and that such traces would be found everywhere these components were moved or stored, and that the P-2 project ended with prototype production once the AEAI realized that mass production of such centrifuges would make it rely heavily on imported steel parts.[48] Aghazadeh followed up his promise to cease all centrifuge construction activities immediately with another pertaining to uranium enrichment activities a week later. Rouhani told Baradei that he would submit new information about Iran's nuclear program later that month and again in mid-May.

When the IAEA team arrived in Iran in mid-April it found that the Iranians had ceased their centrifuge manufacture and uranium-enrichment activities. In return, the Iranians expected that their file at the IAEA would either be closed or put lower down the agenda.

Instead they found that, in his report to the IAEA Board of Governors in mid-June, Baradei referred to his inspectors discovering traces of highly enriched uranium and undeclared Iranian activity on advanced P-2 centrifuges, which, in his view, showed a concealment pattern in Iran's behavior.

As a consequence, the IAEA Board adopted a resolution deploring Iran's failure to cooperate fully with the investigation of its nuclear program.

This disappointed Tehran. It resumed manufacturing centrifuge parts in July, insisting that carrying out a stable fuel cycle was fundamental to its nuclear power program.[49] In response, the EU suspended its talks on the TCA with Iran.

Meanwhile, following the U.S. accusation, based on its satellite images showing that the buildings in Lavizan near Tehran allegedly used for nuclear activities had been razed between August 2003 and March 2004, the Iranians claimed that site was used first as a military physics institute and then as biotechnology research and development facility, and that it was demolished by the local authority to make a public park after it had settled its dispute with the military.

While Washington constantly pressured the EU Troika to refer Iran to the UN Security Council on its alleged nuclear transgressions, the worsening security situation in Iraq made it vulnerable to Tehran's designs in that troubled country. As described earlier (in Chapter Eight), Tehran managed to keep its feet in both the Anglo-American camp through the Supreme Council of Islamic Revolution in Iraq (SCIRI) and its opponent (through Muqtada al Sadr).

When the Bush administration accused Iran of inciting unrest in Iraq in mid-April 2004, Khamanei rebutted the charge: "There is no need for incitement. You yourself are the biggest and dirtiest of provokers of the Iraqi nation. Why did you enter its home? Why did you tell lies about being after their weapons of mass destruction? Where are they? . . . It must be known that, sooner or later, the Americans will be obliged to leave Iraq in shame and humiliation . . . And, God willing, we shall witness the day when an independent and free Iraq is living under Islam."

This was a nightmare scenario for Washington. Asked what would happen if the interim Iraqi government sought closer ties with Iran, Marc Grossman, Undersecretary of State for Political Affairs, told the Senate Foreign Relations Committee: "That is why we want to have an American ambassador in Iraq"— meaning Viceroy, backed up by 140,000 U.S. troops—who would not tolerate such an Iraqi policy.[50]

Iran's interest in Iraq deepened as a consequence of the Shia uprisings in Iraq in April-May. Shias in Iran marched in their tens of thousands to show solidarity with their coreligionists in Iraq. This was one of the factors that led the U.S. occupation authority led by Paul Bremer to agree to a ceasefire with al Sadr in late May.

In between came the expose of the U.S. troops' abuse and humiliation of Iraqi prisoners at the Abu Ghraib prison. "The very brutal actions of American soldiers—their systematic plan to torture Iraqis, to kill them, to rape them—are outrageous," said

Kharrazi in early May. "If Americans are in Iraq to promote democracy, is this the way to do it?"[51]

In a bizarre twist of affairs, the Iraqi authorities tried to implicate Ahamd Chalabi, the one-time poster boy of the Pentagon neoconservatives, as an agent of the Iranian intelligence and as someone who had been involved in forging currencies. "The U.S. charge of Chalabi and his associates spying for Iran is a pretext that serves two purposes: to sever all ties with Chalabi and to find an excuse to accuse Iran of meddling in Iraqi affairs," noted the Tehran-based *Iran News* on May 23.

Iranian leaders, however, continued to speak with a forked tongue on Iraq. On June 21, Rafsanjani described the UN Security Council Resolution 1546 of June 8, endorsing the Interim Iraqi Government led by Iyad Allawi, as "a step forward toward getting the Iraqis and Americans out of the hell created by the U.S."[52]

By contrast, Gen. Yahya Safavi, commander of the IRGC, described the Allawi government as "U.S.-imposed, treacherous, and perfidious." Calling the Allawi cabinet "a lackey," Khamanei said, "That is what happens when you remove clergy from government."[53]

Washington, in return, redoubled its efforts to persuade the EU to stop negotiating with Iran on the nuclear issue and take it to the UN Security Council. This led Rouhani to fly to The Hague on September 6 to meet with top officials of the EU whose rotating chairmanship was then held by Holland, to counteract America's move. Washington's position was buttressed by Baradei's confidential report to the IAEA Board. Its prematurely leaked version contained "clear reservations" about Tehran's nuclear programs, and concluded that Iran had failed to cooperate fully.

Tehran made a last-minute effort to reassure the IAEA Board that it had no intention of producing nuclear weapons. On September 12, Khamanei issued a fatwa that it was "un-Islamic" to use an atom bomb.[54] Four days later, Hussein Mousavian, head of the foreign policy committee of Iran's Supreme National Security Council, told a press conference in Vienna that Iran's religious leaders had issued a fatwa in 1996 that forbade the use of all weapons of mass destruction. "For Iranians, a religious fatwa is more important than any international convention," he said.[55] But Iran's ploy failed to impress the IAEA Board.

On September 18, the IAEA Board adopted a resolution demanding that Iran should answer all the IAEA's questions and suspend all uranium-enrichment activities by its next scheduled meeting on November 25. While reiterating that Iran's enrichment suspension would be "a necessary but voluntary confidence-building measure rather than an obligation," it warned of "further steps" if it found Iran's response unsatisfactory.

Tehran denounced the resolution, accusing the IAEA of bowing to U.S. pressure, and the EU Troika of failing to keep its part of the October 2003 agreement.

Its officials then conducted marathon negotiations with the representative of the EU Troika in Paris, dragging them out to the last minute before the finalization of Baradei's report on November 15. Iran agreed to suspend its uranium-enrichment and reprocessing programs until there was a "grand bargain" between it and the EU Troika, with the EU guaranteeing nuclear, political, and trade concessions to Iran in return for Tehran's indefinite suspension of these programs. The deal killed the Bush administration's plan to refer Iran to the United Nations Security Council for its lack of full cooperation with the IAEA.

By clinching a deal with the EU, Tehran achieved two strategic objectives: to improve Iranians' living standards by signing a Trade and Cooperation Agreement with the EU whose $13.2 billion worth annual trade with Iran makes it Tehran's leading trading partner; and to forestall America's hegemonistic designs by contributing to the widening of the gap between it and the EU. On the other side, what largely motivated the EU Troika to stay on the diplomatic path was to protect the interests of its companies which had lucrative contracts in Iran's oil and gas industry and were hopeful of securing more in the future.

On November 29, the IAEA Board welcomed Iran's decision "to continue and extend its suspension of all enrichment-related and reprocessing activities," and stated that the suspension was "a voluntary confidence-building measure, not a legal obligation." It reaffirmed Iran's right to develop peaceful nuclear energy programs, while criticizing it for failing to cooperate fully with the IAEA, and leaving open the possibility that Iran had an "undeclared" nuclear program that could be used to make nuclear weapons.[56]

Welcoming the IAEA decision, President Khatami described it as "a definite defeat for our enemies who wanted to pressure Iran by sending its case to the UN Security Council." Leader Khamanei went further by asserting that Iran would proceed with its nuclear program in defiance of the U.S. "The people and officials [of Iran] are not afraid of the political threats made by Powers in the service of [world] oppression," he said. "Iran will never abandon its nuclear program. This is our red line."[57]

Khamanei's hard-line views on America were not widely shared by the Iranian public. The first and last opinion poll on the subject in October 2002 by the National Institute for Public Opinion Research, established by the Ministry of Culture and Islamic Guidance, and commissioned by Muhsin Mirdamadi, head of the Majlis Foreign Affairs and National Security Committee, showed that 74 percent favored "the opening of negotiations with America."[58]

My own straw poll on the interrelated subject of Iran, America and Iraq in July 2004 indicated a favorable view of the U.S. especially among young Iranians. Azim Habibi, the youthful, oval-faced owner of Zaiytoon Pizza and Coffee Shop in the provincial town of Delijan, which plays Iranian pop music, said, "America is a powerful country, and so if the Americans invest money in Iran, it will create jobs here." Hooshang Fallahi, a twenty-two-year-old shopkeeper with a scraggly beard, selling imported watches in Tehran's Grand Bazaar, said, "If Americans stay in Iraq, and thereby impact on Iranian politics, then that will be good for both countries."

Iranian Youth and Women:
The Future

◆ CHAPTER 10 ◆

A visit to the main campus of the Tehran University along Inqilab-e Islami (*lit.*, Islamic Revolution) Avenue—formerly Reza Shah—tree-lined and tranquil, always brings back a flood of memories dating back to the immediate aftermath of the 1979 revolution.

I still recall the wide variety of political literature—leaflets, pamphlets, books, posters—being hawked by young, eager Iranians along Inqilab Avenue throughout the week until late in the evenings. Most of what was on offer was left-wing, rooted in Marxism. It was the same inside the campus, with posters and handwritten slogans offering viewpoints that ranged from Stalinism to Trotskyism, from the thoughts of Chairman Mao Tsetung to the vagaries of his ultra-leftist Defense Minister Lin Piao, and from the pro-Moscow Tudeh Party to maverick Enver Hoja of Albania, aligned with China.

Farhad Ganji, the lean, bespectacled postgraduate student with a bristling mustache, who often accompanied me on such trips, proudly told me that he belonged to the Fedia Khalq (Popular Self-sacrificers), a hitherto clandestine organization formed a decade earlier which, inspired by the revolutionary movements led by Fidel Castro in Cuba and Vo Nguyen Giap in Vietnam, believed in the "Propaganda of the Deed" doctrine of Ernesto "Che" Guevara, originating with the anarchist thinkers of the nineteenth-century America and had carried out guerrilla attacks on selected targets in the hope that the resulting repression by the Shah would lead to increased resistance by the masses, culminating in a people's revolution. Now, he and many other Marxists perceived the recent overthrow of the Shah's regime as the first stage toward a Socialist revolution that would follow.

Then there were other groups that combined Marxist analysis

with Shia Islam, the most important being the Mujahedin-e Khalq Organization (MKO, People's Combatants), which believed that Shia Islam would play a major role in inspiring the masses to join the revolution. Its chief ideologue, Ahmad Rezai, argued that the rebellions led by Shia Imams, especially Hussein ibn Ali, were as much against the usurping Caliphs—who had abandoned the goal of establishing the Order of Divine Unity (worship of One God and the founding of a classless society for universal good)—as they were against feudalists and rich merchants. In modern times, true Muslims must strive to create a classless society by struggling against imperialism, capitalism, dictatorship, and conservative clericalism.[1]

But three years later, the walls of the Tehran University Campus carried well-painted slogans from the official list: "War is as holy as prayer," "Iran will be the cemetery of America," and "Prayer and Blessing for Prophet Muhammad's Family bring you close to being a devotee of God." This was one of the minor achievements of the University Jihad launched in the wake of Ayatollah Ruhollah Khomeini's appointment of the seven-member Cultural Revolutionary Committee (CRC) of clergy and scholarly laymen in June 1980. Its task was to end cultural imperialism of the West on the East, and to imbue universities with Islamic values.

The CRC redesigned curricula, sponsored new textbooks or modified the existing ones in the light of Islamic teachings, and made the teaching staff gain a better understanding of Islam. By mid-1983, the Center of Textbooks had produced three thousand textbooks, either original or in translation.

I gained an insight into how the Islamization process at Iranian universities had proceeded on a warm, sunny July morning in 2004—from Dr. Gholam Abbas Tavassoli, professor of sociology at Tehran University's smaller Ale-Ahmad Campus. A short, muscular, soft-spoken man, with graying beard and hair, he had just published a study of the new generation of Iran. "I was the chairperson of the humanities and social sciences during the three years of cultural revolution when the universities were closed so that all textbooks could be examined [from an Islamic viewpoint] and new ones prepared, if necessary," he said.

There were also political considerations, which Tavassoli left unmentioned. Universities and colleges were the main breeding grounds of the MKO and other opposition parties. By shutting them the Islam regime inhibited the growth of its opponents. Had these institutions been open at the time of President Abol Hassan Bani-Sadr's ouster in June 1981, the authorities would have faced a much bigger challenge than they actually did.[2]

The new regime wanted to reform the whole educational system from the primary level upward. It provided fresh Islamic materials to primary schools within a few months of the revolution. It showed similar speed in furnishing secondary schools with Islamic textbooks.

"As for universities," continued Tavassoli, "we compared our courses with those in Algeria, France, America, and others. We went through all the courses in humanities and social sciences— economics, sociology, law, political science, psychology, education, etc. We called some leading clergy to Tehran University. Then we had discussions with the clerics in Qom on the ideological aspect. We agreed that anything against Islam in social sciences was out. But, overall, we only changed 10–15 percent of the courses. We introduced courses in Islamic morals, Islamic ethics, and so on. That is the only change we made. Also we agreed that women were not to be examiners."

It was not all smooth sailing, however. "Initially, the clergy said that universities must be Islamized," Tavassoli said. "Clerics are very narrow in their views, they know little about the outside world. They believed that social sciences contained Western ideology or were based on Western ideology and that they were not independent disciplines. Initially they wanted to start new courses like Islamic economy, Islamic sociology, even Islamic physics and Islamic chemistry, and so on, which was to be ideological. We thought this to be impracticable. It took them time to absorb our reasoning. We said, 'We recognize that Iran is 98 percent Muslim, but it contains pre-Islamic influences and it has also been influenced by the West. So there is a mixture of influences, and you cannot separate these three strands. On the other hand we accept that we must indigenize Western ideas and techniques in the light of our own history and culture, but you cannot create a parallel discipline.' Finally they came around to accepting our argument. And when universities reopened we cut ourselves off from the clergy." By then, however, some forty thousand teachers, considered insufficiently Islamic, were dismissed.[3]

As it was, universities reopened in stages. During my 1983 visit, I discovered that of the five universities and eleven colleges in Greater Tehran, twelve were partially open—that is, their physical sciences, engineering, technology, and medicine faculties were functioning. They were readmitting only old students. Those linked to the secular or Islamic leftist groups were executed, arrested, tortured, or forced into the underground. The eighteen thousand-strong student body at Tehran University was reduced to four thousand five hundred, all of them exempted from paying fees, and three-fifths of them receiving government grants. They now owed their loyalty to the university's Islamic Association. Though these associations appeared much later than secular, leftist groups on university campuses under monarchy, they quickly consolidated their hold over students after their first national conference in September 1979.

At Tehran University the Islamic Association worked closely with the Central Committee of the University Jihad. "Jihad in our case means cleansing the universities of un-Islamic ideologies and persons," explained Muhsin Shaikhpour, the earnest Central Committee Secretary-General with thick raven hair and beard.

"We tend to concentrate on keeping out the counterrevolution-aries." By this he meant the MKO—called *munafqeen* (hyp-ocrites), those who claim to be Muslim but are inspired by un-Islamic ideologies. Those now active in the Jihad movement had proved their Islamic credentials long before the establish-ment of the University Jihad: they had fought pitched battles with the MKO, Fedai Khalq, and other leftist groups on cam-puses. At the same time they had started vetting their teachers. "We don't mind if a student holds different political ideas from ours; but he must not actively oppose the Islamic state," Shaikh-pour told me emphatically. Little wonder there was no dissent on the campus. The unanimity with which students and teachers headed for the Tehran University mosque for the 12.06 P.M. prayer illustrated this to me dramatically.

When I visited the mosque twenty-one years later, I found it spruced up, with its stone minarets glinting in the bright sun-shine, and its entrance embellished with the sign "Allah, Ali, Muhammad, Hussein, Ya Mahdi" written in Arabic calligraphy. Its football pitch inside the campus had been turned into a vast meeting place, covered with tarpaulin supported by steel rods, for the Friday prayer congregation, with an enclosed dais for the speakers next to a raised platform for invited guests and televi-sion crews. On the rear of the platform were inscribed the words in Persian and English: "Message of the Leader of the Revolution, 'In Islam, propagation means showing the world the truth about Islam and intraducing [*sic*] Islamic revolution to the world.' "

This, indeed, was the first statement I read as I entered the campus at its main entrance, now marked by a large billboard, dis-playing the words Girami Abad (in Persian) and JOBIRAN www.Jobiran.com (in English). The juxtaposition reminded me of Tavassoli's statement: "On one hand some clerics want Islam to cover all aspects of life and education; on the other hand all of them want modern science and technology, the very latest." So,

Internet, e-mailing, Internet cafes, and mobile phones are very much in vogue in Tehran and other urban centers throughout Iran.

Outside the Department of Legal and Political Sciences, I came across a group of four students, two male and two female. Both women were wearing discreet makeup and—instead of the gloomy, forbidding chador—a fashionable two-part dress, called *roopash*, consisting of a *roosari*, a head scarf that is often silken, and a *maantean*, a three-quarter-length raincoatlike jacket made of light-colored material, buttoning down the front, with a string close to the bottom of the rib, that can be tightened to make the jacket hug the body. ("What eighteen-year-old girls do is to go to a clothes shop and pick up a coat which is supposed to be for a twelve-year-old," explained the wife of a South Asian diplomat. "That means the length of the coat also gets shortened.")

Ghazal Mihrani was a pretty French-speaking woman with discreet makeup, and Kiana Jalaliyan, a small and plain looking, yet lively woman, fluent in English, equally restrained in her makeup. Both were studying law—specifically law in Shia Islam, known as the Jaafari Code, named after the Sixth Imam Sadiq al Jaafar. They hoped to work with legal firms in Tehran, and saw no impediment in their professional career, except that as women they could not become judges—although they could assist judges. One of their professors, whom they greatly admired, was Shirin Ebadi, a round-faced, matronly, fifty-six-year-old human rights lawyer in Iran, who won the Nobel Prize for Peace in 2003.

Born into a family of academics in Hamadan, Shirin Ebadi grew up in Tehran. She secured her law degree from Tehran University at twenty-one, and became a junior judge after a six-month apprenticeship in adjudication. Two years later she obtained a doctorate with honors in private law from the same university. After serving in various jobs in the Justice Department, she was appointed President of Bench 24 of the Tehran City Court, the first woman in Iran to hold such a position.

Since the Islamic regime did not allow women to become judges, Ebadi and other female judges were demoted to clerks. When they protested, the authorities promoted them to "experts" in the Justice Department. She resigned. In the absence of the Bar Association, which became moribund after the 1979 revolution, she applied for an attorney's license to the Justice Ministry. It rejected her application.

She became a full-time homemaker and mother. She also published books on different aspects of the law, from medical practice to architecture to workers' rights. It was not until 1992 that she was able to secure an attorney's license. She became involved in human rights violation cases, and was appointed an observer for the New York-based Human Rights Watch in 1996. She represented the families of the murdered Dariush Foruhar, an old leader of the secular National Front, and his wife Parvane, in late 1998. She also took up the case of Ezzat Ebrahimi-Nejad, killed during the attack on the Tehran University dormitory in July 1999, and worked hard to trace the main culprits behind the dormitory raid.

A year later she was one of the two lawyers specializing in human rights who were charged with disruption of the political situation in the country by colluding with Ilah-e Sharifpour Hicks, a New York-based Human Rights Watch representative, during her visit to Tehran in May 2000, to produce and distribute a videotape providing damaging inside information by Amir Farshad Ibrahimi, a former member of the Ansar-e Hizbollah, about the functioning of the right-wing vigilantes, and detained briefly.[4]

Later that year, she published *History and Documentation of Human Rights in Iran* in the United States. Her Nobel Prize for Peace made her the first Muslim woman ever to win the prestigious award. Yet the state-run broadcasting media held back the news for several hours, and then mentioned the prize as a fifteen-second item before the weather report, without stating what the award was for. She was in Paris when she heard the news. On her return home, she was warmly received by well-wishers at the airport. But the official reaction remained at best lukewarm.

Firmly rooted in Iranian soil and history, she treats Islam as her primary premise, and argues for new interpretations to align the Islamic Law with human rights, democracy, and freedom of speech and association. In her speeches abroad, Ebadi has been critical of the double standards of the West, particularly America—a fact that both Ghazal Mihrani and Kiana Jalaliyan seemed well aware of. So was Ghazal's boyfriend, Eiman Pirouzkhawa, a clean-shaven, square-shouldered man, also studying law. Since they were not married yet, they could not be seen holding hands on the campus, a restriction that the members of the Baseej unit posted at the campus enforced rigidly.

It was in 1988, when Khomeini decided to put in place measures that would secure the future of the Islamic Republic, that he ordered the establishment of Baseej units on campuses. "Imam Khomeini had a strong belief in the struggle against those who, with the support of the East and West, would exploit the people," said Hamid Chizari, a Baseej leader in north Tehran, in an interview with Geneive Abdo, a resident American journalist, in 2000. "He believed that the only force to stop them was the Baseej. That is why he decided to form the Baseej on the university campuses. The university is the scene of science, intellect, and a battleground for the cultural struggle. As has been ordered by Imam Khomeini, the Baseej has tried its best to establish spiritual values in accordance with our Islamic faith. All the students in the universities are Muslim, and we have done our best to fight global arrogance."[5]

"Global arrogance" is the substitute term for American imperialism that the Islamic regime, keen to distinguish itself from secular Left at home and abroad, uses routinely. It is a protocol inherited from Khomeini who, instead of saying "the exploited," used the term "the needy" or "the deprived"—again to separate himself from the terminology of the Left.

Actually, the Baseej on the campuses do more than enforce the Islamic dress code and other social behavior. "They collect information—especially about the extracurricular books students are reading—for their files and for the Intelligence Ministry," Sadiq Zibakalam, a slim, clean-shaven, bespectacled professor of political science at Tehran University, told me.[6]

Dissidents were often to be found in the faculty of political science, which at Tehran University was part of the Department of Legal and Political Sciences. Amidst the group I talked to at the Tehran University campus, Ali Anwari, a tall, slim man with sharp features, turned out to be a student of political science. While discussing international relations and diplomacy, he showed uncommon maturity. "Every country has its own interests, and pursues them irrespective of the religion of the majority," he said. "In Iran there are two groups, and each one has different ideas about how to deal with America." Others agreed. "America will be inimical to Iran so long as it has not found some other country to focus on as an enemy," said Kiana Jalaliyan.

This was a safe subject for students to discuss with a lone, visiting foreign journalist who was escorted neither by a government minder nor a university's public relations official or a local translator. What was not safe to broach was the fifth anniversary of the 1999 student protest which had just passed—almost unnoticed in the capital and elsewhere.

The Six-Day Tremor and After

On July 7, 1999, the Majlis passed the first reading of a bill to amend the 1985 Press Law by 125 to 90 votes. The amendments required newspaper publishers to submit the list of their employees to the judiciary, and journalists to reveal their sources, and empowered the Press Court to overrule jury verdicts, conduct summary trials, and pass on extremely serious cases to Revolutionary Courts dealing with accusations of treason and endangering national security. What had goaded the conservative majority in the Majlis to adopt these amendments to the Press Law was the doubling of the number of publications to 1,200, following Muhammad Khatami's election as President, most of the new ones favoring reform.[7]

The Majlis's move coincided with the closure of the Salaam, edited by Ayatollah Muhammad Khoeiniha, by the Special Court for Clergy (SCC) after it had published a secret memorandum that detailed efforts by Said Emami of the Intelligence Ministry to rein in the pro-Khatami media.[8] The SCC, charged with trying clerics, upheld the Intelligence Ministry's complaint that by publishing a confidential document the Salaam had created doubts in the public mind and endangered national security.

Late on July 8, about five hundred Tehran University students held a peaceful protest meeting about the Salaam's closure at the university dormitory complex in Amirabad, a Tehran suburb, several miles (kilometers) from the downtown campus. They were attacked by Ansar-e Hizbollah vigilantes while the Law Enforcement Forces (LEF) looked on.

During the night of July 8–9, some four hundred men in black trousers and white shirts, wielding long rubberized green clubs broke into the dormitories, vandalized them, and beat up students. At first the LEF watched but later joined the assailants. Shots rang out and claimed the life of an off-duty soldier who was a guest. Many students were injured and about two hundred were arrested. According to the LEF, some officers had entered the dormitories earlier without authorization and were taken hostage, and so other officers, also acting without orders, stormed the dormitories to rescue their colleagues. Still and television pictures recorded many vandalized rooms, and broken furniture and windowpanes, and some rooms that were gutted.[9]

On July 9, while the Education Ministry criticized the LEF, thousands of students assembled outside the Amirabad dormitories, chanting "Death to Dictators." They then marched to the main campus in central Tehran. Here, protesting students were joined by their colleagues from other universities and colleges. The single most important student body was the pro-reform University-Seminary Unity Consolidation Bureau—or Unity Consolidation Bureau (UCB), for short—which had emerged after the Iran-Iraq War from the earlier Islamic Associations among students, with the aim of bringing together universities and seminaries. The UCB operated from a modest building in central Tehran, the office of its six officials elected by its fifty thousand members nationwide.

At the central Tehran campus some ten thousand students rallied and blocked the main thoroughfare. Others began a sit-in. When Leader Khamanei's representative arrived to address them, he was heckled and driven away. The protesters then marched to the Interior Ministry (in charge of the LEF), shouting, "Death to despotism, death to dictators," clashing with the LEF on the way. Some protesters shouted, "Freedom or death" while others, more daring, *Khamanei haya kon, Rahbari ro raha kon* (Khamanei have shame, let go leadership).

Starting with a demand to punish those who had attacked the university residence halls, the students added thirteen more, including "making secretive state institutions, all the way up to the Assembly of Experts, give full public accounting of their activities and decisions; public investigations into intelligence and security operations against dissidents; freedom for all political prisoners; an end to house arrests; and an end to the bans on any newspapers; the repeal of the new press law and the firing of the head of the Iranian radio and television."[10] This led to the resignation of the Education Minister.

The pro-reform press gave extensive and prominent coverage to the events.

On July 10, the Supreme National Security Council (SNSC), which included two personal representatives of the Leader, chaired by President Khatami, condemned the LEF raid, and appointed a committee of inquiry. Khatami's statement, read on the state-run radio, stated that the SNSC had dismissed the LEF captain whose unit had stormed the student dormitories, reprimanded the LEF commander of the Tehran region, Brig. Gen. Farhad Nazari, ordered the release of all detained students, and promised compensation for those injured. The SNSC also promised to scrutinize radical right-wing vigilante groups like the Ansar-e Hizbollah. Later, the LEF Commander in Chief, Gen. Hedayat Loftian, would tell a closed session of the Majlis that ninety-nine LEF personnel had been arrested for raiding the dormitories. And the number of Ansars arrested would reach one hundred. The SNSC coupled its statement about the dismissals and arrests with a warning that no further demonstrations should be held without the prior permission of the Interior Ministry.

But this did not satisfy the students. On July 11, thousands assembled for a rally at Tehran University's main campus. Some chanted, "Either Islam and law—or another revolution," while others shouted, "Ansar commits crimes, and Leader supports them; O Great Leader, shame on you." This brought a riposte from Hojatalislam Hassan Rouhani, Secretary-General of the SNSC. "Offending the status of velayat-e faqih is tantamount to offending the entire nation, is tantamount to offending all Muslims," he said. "Offending the pillar is tantamount to offending our revolutionary values." [11]

Street protest spread to universities in seventeen other cities, including Hamadan, Isfahan, Mashhad, Shiraz, Tabriz, and Yazd, despite the fact that Khamanei condemned the dormitory raids as "a bitter and unacceptable incident." The authorities imposed a blanket ban on meetings and demonstrations as the number of arrested students reached one thousand. (Most of them would be released but only after they had signed a declaration that they would not participate in politics in the future.) Among the protesters, a split developed, with the moderate majority arguing that they had achieved their aim of highlighting their backing for the *Salaam* and political reform. Among their leaders was Ali Afshari, a mature student. "They [conservatives] want to show that the protests were aimed at overthrowing the system even though they were not," he told Geneive Abdo in September.[12] It was the radical minority among university students that disagreed and took to the streets, inadvertently providing a foil for disgruntled nonstudents to escalate the protest and turn it into a violent episode.

On July 12, journalists working for some twenty newspapers declared a national strike starting the next day. The Tehran University campus drew a bigger crowd than before. When Khamanei's emissary tried to read the Leader's statement, he was silenced by loud shouts of "Commander in Chief, resign!" and "Down with dictator."

With the LEF besieging the campus on foot, motorcycle-borne Ansars patrols circling around the security forces' noose, and LEF helicopters clattering overhead, a bloody confrontation was in the making. As student protestors started marching toward the city center, the LEF, in full riot gear of helmets and shields, pounced on them, forcing them to retreat to the campus grounds, where they erected barricades hastily. To block the LEF and the Ansars, they burnt old tires at the main entrance. The LEF retaliated with tear gas as the Ansars, getting off their vehicles, and wielding clubs, chains, cables, and metal rods, chased the students. Mayhem ensued. The LEF forced the protestors into cages stashed on pickup trucks, which sped off to various jails, and arrested photographers trying to record the scene on film.

Khatami broke his silence by describing the assault on the

student residence halls as "one of the most bitter and unacceptable events since the revolution," and urged restraint. "Now students should cooperate with the government and allow law and order to be established," he said. "You should not commit illegal acts so that in calm fashion we can make a firm decision in the interests of the system." That night the state-run television aired a stern warning: "The Law Enforcement Forces have been ordered to create order and stability—and to prevent any unlawful gathering."[13] The authorities locked all the gates to the Tehran University.

That did not deter the students. On July 13, they gathered outside the main entrance to Tehran University, shouting, "People are hungry, but the clergy live like kings," "We don't want mercenary police," and "We don't want government of force." They were joined by nonstudent residents of the capital, who chanted, "Students, students, we support you." On the other side, the LEF were backed not only by the Ansars, bearing assorted clubs, chains, cables, and even meat cleavers, but also the Baseej militia and the Islamic Revolutionary Guards as well as plainclothes policemen and intelligence operatives—all of them directed by LEF officers aboard low-flying helicopters. As before, LEF riot squads fired tear gas canisters at the demonstrators and fired their guns into the air, a signal to the Ansars and Baseej militia to chase the protestors. Running battles ensued between the protestors and the LEF, with the angry agitators smashing shop windows, overturning buses and LEF vehicles, and targeting banks. Ahmad Batebi, a student leader, sporting a goatee beard and a bandana, held up a blood-stained T-shirt of a classmate behind his long-haired head, for the cameras—an image that would be distributed by international news agencies and be splashed on the cover of the *Economist* weekly. He would soon be arrested, tortured, and sentenced to death, the latter being commuted one to fifteen years in jail after appeals were made to Khamanei for clemency.[14]

As demonstrations occurred elsewhere—outside the Interior Ministry and at the Inqilab (i.e., Revolution) Square and the Grand Bazaar, where rioters set ablaze two banks and caused an instant shutting down of the bazaar—the personnel of the LEF and its supporting agencies spread out to the north and south of the university campus to cover a large area of the capital. This in turn led to a large-scale closure of offices, gas stations, and shopping centers, and a suspension of public transport.

The state-run broadcasting media repeatedly aired a speech by Khamanei urging an end to violence, and blaming foreign enemies, especially America, for the rioting. By sunset, the LEF had restored law and order, with the Baseej and the Ansars aiding them to patrol the streets all through the night while chanting, "We donate the blood of our veins to the Leader."[15] By then the street protest had resulted in fourteen hundred arrests.

That evening in a television speech Khatami deplored the destruction of buildings in the city center and the Grand Bazaar, and pointed out that some of those arrested had no links with academic circles and were not even students. He added that a peaceful protest by students had degenerated into a riot led by "people with evil aims [who] intend to foster violence in society," and declared, "We shall stand in their way."

Defense Minister Ali Shamskhani added his voice, saying that order would be restored "at any price." In practice, the security forces achieved this aim without having to resort to shooting. As Tehran's LEF commander, Brig. Gen. Farhad Ansari, would note later, "The turmoil that followed the attack on the students' dormitories on July 9 was controlled by the LEF without the firing of a single bullet."[16] A fortnight later, Khatami would make the same point in a speech in Hamadan: "Today in order to put down the riots and in order to put out the flames of violence for the nation, others use tanks, armored cars, and heavy weapons, but our forces did not use firearms to tackle the rioting." Those familiar with the ways of the police in Third World countries found the Iranian LEF's overall behavior restrained.

Nonetheless, the episode created tensions within the ruling establishment. It emerged later that twenty-four Islamic Revolutionary Guard Corps commanders addressed a private letter to Khatami warning him that their patience was running out and that he must curb violations against the Islamic system.[17]

On July 14, the political-clerical establishment banded together. The followers of both Khatami and Khamanei joined hands to organize a popular show of support for the regime. In Tehran between five hundred thousand and one million people participated in a peaceful march, chanting, "Death to America!," "Death to Israel!," and "Death to hypocrites!" They carried white banners proclaiming, "My life belongs to the Leader."

Addressing the vast rally, Rouhani, said, "We will resolutely and decisively quell any attempt to rebel." He coupled this with a promise that "security agencies will continue probing the tragic dormitory incident until all the roots which caused the incident are investigated and reported to the public." (The SNSC committee's report later cleared Gen. Hedayat Loftian, and blamed a number of Tehran LEF captains, who acted "more out of anger than necessity." Also, it concluded, the far-right vigilantes—meaning Ansar-e Hizbollah—played a significant role in provoking the LEF to attack the students, and called on the Intelligence Ministry to investigate them. In a message read out to the rally, Khamanei warned that the trouble might not be over yet, and added, "My Baseej children must reserve the necessary readiness and be present at any scene where they are needed to intimidate and crush the enemies."[18]

Three weeks later, the fifty thousand-strong Baseej force in Tehran conducted the largest military maneuvers ever conducted. They carried out drills to break up demonstrations, staged mock commando raids and parachute drops.

A wide-ranging reaction by the authorities to the street protest had followed earlier. On August 3, 1999, the conservative judiciary chief, Ayatollah Muhammad Yazdi, endorsed a bill passed by the Majlis that described political crimes as "any violent or peaceful act by a person or group against the regime," and outlawed "any contact or exchange of information, interviews or collusion with foreign embassies, organizations, parties, or media which could be judged harmful to Iran's independence, national unity or the interests of the Islamic Republic."[19] Later that month, the Special Court for Clergy banned senior editors of the *Salaam* from journalism for five years.

In the Majlis, the conservatives reneged on a painstakingly negotiated compromise that would have weakened the Guardians Council's authority to vet candidates for office at the national level.

On the student front, the authorities used Islamist students to infiltrate the UCB. Within a year, the UCB split between moderates and radicals, and this weakened its role. The division solidified when Khamanei intervened to kill the new liberal press bill in August 2000, and Khatami admitted on television that he lacked the authority as President to perform his job of implementing the constitution.

Meanwhile, in its *Hoviyat* (Identity) magazine program, the state-run television aired statements by the arrested student leaders in which they admitted receiving money from American sources and that it was their followers who had triggered street violence that they then blamed on the Ansar vigilantes.

While these apparently stage-managed admissions failed to convince either pro-reform journalists or a majority of the public, thus highlighting the conservative authorities' inability to terrorize the citizenry, overall, the street protest of July 1999 resulted in diminishing students' power to shape the sociopolitical system.

As a token concession, the authorities allowed some cultural freedom. They allowed indigenous Persian pop music to be recorded and sold once it had been cleared by the censors, thereby providing young Iranians with an indigenous alternative to foreign pop music.

Such a gesture, however, was insufficient to dissipate the underlying disaffection. This became apparent when the Majlis elections in February–May 2000 became highly charged, and many reformist publications were closed down in between the first and second runs of the poll.

On the eve of the first anniversary of the student protest, Khatami expressed his opposition to the far-right vigilantes and their thinking. But that had no impact either on students or on Ansars. On July 8, 2000, the protesting students, bolstered by thousands of disgruntled nonstudents from the capital's poorer neighborhoods, faced the Law Enforcement Forces, backed by the Ansars, at the Inqilab (i.e., Revolution) Square. A popular slogan of the past year—"People are hungry, but the clergy live like kings"—reappeared along with a new one: "Khatami, show your power or resign." As in the past, the LEF fired tear gas canisters while the Ansars chased the demonstrators with broken bottles, chains, and knives. The day ended with several dozen arrests and injuries to many. Commenting on the riot, Leader Khamanei warned that Western powers were behind plans to bring down the Islamic system just as the Soviet system had been brought down.[20]

Khamanei's reference to the Soviet Union was pertinent but his placing of the blame on the West was flawed. Under reformist Mikhail Gorbachev (r. 1986–91), the Soviet Union entered a period of glasnost (*lit.*, transparency) and perestroika (*lit.*, restructuring). The disclosures and condemnations of the past injustices and cruelties that the Soviet people had suffered during several decades of a repressive, totalitarian rule under the Communist Party of the

Soviet Union surfaced with such an unrestrained force that they severely undermined popular faith in the seventy-year-old Marxist-Leninist system per se, and paved the way, inadvertently, for the collapse of the Soviet Union in 1991. While willing to liberalize the Islamic system in Iran, both economically and politically, Khamanei and his close aides apparently wanted to control the speed and direction of the process to avoid the recent fate of the Soviet Union as well as a severe backlash by conservatives.

Generational Problem

During the 1999 student unrest, Iranian leaders reiterated the outstanding role that students played in society. Students also formed an increasingly large segment of the nation, according to the figures released by the Education Ministry. Between 1979 and 1999, when the population doubled, the student body rose almost threefold, from 7 million to 19 million. The overall literacy rate jumped from 58 percent to 82 percent, and the number of university graduates grew ninefold, from a base of 430,000. At any given time, three-quarter million Iranians were enrolled at universities and colleges. "Students are the engine of change," said Nasser Hadian, a political scientist at Tehran University. "Their sheer numbers give them more weight than in other societies—or even compared with the student movement during the revolution."[21]

Sexual segregation, introduced by the authorities after the revolution at all levels of education, resulted in a dramatic jump in the registration of girls from rural or socially conservative urban background in primary and secondary schools. Between 1976 and 1996 (both being census years), literacy rate among women almost tripled, from 28 percent to 80 percent.

So swift was this growth that colleges and universities could not cope with the influx. With increased competition for limited seats, university places became highly prized. The government compounded the problem by giving priority to the children of those who died or suffered injuries in the Iran-Iraq War (amounting to one million), clerics, military and security officers, civil servants, bazaar traders, and the indigent.

After an applicant had passed the university entrance exam, he/she had to prove his/her moral suitability in Islamic terms. This comprised of the applicant establishing that the environment at home was Islamic—that is, his/her parents abstained from alcoholic drinks and prayed regularly, and that the mother veiled herself on leaving the house—and declaring his/her loyalty to the Islamic regime and its institutions and pledging to have no ties to any opposition group at home or abroad. To check the veracity of the applicant's statements, the authorities often dispatched investigators to interview his/her relatives, friends, and neighbors. Given such a strict selection process, it was a shock for the regime's leaders to encounter an open protest by university students in Tehran. On the other hand, they were not totally unaware of the emerging political disaffection on campuses. In 1998, the Majlis passed a law that authorized a considerable rise in the number of Baseej militia posted at campuses, and provided for financial and professional assistance to them from the Defense, Education, and Health Ministries as well as the Islamic Revolutionary Guard Corps.

In his *A Study of Student Political Behavior in Today's Iran*, published in Tehran in 1999, Iranian political scientist Majid Muhammadi concluded that university students fell into three categories defined primarily by their parents' social background: (a) those brought up in traditional Islamic culture that is prevalent among working and traditional middle classes; (b) those raised in secular or nominally Islamic culture predominant among established or emergent modern middle classes; and (c) those reared in a hybrid environment. The first traditionalist category was actively loyal to the Islamic regime and its Leader, and was disinclined to ask questions or raise doubts. It had much in common with, say, the students of the Marvi Seminary near the Grand Bazaar.[22] The second group kept a very low profile and shunned politics. Unlike these groups, the last category was caught in a dilemma: while it was linked to Islam through tradition it was also attracted to modern, Westernized culture, politically and socially. In the process of trying to resolve this conflict, members of this group became politically active. They strove to enlarge the area of political and social freedom as a means to counter social repression and administrative corruption and make the system more transparent and accountable.

An example of applying Western political culture to Iran was the agitating students' demand to make secretive state institutions—all the way up to and including the Assembly of Experts, which elects the Leader—give full public accounting of their activities and decisions. What was involved here was the twin concept of accountability and transparency.

The mechanism for choosing the Leader and his powers was a subject of heated discussion among politically conscious students. Summing up a prevalent view among such students, Ali Tavakoli, a plump student activist sporting a brown beard, said, "When Imam Khomeini was alive, because of his special characteristics, no one asked if he was supreme or not. But afterward, people believed that the Leader should operate according to the constitution—where the duty and position are clear. He is subject to it, like everyone else."[23]

Actually, the radical faction in the Unity Consolidation Bureau favored abolishing the Leader's office and instituting greater separation between Islam and politics than was the case then. While maintaining that Islam reduced people's rights, student radicals did not advocate abandoning it altogether and opting for secularism.

Others like Heshmatollah Tabarzadi, head of the Union of

Muslim University Students and Graduates, a narrow-eyed, bearded pious leader rarely without his prayer beads and with a long history of political activism, advocated amending the constitution to allow Iranian voters to elect the Leader and strictly define his powers. Such a viewpoint gelled with what Abdul Karim Soroush, a leading Islamic thinker, had been advocating: the ideal Islamic Republic should be ruled by whosoever is the best Leader, whether secular or religious, and that every citizen should have an equal right to run. (These views were expressed before April 2000 when the newly amended Press Law outlawed criticism of the constitution or the Leader.)

Leaving aside these radical views, the mainstream rank and file UCB members were agreed on curtailing mullahs' political role, and expanding freedom of expression and other constitutional rights mentioned in the constitution.

Overshadowing these sophisticated arguments, however, were some bald facts. In 1999, roughly half of Iran's population of sixty-five million were under twenty-one, and two-thirds were under twenty-five. They had no direct experience or memory of the pre-Islamic regime of the Shah, and therefore their commitment to the Islamic regime was less than total. "The clergy have yet to find a way to get through to them," Shirzad Bozroughmehr, the amiable editor of the *Iran News*, told me in Tehran in August 1999. "The postrevolutionary educational system has not socialized them in the way they would like." This was borne out by a study done earlier that whereas 83 percent of university students watched television, only 5 percent watched religious programs. Of the 58 percent who read extracurricular books, barely 6 percent showed interest in religious literature.[24]

The gap between the pre- and postrevolution generations was aptly summarized by Sadiq Zibakalam, who was imprisoned for his political views under the Shah. "My generation is not going to turn its back on the revolution because if we did, we would be like mothers saying goodbye to our children, we would be saying goodbye to our existence," he said. "But the younger generation has no attachment, no feeling for the revolution. They were just babies. When I teach the revolution in my class, many of my students just look out the window and watch the clock for the lesson to end. They say, 'What about us? You had your revolution and your war. What's in it for us?' And I can't give them the answer."[25]

A suggestion to rectify the situation came from a student at the conservative Marvi Seminary in Tehran. "Given the religious fabric of most families, young people are actually suited for religious education, just as was the case before the revolution," he said. "I think the gap created by the clergy's other activities after the revolution consists of insufficient contact between the clergy and the youth."[26] In other words, if clerics were to channel less of their time and energy into day-to-day politics, and more into education and stay in close touch with students, then the young people's interest in Islam would rise. This is a debatable point.

On the other hand, what indisputably impinges on the daily lives of university students and other young Iranians are the restrictions on their social and personal freedoms: going to mixed sex parties, holding hands of someone other than a marriage partner, drinking alcoholic beverages, listening to modern Western music, watching foreign television channels via satellite, and having extramarital sex.

While reformers recognized that such restrictions were alienating the young from the regime, their conservative opponents justified them as necessary to uphold Islamic morality.

In practice, however, these prohibitions were being undermined, partly through the use of satellite dishes to receive foreign television channels, and partly through bribes to the Law Enforcement Forces. A ban on satellite dishes imposed in spring 1995 had not stopped their use. Depending on the diameter of the receptor, an Iranian family could watch up to thirty Western and Asian channels, including the pop music channel MTV, Rupert Murdoch's Star TV, and the BBC World Service. "If you live in high-rise blocks in north Tehran, you go for a dish on the roof which is then branched out to different apartments," explained Bozroughmehr to me in July 2004. "Then those with their own mansions with high walls put up these dishes on balconies. In [affluent] North Tehran probably one out of two houses has a satellite dish connection. Every so often these are taken down by the authorities and owners fined about ten thousand Iranian rials [twelve U.S. dollars]. Often the offenders submit old equipment which is then confiscated. Even in South Tehran there are now satellite dishes, although very much fewer." Two months earlier, while the authorities banned *Marmoolak* (Lizard), a Persian-language movie that satirizes mullahs after it had proved a record hit with moviegoers in Tehran and elsewhere, its CD-ROM was freely available in Tehran's stores. I got one.

When the new Voice of America (VOA) television program in Persian proved popular in 1996, with pirated versions being rented out in Tehran and elsewhere, the government launched a crackdown. Although the VOA broadcasts were apolitical, it acted swiftly to stifle any political aftereffect that might follow. At the same time, the popularity of this VOA program in Persian made the Iranian broadcasting officials sit up and take notice. It made them realize that their audiences, especially the young, wanted programs that were less moralizing and rigid and more entertaining. But they did not know how to achieve this without transgressing what they perceived as fundamental values of the Islamic revolution. Nonetheless, as a tentative start, they decided to permit the Islamic Revolutionary Guard Corps to run its own national television channel with stress on light entertainment and music almost free of ideological content. To balance this, they considered establishing a nationwide Islamic radio network with its headquarters in the holy city of Qom.

None of this lowered university students' interest in foreign television channels. "Most university students are affected by propaganda by non-Islamic media," Professor Gholam Abbas Tavassoli told me in July 2004. "They are exposed to the outside world, to the monarchist viewpoint, to the Mujahedin Khalq Organization viewpoint, and so on. Many people have access to satellite TV. And so they are exposed to the BBC, CNN, VOA, and other Western broadcasting media. Also there is a reaction against the clerical rule among students. In the last five years, there is a move among university students towards secularism. They are moving away from Islam and want pure democracy [not Islamic democracy]. This is a problem for the leadership."

Evidently, many university students have also been exposed to the ideas of Abdul Karim Soroush. A balding, bearded, bespectacled man with a prominent nose, he was at one time head of the Research Faculty for History and Philosophy of Science at Tehran University. Born in 1945 to a grocer father and a highly religious mother in south Tehran, he obtained a degree in pharmacology. After working in a pharmaceutical laboratory in Tehran, he went to London in the early 1970s to study analytical chemistry, but soon switched to philosophy. After securing a doctorate, he published a book, *The Restless Nature of the World*, in which he dealt with the constant flux of the universe and time as the fourth dimension. In the fall of 1978 he traveled to Paris to meet Khomeini, who later appointed him to the Cultural Revolution Committee. As its spokesman, he had periodic meetings with Khomeini.

Once mullahs had lost the leadership of charismatic Khomeini with his death in 1989, they came under critical scrutiny by Islamic intellectuals such as Soroush. He found that since some of them were not particularly scholarly and some were less than pious, their comprehension of Islam did not deserve to be accepted unquestioningly.

His own study of Islam and Islamic thinkers had turned him

into a disciple of India-born Sir Muhammad Iqbal, a pious layperson, who published a seminal book, *The Reconstruction of Muslim Thought*, in 1937, and who differentiated between religion and science of religion—that is, thoughts of religion. Taking his cue from Iqbal, Soroush distinguished between religion, which was eternal, and *maarifat-e dini* (religious knowledge), which resulted from applying "knowledge of the day" to the study of the core scriptures. Therefore, he reasoned, there could be no official guardianship of religious thought in Islam, the foundation on which the Iranian constitution rested. Those who insisted on such guardianship needed to answer the crucial question, "Who guards the guardians?"

He also argued that there should be multiple interpretations of Islam because no understanding can be the final and most complete one, and that interpretations need constant renewal. In the ensuing multiple understandings of Islam, which must be tolerated and accepted, his own choice lay with incorporating modernity and pragmatism into religion. In his Persian-language book, *Qabzo Bast-e Theorik Shariat* (Contraction and Expansion of the Theory of Sharia), published in 1990, he tried to adapt the eternal nature of Islam to the modern conditions of popular revolts and globalization. His approach was perceived by many as paving the way for a pluralist Islamic society where different understandings of Islam were represented in various state organs.[27]

Soroush's commonsensical thesis offered a convincing explanation for the gap that often existed between the interpretations given by the older jurisprudents, educated in earlier times, and the younger ones, educated more recently. He advocated that religious knowledge be pursued vigorously by clerics and lay believers alike freely, and whatever impeded that objective ought to be removed. He argued, for instance, that since using religion as a political ideology limited religious knowledge of the believer it should be discontinued. He found religiously based methodology in governing a modern state inadequate, and concluded that there were no specifically religious methods of governance. The only institutional role for religion in government he was prepared to concede was that of establishing a legal code that incorporated the fiqh, and was in compliance with it.[28]

Soroush began propagating his views in the mid-1990s, arguing that it was neither the state's right nor its duty to impose one particular understanding on its citizens, and questioning the powers of the Guardians Council and the Assembly of Experts, and demanding that "Islam should not be used to meddle in private lives or control public thinking." This was a time of fermentation among Iranian intellectuals, writers, and artists.

As a result of the efforts by eight writers over a year, 134 authors, novelists, poets, journalists, scholars, and literary translators signed an open letter—"We Are Writers"—and sent it to forty publications and the Ministry of Culture and Islamic Guidance in late 1994. In it they appealed to the government to end censorship, and stop interfering in writers' private lives and allow them to form an association. No Iranian publication printed the letter, but a summary was broadcast by the Persian Service of the BBC and the VOA. During his Friday prayer sermon, Ayatollah Ahmad Jannati, an arch conservative, lashed out. "You want to write lies, to make accusations, to mar others' reputations and to weaken the foundations of our young people's beliefs," he said. "But our people and our officials are not going to let you do that . . . If you don't observe the limits and if you keep doing what you are doing, then the Hizobollah people will definitely come to perform their duty."[29] By this, Jannati meant that the Ansar-e Hizbollah would use intimidation and violence.

Even though, within a month ten writers withdrew their signatures publicly, the issue did not end. Indeed, in mid-1995, over two hundred movie directors and actors publicly appealed to the Ministry of Culture and Islamic Guidance to end its strict control of the film industry. It was published in the local press. The ministry responded by banning the export of any movie projecting a "negative image of Iran." It transpired in August 1996 that virtually none of the fifteen hundred fiction manuscripts and screenplays submitted to the ministry had been approved for publication or production.[30] The situation would change only after the election of Khatami as President in spring 1997.

When asked by students at a university in Rasht, a Caspian port, in December 1995, why the revolutionary spirit had cooled, he replied, "The seminaries are stagnant . . . You must not rely only on the clergy. You have to teach yourselves . . . The clergy has no feeling about the rights of the people. For them, it is the logic of power, not the logic of liberty." His remarks were considered so damaging that Khamanei publicly criticized him.[31]

In essence, in his lectures and articles in the pro-reform press, Soroush was arguing for separation of religion and politics, a taboo subject in Iran. The Ansars attacked him at a Tehran University meeting in late 1995. In an open letter published in a conservative newspaper, they claimed that Soroush was not propagating philosophy but "secular and vulgar temptations" that undermined the Islamic state. His "deviant ideas" negated "all that is sacred" and created "a whirlpool of doubt and confusion." The letter concluded, "We are not prepared to sell out the ideas of revolution or the blood of the martyrs to secularism."

In early 1996, Soroush lost his three academic jobs and was questioned by intelligence officials. He disappeared from Tehran in May 1996, and got a teaching post at University of Toronto, and spent 1997 abroad, giving lectures in Muslim countries and the Western world, including America.

It was only in 1998, after Khatami had settled into his presidential office, did Soroush return home. The *Jame* newspaper, set up by some of his followers, was doing well, so also the weekly *Kiyan*. But when he was invited to address students at Amir Kabir

University in Tehran, the Ansars turned up. Soroush felt so threatened that he resorted to taking different routes to his workplace as well as his changing his daily routine for personal security.

Conservative deputies in the Sixth Majlis feared that a debate along the lines suggested by Soroush would raise the possibility of a divorce between religion and politics, and threaten the system dominated by clerics. That had to be nipped in the bud. With that in view, they outlawed criticism of the constitution in April 2000.

Though Soroush and other reformist thinkers have been silenced, the problem of growing alienation of the young generation persists. This expresses itself partly in young people taking drugs. Officials concede that there are around 1.2 million addicts, most of them on opium and heroin originating in Afghanistan, with a shot of heroin available at U.S. 50 cents. This means the figures are back to the days of the Shah when, with a population of thirty-six million, there were an estimated five hundred thousand to eight hundred thousand heroin addicts. After the revolution, the regime mounted a campaign against drugs, which are forbidden in Islam. The execution of two hundred drug traffickers during May to July 1980 had a dramatic effect. But the problem did not disappear altogether. My visit to the Center for the Rehabilitation of Drug Addicts at Shourabad near Tehran in 1983 showed that there were 1,100 patients there. Though most of them were men in their early thirties to late fifties, who had acquired the habit during the Shah's rule, there were some young men in their early twenties as well.[32] A generation later, the proportion of young addicts has gone up considerably. Sexual frustration, resulting from strict observance of Islamic edicts, is a factor that tempts young men to try what is forbidden, partly as a gesture of defiance.

"The [Islamic] leadership realizes that in the social sphere it must give young people certain freedoms, and that too much restriction will create severe problems," said Tavassoli. "For instance, in the beginning the authorities were very strict about hijab and makeup for women, and also about mixing between sexes. They did not allow boys and girls to sit in the same classroom. But now they have changed their policy on this issue." However, this does not amount to wholesale reversal of the previous position. It simply means being prepared to make exceptions where the situation demands.

The overall scene has changed dramatically over the past quarter century. "At the university level, women are 60 percent of the student body," Tavassoli continued. "At Tehran University, women are in the majority in all faculties, including science. In the humanities, they are 90 percent."

Iranian girls are faring better than boys at the university entrance examination, also on the Islamic morality test. Additionally, they have a stronger motivation for enrolling at a university than boys. The most likely alternative after high school graduation is sitting at home, waiting to get married since jobs for high school graduates are few and far between.

Women's Role

Among the subject that engaged Iranian intellectuals in the cultural fermentation that occurred in the mid-1990s, women's status in society emerged as one of the most important—thanks largely to the lobbying by the weekly *Zan* (Women) and the quarterly *Farzaneh* (Wise). The *Zan* was edited by Faizeh Rafsanjani, a fair-skinned, plain-looking, athletic woman of thirty-one, and daughter of President Ali Akbar Rafsanjani, and the *Farzaneh* by Mahboubeh Abbas Qolizadeh, a high-cheeked woman with a pleasant demeanor. These publications argued that the centuries-old interpretations of Islam were erroneous, and that a series of misinterpretations of Islam had been perpetrated by male scholars to rationalize male domination of Muslim society. Sensitive to enlightened female opinion, Rafsanjani had appointed thirty-five-year-old Shahla Habibi as an adviser on women's affairs with the status of Deputy Minister.

But a boost for women's roles would come in the late 1990s with a series of fatwas issued by the Qom-based Grand Ayatollah Saanei. In it he illegitimized discrimination based on gender, race, or ethnicity, and declared that women could hold all jobs, including his own and the Leader's. "It is my interpretation from the Quran that all people have equal rights," he told Robin Wright. One result of his fatwas was that for the first time the Guardians Council allowed women and nonclerics to apply for candidacy to the Assembly of Experts in 1998 provided they passed a religious test. As stated earlier (in Chapter Five), all of them failed the test. But their right of eligibility was established.

Also, Saanei raised the age of puberty for girls from nine to thirteen, and declared that a woman should be allowed to divorce her husband if he married more than one wife without the first wife's consent.[33] He permitted abortion in the first trimester. "Generally abortion is forbidden," he explained. "But Islam is not a religion of hard rules. Islam is a religion of compassion and if there are serious problems, then God does not require his creatures to practice his law. So under some conditions—such as parents' poverty or overpopulation—then abortion is allowed. This does not mean we are changing God's laws. It just means we are interpreting laws according to the developments of science—realities of the times."

There were echoes here of what Soroush had said earlier. But there was a basic difference. "I have reached these ideas with the same methods of study and thought taught in the seminaries throughout the ages," he said. "Only my interpretation or what I have found in the sacred texts is different. But my conclusions are just as purely Islamic. I am saying the same in the seminaries."[34]

Unlike the majority of his peers, he was in tune with the rising generation of mullahs, most of whom felt that Iran's Islamic system must adapt to changing times to survive. Little wonder that protesting students in 1999 approached him for advice. Radicals among them proposed that the veil for women should be voluntary, an idea that failed to get off the ground.

Some years earlier, when roopash as an alternative to the oppressive chador was being perfected by women designers in the affluent north Tehran, Dore, a strictly indoor fashion model, explained the nuances and overarching implications of the hijab to Tira Schubert, a visiting American television producer. "If you go down to the [Grand] Bazaar area, where women are strict about hijab, you don't push your sleeves to your elbows as I like to do when I'm in north Tehran. . . . The roopash now has epaulettes and big buttons. I know it looks ugly, but I like it . . . It's a way of creating a different identity for yourself because these people, the government, are trying to force something on you, asking people to be religious when they aren't. You either believe in something or you don't. Hijab is really hard to believe in. You have to feel comfortable with your clothes. Our servant does not feel comfortable without hijab. She has the head scarf on even if she is alone in the house ironing. She is used to it. I'm not, and my friends aren't. But we don't have a choice."[35]

An alternative viewpoint on the hijab and the revolution came from Massoumeh Goolgiri, an articulate mother of four, living in Qom. "The revolution opened up opportunities [for women]," she told Robin Wright. "The hijab frees me to be a person judged not by beauty but by actions and thoughts. My life has been much improved. Now that more women are on the path to becoming an ayatollah, the revolution is introducing real equality."[36]

Clearly, the subject is bound up with social class. Yet there is paucity of class analysis in Iran today. Debates are always conducted within the framework of Islam, be it banking, male-female relations, or sports—a subject that came to the fore primarily because Faizeh Rafsanjani, the foremost champion of women's causes, was a former volleyball coach. As President of the Solidarity Council for Women's Sport Organizations, she organized the first Islamic Women's Olympics in Tehran in 1993. It was attended by seven hundred athletes from eleven Muslim countries, and became a triennial event. "In most of the Islamic world, women have cultural problems," she told a visiting *New York Times* reporter in January 1995. "They are regarded as a commodity, often forced into domesticity. [But] for Iranian women, the values have changed." Prodded by her, the national government gave strong support to women's sports. An example was the five-acre (two-hectare) Bahman cultural complex in the underprivileged south Tehran, with a sports center that had more facilities for women than men. She went on to become a Majlis deputy in 1996 from Tehran, securing the second largest number of votes. She was reelected in 2000.

Bare statistics about women showed that having to wear a veil in public had not stopped them from advancing socially and economically—or even skiing on the slopes of Elborz Mountains north of Tehran.

In 1994 about a third of civil servants were women. Among university students 40 percent were female—versus 12 percent just before the revolution. The government had removed restrictions in higher education to let women train as engineers and assistants to judges—but not judges (in accordance with the official interpretation of the Sharia).

Furthermore, faced with the unprecedented population growth of 3.9 percent in the 1980s, the authorities had encouraged family planning to the extent that the rate fell to 1.8 percent in the mid-1990s.[37] After the revolution, Khomeini favored high birth rate by saying, "My soldiers are still infants," and citing Prophet Muhammad's saying, "Marry and multiply, for I shall make a display of you before the nations on the Day of Judgment." Due to this, and the lowering of the female marriage age from eighteen to nine, the age of puberty according to Islam, the population of thirty-six million rose by a third in seven years, with an average woman bearing seven children.

Pressures of war and population explosion became too much to bear for the Iranian government led by Prime Minister Mir Hussein Mousavi. Yet so strong were the influences of traditional Iranian attitudes and religious ideology toward procreation that the cabinet voted for birth control in 1988 only by a single vote after a long and heated debate. Mousavi withheld announcing the cabinet decision as he scrambled for a religious decree by a preeminent mullah.[38]

As pragmatism prevailed over ideology following Khomini's death, the Iranian leaders' decision to launch a state-sponsored family planning program signaled maturing of the revolution.

The policy reversal became firm under Khamanei, who reportedly discovered that in 1980 Khomeini had declared that "Islam allows birth control as long as the wife receives the consent of her husband and that the chosen method does not damage her health," and then issued his own fatwa in the form of questions and answers on different forms of contraception. "When wisdom dictates that you do not need more children, a vasectomy is permissible," he said, answering a question.[39]

In 1993, the Majlis passed a law that withdrew paid maternity leave, social welfare subsidies, and food coupons to a couple after their third child. In addition, unmarried couples were required to attend contraception classes before wedlock. Iran adopted an annual Population Week to coincide with the UN Population Day in July when mosques and seminaries stressed the significance of small families. To make a success of its family planning campaign the government licensed an Iranian company to manufacture condoms. Its annual output of seventy million condoms, produced in a variety of flavors and textures, is deliberately packaged in English or French to make it appear risqué. Consequently, the birth rate fell further to 1.47 percent, with the average number of children born to a woman declining to 2.7, in 1998.

By then, changes in the Muslim personal law had given greater rights to women than before—and, with President Khatami appointing Massoumeh Ebtekar as the first woman Vice President in 1997, women had acquired a highly visible role model.[40]

The 1998 Family Law strengthened women's position. It required that a legal divorce could only be granted by a court and not by a mere statement of the husband, "I divorce you, I divorce you, I divorce you." Secondly, if a husband petitions for a divorce without his wife's agreement, then she is entitled to half of his property as compensation for her work in the home and child rearing. In all such cases, investigation must be carried out by a woman assistant judge. Finally, working women cannot be dismissed for family reasons, and must be given the options of part-time employment or early retirement with pension.

Interestingly, Vice President Massoumeh Ebtekar dealt not with women's affairs but with environment protection. She applied herself to the job with extraordinary vigor and enthusiasm, and dealt with the problem of smog that regularly blighted Tehran during winters. At her behest, in April 2000, the cabinet adopted a ten-year plan to tackle air pollution head-on. It involved educating the public and securing their cooperation. "Now some 230 nongovernmental organizations are involved in anti-air pollution schemes, with more than fifty based in Greater Tehran," she told me in her tastefully furnished office in the capital in August 2001. "All this is part of the opening up of civil society when different voluntary groups are speaking out on matters of public concern like air pollution."

Distinguished by her drooping eyelids and winsome smile,

Ebtekar first made her mark on public life at the age of nineteen, when she was a student at Tehran's Polytechnic University. She acted as a spokesperson for the militant students who seized the U.S. Embassy in Tehran in November 1979, and took diplomats as hostages. They were intrigued by her American East Coast accent, a result of her education at the Highland Park Elementary School in Philadelphia, where her father researched and wrote his doctorate in engineering. Ayatollah Khomeini awarded her militancy with an appointment as an editor at the *Kayhan International* daily. After a brief crack at journalism, she enrolled in the medical faculty of Tehran University and earned a doctorate in immunology. Then she became a medical teacher at Tehran University. She married and had two children. Simultaneously, she actively promoted women's causes. At the university she was instrumental in introducing women's studies for which she designed a curriculum. She established the Center for Women's Study and Research, and founded the *Farzaneh* quarterly journal as a forum for women's issues.

During my interview with her in August 2001, she illustrated her point about Iranian women increasingly getting into professions by referring to the medical faculty of Tehran University where she lectured once a week: about a third of the faculty was female as were half of the students.

The reason why Khatami chose to name her Vice President and not Cabinet Minister was that in the latter case he would have to gain the endorsement of the Majlis which, given its conservative majority, seemed disinclined to oblige the President on this issue. Nonetheless, she attended cabinet meetings, and was treated on a par with her male colleagues.

On the other hand, Ebtekar's testimony in court was worth only half that of any man's; and, if murdered or killed accidentally, the blood money to be paid by her killer would be only half that of a man's, as stated in the Sharia. Also, as a married woman, she could not travel abroad without her husband's written permission. While riding a bus, she was required to sit in the rear, reserved for women. And on any train, her place was in the compartment reserved for women. She did not shake hands with me, something she could only do with the men closely related to her. But, if by any chance, she found herself standing at major road junctions in Tehran to ride a shared taxi, she would end up sitting squashed in between strange men. In her department, as in all public offices and factories, mosques and prayer halls, men and women pray separately. The logic behind this edict is that sexual attraction diverts the believers' attention away from the demanding task of praying (or learning.)

On her marriage, Massoumeh Ebtekar did not adopt the surname of her husband, a common practice among married women in Iran, which their Western counterparts may as well emulate.

Like Ebtekar, hundreds of thousands of Iranian women, clad in black chadors, marched in the streets during the revolutionary movement of 1978 to 1979, a legacy captured in the still and moving pictures of the period. They were responding to the calls made by Khomeini from his exile in Najaf and a Paris suburb. This was a welcome change from his stance in 1963 when he opposed the franchise for women. Later, indeed, in his *Pithy Aphorisms: Wise Sayings and Counsels*, Khomeini would express his gratitude to women in bringing about the Shah's downfall thus: "Iranian women have a larger part than men in this movement and this revolution. Our men are indebted to the bravery of you lionhearted women."[41]

Following the revolution, on March 8, 1979, the International Women's Day, Khomeini banned coeducation, and suspended the progressive Family Protection Law of 1967/1975, which raised the marriage age for girls to eighteen, gave women the right to apply for divorce without the husband's permission, restricted polygamy by requiring a man to secure the permission of the first wife before marrying again, and transferred family affairs from the Sharia courts to secular courts.

Khomeini also ruled that women employees in government ministries must dress "according to Islamic standards," that is, wear a veil. That set off protest demonstrations by women. Day after day thousands of women marched through the streets of Tehran. A demonstration on March 11 was met by the security forces firing over the heads of the protesting women. The next day, the demonstrators were stoned and attacked by knife-wielding men. On March 13, responding to public protest and private pleas, Khomeini's office announced that the ayatollah Khomeini had said that a chador was a desirable, not compulsory, form of dress for women.

This would prove to be a temporary retreat, however.

Aware of the religious atmosphere prevailing during Ramadan the following year, the government ordered in early July that all women in government and public offices must wear a hijab (veil). The five hundred thousand urban women above the age of twelve who had such jobs as well as employment in workshops and factories constituted 9 percent of the female population. A large majority of them worked in small, all-female workshops or sections of factories. So the government order affected about 3 percent of the urban female population aged twelve or more.

Due to this, and the frequent reiteration by the mass media that prescribing a proper dress for women had the sanction of the Quran, resistance to the government fiat collapsed. The appropriate verses in the Quran (24:30–31) states: "And say to the believing women that they cast down their eyes, and guard their private parts . . . and let them cast their veils over their bosoms, and reveal not their adornment (*zinah*) save to their husbands, or their fathers, or their husbands' fathers, or their sons, or their husbands' sons, or their brothers, or Islamic dress their brothers' sons, or their sisters' sons, or their women . . . or children who have not yet attained knowledge of women's private parts."[42] The intention is to avoid arousing sexual passion between men and women who are not present or potential partners. The hijab traditionally worn by Muslim women in public always covers the head but not necessarily the face.

Addressing the Friday prayer congregation in Tehran, Hojatalislam Ali Khamanei, the prayer leader, said, "Hijab is an Islamic duty. Wearing of ornamental trinkets, elaborate hair styles and makeup is un-Islamic." A year later—in 1981—the Majlis passed the Islamic Dress Law, which applied to all women in Iran, whether Muslim or not. The maximum penalty for violating the law was a jail sentence of a year. The law remains in force and is applied with varying degrees of severity. Khamanei reiterated his socially conservative views nearly two decades later while answering twenty-nine questions on Islamic morality to *Jebhe* (Front), a weekly journal of the Ansar-e Hizbollah. "Women should avoid colors that attract attention," he said. "Women riding bicycles or motorcycles would spread corruption and so it is banned."[43]

The more severe examples of veiling are the *niqab* (*lit.*, mask), a black veil that covers the face and obscures all but the eyes from public view, worn by some Arab women, and the burqa, an all-enveloping, top-to-toe garment that allows the wearer to see through a threaded gauze, common among Afghan women. Actually, the custom of veiling of women existed in pre-Islamic times and non-Muslim societies, during the Sassanian and Byzantine Empires, and in European Mediterranean and India. Its persistence in Muslim communities is attributed to the sanctification offered by the Quran and its usefulness as a form of rebellion against Western cultural imperialism. Even then, peasant and nomadic Muslim women seldom accepted the veil. Indeed when the seminomadic Seljuk, Mongol, and Timurid Dynasties ruled Iran from 1037 to 1500, the unveiling of women spread among the local elite and lower ranks. After that veiling and seclusion of women became the ideal for those women who did not labor in fields or elsewhere.

On May 30, 1982, the Iranian cabinet approved comprehensive plans to introduce Islamic legislation into the current penal and legal codes, civil law, and trade law, and decided that adherence to Islamic dress was to be enforced strictly. The following year, when the Family Protection Law of 1967/1975 was abolished, a woman's right to divorce her husband was restored if this provision was inserted in the marriage contract.

Over time, the strictness with which the hijab is enforced has become the barometer of the state of the regime. When it feels threatened externally or internally, the Law Enforcement Forces mount a campaign to rid society of "bad hijab." When LEF men encounter instances of bad hijab, they often deliver a warning to those violating the law along with a short lecture. But when LEF women come across those breaching the law, they rustle the miscreants into their vehicles and rush them to the headquarters where they are fined the equivalent of $2 to $20.[44]

Relationships between men and women had to conform to what the Quran has stated. "Men are the managers of the affairs of women: for that God has preferred in bounty one of them over another, and for that they have expended of their property," reads verse 38 of Chapter Four, titled "Women," of the Quran. "Righteous women are therefore obedient . . . And those you fear may be rebellious, admonish, banish them to their couches, and beat them."

Women's legal and financial positions too are defined by the Quran. "God charges you, concerning your children: to the male the like of the portion of two females," reads verse 11 of chapter four. "And call in to witness two witnesses, men; or if the two be not men, then one man and two women, such witnesses as you approve of, that if one of the two women errs, the other will

335

remind her," reads verse 282 of Chapter Two. Following another Quranic verse, the Islamic regime dismissed all women judges. It also barred women lawyers from practicing, a ban that would later be rescinded. It laid great stress on women as mothers and homemakers, and encouraged them to stay at home.

But the manpower demands of a long conflict with Iraq led Khomeini to modify his views on women in order to gain their active support for the war effort and to encourage them to take up work outside home. He appealed to them to make the most innovative use of the strictly rationed necessities, and urge their sons, brothers, and husbands to join the military and its auxiliary forces. Much to the approval of women, he ruled that, contrary to the Sharia—which requires orphans to be placed in the custody of the nearest male relative—the orphaned children of the war dead must remain with their mothers.

He went on to proclaim, "In an Islamic order, women enjoy the same rights as men—right to education, work, ownership, to vote in elections and to be voted in. Women are free, just like men, to decide their own destinies and activities."[45]

As an illustration of the first statement, Khomeini's followers could point out that Zahra, one of his daughters, was a university graduate who, after her marriage, continued to work for a research institute in Tehran along with her husband, and that his granddaughters acquired postgraduate degrees and became working women. But contrary to Khomeini's second statement about women being free "just like men," female singers cannot give solo performances in public, and women cannot model in advertisements or allow themselves to be used in any fashion to promote a product. That explained why in my 3,000-mile (4,800 km) long journey through Iran in the summer of 2004, I never came across a single female face or body in advertisements even when they dealt with kitchenware or washing machines.

When it came to education, Khomeini was as keen to secure

women full access to all faculties at universities as he was for them to pursue religious education at seminaries. During the Pahlavi era, women were treated as adjuncts in classes at the seminaries in Qom, which lacked any female teachers. This was in line with Twelver Shia tradition in Iran. Stating that Twelver Shiaism had "some features that might be considered favorable to women," Nikki R. Keddie, an American academic, notes that "orthodox women religious leaders [in Twelver Shiaism] have held a position closer to that of male religious leaders than in most Sunni countries. These leaders, among Shias called mullahs like their male counterparts, preside over women's religious ceremonies. In Iran there are special women's *rowze-khanis* where stories of the Imams, especially the martyred Imam Hussein, are recounted and women's *surfihs* (ceremonial meals), involving vows at which women mullahs read from the Quran and explicate it."[46]

After the revolution, Khomeini decreed that women should have their own seminaries, and that they should be encouraged not only to study Islam but also to teach.

This led to the establishment of the Zahra Seminary in a back alley of Qom behind an entrance embellished by turquoise and navy blue tiles. It attracted students nationally and internationally. Indeed, in 1993, nearly two-thirds of its 1,100 students were from abroad. Most Iranian students, Elaine Sciolino of the *New York Times* discovered in the mid-1990s, were wives and mothers who lived nearby. They found the free day-care facility for their children at the seminary, named after a daughter of Prophet Muhammad, very convenient, and showed scant interest in turning themselves into erudite religious-legal scholars in search of independent interpretations of the Sharia. No wonder that one student told Sciolino that "restrictions for women exist because Islam respects women."[47]

Khomeini also decreed that women could join the Baseej militia, a decision of great import. That in turn produced a crop of images of Iranian women in black chador, carrying sub-machine-guns and marching in military formation in the streets of Tehran, and doing weapons-handling exercises at military garrisons.

"In ways never anticipated, Iran's upheaval did succeed in creating a climate for revolution within the revolution—in women's rights, the arts and social customs, among the young and, most important, within Islam itself," concludes Robin Wright in her book *The Last Great Revolution*. "Through these other movements, Iranians took bigger steps in defining a modern Islamic democracy than any other Muslim country."[48]

Since Muslim-majority countries, stretching from Indonesia to Algeria, possess 75 percent of oil and 45 percent of natural gas reserves of the world, it is in the interests of the West to see that the attempts being made in Iran to meld political Islam with democracy succeed.

Overview

The Iranian revolution stands apart from similar upheavals in the Middle East. During 1952 to 1962, the monarchs of Egypt, Iraq, and North Yemen were overthrown by groups of nationalist military officers who established Republics. These coups were welcomed by the public at large; and they set the scene for widespread political and economic reform. The resulting change came about at the initiative of the military juntas, not a popular movement or party. In Iran, however, the involvement of millions of people in the process of toppling the Pahlavi dynasty made a qualitative difference.

Like revolutions elsewhere, the Iranian revolution destroyed the old power structure, consisting of the Shah, the aristocracy, and the Westernized upper and upper middle classes. In the new power structure, the lower middle class—both traditional and modern—acquired a preeminent place. The Iranian revolution shared this feature with the republican revolutions in Egypt, Iraq, and North Yemen. There the ruling elite, consisting of the monarch, aristocrats, feudal lords, and urban rich, was replaced by military officers mainly from lower-middle-class families. Once in power, these officers implemented policies that hurt the old propertied classes and benefited, primarily, the lower- and middle-middle classes, the petty bourgeoisie. That is, the interests of the petty bourgeoisie were advanced by the members of this class wearing military uniforms. A similar process unfolded in Iran, with one crucial difference: the interests of the petty bourgeoisie were served by the members of the same class wearing Shia clerical robes.

A large majority of Iran's clerics come from urban or rural petty bourgeoisie families, who are often related to traders or shopkeepers. Those who come from better-off homes are linked with rich merchants or landlords. So, though the petty bourgeoisie is the dominant class in the Islamic camp, it has to contend with the interests of the mercantile bourgeoisie and rich landlords. Therein lay the root of conflict between conservatives and radicals between the ruling Islamic Republican Party (IRP) and the Guardians Council—a conflict that came to the surface on land distribution, foreign trade nationalization, and confiscation of the exiles' properties. Though the overall basis of the regime was, and remains, toward the working and lower middle classes (both traditional and modern), it is unwilling to alienate bazaar merchants, who have traditionally been close to clerics and the mosque, and have supported them.

In contrast to the social setup in the Pahlavi era, when the working class and the petty bourgeoisie were powerless, the post-Pahlavi regime has inducted them into such powerful revolutionary organizations as the Islamic Revolutionary Guard Corps (IRGC) and the Baseej, and armed them. For the first time in Iranian history, they felt they had a stake in the political-administrative system. Most of them, being religious, were loyal to Ayatollah Ruhollah Khomeini, whom they considered a divine figure, an aide to the Twelfth Imam, whose success in overthrowing the Shah they regarded as a superhuman feat.

Though all public buildings and offices carry equal-size portraits of Khomeini and his successor Ayatollah Ali Khamanei, with his flowing white beard and thick tortoiseshell glasses, nobody in Iran or outside puts the two of them on a par. While Khamanei has inherited the clerical network, he does not enjoy the supreme clerical status that Khomeini did. A towering Islamic personality, Khomeini ruled as much by sheer personal magnetism as by activating the Shia religious network.

It was Khomeini's religious standing and charisma that enabled him to rally the nation to resist the invasion by President Saddam Hussein of Iraq in 1980, merge nationalism with Islam, inspire his people to keep fighting for years on end, and thus consolidate the foundation on which his fledgling Islamic Republic, trying to cater for both temporal and spiritual needs of its citizens, then stood. He complemented his personal magnetism with a strong grip over governmental machinery, the broadcasting media, and the Shia religious network. He cunningly eliminated or neutralized his secular and religious opponents in stages. When challenged violently by opposition groups such as the Mujahedin-e Khalq—who claimed killing twelve hundred religious and political leaders of his regime within three years of the revolution—Khomeini proved ruthless in his retribution. "When Prophet Muhammad failed to improve the people with advice, he hit them on the head with a sword until he made them human beings," he said. The number of the executed MKO members reached four thousand.[1] By the time the war ended after eight years, it had resulted in three hundred thousand Iranian deaths and injuries to seven hundred thousand more, affecting one in ten families. It thus helped rejuvenate in modern times the cult of martyrdom, a concept highly revered in Shia Islam. In addition, the war created a vast pool of soldiers with battlefield experience—a national asset that will prove invaluable to Iran's leaders if their country becomes a target of U.S. President Bush's policy of waging "preventive wars" to bring about "regime change" in the countries he has included in his "axis of evil."

On the other hand, when an ailing Khomeini realized in the summer of 1988 that if he continued to fight Iraq, the U.S. would enter the fray openly on Baghdad's behalf, and that this development, combined with the Iraqis' continued large-scale use of chemical weapons would break the will of his forces on the front lines, leading to the collapse of the military and the Islamic Republic he had founded. So he performed a U-turn. He did so also because of his realization that his successor would lack the courage and charisma to stop fighting and that would only make the situation worse. While spurning several attempts by the Islamic Conference Organization to mediate in a war between Muslim nations, Khomeini accepted a ceasefire brokered by the United Nations, a non-Muslim body. In the final analysis, therefore, despite the stern, unyielding image he projected in the West, Khomeini proved to be a pragmatist.

There were other examples of his pragmatism. He reversed his stance on women's enfranchisement. Having opposed votes for women in 1963, he went on to uphold their rights during the revolutionary movement and after, opening the ranks of the Baseej militia to them. After crushing the violent opposition to the Islamic Republic ruthlessly, he issued a decree upholding citizens' civil rights.

All along, Khomeini ensured that his regime received periodic mandate from the people through elections to the Majlis and the presidency.

Though the Majlis had existed in Iran since 1906, it really came into its own in the 1940s. It was as a parliamentarian that Muhammad Mussadiq emerged as the first truly popular leader of Iranians in modern times with his commitment to gain Iran economic independence by nationalizing the British-owned Anglo-Iranian Oil Company, and rid the country of the oligarchic rule.

When the freshly established National Iranian Oil Company

(NIOC) took over the assets of the AIOC in October 1951, the British government of Prime Minister Winston Churchill tried to co-opt the U.S. administration of President Harry Truman to reverse the nationalization of the AIOC in 1951. It failed. Churchill then raised the alarmist bogey of an imminent Communist takeover of Iran. President Dwight Eisenhower, a staunch anti-Communist, swallowed the bait unhesitatingly.

The CIA-engineered overthrow of Mussadiq's constitutional government in August 1953 blocked the development of Iran as a multiparty, democratic state. The unveiling of the dictatorial rule of Muhammad Reza Shah—backed by Washington and reinforced by a consortium of Anglo-American oil corporations—estranged most Iranians, urban and rural, from the U.S. By closing all secular avenues of opposition to his autocracy, the Shah inadvertently encouraged a section of the clerical establishment to become politically active. By expelling their leader, Khomeini, in 1964, the Shah gained time for his regime.

The next decade saw his power and authority rise higher and higher at home and in the region. With the planned withdrawal of the British from the Persian Gulf in 1971, where it had been the leading foreign power for a century and a half, both Washington and London decided to make him the bulwark of the status quo, to check revolutionary forces, whether Marxist or Arab nationalist. With this, Iran under the Shah became an integral part of America's regional strategy, which came to rest firmly on the tripod of Israel, Saudi Arabia, and Iran, the prime agenda of this alliance being maintaining political stability in the oil-rich Gulf and the rest of the Middle East. This and the dramatic rise in oil prices from 1973 to 1974 stoked the Shah's ambitions to the extent that he lost touch with reality.

The loss of the Iranian leg of the tripod created a crisis for American policy makers—all the more so when a revolutionary movement rooted in Islam, and virulently opposed to the U.S.

hegemony in the region, emerged triumphant. There was no precedent for such a popular movement in modern times.

However, on one strategic aim Islamic Iran and the U.S. were united: both wanted to minimize or expel Soviet influence in the Persian Gulf. Significantly, while pursuing an anti-imperialist line abroad, and making repeated statements in favor of the poor at home, Khomeini deliberately did not use phraseology that could conceivably be termed Marxist. He avoided such terms as capitalists, landlords, bourgeoisie, toilers, working class, proletariat, and feudal. Instead of talking about exploiters and exploited, he referred to oppressors and oppressed. In general, he championed the cause of the lower classes. Yet he also said, "The foundation of an Islamic state is based on no one class being dominant over other classes."[2]

Where Tehran and Washington clashed head-on was on the question of regional leadership. Iran under the ayatollahs wanted to be the regional superpower, a position it thought it deserved: it was the most strategic country in the area, its shoreline covered not only the Persian Gulf but also the Arabian Sea, its population was one-and-a-half-times the total of the remaining seven Gulf states, and it shared the same religion—Islam—with its neighbors.

Firmly committed to the long-term strategy of not allowing any state to become the dominant power in the region, the U.S. did its utmost to frustrate Tehran's ambition. In this, it had the active support of the Gulf monarchies whose Arab subjects had been historically antipathetic toward Persians/Iranians, and whose rulers were alarmed by Khomeini's condemnation of monarchy as un-Islamic. Though Saddam Hussein governed a Republic, he was hostile to ethnic Persians and apprehensive of the Shia majority in Iraq asserting itself. He benefited from Washington's determination not to allow Iran to become the regional superpower and its adoption of the zero-sum doctrine concerning Iraq and Iran—that is, strengthening one meant weakening the other. That is why Washington began siding with Baghdad during the Iran-Iraq War when Tehran acquired the upper hand in the conflict, raising the possibility of becoming the unchallenged leader in the Gulf.

In the absence of being accepted as the region's leader, Tehran insisted that the security of the Gulf should be the exclusive responsibility of the regional states, and that nonregional countries should stay out. Washington disagreed strongly. It regarded the Persian Gulf and the Straits of Hormuz as international waterways. And it made no bones about its economic and strategic interest in the continued supply of Gulf oil and gas at comparatively cheap prices to it and the rest of the Western world and Japan—an objective in which it was actively aided by the ruler of Saudi Arabia, possessing a quarter of the globe's oil deposits, and acting as the swing producer in the Organization of Petroleum Exporting Countries (OPEC).

If it was merely a question of coexisting or even allying with a regime that administered the state along Islamic lines, America had enjoyed excellent relations with the Saudi kingdom, which had been run strictly according to the Sharia since its inception in 1932. Both Washington and Riyadh shared a deep hatred of Marxism and were committed to maintaining the political status quo. With U.S. oil corporations running the Saudi petroleum industry, the economies of the two countries were interlinked.

But Saudi Arabia was, and remains, a royal autocracy whereas America is a secular, democratic Republic.

In strictly ideological terms, the U.S., committed to promoting democracy worldwide, should feel an affinity with the Islamic Republic of Iran since the latter has had a representative government based on universal franchise (extended to fifteen-year-olds) since the 1979 revolution.

During the first two decades of its history, it held three referendums (on establishing an Islamic republic, and adopting a constitution framed by a popularly elected body in 1979, and then on endorsing an amended constitution a decade later) and seventeen elections (four for the Assembly of Experts Assembly, seven for the President, five for the Majlis, and one for local councils). Even during the war with Iraq, the Iranian regime did not alter the electoral timetable. And in all polls voters had a choice of candidates, the only exception being the election of the Leader by the Assembly of Experts.

Indeed, when it comes to choosing the highest official, both Iran and America confer this privilege on an electoral college. In the case of Iran, the directly elected Assembly of Experts (of Islam) acts as the electoral college to elect the Leader (of the revolution); and in the United States of America the member states constitute one on the basis of their respective populations. The only difference is that an electoral college comes into being in the U.S. only to elect the chief executive whereas the Iranian Assembly of Experts has tenure of eight years and monitors the performance of the Leader (but does not make it public).

Such similarities matter little. What matters is Iran's anti-U.S. policy has extended beyond the region. Describing America as a hegemonist (not imperialist—the term used by the secular Left worldwide) power, Khomeini encouraged, within Iran's limited resources, anti-American, Islamic forces in the Muslim world. His most notable contribution was in Lebanon (where the Hizbollah would succeed in securing Israel's unconditional evacuation of south Lebanon in 2000, after twenty-two years of occupation) and in the Occupied Palestinian Territories where, to the chagrin of Washington, he supported Hamas and Islamic Jihad. His successor, Khamanei, has continued the policy.

On its part, the U.S., whether ruled by a Democratic or Republican President, remained consistently hostile to the Islamic Republic for almost two decades—from imposing economic sanctions against it in late 1979, following the American hostage-taking in Tehran, to the adoption of the dual containment policy in 1993 to the 1996 Iran-Libya Sanctions Act (ILSA).

The thaw in relations that started in early 1998, with President Muhammad Khatami expressing regret at the American hostage-taking, has yet to result in talks at a government-to-government level, a preamble to normal ties between the two countries. United States President George W. Bush's inclusion of Iran in his "axis of evil" in early 2002 soon after Tehran's covert assistance to the Pentagon to bring about the overthrow of the Taliban regime in Afghanistan cancelled any progress toward normalization that had been made gradually over the past four years.

Meanwhile, the subject of relations with the "Great Satan"— the defining term routinely used by Khomeini for America— continues to engage Iranian politicians and journalists.

The Domestic Scene

Having unveiled a sociopolitical system that combines salient features of Islamic jurisprudence with the basics of democracy— universal suffrage, representative government, freedom of speech and association, albeit within the strict limits of Islam as defined by the Leader and the Guardians Council—the leaders of the Islamic Republic have seen it evolve as the polity has grappled with changing circumstances, from revolution to war to reconstruction. Indeed, by amending 40 of the 175 articles of the 1979 constitution, and adding two more, within a decade of its promulgation, the regime had acknowledged the indisputable need for change. Later, in the economic field too the government and lawmakers showed sufficient flexibility to come up with the "buy back" proposition in their dealings with non-Iranian oil companies, thereby guaranteeing them attractive returns on their capital investments while abiding by the constitutional requirement of not letting foreigners own Iran's natural resources.

The evolution of Iranian politics was summarized by Sadiq Zibakalam, professor of political science at Tehran University, thus: "After the revolution President Abol Hassan Bani-Sadr antagonized the mullahs, and the Mujahedin-e Khalq went on a warpath, and then came the war with Iraq. So the issue of political freedoms got marginalized. After the war, during his two terms, President Rafsanjani focused on reconstruction. It is only after Khatami's election [in 1997] that the issue of political reform got back on the agenda. Actually, this is not surprising. After all this is what the Iranian revolution was about. During the late 1970s we discussed such subjects as Islam and freedom, and Islam and the role of women."[3] But the nature of freedom is highly complex and shifting as it must consider not only the culture and history of a society but also its stage of economic development. Furthermore, since the reported differences between Khamanei and Khatami on the subject remained unresolved, the issue is unlikely to be resolved soon and without further furies.

Seen in a positive light, this can be described as the dynamic of Iranian politics. Since the early days of the Islamic Republic there have been two main currents within Islamic politics: Right/conservative/hard-line and Left/reformist/moderate. Measured by the size of Majlis deputies, their fortunes have varied.

In the First Majlis (1980–84) conservatives were in a minority even though clerical deputies enjoyed a slim majority. That was why it rejected President Ali Khamanei's first choice of Prime Minister, conservative Ali Akbar Velayati, albeit by a narrow margin. On the other hand, left-of-center Mir Hussein Mousavi was accepted by 115 votes to 39 in October 1981. Though neither faction had a majority in the Second Majlis (1984–88), it again endorsed Mousavi after President Khamanei presented him as his choice following his reelection in 1985. In the Third Majlis (1988–92), the leftist camp, which now included moderates, claimed the loyalty of two-thirds of the house.

This changed when, as explained earlier (in Chapter Two), Khamanei and Rafsanjani together used the Guardians Council to bring about the downfall of leftists. Their strength declined to 90 in the Fourth Majlis (1992–96) while the conservatives' total rose to 150.

With the formal split in the traditional Right, leading to the formation of the Servants of Construction in 1996, a centrist force, backed largely by the modern middle class, emerged in Iranian politics. In the Fifth Majlis (1996–2000), right-wingers at 120 lacked a majority, but were more than the 70 left-wingers and centrists.

The changing fortunes of different factions, the emergence of a centrist trend, the shift in the public debate from economic to political liberalization—all these were signs of a functioning democracy within an Islamic framework. With major battles on running the economy behind them, the different factions had converged on such vital issues as further privatization (to include such sectors as telecommunications, railways, and petrochemicals) and maintenance of highly popular subsidies on essential items like foodstuffs, fuel, and medicine.

It was in the arena of political reform that the factions were at loggerheads. Fundamentalists and right-wingers wanted to maintain the status quo while centrists and leftists advocated widening of the freedom of expression, association, and assembly within the constitution. The former warned that if the regime allowed political liberalization to advance unchecked, it would end up losing power, and regress to the last days of the Shah, when he conceded too much too quickly to his opponents.

Their opponents referred to Articles 19–42 in the 1989 constitution, which guaranteed press freedom as long as it was not detrimental to "the basic principles of Islam or the rights of the public," and freedom of assembly provided it was peaceful and "not detrimental to the basic principles of Islam."

After Khatami's election as President in 1997, the term "reformist/reformer" came into vogue to encompass everybody who was not a conservative or hard-line fundamentalist.

An all-encompassing yet profound definition of the term "reform" was provided by Professor Hadi Semati in Tehran. According to him, reform consists of finding ways of reconciling democracy with Islamic revolution, bringing about reformation in Islam, and progressing economically and politically in an increasingly secular world with a global, interdependent economy without losing the religious and ethical content of Islam in order to avoid the moral decadence that has, in his view, developed in the Christian West—a tall order. A broad solution, in his view, lies with "domestication" of democracy, meaning fostering "a democracy that is homegrown and compatible with our culture."[4]

Allied to this issue is the element of the time frame. "One of our serious problems historically in Iran is that social movements become hollow [soon]," said Ibrahim Shaikh, a student leader, in 2000. "Look at the Constitutional Revolution. To create reform today, given our history of despotism, we need at least two decades . . . We cannot act so quickly. This is the reason the students should not try to force change through radicalism. We move ahead of society, and society is not ready for profound change."[5]

Part of the reason why institutional changes are slow to materialize in Iran is that, contrary to the prevalent view in the West of an authoritarian regime in power in Tehran, the Iranian constitution has more checks and balances than many of its Western counterparts. That is what Rafsanjani, elected by an almost unanimous vote in 1989, discovered.

There are five primary centers of power in Iran: the Leader, who is both the spiritual and temporal ruler of Iran, the ultimate arbiter of power; the Assembly of Experts, which elects him and monitors his performance; the President, the chief executive; the Majlis, the legislative organ; and the judiciary. And there are two secondary centers of power: the Council of Guardians (of the Constitution), which ensures that legislation is compatible with the Sharia, the Islamic law, and the Iranian constitution, and supervises elections to the Assembly of Experts, the presidency, and the Majlis; and the Expediency Council, which resolves differences between the President, the Majlis, and the Guardians Council. All of the Expediency Council members and half of the Guardians Council members are appointed by the Leader, as is the judiciary chief. Given the multiplicity of its centers of power, Iran resembles more the United States than China.

Then there is the cultural-religious aspect of Iran, where nine out of ten Iranians are Shia, and where there is a long tradition of the ayatollahs and grand ayatollahs of Shia Islam offering varying interpretations of the Sharia, Islamic law. "Iranian culture is simply too argumentative, too full of escape hatches and private corners in which dissidents can hide, both literally and intellectually," concludes Elaine Sciolino in her book *Persian Mirrors*. "So, even the hard-liners had to adapt, leaving room at time for more than one party line and room for people to choose—even with difficulty—between them. In addition, even at its most rigid, the character of repression and surveillance has been episodic, rather than omniscient and pervasive."[6]

However, this episodic surveillance and repression was not acceptable to reformist politicians who came to the fore in the late 1990s. Once they had acquired an overwhelming majority in the Sixth Majlis (2000–2004), they were hopeful of widening the boundaries of social and political freedoms. They made some progress but not much. It became obvious to them that their powers and those of President Khatami were limited.

They lost to the conservative forces, embedded into the Guardians Council and the judiciary, because the latter trumped their strategy. The reformist strategy, masterminded by Saeed Hajjarian, was: build up pressure steadily from the grass roots by mobilizing students and workers, take it to the crisis level, and then negotiate the surrender of conservatives on reformists' terms. Conservatives adopted the reverse strategy: they exercised their authority at the top against reformers and squeezed them while at the same time, using their extensive clerical network, they mingled with working- and lower-middle-class people socially, and defused the pressure their reformist adversaries had planned on increasing to an unbearable level. The fact that not a single supportive public demonstration occurred during the weeks that the reformist deputies staged their sit-in at the Majlis complex in early 2004 illustrated the effectiveness of the conservatives' strategy. They were also on the whole more adept at negotiating than reformists. This was as true of them in the domestic arena as it was in foreign affairs—as exemplified in their dealings with the European Union Troika on the nuclear issue.

In the Seventh Majlis (2004–), the reformist bloc shrank to 50 while the conservative one rose to nearly 190—with three-quarters of them being mainstream conservative, and the remaining divided equally between hard-line ideologues and pragmatists. Significantly, at 11 percent, the proportion of clerical deputies in this Majlis was a fifth of what it was in the First Majlis. Over the past generation it had become clear to most Iranians that clerics as politicians were no different from non-clerics, and that they shared the same mundane motives as their nonclerical counterparts for turning to politics, and that there was nothing spiritual about them—a healthy development.

Though reformers were on the retreat, the debate on political reform was far from over. Press freedom remained of primary concern to those pushing for political and social liberalization. The reason was as much ideological as pragmatic. "We must not expect the people to behave as we would like and [threaten] to suppress them if they do not," Khatami said. "People must be allowed to speak freely and criticize their government. If people are left unsatisfied, this will one day lead to an explosion."[7] Though Khatami made this statement in mid-2000, it remains as valid today as it did then.

And opposition to it also comes from the same quarters as before: the conservatives in the Majlis as well as the judiciary where they are in a majority. Since Iran's legislation is based on Islamic canons, dispensation of justice comes exclusively from qualified clerics.

A side effect of their continued anti-reform verdicts is that it has enabled the proponents of the regime to claim that the three organs of the state—executive, legislative, and judicial—in Iran are indeed separate, a salient feature of Western democracies.

There were of course several major differences between secular democracies in the West and the emerging Islamic democracy whereby, in Khatami's words, Iran was unprecedently trying to "formulate democracy in the context of spirituality and morality." One of them was that, unlike in Europe and North America, in criminal cases the roles of the investigator, prosecutor, and judge were played by the same person, a practice dating back to medieval times in tribal societies and sanctioned by early Islamic religious-scholars.

But a far greater difference lay in the fact that there was an overlay of mullahs in all important aspects of Iranian state and society. The Leader, who had to be a senior cleric, appointed his personal representatives not only to all the important institutions of the state at the national and provincial levels but also to the major private and quasi-official foundations, which possessed enormous assets. Mullahs were attached to the regular military as well as the IRGC, Baseej, and Law Enforcement Forces. They, of course, ran the Islamic Propagation Organization. They were on the payrolls of the Ministry of Culture and Islamic Guidance, which had its representatives in most of the thirty-three thousand villages, not to mention seven hundred towns and twenty-five cities. In addition, they were on the staff of the private and official foundations, including the richly endowed Foundation for the Deprived and Disabled. Finally, there were many seminaries where all teachers and many administrators were clerics.

In political terms, Islam provides the Iranian regime with an ideology and social cement. The image of women clad in chadors in the street—however repugnant to the Western eye—is the most dramatic and ubiquitous manifestation of Islam in daily life. The absence of alcohol and gambling (in public) as well as nightclubs is another.

In an Islamic state, the Sharia governs the life of a Muslim completely. Having studied all human actions, the early jurisprudents categorized them as: obligatory, recommended, allowed, unspecified, undesirable, and prohibited. From this they graduated to prescribing exactly how the obligatory, recommended, and allowed acts were to be performed. The simple edict of Prophet Muhammad that a believer must undertake ritual ablution with water (or sand) before prayers became enmeshed into a profound debate on the purity and pollution of the human body. Religious jurisprudents conducted minute examination of all bodily functions—eating, drinking, breathing, washing, urinating, defecating, farting, copulating, vomiting, bleeding, shaving—and prescribed how these were to be performed, the main stress being on keeping the body "pure." Along with this went a code of social behavior, including contact between opposite sexes, which too was all-encompassing. (The twin codes were so demanding that, even with the best will in the world, a believer could not abide by them all the time. On the other hand it was the introduction of these codes into the lives of those who embraced Islam that led to common behavioral patterns among Muslims whether they lived in the Mauritanian desert or Indonesian archipelago.) What emerged within a century of the rise of Islam in 622 A.D. was Islamic fiqh (jurisprudence), which included all aspects of religious, social, and political life—covering not only ritual and religious observances, the law of inheritance, property and contracts, and criminal law, but also constitutional law, laws concerning state administration, and the conduct of war.[8]

When it comes to interpreting the Sharia—that is practicing ijtihad (interpretative reasoning)—there is often no difference between jurisprudents on the obligatory and prohibited subjects. Differences usually arise in the gray area of "allowed, unspecified, and undesirable." Whether a woman is entitled to become President of Iran or a member of the Assembly of Experts falls into this category. As stated earlier, at least one senior theologian, Grand Ayatollah Yusuf Saanei said, "Yes" to both. In general, though, older jurisprudents are conservative, sticking to traditional interpretations, whereas younger ones are flexible and progressive.

Then there is the specific issue of the concept of vilayat-e faqih (rule of the religious jurisprudent) that forms the backbone of the Iranian constitution adopted in 1979. This doctrine, developed by Khomeini in 1971 in his book *Hukumat-e Islami: Vilayet-e Faqih* (Islamic Government: Rule of the Jurisprudent), specifies that an Islamic regime requires an Islamic ruler is thoroughly conversant with the Sharia and is just in its application: a Just Faqih. He should be assisted by jurisprudents at various levels of legislative, executive, and judicial bodies. The function of the popularly elected Majlis and presidency, open to both lay believers and clerics, is to resolve the conflicts likely to arise in the implementation of Islamic precepts. However, judicial functions are to be performed only by jurisprudents conversant with the Sharia. Such jurisprudents would also oversee the actions of the legislative and executive branches. The overall supervision and guidance of the Majlis and judiciary rests with the Just Faqih (later officially called Rahbar (Leader), of the Islamic Republic), who must also ensure that the executive does not exceed its powers.

An important amendment to the constitution's Article 107—authorizing the Assembly of Experts to choose the Leader—incorporated after Khoemini's death in June 1989, included the sentence, "The Leader is equal with the rest of the people of the country in the eyes of [the] law." As such, those clerics who argue that the Leader is divinely chosen and not accountable to the people can only be a minority. Equally small is the number of those who are advocating an end to the monopoly over ijtihad (interpretative reasoning) that jurisprudents have so far enjoyed.

In this debate, Professor Abdul Karim Soroush has stood out for the boldness, if not originality, of his thought. It draws a line between religion, which is eternal, and maarifat-e dini (religious knowledge), which results from applying "knowledge of the day" to the study of the core scriptures. Summarizing Soroush's thesis, Valla Vakili, an Iranian scholar at Britain's Oxford University, writes, "While religion itself does not change, human understanding and knowledge of it does. Religious knowledge is but one among many branches of human knowledge . . . [It] is the product of scholars engaged in the study of the unchanging core of Shia Islamic texts—the Quran, the hadiths [Sayings and Doings of Prophet Muhammad] and the teachings of the Shia Imams. These scholars interpret the text through the use of various methods, ranging from the rules of Arabic grammar to inferential logic, from Aristotelian philosophy to contemporary hermeneutics. Religious knowledge changes then as a function of these methods. But it is also influenced heavily by the worldview that informs each scholar [i.e., his understanding of other human sciences] . . . Religious knowledge changes and evolves over time, as more comprehensive understandings replace previous, more limited interpretations. Yet all interpretations are bound by the era in which a religious scholar lives, and by the degree of advancement of the human sciences and religious studies within this era."[9]

Soroush began proposing that religious knowledge be pursued as vigorously as possible by clerics and lay believers alike in a free-flowing environment. He argued in his articles in the pro-reform press for separation of religion and politics. The conservative deputies in the Fifth Majlis (1996–2000) feared that a debate along the lines suggested by him would raise the possibility of a divorce between religion and politics, and threaten the system dominated by clerics, and had to be nipped in the bud. They had the backing of the Leader's office.[10] So they tightened up the Press Law in July 1999 and April 2000.

Seen in a historical perspective, the Soroush-inspired debate was a rerun of the one that had engaged the Shia community in the eighteenth century. As mentioned earlier (Chapter Six), in the debate between traditionalists who, subscribing to the literal acceptance of the scriptures, argued that pious Shias could interpret the Sharia for themselves, and mujtahidis or usulis (those believing in principles), who insisted that mujtahids were needed to interpret the principles of Islam, mujtahidis won.

That school still holds sway. As Hojatalislam Ruhoallah Husseinian, a conservative intellectual, explained, Iran, being an Islamic republic, was a Republic that was to be guided and supervised by the Guardians Council to ensure it did not deviate from the Islamic framework. Since these guardians were selected by the Leader on the basis of their expertise in Islam, their interpretations and opinions overrode those of all others.

A more basic conflict has been noted by many between "Islamic" and "Republic" in the country's official title. According to Khatami, Khomeini had a choice between "Islamic State of Iran" run exclusively by clerics, and "Islamic Republic," governed by the people, and that he opted for "Republic." This principle is enshrined in Article 56 of the 1979 constitution (and unchanged in the 1989 version): "Absolute sovereignty over the world and man belongs to God, and it is He who made man master of his own social destiny . . . The people are to exercise this divine right in the manner specified in the following articles [concerning the Leader, the President, and the Majlis]."

Yet, commenting on the landslide victory of Khatami in May 1997, Ayatollah Ahmad Jannati, the arch conservative head of the Guardians Council, said, "Difference of [political] preference is one thing. The ruling system—the Islamic Republic, Imam Khomeini's path and such matters—are another . . . All must know that this state is the state of the vilayat-e faqih . . . Mr. President-elect must bear in mind that now the creditors start . . . . The first creditor of anyone who has been given a position by God is God Almighty. The second is the eminent Leader, the vali-ye faqih. After that, comes the electorate."[11]

But then the same Jannati defied the Leader in early 2004. When Khamanei publicly instructed Jannati and the rest of the Guardians Council to examine carefully the credentials of the sitting Majlis deputies while reconsidering the cases of those applicants whose candidacy for a Majlis seat the Council had rejected, the Council went on to raise the number of the rejected sitting parliamentarians. A decade earlier, in the religious field, rebuffing political pressures, the Association of Qom Teachers had refused to raise the status of Leader Khamanei to marja-e taqlid (source of emulation), thus underscoring their independence from the state—a long-established tradition in Shia Islam.

The office of the Leader and his powers are also issues that many Iranians would like to discuss. But the ban on criticism of the Leader and the constitution imposed in April 2000 inhibits public debate. Even in political science classes, students and teachers are barred from challenge the doctrine of vilayat-e faqih.

"If there were a referendum tomorrow, and people had to say whether or not they wanted to have a Faqih, may be 70 percent would say yes," said Zibakalam on the polling day for the Assembly of Experts in October 1998. "The concept is not at stake—yet. But its functions, powers and term in office are. It is all progress that people are saying these things."[12]

Before the ban, such subjects were freely discussed by the members of the influential, semiofficial University—Seminary Unity Consolidation Bureau, in the wake of the election of Khatami, who was seen as a conciliatory figure bridging the pre- and postrevolution generations, an extremely valuable political asset, once any revolution, secular or religious, has passed its twentieth anniversary.

The radical faction within the UCB advocated abolishing the Leader's post, and demanding more of a separation between religion and politics than existed. Reza Hojjati, a leading member of this faction, believed that the core conflict could be resolved only by confrontation, but was conscious that there was no mass support for a return to the armed struggle of the late 1970s and early 1980s. "The students have to create public awareness," he said. "Many members of the lower classes of society don't have any understanding of reform and development. As a result, they are not ready to fight and suffer even though their rights are being violated."[13]

Here was the nub of the challenge for young reformers. The reform movement had remained an urban modern-middle class phenomenon, with scores of affluent businessmen ready to finance newspapers to advocate political and social liberalization, and had failed to strike a chord among working and lower middle classes in cities and small towns and villages.

As it was, at the turn of the twenty-first century as the Islamic revolution entered its third decade, even the harshest critics of the government conceded that the social-political situation had normalized to the point that the regime tolerated former monarchists and Marxists, Westernized aristocrats, and Western-educated intellectuals and artists so long as they did not defy the system or the law blatantly, and practiced peaceful coexistence by finding ways to circumvent the rules in an unobtrusive way. The improvement in the economy due to consistently high prices of oil since March 1999 too has helped to ease tensions as middle-class men become more focused on improving their economic condition and less interested in politics than before.

The authorities too have taken to turning a blind eye to Iranian Muslims drinking at home or at diplomatic parties. In any case, it has become common practice to bribe the law enforcement agents. Strict implementation of "good hijab" and segregation of unmarried men and women is no longer de rigeur, nor is the ban on satellite dishes enforced strictly. "Look at what's happened with videos in this country," said Ali Reza Shiravi of the Ministry of Culture and Islamic Guidance in Tehran. "In the beginning of the revolution, they were banned. But people didn't care. Videos became widespread. By the time the government lifted the ban, it was too late."[14] Today, Internet is everywhere in Iran, and so also are mobile phones.

Taken as a whole, how has the Islamic revolution fared over the past quarter century?

From religious point of view, the new regime has raised Islamic consciousness among the public at large.

Besides the universally observed Muslim festivals of Eid al Fitr and Eid al Adha, the Iranian regime and media also commemorate the birth- and death-anniversaries of Prophet Muhammad and Twelve Shia Imams as well as those of Fatima, a daughter of Prophet Muhammad and the wife of Imam Ali, and Fatima Massaumeh, and the first ten days of Muharram culminating in Ashura.[15] Every several miles (km) on highways, quotes from the Quran in white Arabic letters with green background appear on large signboards: "There is no god but Allah, Muhammad is His Messenger"—the Islamic credo; and "God is great." Even radical students do not want to abandon Islam, all they want is that it should not be manipulated by conservative clerics to diminish the believers' civil and human rights.

Going by the statistics for education and public health, it has done very well. Unexpectedly, the imposition of the veil and sex segregation in classrooms boosted education among women. Equally impressive was the explosion in telecommunications, with the number of landline telephones registering fourfold increase during the decade of 1991 to 2001.[16] But, in per capita income the Islamic Republic is still way behind the level Iranians enjoyed in the last years of the Shah's rule.

In class terms, the revolution empowered the previously powerless working class and petty bourgeoisie. These are the classes that have provided, and continue to provide, the vast bulk of recruits for the predominantly volunteer fighting forces of the 125,000-strong Islamic Revolutionary Guards Corps and its auxiliary three hundred thousand-strong Baseej, on whom, in the final analysis, the Islamic regime relies. While safeguarding Iran's borders, the IRGC, assisted by the Baseej, is also trained to curb serious domestic disorder, and did so in July 1999. At 425,000, the strength of the two forces far exceeds that of the regular military (at 395,000) once the nearly 200,000 conscripts are excluded.

When the chips are down, it is the IRGC and the Baseej who would man the barricades and shed blood to preserve the theocratic regime. This is as true of an internal threat to the regime as an external attack, which remains a possibility as far as the reelected George W. Bush administration remains committed to pursuing its doctrine of "preventive wars." In any case, Washington's intimidation of and threats to the Islamic Republic continue. The net effect of this U.S. policy is to strengthen the hands of conservatives and hard-liners at the expense of reformists and moderates.

In international affairs, the Islamic regime has truly turned Iran into an independent state, conducting its affairs with such giants as the European Union, China, and India on equal terms. So Iranians strongly resent interference in their affairs by America—at both official and popular levels.

Having gained a two-thirds majority in the Seventh Majlis, and maintaining their traditional predominance in the judiciary, conservatives now control two of the three state organs. Reformist President Khatami is constitutionally barred from running for the presidency for a third term in the poll due in May 2005.

In that campaign the nuclear issue is likely to figure prominently. If negotiations with the EU being conducted by Hojatal-islam Hassan Rouhani, the Secretary-General of Iran's Supreme National Security Council, result in a successful "grand bargain" between the two parties, the chances of him emerging as the favorite for the presidency will improve. A cleric who obtained a doctorate in law from Glasgow University in Scotland, he is a pragmatic conservative in the mold of Rafsanjani.

Having captured all three organs of the state, the conservatives are likely to compromise on social and economic reform while insisting on retaining monopoly of political power.

That seems to be the most likely scenario for the Islamic Republic of Iran in the near future.

Epilogue

The Iranian-European Union Troika (EU3) talks, begun in mid-December 2004, centered round the concessions to Iran on technology transfers, trade and cooperation, and security and political issues in return for its voluntary surrender of its right to produce nuclear fuel to run its reactors for civilian purposes, as allowed by the nuclear Non-Proliferation Treaty (NPT) it had signed. U.S. President George W. Bush regarded such a deal as tantamount to "rewarding" Tehran for giving up activities that, in his view, were a cover for a nuclear arms program—an assertion for which the International Atomic Agency (IAEA) had found no evidence.

The Europeans soon realized that, given America's occupation of Afghanistan and Iraq, their discussion of Iran's security was meaningless without Washington's direct or indirect participation. That Tehran's security was at the core of the problem was stressed by Joschka Fischer and Peter Struck, respective Foreign and Defense Ministers of Germany, an EU3 member. At the Munich Security Conference in mid-February 2005, they said that Iran would abandon its nuclear ambitions only if its legitimate security interests were safeguarded.[1] Regarding trade and cooperation with the EU, where Tehran was seeking support for its membership of the World Trade Organization (WTO), the role of America was crucial. Iran's application could only be considered if there was no a priori objection by any of the WTO's leading members, such as America. But Washington refused to oblige.

Overall, the Bush administration had five options on Iran: (a) constructive engagement following the European approach; (b) tightening economic and military sanctions through the United Nations; (c) increasing support for proxy opposition groups to destabilize the regime; (d) pinprick strikes against specific nuclear and military targets; and (e) outright invasion.

Given the paucity of spare soldiers, the Pentagon was not in a position to invade Iran. Nonetheless, U.S. Defense Secretary Donald Rumsfeld had ordered the Centcom headquarters to update contingency plans for invading Iran, which had hitherto visualized American troops entering Iran along its shoreline. In Iran, the leaders' earlier fear of being surrounded by the American troops had subsided as the Pentagon became mired in Iraq. However, the commander of the Islamic Republican Guard Corps (IRGC) was realistic enough to concede publicly that Iran could resist an American invasion only for a few weeks, and that it would be the guerrilla warfare by the Guards and the Baseej militia that would make it impossible for the Americans to occupy Iran.

It soon emerged that Washington's favored choice was surgical strikes on Iran.

Revelations in the *New Yorker* and the *Washington Post* in January–February 2005 showed that the Pentagon had been flying drones over Iran since April 2004. They used radar, video, still photography and air filters to test Iranian defenses and seek traces of nuclear activity. Iranians noticed drones in the Caspian region, Natanz, Isfahan, and along the Iraq border, and the local press ran stories about unidentified flying objects (UFOs). An unnamed Iranian security official told the *Washington Post* that the security chiefs decided not to engage the drones because to do so would give information about the country's air defense capabilities. Iran protested through the Swiss embassy, which has an American Interests Section.[2]

America's aerial reconnaissance was complemented by ground action. In his mid-January article in the *New Yorker*, Seymour Hersh revealed that undercover American commando groups and other Special Forces units had been conducting clandestine reconnaissance missions inside Iran since at least July 2004. One such task force was working closely with those Pakistani scientists and technicians who had dealt with their Iranian counterparts in the past.[3]

Another American task force, assisted by Islamabad, had infiltrated Iran to search for underground installations and place remote detection devices to sample the environment for radioactive emissions or other evidence of the uranium-enrichment program. The payback for Pakistan was that Washington would not pressure President Gen. Pervez Musharraf to hand over Abdul Qadeer Khan—"the father of Pakistan's nuclear bomb," who had sold nuclear secrets to several countries—either to it or the IAEA for questioning. "Tell us what you know about Iran and we will let your Khan guys go." That was the deal between America and Pakistan, according to Hersh's informant, a former high-level intelligence official. It was the American neocons' version of short-term gain at the cost of the long-term goal of eliminating the black market for nuclear proliferation, the official added.

Washington's aim was to gather information on about forty of Iran's declared and suspected chemical, nuclear and missile sites, with about three-quarters to be destroyed from the air, and the rest, being too close to population centers, or buried too deep, to be targeted by commando units. "The [hawkish] civilians in the Pentagon want to go into Iran and destroy as much of the military infrastructure as possible," a government consultant with close ties to the Pentagon told Hersh. These civilians argued that the only thing the Iranians understood was pressure and that they also needed "to be whacked."

But the attackers could not be sure whether they had hit all the sites or how soon the Iranians could rebuild the destroyed facilities. "Our nuclear technology comes from our scientists [and] we can transfer our nuclear workshops under mountains and carry out our enrichment where no bomb or missile can be effective," Hassan Rouhani, Secretary-General of Iran's Supreme National Security Council, told state TV. "We are seeking to resolve our issues with America. But they are blocking any chance of resolving the issues."[4] While pursuing an active military plan clandestinely, Bush expressed his preference for diplomacy in public.

In her testimony to the U.S. Senate Foreign Affairs Committee in late January 2005, however, the Secretary of State-Designate, Condoleezza Rice, included Iran in her list of the "outposts of tyranny" that the new Bush administration would focus on, the other outposts being Belarus, Burma, Cuba, North Korea and Zimbabwe. (She made no mention of Syria, Uzbekistan, Turkmenistan or Saudi Arabia.) She also expressed her belief in "transformational diplomacy," a code term for regime change.

In his State of the Union speech on February 2, Bush said, "Iran remains the world's primary state sponsor of terrorism— pursuing nuclear weapons while depriving its people of the freedom they seek and deserve," and added, "To the Iranian people I say tonight, as you stand for your own liberty, America stands with you."

Iran's leader, Ayatollah Ali Khamanei, responded by calling America "a global tyrant," which was trying to "deny the talented Iranian nation of progress and to deprive it of existence." Describing the U.S. as "one of the big heads of a seven-headed dragon," menacing Iran under the direction of "Zionist and non-Zionist capitalists," he said, "Bush is the fifth American president seeking to uproot the Iranian nation and the Islamic Republic of Iran. Carter, Reagan, and father Bush and Clinton failed. This president will also fail."[5]

A telling insight into the thinking of the Second Bush administration came during Rice's breakfast meeting with six French intellectuals in Paris on February 9, when she branded Iran as "a totalitarian state." A year before, she added, she would have called it "an authoritarian state," but after the flawed parliamentary elections in the spring of 2004, Iran had moved to "a totalitarian state." (As described in Chapter Two, Iran's Guardians Council first barred leftists and reformers from contesting the 1992 parliamentary poll. So by Rice's logic, Iran became totalitarian in 1992. It was under such conditions that reformist Muhammad Khatami got elected President in 1997!) Rice said that the West had been wrong to accept the Soviet Union on its terms during the Cold War, and it must not make the same mistake with Iran. (Comparing the mighty Soviet Union, one of the two superpowers for nearly two generations and leader of the Warsaw Pact nations, with Iran was a glaring example of a dangerously blinkered view of history.) Recalling the meeting, François Heisbourg, Director of the Foundation for Strategic Research, said, "I tried to explain that Iran was not like the Soviet Union, that the mullahs were deeply unpopular, but, unlike their predecessors [i.e., previous rulers] over the past 150 years, they were not in the hands of the British or the Russians or the Americans. She gave no proof that Iran was totalitarian because she didn't have any. It was scary." Another participant, Nicole Bacharan, an expert on America at the Sciences Po, said, "Rice believes that EU negotiations with Iran are going nowhere and she is very much in favor of regime change."[6]

Washington had coordinated its policy on Iran with Israel, with Douglas Feith, the Undersecretary for Policy at the Defense

Department, working closely with Israel's military planners to pinpoint actual and potential targets. With American connivance, Israel had established a forward spying site in Iraqi Kurdistan.[7]

But their estimations on Iran's nuclear program differed. Whereas Porter Goss, Director of Central Intelligence, told Congress in November 2004 that Iran was "several years away from producing an actual weapon," and most Western intelligence agencies had concluded that Tehran was facing serious technical problems to manufacture uranium hexafluoride (UF6) gas—the material to be enriched to varying degrees—Israeli officials claimed that the Iranians were within a year of completing facilities to produce nuclear arms.[8]

"The Europeans' attitude has been to use the carrot and the stick—but all we see so far is the carrot," complained Israeli Foreign Minister Silvan Shalom to the *New Yorker*, "If they can't comply, Israel cannot live with Iran having a nuclear bomb."

Why is Israel, possessing an estimated arsenal of 200-plus atomic bombs, drawing this red line? Because it wants to maintain its nuclear monopoly in the region in defiance of Paragraph 14 of the UN Security Council Resolution 687 (April 1991), which calls for "steps towards the goal of establishing in the Middle East a zone free from weapons of mass destruction and all missiles for their delivery."

While the immediate objective of the U.S. and/or Israeli attacks would be to destroy or degrade Tehran's plans to go nuclear, the hawkish policy-makers believed that these raids could lead to the overthrow of the clerical regime, especially if they were preceded by increasing support for proxy opposition groups to destabilize it. Given the widespread disaffection with the mullahs' rule, the hawks argued, all that was needed was to show to the suffering Iranians that the clerics were vulnerable. Such a scenario, accepted by Rumsfeld and his deputy, Paul Wolfowitz, had the same delusional aura about it as the one where Iraqis would welcome their Anglo-American invaders with sweets and flowers. As the history of Iraq's invasion of Iran in 1980, outlined in Chapter Eight, shows, a foreign attack on Iran would lead Iranians of all social classes and political colors to rally round their government. On balance, such an event would strengthen the hands of Iranian conservatives at the expense of reformers.

Since the nuclear ambition in Iran was supported by both conservatives and reformists, most Iranians would view military raids as assaults on their aspirations to become a modern, technologically advanced nation and a major regional player. An Iranian official told EU3 negotiators that American military strikes would make "building nuclear weapons an uncontested national cause among Iranians." In his *New York Times* op-ed in late January, Richard Haass, former head of the State Department's policy planning bureau, argued that "even if 'freedom' were somehow to come to Tehran, it is almost certain that free Iranians would be as enthusiastic as the mullahs about possessing nuclear weapons owing to the political popularity of these weapons and their strategic rationale, given Iran's neighborhood."

After discussing Iran with European leaders during his February 20–23 visit to Europe, Bush said, "This notion that the U.S. is getting ready to attack Iran is simply ridiculous...Having said all that, all options are on the table." It is worth recalling that it was the same Bush who told a press conference at his Crawford ranch on August 22, 2002 that he was studying intelligence on Iraq and that there were no war plans on his table, even though he had decided six months earlier to invade Iraq.[9]

In his report to the IAEA's Board of Governors on March 1, Director-General Muhammad El Baradei said that while Iran had not answered all IAEA questions, during two years of near constant on-site inspections the IAEA had discovered nothing to show that Iran was engaged in an active weapons program. Summarizing the report, an IAEA official said, "The facts don't support an innocent or guilty verdict at this point."[10]

On March 11, Rice issued a statement which read: "In order to support the EU3 diplomacy, the President has decided that the U.S. will drop its objection to Iran's application to the WTO and will consider on a case by case basis the licensing of spare parts for Iranian civil aircraft, from the EU to Iran." In return the EU would back Washington in referring Iran to the United Nations Security Council if the latest round of talks failed to secure agreement.[11]

The same day, however, Vice President Dick Cheney said that Iran would face "stronger action" if it failed to respond. This implied that American military action was not ruled out if the issue got deadlocked at the Security Council—just what America had done in the case of Iraq.

The chances of a Security Council stalemate were high. On February 26, at the Haleyle nuclear power plant, Alexander Rumyantsev, head of the Russian Federal Atomic Energy Agency, signed an agreement with Iranian Vice President Gholam Reza Aghazadeh, who also headed Iran's Atomic Energy Organization, on the supply of nuclear fuel plant under which Iran would return spent fuel rods to Russia. Moscow repeated its opposition to Iran being referred to the Security Council. So also did Beijing. With its unquenchable thirst for oil to fuel its fast-rising economy, China has strengthened its ties with Tehran.

As it takes years for an applicant to become a member of the WTO, Washington's concession to the EU on this issue was a mere tactical move. Yet Israeli Prime Minister Ariel Sharon thought that Bush had gone soft on Iran. In protest his aides informed the (London) *Sunday Times* that in February the Israeli inner cabinet gave "an initial authorization" for a combined air and ground attack on the uranium enrichment plant at Natanz. They claimed that the plans had been discussed with U.S. officials who had "indicated" that they would not bar Israel if all diplomatic efforts to halt Iran's nuclear projects failed.[12]

Reviewing the deliberations of the past three months on March 23, the Iranian and European negotiators concluded that sufficient progress had been made to continue talking for at least three more months—that is, past the presidential poll on June 17.

2005 Presidential Poll

When the Guardians Council rejected the applications of all but six of the 1,008 candidates for the presidency, including two leading reformists—Mustafa Moin and Muhsin Mehr Alizadeh—Khamanei publicly instructed it to allow all factions to compete. Moin and Alizadeh were then permitted to contest.

Of the seven candidates who finally appeared on the ballot papers, Ali Akbar Hashemi Rafsanjani, a former President and current head of the Expediency Council, was the favorite. An affluent cleric, derided by his opponents as "Akbar Shah (Great Shah)," he would spend about $5 million on his campaign.

This time Iranians witnessed slick, Western-flavored campaigning. Digitally edited color photos of the candidates printed on large posters, and colorful balloons and badges carrying their names and images became the norm. The odd man out was Mahmoud Ahmadinejad (derived from *Ahmad-i-nehjad*, "race of Ahmad," or "descendants of Ahmad"), the conservative mayor of Tehran since 2003. He mounted an austere campaign. Short and slim, with a big nose and small eyes, a thick mop of black hair and a thin, untrimmed beard, he presented himself as an ordinary pious man, a blacksmith's son, modeling himself on Muhammad Ali Rajai, a bricklayer, who became the second President of Iran. His were the only posters in black and white. In the television documentary on him, he stressed the modesty of his home in the middle-middle-class neighborhood of Narmak in eastern Tehran, furnished with a single chair at the desk he shared with his father. On the election day, he went to his polling station and stood in line like all the others.

Though four of the candidates were conservative, with Ahmadinejad being the most hard-line, they were all aware of the numerical preponderance of women and young people among voters. So they all spoke the language of democracy, market economy, and the participation of women and young people in the political process, with little, if any, mention of Islam. Moin, the leading reformist candidate, promised to release all political prisoners, to put Shirin Ebadi, the Nobel peace laureate, in charge of protecting human rights, and to challenge Khamanei on the issue of the President's constitutional rights.

According to an editorial in the reformist *Sharq* (East), the judges were being "a bit nicer" to dissident journalists, satellite dishes were not being confiscated, and the state-run television had been fairly even-handed, airing a half-hour special documentary on each of the official candidates.[13]

On the eve of the election, the Bush White House said that "Iran's electoral process ignores the basic requirements of democracy" on the basis that 1,002 candidates had been disqualified from running. The statement proved counter-productive. Iran's state-run television presented it as a taunt, implying that Iranians' ballot did not matter. This spurred Iranians to vote.

Nearly two-thirds of the 46.5 million voters cast their ballots. Rafsanjani topped the list with 21 per cent of the vote, followed by Ahmadinejad at 19.5 per cent, Hojatalislam Mahdi Karrubi at 17.5 percent, Moin and Muhammad Qalibaf at 13.9 per cent each, Ali Larijani, former head of the Islamic Republic of Iran Broadcasting, at 6 per cent, and Alizadeh at 4.4 per cent.

The emergence of Ahmadinejad as a runner-up surprised many. It upset Karrubi, a former Speaker of the Majlis and a moderate reformist. Alleging that ballot boxes had been stuffed in

Isfahan, the Baseej had illegally campaigned for "one of the candidates," and Khamanei's son Mujtaba had canvassed for Ahmadinejad, he resigned as advisor to Khamanei.[14]

Observers noted that there was a last-minute surge in favor of Ahmadinejad among the urban working class, attracted by his simple appearance and campaign, and his attacks on corruption ("I will cut off the hands of the corrupt mafia"), which, going by his performance as Tehran's mayor, were convincing. Most of the conservative leaders in cities, who had initially backed Qalibaf, switched to Ahmadinejad and activated the Baseej network to add to the momentum.

During the second round on June 24, Rafsanjani, a pragmatic conservative, tried to rebrand himself as a reformist, claiming that it was during his presidency that the foundation was laid for economic and political liberalization. He argued that his many years of experience in the government made him well qualified for the presidency, and that he alone possessed the influence and adroitness to unify the nation to make a respectful peace with America. He promised to press ahead with "realistic reform." But there was very little he could do to dissipate the popular view that associated him with money-making for himself and his family so long as he continued to display an ostentatious manner and the trappings of power he already possessed.

Set in his ways, seventy-two-year-old Rafsanjani stuck to a top-down strategy in his campaign—a contrast to the bottom-up strategy of his forty-eight-year-old rival, Ahmadinejad, which (as described on pp. 351–52) the conservative activists had deployed successfully in the 2004 Majlis elections against reformers by mixing socially with working and lower-middle class Iranians. Now, Ahmadinejad's camp focused on villages and provincial towns, which contained most of the nineteen million Iranians living below the poverty line, repeating his pledges of "putting oil money on people's tables," shifting state funds away from more developed cities to less developed areas, giving interest-free loans to farmers and small businesses, and maintaining subsidies on food and fuel. To win women's votes, he promised pensions, health insurance, and unemployment insurance for them. His strategy became so effective that it drove Rafsanjani's followers to send out last-minute messages on cell phones warning that if he won he would usher in a Taliban-type government.

This time nearly three-fifths of voters participated. Ahmadinejad trounced Rafsanjani by a factor of nine to five. At 17.3 million votes, he improved his previous score by 11.6 million whereas Rafsanjani added less than 4 million to his earlier figure of 6.15 million—far less than the total of 5.4 million votes won by the two reformist candidates in the first round, who now backed him.

Ahmadinejad picked up most of the 5 million ballots cast for Karrubi, who had promised a stipend of $60 a month to each family, amounting to almost a third of the average monthly salary. Evidently, this time pocket book issues interested the electorate more than social, cultural, and political freedoms advocated by reformists.

The voter turn-out of around 60 per cent in both rounds showed that Iranians were engaged with their political system, a conclusion which clashed with the Bush White House's perception that the bulk of the people were alienated from the regime. "The election result belied the view, especially widespread among Iran's critics in the Bush administration, that Iran's public discourse is essentially a fight between the people, who want freedom, and a repressive state," noted the *Economist*'s correspondent in Tehran. "Nor are there signs that popular discontent is spilling into violence. In contrast with the pre-revolutionary Iran, the Islamic Republic is a partial democracy, and people let off steam on the polling day"[15]

Actually what happened on June 24, 2005 in Iran was far

more than "letting off steam." This poll was a watershed in the Islamic Republic. It was the first time that a second ballot had been held as no candidate won more than 50 per cent of the vote in the initial round. It signaled the arrival of war veterans, who had closer ties with the Iran-Iraq War than with the revolution, at the helm of the state's executive organ. More importantly, it was also the first time in post-revolutionary Iran that the presidential election was decided on the basis of social class—with peasants, workers, and the lower-middle class backing Ahmadinejad, and the middle-middle, upper-middle, and upper classes Rafsanjani.

Mahmoud Ahmadinejad's background fitted this analysis. Born in 1956 in Aradan (pop. 7,000), a village 80 miles (130 km) southeast of Tehran, he was the fourth of seven children of a barber. The following year his father migrated to Tehran where he became a blacksmith. A brilliant student, he ranked 130th among the hundreds of thousands who took the university entrance examination. He enrolled as a civil engineering student at the Iran University of Science and Technology (IUST). He became active in the anti-Shah movement. On the eve of the revolution in early 1979, the whole family fled to a provincial town to avoid his arrest. At the outbreak of the Iran-Iraq War in 1980 he joined the Baseej militia, and then the IRGC where he became chief engineer in the 6th Army. In 1986 he enrolled on an M.Sc. in civil engineering at the IUST, and then won a doctorate in traffic and transportation engineering and planning. After the war he became an advisor to Khatami, then Minister of Culture and Islamic Guidance. In 1993 he was appointed governor-general of Ardebil Province, serving until 1997. He performed well. Following the second municipal election in Tehran in early 2003, won by the conservative Alliance of the Builders of Islamic Iran, he was elected mayor. Refusing to accept the mayor's salary, he lived austerely. He laid roads, gave interest-free loans to the needy, and put religious emphasis on the cultural centers established by his predecessors.

The 2005 presidential election exposed a major weakness of the reformists, who, reflecting the interests and aspirations of the modern middle classes, had neglected the issues that most interested peasants and workers—the wealth gap that had grown wider and more blatant due to increased foreign imports of consumer goods paid for by high oil prices, rampant corruption, and high inflation. With the near collapse of the reformist camp, the center of political gravity shifted sharply to the right in religious-ideological terms and left in the economic sphere, reflecting primarily the values of the emergent urban working class—economically leftist but religiously and socially conservative.

With all three state organs now headed by conservatives and reformists in disarray, the tensions between the reformist and conservative camps that had become the mainstay of Iran's politics were most likely to be transferred to the conservative bloc, which was far from homogenous. As stated earlier (p. 352), of the 190 conservative legislators, nearly 140 were mainstream, and the rest were divided almost equally among hard-line ideologues and pragmatists. Since Ahmadinejad was not a mainstream conservative, he could not take it for granted that the Majlis would always do his bidding.

Khamanei was aware of the radical change wrought by the latest poll, and acted to bring about some balance. He publicly urged Rafsanjani to stay as the head of the Expediency Council.

Ahmadinejad as the Ninth President

On assuming the presidency on August 2, Ahmadinejad refused to move to the official residence in Saadabad Palace in north Tehran. Instead he settled for living in one of the buildings in the well-protected Pastor Square complex of the government.

Three days later the EU3 submitted "The Framework for a Long Term Agreement" to Tehran. It offered commercial incentives and building of light water nuclear power plants conditional on Iran's permanent renunciation of its rights under the nuclear NPT. It also included the demand that Iran must give a legal binding not to quit the NPT under any circumstances.[16]

Tehran rejected the EU3 package because it did not accept "Iran's inalienable right to all aspects of peaceful nuclear technology." It resumed its conversion of uranium oxide, called yellow cake, into UF6 at its plant near Isfahan—but only under the watchful eyes of the IAEA inspectors. This was a clear breach of Iran's agreement to suspend "all uranium enrichment-related activities" while talks between it and the EU3 continued, protested the Europeans.

At their request the IAEA Board held an emergency session in Vienna in late August. Baradei reported that the traces of highly enriched uranium found earlier at the Iranian sites came from contaminated equipment imported from Pakistan and Russia, as the Iranians had maintained.

Rajmah Hussein of Malaysia, chairman of the Non-Aligned Movement (NAM)—to which 116 of the 191 members of the UN are affiliated—reiterated the NAM's position that all countries have "a basic and inalienable right" to develop atomic energy for peaceful purposes—the prime objective for which the IAEA was established in 1957 at the initiative of U.S. President Dwight Eisenhower. Most NAM governors feared that any limitations imposed on Iran could be extended later to all Third World countries.

Since the NAM accounted for twelve governors, including such heavyweights as Brazil (whose uranium enrichment plant at Resende, 200 km from Rio de Janeiro, was on schedule to start operating in January 2006), India, Pakistan, Indonesia, South Africa, and Venezuela, it became evident to the EU3 and America that they lacked the wide majority they were seeking. So they settled for a consensual call to Iran to suspend its activities related to uranium enrichment, and for Baradei to report on the matter by September 3. Ali Larijani, the newly appointed Secretary-General of Iran's SNSC, said that he welcomed talks with all IAEA governors, including NAM members.

Baradei's fifteen-page document submitted to the IAEA Board in early September was a mixed bag. Its harshest comment was: "In view of the fact the agency is not in a position to clarify some important outstanding issues after two and a half years of intensive inspection and investigation, Iran's transparency is indispensable and overdue."[17] This left intact the IAEA's conclusion in March that it had not found evidence that Iran was engaged in an active nuclear weapons program.

An equally mixed message was contained in the story published by the *Washington Post* a month earlier.[18] It revealed that in its latest National Intelligence Estimate on Iran, produced in May after a gap of four years, U.S. intelligence agencies had concluded that Iran was "determined" to build nuclear weapons but that it was not expected to possess such weapons until the early or middle years of the next decade.

Using the UN General Assembly's platform, in his speech on September 17, Ahmadinejad offered "to engage in serious partnership with private and public sectors of other countries in the implementation of the uranium enrichment program in Iran."[19] But at the IAEA Board's quarterly session, starting on September 20, neither the EU3 nor America made any mention of Tehran's offer. The debate on Iran's nuclear issue was unprecedentedly rancorous. There were bitter exchanges between British Governor Peter Jenkins and his counterparts from Malaysia and South Africa, a country which in 1993 voluntarily gave up its nuclear weapons and program.[20] When Jenkins dismissed their criticism as "disingenuous," Rajmah Hussein retorted, "I object to this treatment." Abdul Minty of South Africa complained that the EU and the US were riding roughshod over the others.[21]

On September 24, ignoring NAM governors' appeals to avoid confrontation by delaying a precipitate decision, Britain called a vote on its resolution, and won. Twenty-two voted in favor, and one (Venezuela) against, with the remaining twelve abstaining. All but two of the abstainers belonged to the NAM.

The IAEA resolution found that Iran's "many failures and breaches of its obligations to comply with its NPT Safeguards Agreement…constitute non compliance" with the nuclear NPT, and that "the resulting absence of confidence that Iran's nuclear program is exclusively for peaceful purposes [has] given rise to questions that are within the competence of the Security Council." It called on Iran to reestablish "full and sustained suspension of all enrichment-related activity," and promptly ratify and implement the Additional Protocol.

It was at the insistence of Russia and China that the resolution dropped any reference to when Iran might be referred to the UN Security Council. In return they abstained. (Moscow's close cooperation with Tehran continued uninterrupted, with a Russian space launcher placing Iran's first satellite, Sinah-1, into orbit a few weeks later—followed by a $1 billion deal with Tehran to sell it TOR-M1 missile systems capable of destroying guided missiles and laser-guided bombs from aircraft.) As for the NAM members, their leader, Hussein, left little doubt that their abstention was tantamount to opposition. "Our major concerns and those of like-minded states were not taken on board," he said after the vote.

There were two defections from NAM ranks: Singapore and India. The behavior of Singapore, one of the richest countries, did not surprise many. The contrary was the case with India. "The vote in favor of the resolution by India came as a shock to the Islamic Republic," noted the *Iran News*. "Until yesterday, Iranian diplomats were expressing confidence that New Delhi would be in Tehran's corner." India abandoned its long-held ideology of non-alignment for technological gain. During the Indian Prime Minister Manmohan Singh's visit to Washington in July, President Bush described India as "a responsible nuclear weapons power," and promised to make advanced U.S. civilian nuclear technology available to it. But this could only be done if the Congress voted to make an exception to the existing law which forbids the U.S. to provide nuclear energy assistance to countries with nuclear weapons. Finding India on Tehran's side at the IAEA, the White House threatened not to make the necessary recommendation to the Congress. The ploy worked.[22]

In Tehran, calling the IAEA resolution "unfair," 180 legislators urged the government to resume uranium enrichment activities, and said that the Additional Protocol should not be ratified as demanded by the IAEA. Forming a majority in the 290-strong Majlis, the signatories could block the Protocol's ratification. By contrast, Iran's newly appointed Foreign Minister, Manouchehr Mottaki, expressed his readiness to continue negotiations with a qualification: "Iran will include new countries in the talks." The EU3, backed by America, ruled out expanding the negotiating team.

Following the decree issued by Ayatollah Ruhollah Khomeini, Iran prepared to mark the last Friday in Ramadan (starting October 4) on October 28 as Jerusalem Liberation Day. Two days earlier, Ahmadinejad addressed a conference, titled "The World Without Zionism," at Tehran University. "The establishment of the Zionist regime was a move by the world oppressor against the Islamic world," he said. "There is no doubt that the new wave [of attacks] in Palestine will wipe off this stigma [Israel] from the face of the Islamic world." Referring to Khomeini, he added, "As the Imam said, Israel must be wiped off the map."[23]

His statement was condemned by the U.S., Britain, France, Germany, Israel and UN Secretary-General Kofi Annan. Russian Foreign Minister Sergei Lavrov, who had publicly opposed Rice's proposal of referring Iran to the UN Security Council, said that Ahmadinejad's remarks would provide ammunition for those who wanted the Security Council to act against Iran. Most significantly, Saeb Erekat, the chief Palestinian negotiator, said, "I urge the President of Iran to focus on adding Palestine alongside Israel, not calling for wiping a country off the map."

Other Iranian politicians intervened to do damage control. In his sermon to the Friday prayer congregation on October 28, Rafsanjani said, "If Muslims and Palestinians agree [to a referendum to settle the future of Palestine and Israel], it will be a retreat but let us still hold a referendum." Differentiating between Jews and Zionists, he added, "We have no problem with Jews and highly respect Judaism as a holy religion. We only have problems with the Zionist circles in Israel which we hold responsible for the suppression of the Palestinian nation."[24] Rafsanjani spoke with greater authority than before. Three weeks earlier Khamanei had issued a decree authorizing the Expediency Council to supervise the implementation of policies by all three state organs—as well as the armed forces and the state-run media. By so doing, he placed the Expediency Council, headed by Rafsanjani, above the rest of the government.

Iran's foreign ministry said that Iran would back whatever course the Palestinians chose to resolve the Middle East conflict. But Iran's reformers were not prepared to give Ahmadinejad the benefit of the doubt. "It is becoming more and more clear among reformist politicians and some of his own supporters that Mr Ahmadinejad had neither the political experience nor the knowledge to run the country," said Isa Saharkhiz, a reformist politician and journalist.[25]

On the nuclear issue, Ahmadinejad's government allowed IAEA inspectors to revisit the military complex at Parchin in early November, and let them interview senior officials linked to the earlier black market purchases of the equipment for the nuclear program. Larijani addressed letters to EU3 embassies to restart negotiations, while telling them that Iran was converting a fresh batch of yellow cake.

The State Department in Washington floated the idea of letting Iran convert yellow cake into UF6 but only if the gas was then shipped to Russia for enrichment to produce nuclear fuel for a power plant. Iran was to be allowed to have management and financial interest in the Russia-based factory but not technological control. Iran rejected the proposal, with Larijani insisting, "What matters to us is to preserve nuclear technology in Iranian hands." (Later, Iran would agree to discuss the proposal.)

Stung, the Bush administration revealed that in July its undersecretary for arms control, Robert Joseph, had showed IAEA inspectors information from a stolen laptop from Iran (passed on to the U.S. in mid-2004), containing more than 1,000 pages of computer simulations to design a nuclear warhead compatible with Iran's Shahab ballistic missile. "I can fabricate that data," said a senior European diplomat familiar with the document. "It looks beautiful but is open to doubt."[26] Confirming the meeting, an IAEA official told Reuters, "There was a meeting in July where we were shown information—basically design works on a missile cone, that is, the space where the warhead would go. The information did not seem conclusive, the 'smoking gun.' No one has augmented this data since then, and we are in no position to know whether the data indeed came from the Iranians."

As if to trump the American move, the Iranians handed over to the IAEA a document containing a blueprint that showed how to build the core of a nuclear warhead, saying they had obtained it via the black market in nuclear technology operated by Dr. A. Q. Khan. On November 20, the Iranian Majlis passed a bill by an overwhelming majority that would ban intrusive IAEA inspections if Iran was referred to the UN Security Council.

At the next meeting of the IAEA Board, held on November 24,

the Europeans and Americans decided not to refer Iran to the Security Council. They did this because, due to the rotating system at the IAEA, three pro-western nations were replaced by Belarus, Cuba, and Syria. With the loss of these votes and with Indian set to abstain, the Europeans and Americans could muster only eighteen votes, a bare majority. So by consensus it was decided to give Iran and EU3 time to restart talks.

If this did not happen, and Iran found itself referred to the Security Council, it could face sanctions with varying degrees of severity. The Council could impose a travel ban on those Iranian officials who are directly involved in the nuclear program. Or it could rule that no UN member should give Iran any nuclear help. Such a restriction would not apply to any contracts already signed—otherwise Russia would veto such a resolution. Neither of these measures would hurt Iran to a meaningful degree.

Finally, the Council could impose an oil embargo on Iran, a measure that would severely damage its economy. But what would be the consequences of cutting off supplies from the fourth-largest oil producer in the world and the second-largest exporter within OPEC? Oil prices would pass $80 a barrel and even touch $100 a barrel. "We are seeing desperate measures by Asian countries, mainly China, India and others, to get hold of energy resources and for them Iran is a partner they can't do without," Gernot Erler, deputy foreign minister of Germany, said. "It is dangerous to put restrictions on trade relations which could hurt one's own side more than the other side."[27] So the economies of the West as well as China and India would suffer as well.

Then there is the question of enforcing an embargo on a commodity that is in great demand from a country that has a coastline 900 miles (1,450 km) long, land frontiers with seven friendly states, and fluvial borders with two (Russia and Kazakhstan).

As for Iran's citizens, they have been through sanctions before. Immediately after the revolution, they were sanctioned both by America and by western Europe. They fought an eight-year war with Iraq under very trying economic and diplomatic conditions. Referring to the past, Khamanei told an audience in Qom that "years of sanctions" had led to self-reliance.[28]

For now, Iranians are aware that their government has built up an Oil Stabilization Fund, made up of excess oil revenue over the budgeted figures, and that the fund has been growing due to high petroleum prices yielding a record income of $3.33 billion a month. The authorities have been stockpiling food, medicine and other essential materials to withstand at least three years of sanctions. And Iran's Central Bank has moved its overseas assets, a holding worth $30 billion, from Europe to Asia.

All told, therefore, it is not in the interests of the EU or the U.S. to delve into the modalities of the UN sanctions against Iran for now. Western capitals are apparently content to use the threat of sanctions as a lever to reengage Iran into a meaningful dialogue. High officials at the UN in New York seem aware of this strategy of the West—as also does Baradei in Vienna.

After his meeting with Swedish Prime Minister Goran Persson, following the awarding of the Nobel Peace Prize to him and the IAEA on December 10, 2005, Baradei said, "Part of the negotiations should be providing Iran with security assurances. I hope… that the United States at a certain point will become more engaged. We look at the United States to do the heavy lifting in the area of security."[29]

This boils down to Washington genuinely accepting Iran's Islamic regime in the way Brussels, Moscow, Beijing and New Delhi have done. As starters, it would mean the U.S. ceasing its hostile radio and television programs beamed at Iran and its assistance to Iranian exile groups to destabilize the regime. That is not on the horizon.

Going by the revelations made by James Risen, the *New York Times* reporter on national security, in his book *State of War: The Secret History of the CIA and the Bush Administration*, even the preceding administration of President Bill Clinton was far from reconciled with the continued existence of the Islamic Republic of Iran.

Clinton's administration authorized the CIA to mount its audacious Operation Merlin in February 2000. The CIA dispatched a Soviet-era defector, a former Soviet nuclear weapons engineer, to Vienna where, posing as an unemployed scientist selling nuclear secrets, he was instructed to contact the Iranian representatives dealing with the IAEA. He was carrying doctored Soviet blueprints, leaked to the CIA by another Soviet defector, for a triggering device for an atom bomb. Had the Iranians used these blueprints to build a trigger over the next many years, they would have ended up with a "disappointing fizzle" instead of "a mushroom cloud." However, the Russian scientist spotted the defect in the design and told his CIA handlers. But they advised him to go ahead with the plan. Once in Vienna, afraid that the Iranians would detect the flaw, he opened his sealed document and inserted a note, pointing out the errors in the design. He then delivered the package to the apartment of the Iranian representative without meeting anybody. In the past the CIA had played such tricks on adversaries regarding conventional arms, but it was the first time it had extended this tactic to an unconventional weapon once it had secured authorization at the highest level.[30]

Equally seriously, according to Flynt Leverett, a former Director for Middle East Affairs at the U.S. National Security Council, the Bush administration received a credible Iranian offer of comprehensive negotiations in 2003 after the Iraq War, but it summarily turned it down.[31]

On the other side, the day after Baradei's remarks in Stockholm in December 2005—expanding on Ahmadinejad's offer of partnership with foreign companies in its uranium enrichment program—Iran said that America could take part in the international bidding for the construction of a 360-megawatt light water nuclear power plant in southwestern Iran.[32] Washington rejected the overture instantly.

The Core of the Escalating Crisis

Iran's nuclear issue cannot be examined properly without analyzing the reasons for America's obsession with non-proliferation of nuclear arms. According to Prof. John Marsheimer of Chicago University, a member of the "realist" school of policy analysis, "the implicit aim of U. S. non-proliferation policy" is to prevent limits being placed on Washington's freedom of action in dealing with other countries. "The country that acquires nuclear weapons becomes unattackable," he writes. "It is precisely for that reason that it wants them."[33]

The countries which have acquired nuclear arms outside of the "recognized five" nuclear powers provide evidence to support the above thesis. By claiming to possess a few atom bombs, North Korea has made itself immune from attack by the Pentagon. Pakistan is another glaring example. In a conventional war it is no match for India. But the day it acquired a nuclear bomb it became unattackable. So, in *realpolitik*, the effective value of nuclear weapons lies in dissuasion, in deterring an enemy attack. After all, it was the doctrine of mutually assured destruction (MAD) that maintained peace during the 1946–91 Cold War.

Evidently, Iran's rulers understand this. It was the recurrence of the "war of cities" in 1987 during the Iran-Iraq armed conflict that led them to explore the nuclear option to defend their country in the future. So far, going by the IAEA's findings, Iran has not engaged in a nuclear weapons program. It is fair to assume, however, that Iran's leaders do not want to foreclose on this option. That is why they are unlikely to forgo their right to enrich uranium. "No Iranian government, regardless of its ideology or democratic credentials, would dare stop Iran's nuclear program," write Shirin Ebadi and Muhammad Sahimi, petroleum engineering professor at the University of Southern California, in the *International Herald Tribune*.[34] In any case, keeping the nuclear arms option open provides the Iranian leaders with a strong bargaining chip.

The fact is that the Iranian regime's most hostile adversary is the United States—the only country which, in Baradei's words, can provide it the security it needs. To this one should add Israel—especially after Ahmadinejad's vehement outbursts against it.

At a press conference following a summit of the Islamic Conference Organization in Mecca on December 8, after repeating Iran's proposal that the Israeli-Palestinian conflict be resolved by a referendum of all the inhabitants of Israel, Gaza and the West Bank as well as Palestinian refugees in neighboring countries, Ahmadinejad added, "Some European countries insist on saying Hitler killed millions of Jews in furnaces, and they insist on it to the extent that if anyone proves something to the contrary to that they condemn that person and throw them in jail. Though we don't accept this claim, if we suppose it is true, our question for the Europeans is: Is killing of innocent Jews by Hitler the reason for their support to the occupation of Jerusalem? If the Europeans are honest they should give some of their provinces in Europe—like in Germany, Austria or other countries—to the Zionists and the Zionists can establish their state in Europe. You offer some part of Europe and we will support it."[35]

Raanan Gissin, spokesman for Ariel Sharon, said, "Just to remind Mr. Ahmadinejad, we have been here long before his ancestors were here. Therefore we have a birth right to be here in the land of our forefathers and to live here."

Repeating his refusal to accept a nuclear Iran, Sharon warned, "We have the ability to deal with this and are making all the necessary preparations for such a situation." This was followed by a leak to the (London) *Sunday Times* that Israel's Special Forces were on the highest "G" readiness; that Israeli agents based in Iraqi Kurdistan had through signal intelligence and cross-border operations into Iran identified a number of uranium enrichment sites unknown to the IAEA; and that Israel's military operation would involve ground and air forces against several Iranian nuclear sites.[36]

Following Sharon's brain hemorrhage in early January 2006, his deputy Ehud Olmert became the acting Prime Minister. He immediately formed a three-member ad hoc committee, consisting of himself, Defense Minister Shaul Mofaz, and Military Chief of Staff Gen. Dan Halutz, to supervise the plan to hit the Iranian targets.

When asked about the Israeli plans by the *Guardian* during his visit to London on February 2, Mottaki said, "Iran does not think that the Zionist regime is in a condition to engage in such a dangerous venture, and they know how severe the Iranian response will be to its possible audacity. The Zionist regime, if they attack, will regret it."

A few days earlier, in his interview with the state-run Iranian TV, Gen. Yahya Rahim Safavi of the IRGC said, "The world knows that Iran has a ballistic missile power with a range of 2,000 km [1,250 miles]. We have no intention to invade any country [but] we will take effective defense measures if attacked." He referred to Shahab-3 missiles. "We are producing these missiles and do not need foreign technology for that."[37]

While talking tough about their military option, the Israelis privately conceded that they lacked adequate air power or range to accomplish the task.

For the Pentagon to do the job thoroughly, it would need to mount "something in the neighborhood of 1,000 strike sorties," experts agreed. Its targets would include factories and workshops that made centrifuge parts and yellow cake conversion equipment. There was a strong likelihood that some of the suspect sites would turn out to be innocuous factories or schools. This was all the more likely since, according to Risen's book *State of War*, in early 2004 a CIA officer mistakenly sent information to an agent in Iran—who was a double agent—which helped the Tehran government to uproot the CIA espionage network in Iran, leaving the agency "blind" in the country. Apparently, it was after this debacle that the CIA resorted to reconnaissance drones (mentioned on p. 364).

The consequences of military strikes by America or Israel would be dire. "Given the Iranians' fierce nationalism and the Shias' tradition of martyrdom, any military move on Iran would receive a response that would engulf the entire region in fire," wrote Ebadi and Sahimi. Mottaki was more specific, warning that any military action against Iran would result in an escalating crisis which could further destabilize the Middle East by "intensifying U.S. and British difficulties in Iraq and Afghanistan."

The response of Iran at the popular and official levels would be as much anti-American as it would be anti-Israeli. Israel would face retaliation by the Lebanese Hizbollah armed with Iranian-supplied short-range missiles as well as drones. That in turn would scupper any chance of peace talks between Israel and the Palestinians. By stopping its oil exports in a very tight market, Iran would cause a steep rise in oil prices.

Overall, military strikes against Iran would raise anti-Israeli and anti-American feelings in the world of Shias—who are an important minority in Pakistan, Afghanistan, Kuwait and the oil-bearing eastern region of Saudi Arabia—at a time when anti-U.S. sentiment is running high among Sunnis in the region due to the

Pentagon's occupation of Iraq. Given the infiltration of Iranian agents into a wide variety of Iraqi factions, Iran would activate its covert alliances in Iraq, resulting in attacks on the American forces by Shia partisans and a further destabilization of Iraq.

In any case, the military strikes will merely delay Iran's nuclear program, not eliminate it. And they would alienate Washington's allies in the West and the Muslim world, and turn many Iranians, who dislike the theocratic regime, into America's enemies.

Their immediate impact would be to make the Iranian nation rally round its hard-line leaders. Actually, this is already happening.

Iran and the UN Security Council

Western pressure on Iran on the nuclear issue strengthened the power of Ahmadinejad, who, instead of falling in line with the establishment conservatives, struck out on his own. He ignored the conservative lobby's nominees for crucial ministries, and nominated only those he knew and trusted, with most of them having Baseej, military, or intelligence background. Little wonder that only one minister from the previous cabinet appeared in the list of twenty-two he submitted to the Majlis. All but four won parliamentary endorsement. Those rejected included his nominee for the vital petroleum ministry.

The new cabinet members carried out wholesale dismissal of the deputy ministers they inherited. The accompanying purge saw the sacking of the presidents of seven state banks and heads of state insurance and privatization. Ahmadinejad's anti-corruption drive resulted in hundreds of experienced managers being replaced by their young, inexperienced subordinates.

"A tendency in Iran is trying to banish competent officials and it is harming the country like a plague," said Rafsanjani. "Our society has been divided into two poles and some people are behaving aggressively."

Khamanei warned vaguely that "irregularities" in the government will not be tolerated.[38] Taking heed, Ahmadinejad compromised by presenting Kazem Vaziri Hamaneh, a deputy oil minister from the earlier government who had been running the ministry since August, to the Majlis. He won 177 of the 259 votes.

Though the decision to harden Iran's policy on the nuclear issue was taken by Khamanei before the presidential poll, its later implementation under Ahmadinejad's presidency associated the newly elected president with that stance.

As nationalist fervor rose in the face of Western pressure—which escalated sharply after Iran broke the seals of the uranium enrichment plant at Natanz in the presence of IAEA inspectors on January 10—Ahmadinejad gained politically, inhibiting his opponents from voicing their criticism of his policies too stridently.

That encouraged him and his allies to continue blazing the new trail. "They have taken their appeal directly to the poor and middle class masses generally disgusted with a system widely viewed as corrupt and uncaring," said an unnamed professor of political science in Tehran. "Ahmadinejad is an individual representing a new body in the whole Iranian political system that had been marginalized and disorganized. They are in the process of making their identity—and making history."[39] In other words, the urban working class and peasantry—*mustazafin*, needy or oppressed, in the terminology of Khomeini—were being empowered as never before. In his first budget Ahmadinejad attempted to deliver what he had promised: more money to meet ordinary citizens' immediate needs.

Deriving his inspiration from Khomeini, he tried to resurrect the popular fervor of the early years of the Islamic revolution. He substituted "World Oppressor" for the "Great Satan" used by

Khomeini to describe America. Reversing the policy pursued by his two predecessors, he started turning away from Europe and toward Asia. A similar trend was in progress in Saudi Arabia, albeit for different reasons.

The events elsewhere in the region boosted the morale of hardliners in Iran, assuring them that political Islam was the wave of the future in the region. They gladly noted the success of the Islamic parties in the electoral politics of the Middle East—from Iraq (the Shia United Iraqi Alliance and the Sunni Iraqi Islamic Party) to Lebanon (Hizbollah) to Egypt (Muslim Brotherhood) and Palestine (Hamas). They registered too the worldwide anger of Muslims at the publication of the cartoons deriding Prophet Muhammad first in a Danish newspaper and then reprinted in publications in other European countries.

By happenstance, the passage of the IAEA Board's resolution to "report" Iran to the UN Security Council for its "many failures and breaches of its obligations" under the nuclear NPT, and expressing "the absence of confidence that Iran's nuclear program is exclusively for peaceful purposes" on February 4, 2006 coincided with violent demonstrations by Muslims in many cities protesting against the offending cartoons.

Responding to Moscow's concerns, the EU3 had dropped the term "non-compliance" from its draft resolution for the IAEA Board, and changed "refer Iran to the UN Security Council" to "report…," thereby winning the backing of Russia, whose lead was then followed by China. (The difference between these two terms was that "reporting" lacked legal weight and any potential for "consequences" detrimental to Iran.)

At the emergency IAEA Board meeting on February 2–4, Britain, the sponsor of the resolution, faced opposition from the sixteen-member Non Aligned Movement bloc. It wanted (a) all references to the Security Council to be removed or at least delayed until Baradei's full assessment of Iran's case for the

IAEA's quarterly meeting on March 6, and (b) a statement to be inserted saying that "a solution to the Iranian nuclear issue would contribute to the goal of a Middle East free of all weapons of mass destruction and their means of delivery." The final, amended resolution required the Security Council to postpone discussion on the subject until after the March 6 IAEA meeting. To reassure NAM members that the demands made on Iran would not be extended to any of them in the future, Britain inserted a sentence saying that "Iran is a special verification case."[40] Yet only half of the NAM bloc backed the amended resolution, with three of them voting against (Cuba, Syria, and Venezuela), and five abstaining. India was among the twenty-seven who voted for the resolution.

As anticipated, in accordance with the parliamentary law passed in November, the Iranian government suspended all voluntary measures and extra cooperation with the IAEA, terminating surprise IAEA inspections, and resuming "all the peaceful nuclear activities without any restrictions." The fact that the Iranian delegation met Baradei at home on the night of February 1 to find a face-saving formula by allowing Iran to keep the Natanz plant open but nonoperational, but failed, would help Iran's leaders to convince their people that they were being reasonable.[41]

"Adoption of the policy of resistance does not mean we are on non-speaking terms or noncooperative," said Mottaki. The foreign ministry spokesman confirmed that the Iranian officials would attend talks in Moscow on February 16 to discuss the proposal for the enrichment of uranium inside Russia for shipment to Iran.[42]

But it is unlikely that Tehran would abandon its right to complete the nuclear fuel cycle, which involves enrichment of uranium at home. On this issue there is political consensus in Iran. If there is further outside pressure, then Iran will most likely leave the nuclear NPT. After all, Israel, India and Pakistan never signed this treaty. If there is an oil embargo on Tehran, its impact will prove more harmful to the West and other countries than to Iran. And if there are military strikes against the Islamic Republic, the consequences will be grave for the region and the rest of the world.

All in all, a major crisis is in the making.

Notes

INTRODUCTION

[1] Dilip Hiro, *The Longest War: The Iran-Iraq Military Conflict*, Harper-Collins, London; Routledge, New York, 1991, pp. 219–20.

[2] President Bill Clinton addressing a fund-raiser by Iranian-Americans in California, on March 4, 2000, cited in Elaine Sciolino, *Persian Mirrors: The Elusive Face of Iran*, Simon & Schuster, New York and London, 2000, p. 336.

[3] Even during the eight-year war with Iraq, Iran held its elections on time whereas during World War II, Britain postponed its general election.

[4] *New York Times*, March 18, 2000.

[5] Cited in *Middle East International*, July 11, 2004, p. 16.

CHAPTER 1

[1] "Bazaar" is a Persian word.

[2] The inspiration for political reform had come from Russia where Tsar Nicholas had agreed to convene a parliament with legislative powers in October 1905 in the wake of his defeat in the Russo-Japanese War of 1904 and massive revolutionary ferment across the Tsarist Russian empire.

[3] The book did not even carry the publisher's name.

[4] Cited in Shahrough Akhavi, *Religion and Politics in Contemporary Iran:*

Clergy-State Relations in the Pahlavi Period, State University of New York, Albany, N.Y., 1980, pp. 29–30.

5 Stephen Kinzer, *All the Shah's Men: An American Coup and the Roots of Middle East Terror*, John Wiley, Hoboken, N.J., 2003, p. 178.

6 Cited in Dilip Hiro, *Iran Under the Ayatollahs*, Routledge & Kegan Paul, London and New York, 1985; and toExcel Press, New York, 2000, p. 61.

7 Robert Graham, *Iran: The Illusion of Power*, Croom Helm, London, 1979, p. 224.

8 Outside, many Chinese restaurants resorted to serving beer in teapots, a common practice during the prohibition era in America.

9 Komiteh is a variation of *comte*, the French word for "committee."

10 *Ettilaat* (Information), March 23, 1983.

11 *Iran Press Digest*, March 27, 1983, pp. 3–4.

12 *Guardian*, July 30, 1983. Soon thirteen bazaar merchants, found guilty of hoarding, were fined $540,000. *Middle East Economic Digest*, July 15, 1983, p. 8.

13 *Sunday Times*, January 10, 1983.

14 *Middle East Economic Digest*, October 18, 1984, p. 23.

15 *Middle East International*, February 16, 1990, p. 12.

16 Interview in November 1989.

17 *Sunday Times*, December, 4, 1994.

18 *Washington Post*, September 7, 1998.

19 The twelve Imams of the Twelver Shias are: Ali, Hussein, Hassan, Zain al Abidin, Muhammad al Baqir, Jaafar al Sadiq, Mousa al Kazem, Ali al Reza, Muhammad al Taqi Javad, Ali al Naqi, Hassan al Askari, and Muhammad al Qasim.

20 Since the 1979 revolution, there have been four elections to the Assembly of Experts, eight for President, seven for the Majlis, and two for local councils.

CHAPTER 2

1 The Web site address of the Majlis is www.majlis.ir

[2] The corridor surrounding the chamber carries the pictures of all the seventy-four Islamic leaders, including the thirty-four Majlis deputies killed in the June 28, 1981, bombing at a gathering of the ruling Islamic Republican Party officials.

[3] Cited in Shahrough Akhavi, *Religion and Politics in Contemporary Iran*, p. 26.

[4] Twelver Shias follow the law codified by Imam Jaafar al-Sadiq (699–765), the sixth Imam. So they are also called Jaafari Shias.

[5] It was not until 1950 that the first Senate convened.

[6] In early 1921, the same Majlis ratified the Iranian/Persian-Russian Treaty after the Bolshevik regime had remitted all the Tsarist loans to Iran and had satisfactorily delineated common borders.

[7] Interview with the caretaker of Muhammad Mussadiq's estate in Ahmadabad, July 2004.

[8] Dilip Hiro, *Iran Under the Ayatollahs*, p. 157.

[9] Geneive Abdo and Jonathan Lyons, *Answering Only to God: Faith and Freedom in Twenty-First-Century Iran*, Henry Holt, New York, 2003, p. 117. In the 1990 Assembly of Experts poll too, the Guardians Council's Competence and Qualification Committee had disqualified many.

[10] Anoushirvan Ehteshami, *After Khomeini: The Second Iranian Republic*, Routledge, London and New York, 1995, p. 61.

[11] Interview in Tehran, July 2001.

[12] *Middle East International*, January 28, 2000, pp. 16–17, and February 25, 2000, pp. 4–6.

[13] Cited in Elaine Sciolino, *Persian Mirrors*, p. 311.

[14] Ibid., p. 312.

[15] Cited in *Middle East International*, March 10, 2000, p. 15.

[16] *International Herald Tribune*, August 7, 2000.

[17] Ibid.

[18] Interview in Tehran, July 2004.

[19] *Financial Times*, February 11, 2004.

[20] *Vaqa'ye Itifaqiyeh* (Past Events), July 22, 2004.

CHAPTER 3

[1] It is the wish of every Shia in the world to be buried in Najaf. Failing that, soil from the holy city should be thrown into the grave to sanctify it.

[2] In his book *The Imperial Shah: An Informal Biography*, Gerard de Villiers describes Muhammad Mussadiq as "pint-sized troublemaker" who possessed "the agility of a goat," and "who pranced before journalists." Little, Brown, Boston, Mass., 1976, p. 156 and p. 170.

[3] C. M. Woodhouse's interview with Robert Fisk, published after his death, *Independent*, September 2, 2003.

[4] The government's legally sanctioned decision could only be overturned by a majority of the seventy-nine elected members. This did not happen.

[5] L. P. Elwell-Sutton, *Persian Oil: A Study in Power*, Lawrence and Wishart, London, 1955, p. 310.

[6] Stephen Kinzer, *All the Shah's Men*, p. 6 and pp. 162–63.

[7] Cited in Stephen Kinzer, op. cit., p. 6.

[8] Ibid., p. 13.

[9] "The mob that came into north Tehran [from the south] and was decisive in the overthrow was mercenary," said Richard Cottam, who was on the Operation Ajax staff in Washington. "It had no ideology, and that mob was paid with American dollars." Ibid., p. 180.

[10] Dilip Hiro, *Iran under the Ayatollahs*, p. 36.

[11] *Ettilaat*, August 20, 1979.

CHAPTER 4

[1] Cited in Dilip Hiro, *Iran Under the Ayatollahs*, p. 24.

[2] Dilip Hiro, op. cit., p. 27.

[3] T. H. V. Motter, *The Persian Corridor and Aid to Russia*, Office of the Chief of Military History, Department of the Army, Washington, D.C., 1952, p. 161.

[4] Nikki R. Keddie, *Roots of Revolution: An Interpretive History of Modern Iran*, Yale University Press, New Haven, CT, and London, 1981, p. 111.

[5] *Christian Science Monitor*, May 28, 1963; and Mohamed Heikal, *The Return of the Ayatollah: The Iranian Revolution from Mossadeq to Khomeini*, Andre Deutsch, London, 1981, p. 70.

[6] Dilip Hiro, op. cit., p. 40.

[7] Cited in Ali Reza Nobari (ed.), *Iran Erupts*, The Iran-America Documentation Center, Stanford, CA, 1978, p. 70.

[8] This U.S.-Iran arrangement, secured by the American President's executive order, did not require the Senate's consent, and was within the parameters of the Eisenhower Doctrine announced in January 1957.

[9] Robert Graham, *Iran*, p.40; and Eric Hooglund, *Reform and Revolution in Rural Iran*, University of Texas Press, Austin, TX, 1982, p. 17 and p. 22.

[10] Michael M. J. Fischer, *Iran: From Religious Dispute to Revolution*, Harvard University Press, Cambridge, MA, and London, 1980, p. 188.

[11] Ruh Allah Khumayni, *Islam and Revolution*, (tr., Hamid Algar), Mizan Press, Berkeley, CA, 1981, p. 176.

[12] Marvin Zonis, *The Political Elite of Iran*, Princeton University Press, Princeton, N.J., 1971, p. 63, note 45.

[13] Cited in Zonis, op. cit., p. 46

[14] "Mousavi" means "a descendant of Imam Mousa al Kazem," the Seventh Imam of Twelver Shias. Sayyid Ahmad Mousavi was called *al-Hindi* (the Indian) because he was born in the Oudh province of northern India where his forefathers had migrated from the Iranian province of Khurasan many decades earlier at the invitation of the Shia ruler of Oudh.

[15] Dilip Hiro, op. cit., p. 55.

[16] *New Republic*, September 1, 1973, p. 7.

[17] Dilip Hiro, op. cit., p. 60.

[18] Ibid.

[19] In addition, there were sixty thousand foreign managers and technicians in Iran. Ervand Abrahamian, *Iran Between Two Revolutions*, Princeton University Press, Princeton, N.J., and Guildford, 1982, p. 434.

[20] Ervand Abrahamian, op. cit., pp. 434–35.

[21] Robert Graham, op. cit., pp. 250–51.

[22] Later, its author turned out to be none less than Information Minister Dariush Humayun.

[23] Cited in Nikki R. Keddie, op. cit., p. 243. The reference to India had to do with Khomeini's grandfather, Ahmad. Also see Note 14.

CHAPTER 5

[1] Shia clerics who did not claim lineage from Prophet Muhammad wear white turbans.

[2] PBUH = Peace Be Upon Him.

[3] Cited in Ruh Allah Khumayni, *Islam and Revolution*, p. 170.

[4] Cited in Shahrough Akhavi, *Religion and Politics in Contemporary Iran*, p. 101.

[5] Cited in *Time*, January 14, 1980, p. 14.

[6] Cited in Ruh Allah Khumayni, op. cit., p. 170.

[7] Nikki R. Keddie, *Roots of Revolution*, p. 107.

[8] Pages 254–55. Ramadan, the ninth month in the Islamic calendar, is regarded holy because it was during this month that the first divine revelation was made to the Prophet Muhammad. During this month, between sunrise and sunset all adult Muslims are required to abstain from eating, drinking, smoking, and conjugal relations.

[9] Page 194.

[10] Cited in Ruh Allah Khumayni, op. cit, pp. 234–36

[11] Dilip Hiro, *Iran Under the Ayatollahs*, pp. 78–79.

[12] Cited in Ruh Allah Khumayni, op. cit., pp. 240–41.

[13] Cited in Dilip Hiro, op. cit., p. 82

[14] Dilip Hiro, op. cit., pp. 87–88.

[15] The Shah had delayed his departure by about a week partly to finalize plans for a coup and partly to take with him the royal crowns, the largest one studded with 3,380 jewels, which were stored in the underground vault of the Central Bank whose employees had gone on an indefinite strike. In the end, he failed

because the bank officials who knew how to operate the combination locks could not be found.

16 Page 177.

17 There was no evidence that Abol Hassan Bani-Sadr had accepted any money from the CIA. But the mere fact that the CIA had considered him suitable to "cultivate and recruit" as an informer, first in Paris and then in Tehran, was a vital contributory factor to turn Khomeini decidedly against him.

18 *The Times*, June 9, 1981.

19 *Boston Globe*, March 5, 1986.

20 After Khomeini's death, Leader Ali Khamanei moved his office to the complex near the Pasteur Square named after Louis Pasteur, the French scientist whose technique for sterilizing milk is used throughout the world. Significantly, the Islamic authorities have left the name unchanged.

21 Cited in John Simpson and Tira Schubert, *Lifting the Veil: Life in Revolutionary Iran*, Hodder & Stoughton, London, 1995, p. 305.

22 Since the lunar Islamic calendar is shorter than the solar Christian calendar by about eleven days, it takes roughly thirty-four lunar years to equal thirty-three solar years.

23 Dilip Hiro, *Neighbors, Not Friends: Iraq and Iran after the Gulf Wars*, Routledge, New York and London, 2001, pp. 206–7.

24 Geneive Abdo and Jonathan Lyons, *Answering only to God*, p. 58.

25 Cited in ibid., p. 74.

26 Associated Press, October 26, 1998.

27 Arthur J. Arberry, *The Koran Interpreted*, Oxford University Press, Oxford and New York, 1964, p. 107. "Anyone who renounces the fundamental precepts of Islam must be seen as an apostate—and death will be his punishment," said Leader Ali Khamanei. Agence France-Presse, September 5, 1999.

28 Reuters, October 1, 1999.

29 March 24, 2000, p. 14.

30 Indeed, the Berlin conference was seen by government officials as a

means to improve relations between Iran and the European Union on the eve of President Muhammad Khatami's state visit to Germany in July.

31 Associated Press, April 20, 2000. Some pro-reform newspapers had alleged that the instructions to kill Saeed Hajjarian were given at a religious center in Islamshahr located near Tehran. *International Herald Tribune*, July 20, 2000.

32 May 5, 2000.

33 Cited in *Middle East International*, May 19, 2000, p. 17.

34 Interviews in Tehran, July 2001.

CHAPTER 6

1 Being a north Indian, I am racially indistinguishable from an Iranian. Also Farhad Ganji was especially friendly with me chiefly because his sister, then enrolled as a postgraduate student in chemistry at Chandigarh University in India, sent glowing accounts of her stay in that country.

2 AH, After Hijra: The Islamic era began with the migration of Prophet Muhammad from Mecca to Media on July 15, 622 AD.

3 Majority Sunnis and minority Shias differ in doctrine, ritual, law, theology, and religious organization. See further Dilip Hiro, *The Essential Middle East: A Comprehensive Guide*, Carroll & Graf, New York, 2003, entries on Shia, Sunna, and Sunnis, respectively on pp. 485–86, 501–02.

4 By contrast, there were eighty-five thousand qualified clerics, itinerant preachers, Friday prayer leaders, and Ashura procession organizers in Iran in 1978.

5 In the late 1990s Ayatollah Hussein Ali Montazeri set up his own Web site to express his views and communicate with others. In early 2003, the authorities lifted restrictions on his movements.

6 His Web site address is www.saanei.org.

7 Robin Wright, *The Last Great Revolution: Turmoil and Transformation in Iran*, Vintage, New York, p. 291.

8 Ibid., p. 293

[9] Geneive Abdo and Jonathan Lyons, *Answering Only to God*, p. 38.

[10] Robin Wright, op. cit., p. 292.

[11] Cited in *Middle East International*, October 15, 1999, p. 12.

[12] Geneive Abdo and Jonathan Lyons, op. cit., pp. 36–37.

[13] Cited in Dilip Hiro, *Neighbors, Not Friends*, p. 272.

[14] Reuters, January 14, 1999.

[15] *Middle East International*, October 15, 1999, p. 23.

[16] *International Herald Tribune*, July 20, 2000

[17] Elaine Sciolino, *Persian Mirrors*, p. 239. By far the most courageous was Akbar Ganji, a forty-year-old investigative journalist, whose daring columns in 1999 began naming high-ranking individuals behind the assassinations. They included former Intelligence Minister Ali Fallahian. When Ali Akbar Hasehmi Rafsanjani, then head of the Expediency Council, denied that no such murders had been committed during his presidency, Ganji wrote, "Rafsanjani should clearly and openly apologize to the public for the serial murders committed by the gang members." P. 241. In early 2000, Ganji was sentenced to ten years in prison and five years in internal exile for "defaming the state."

[18] Muhammad Khatami's candidacy was approved by six votes to five, with one member abstaining. Geneive Abdo and Jonathan Lyons, op. cit., p. 60.

[19] Elaine Sciolino, op. cit. pp. 250–51.

[20] Ibid., p. 260.

[21] Ibid., p. 258.

[22] Cited in *Middle East International*, December 25, 1998, p. 16.

[23] July 2, 1999, pp. 15–16.

[24] Reuters, November 29, 1999.

[25] Cited in Geneive Abdo and Jonathan Lyons, op. cit., pp. 192–93.

CHAPTER 7

[1] Dilip Hiro, *Iran Under the Ayatollahs*, p. 16. The outrage in Iran was so vehement that the Shah was forced to cancel the concession.

[2] There is no mention of this cable in Arnold S. Wilson's *Persia: Letters and Diary of a Young Political Officer, 1907–1914*, Oxford University Press, London, 1941.

[3] The Soviets argued that once the Shah had signed the agreement, the oil concession to them became operational, and all that was needed was the formation of a joint Soviet-Iranian company; but Tehran refused to budge.

[4] Cited in L. P. Elwell-Sutton, *Persian Oil*, p. 119.

[5] Daniel Yergin, *The Prize: The Epic Quest for Oil, Money, and Power*, Simon & Schuster, New York and London, 1991, pp. 451–52.

[6] Manuchehr Farmanfarmaian and Roxane Farmanfarmaian, *Blood and Oil: Inside the Shah's Iran*, Modern Library, New York, 1999, pp. 184–85.

[7] *Middle East International*, December 3, 1993, p. 10, and January 7, 1994, p. 13.

[8] Interviews in Tehran, August 1999.

[9] In contrast, during the Iran-Iraq War, the government actually reduced its foreign debts of $15 billion it had inherited from the Shah's regime. Inter Press Service, June 15, 1993.

[10] America's unilateral sanctions derive from its national emergency legislation of 1897 passed during its war with Spain, giving the President wide powers. The excessive use of this law in the 1980s and 1990s resulted in the U.S. imposing sanctions against seventy-five countries. *Los Angeles Times*, January 21, 2001.

[11] Unless Iran showed signs of changing its terrorist behavior, after the first year of ILSA the limit on investment in its oil and gas industry was to be halved to $20 million a year.

[12] *Middle East International*, April 18, 1997, p. 12, and May 16, 1997, p. 17.

[13] Interviews in Tehran, August 1999.

[14] Between 1986 and 1990, of the $2.9 billion that Tehran spent on foreign weapons, just under $1.5 billion went to China.

[15] *New York Times*, November 8, 2004; *Financial Times*, November 11, 2004.

16 *The Middle East and North Africa, 2002*, Europa Publications, London and New York, 2003, p. 373.

17 See further entry on "Oil and gas industry (Iran)" in Dilip Hiro, *The Essential Middle East*, pp. 375–76.

18 Interview in Tehran, August 1999.

19 *Financial Times*, November 10, 2004.

CHAPTER 8

1 *Toronto Star*, September 28, 1986.

2 Dilip Hiro, *The Longest War*, p. 16.

3 Dilip Hiro, op. cit. p. 17.

4 The six Shia holy shrines are one each in Najaf, Karbala, Kufa, where Imam Ali lived, and the Kadhimiya neighborhood in Baghdad, and two in Samarra.

5 Dilip Hiro, op. cit., p. 39.

6 See further entry on "Martyrdom" in Dilip Hiro, *The Essential Middle East*, p. 317.

7 *Guardian*, July 22, 1983; *New York Times*, March 29, 1984.

8 Dilip Hiro, *The Essential Middle East*, p. 156.

9 *Toronto Star*, September 28, 1986.

10 *Wall Street Journal*, February 18, 1986.

11 Ibid. Given these perks, and the fact that each year 422,000 Iranians reached the conscription age of eighteen, there was no dearth of manpower to conduct the war.

12 The record was held by Sayyid Ahmad Hussein, a sixty-year-old canteen worker, who has been to the front nine times for spells ranging from three weeks to four months, when he was assigned to a canteen serving combatants or support units.

13 By chance, Muharram started on September 15, and the seventh day fell on September 22.

14 *The Economist*, October 11, 1986, p. 39.

15 *International Herald Tribune*, November 14, 1986.

16 *Foreign Broadcast Information Service*, November 20, 1986.

[17] Dilip Hiro, *The Longest War*, p. 183.

[18] Dilip Hiro, *The Essential Middle East*, p. 156.

[19] The U.S. Defense Department asserted that Iran was partly responsible for the atrocity. Dilip Hiro, *The Essential Middle East*, p. 176.

[20] In July 1990 Iraq's Deputy Premier Tariq Aziz would put the military imports at $102 billion.

[21] Dilip Hiro, *The Longest War*, p. 297.

[22] After the war, Iran kept these planes as a fraction of the compensation for war damages.

[23] Cited in Dilip Hiro, *Desert Shield to Desert Storm: The Second Gulf War*, HarperCollins, London/Routledge, New York, 1992; Authors Choice Press/iUniverse, New York and Lincoln, NE, 2003, p. 382.

[24] *New York Times*, March 8, 1991.

[25] Tehran Radio claimed that Saddam's forces had killed twelve thousand to sixteen thousand civilians in recapturing Najaf and Karbala alone.

[26] *Iran News*, January 15, 2000.

[27] *International Herald Tribune*, October 16, 2000.

[28] *Middle East International*, June 27, 2003, p. 14.

[29] Reuters, April 9, 2004.

[30] Cited in *Middle East International*, April 30, 2004, p. 18.

[31] *Sunday Times*, August 8, 2004.

CHAPTER 9

[1] Mohamed Heikal, *The Return of the Ayatollah*, pp. 16–19.

[2] The whole cache was later published in fifty-four volumes in English and Persian.

[3] Of the fifty-three hostages, fifty were held at the U.S. Embassy and rest at the Foreign Ministry—for their own safety.

[4] Zbigniew Brzezinski, *Power and Principle: Memoirs of the National Security Adviser*, Weidenfeld and Nicolson, London, 1983, pp. 488–89 and p. 284.

[5] *Guardian*, July 31, 1980.

6 Cited in James Bill, *The Lion and the Eagle: The Tragedy of American-Iranian Relations*, Yale University Press, New Haven, CT, and London, 1988, pp. 18–19.

7 Dilip Hiro, *The Longest War*, p. 120.

8 *The Times*, July 31, 1985.

9 Cited in Dilip Hiro, *The Longest War*, p. 186.

10 *Independent*, September 15, 1990.

11 Dilip Hiro, *Desert Shield to Desert Storm*, p. 437.

12 Cited in Dilip Hiro, *Neighbors, Not Friends*, pp. 69–70.

13 It was not until May 2000 that the World Bank reversed its policy, saying "the bank's charter says that only economic considerations should be taken into account in lending decisions." It granted $230 million loans for infrastructure projects. *The Middle East and North Africa, 2002*, p. 394.

14 *Independent*, January 11, 1995; *Guardian*, March 24, 1995; *Sunday Times*, August 11, 1996. Actually, the Kelaye Electric Company facility in Kelaye was near Karaj; it would later turn out to be a laboratory for testing centrifuges for enriching uranium.

15 *Guardian*, February 22, 1996; *Independent*, June 27, 1996; *Middle East International*, July 5, 1996, pp. 7–8; and interview with Dr. Mustafa Alani, a Gulf specialist at the Royal United Services Institute, London.

16 Three of them had participated in the jihad against the Soviets in Afghanistan in the 1980s after receiving training in the Pakistani camps run under the supervision of the U.S. Central Intelligence Agency.

17 *Observer*, August 4, 1996.

18 April 12, 1997.

19 *USA Today*, March 30, 2004; Dilip Hiro, *Neighbors, Not Friends*, pp. 265–66.

20 The Anti-terrorism and Effective Death Penalty Act, 1996, also stipulated that the American representatives on the international financial institutions should lobby against extending credit to the states sponsoring terrorism.

[21] Cited in *Middle East International*, January 16, 1998, pp. 10–11.

[22] Dilip Hiro, *Neighbors, not Friends*, p. 232.

[23] *Washington Post*, May 1, 1998.

[24] Inter Press Service, May 26, 1998.

[25] To show that he was not totally helpless in punishing those trading with Iran, in July—after Iran test-fired a medium-range missile, Shahab-3—President Clinton signed an executive order under the 1992 Iran-Iraq Non-Proliferation Act, barring seven Russian organizations, including the Baltic State Technical University in St. Petersburg, from receiving U.S. financial assistance or trading their goods in America for having assisted Tehran in its missile program.

[26] Robin Wright, *The Last Great Revolution*, pp. 248–49 and p. 250.

[27] Agence France-Presse, November 4, 1998. Earlier, in his conversation with twenty American journalists at the UN on September 21, Khatami made it clear that Tehran had no intention of opening a "political dialogue" with America until it had taken "concrete steps to change its policies toward Iran." *New York Times*, September 22, 1998.

[28] Cited in the *Nation*, November 15, 1999, p. 4.

[29] In 2001, the thirty countries that operated 438 nuclear-fueled electricity plants included Argentina, Brazil, France, India, Mexico, Pakistan, South Africa, the UK, and the U.S. Many countries also operated research or test reactors to produce radioisotopes for medical, industrial, and agricultural use.

[30] Since, of every one thousand atoms of uranium, 993 are atoms of the heavier U238, and only seven are the lighter U235, required to generate a fission chain reaction in a nuclear power plant or weapon, 1,525 tons of uranium are needed to produce 33 pounds (15 kg) of 90 percent pure U235 to fabricate one nuclear bomb.

[31] *Washington Post*, March 18, 2000.

[32] BBC News, March 25, 2000.

[33] During his stay in New York, Karrubi met the representatives of Conoco, ExxonMobil, and Chevron, which maintained close contacts with the NIOC at its London office.

[34] *Washington Post*, September 15, 2001.

35 Dilip Hiro, *War without End: The Rise of Islamist Terrorism and Global Response*, Routledge, London and New York, 2002, p. 311.

36 *Guardian*, October 9, 2001.

37 Seymour Hersh, *Chain of Command: The Road from 9/11 to Abu Ghraib*, HarperCollins, New York; Allen Lane, London, 2004, p. 342.

38 Dilip Hiro, *War without End*, p. 364.

39 See http://www.whitehouse.gov/news/2002/01/20020129-11.html.

40 *New York Times*, February 4, 2002.

41 The treaty obliges China, France, Russia, the UK, and the U.S. to take significant steps toward nuclear disarmament,' says Frank Barnaby—but he fails to add that these Powers have done absolutely nothing in that direction. *How to Build a Nuclear Bomb and other Weapons of Mass Destruction*, Granta Books, London, 2004, pp. 96–97.

42 For different views of the Iranian nuclear power plant at Haleyle near Bushehr, visit http://iran.motime.com/archive/2003-11 and http://www.members.cox.net/nabard-english/images/bushehr.jpg.

43 For Israel's arsenal of weapons of mass destruction, see Dilip Hiro, *The Essential Middle East*, pp. 325–26.

44 In the nuclear reaction that fuels electricity generating stations, uranium-235 is converted to plutonium-239 and 241. It is estimated that by the end of two to three years' operation, little uranium is left and about a third of the power produced by the reactor comes from the plutonium. See "Nuclear Issues Briefing Paper" June 18, 2002, from the Australian Uranium Information Center at www.uic.com.au/nip18.htm. In short, plutonium can be and is used as a fuel in a nuclear reactor. But there are no commercial power stations fueled only by plutonium.

45 Cited in *Middle East International*, November 7, 2003, pp. 16–17; and interviews in Tehran, July 2004.

46 *New York Times*, February 13, 2004.

47 The IAEA also discovered that the Iranians were planning to build a heavy water 40 MW research reactor at Arak. They were not breaking the nuclear NPT, but they should have informed the IAEA about this activity.

48 Reuters, April 3, 2004. The IAEA asked Islamabad to let it take Pak-

istani samples to verify Tehran's claim, but Pakistan, a nonsignatory to the nuclear NPT, refused.

49 *Iran News*, July 19, 2004.

50 *New York Times*, April 24, 2004.

51 Ibid., May 3, 2004.

52 *Financial Times*, June 22, 2004.

53 This was an indirect reference to the removal of Shia ministers from the Communications and Health Ministries which they had held in the earlier cabinet.

54 BBC World Service Radio, *NewsHour* program. Its Persian services head, Sadiq Sabah, elaborated on the news story.

55 *New York Times*, September 17, 2004.

56 Finding herself in a minority of one in the thirty-five-strong Board of IAEA Governors, the U.S. Governor Jackie Sanders swiftly followed her very reluctant "yes" to the resolution with a nine-page statement asserting repeatedly that Iran had a clandestine nuclear weapons program without offering any backup evidence. *New York Times*, November 29, 2004.

57 Ibid., November 29, 2004.

58 Following the dissemination of this result by the official Islamic Republic News Agency, Behrouz Geranpayeh, Director of the National Institute for Public Opinion Research, was accused of "spreading lies to incite public opinion," and arrested. The judiciary closed down the Institute. *Middle East International*, October 25, 2002, p. 22.

CHAPTER 10

1 See further entry on "Mujahedin-e Khalq" in Dilip Hiro, *The Essential Middle East*, pp. 339–41.

2 Dilip Hiro, *Iran Under the Ayatollahs*, p. 217.

3 *Boston Globe*, March 5, 1986.

4 Shirin Ebadi, the other Iranian lawyer, and Ilah-e Sharifpour Hicks

were also charged with coercing Amir Ibrahimi to make a confession on tape.

[5] Geneive Abdo and Jonathan Lyons, *Answering Only to God*, p. 222.

[6] Interview in August 1999.

[7] In early 2000, there were twenty-four newspapers in Tehran alone.

[8] It was the same Said Emami who had been allegedly implicated in the assassinations of the dissident intellectuals.

[9] My visit to the site in early August 1999 confirmed the damage done.

[10] Cited in Robin Wright, *The Last Great Revolution*, pp. 264–65.

[11] Cited in Geneive Abdo and Jonathan Lyons, op. cit., p. 206.

[12] Ibid., p. 224.

[13] Associated Press July 12, 1999; Agence France-Presse, July 12, 1999; Reuters, July 13, 1999.

[14] In his letter to Ayatollah Muhammad Shahroudi, appointed judiciary chief in mid-August 1999, Ahmad Batebi wrote, "On the first day of my arrest by plainclothesmen, I was brought inside the university where they confiscated all my documents and possessions. While taunting me with insults, they beat me about my testicles, my legs, and abdominal area. When I protested, they said this is the land of the velayat [Islamic Jurisprudent] and that I should be blinded and not be allowed to live here, Later, they transferred me in a van along with other people arrested. They blindfolded us with our shirts tied around our necks . . . and beat us with batons. The soldiers bound my hands and secured them to plumbing pipes. They beat my head and abdominal area with soldiers' shoes. They insisted I sign a confession of the accusations made against me. Next they threw me on the floor, stood on my neck, and cut off not only my hair but also parts of my scalp causing it to bleed. Once again they insisted I confess. When I again protested, they beat me with a [metal] cable . . . I asked to go to the bathroom, but they would not let me close the door saying I might commit suicide . . . Then they began lashing me. I resisted and punched one of them in the face. At this point, they took me and

ducked my head into a closed drain full of excrement. They held me under for so long, I was unable to hold my breath, and the excrement was inhaled through my nose and seeped into my mouth." Geneive Abdo and Jonathan Lyons, op. cit., pp. 229–30.

15 Reuters, July 13, 1999.

16 *Tehran Times*, August 26, 1999.

17 IRGC commanders' confidential letter was published by conservative papers within a fortnight, but the Press Court failed to take action against any of them for divulging sensitive information. *Middle East International*, July 30, 1999, pp. 17–18.

18 *New York Times*, July 15, 1999.

19 Agence France-Presse, August 3, 1999.

20 *Middle East International*, July 14, 2000, pp. 18–19; *The Economist*, July 15, 2000, p. 70.

21 Geneive Abdo and Jonathan Lyons, p. 258, and p. 260.

22 See Chapter One, pp. 19.

23 Cited in Robin Wright, *The Last Great Revolution*, p. 259.

24 *Middle East International*, July 30, 1999, pp. 20–21.

25 Cited in Elaine Sciolino, *Persian Mirrors*, p. 289.

26 Cited in Geneive Abdo and Jonathan Lyons, *Answering Only to God*, p. 47.

27 See further Farhand Rajaee, "A Thermidor of 'Islamic Yuppies'? Conflict and Compromise in Iran's Politics," *Middle East Journal* (Washington, D.C.), Spring 1999, pp. 222–23.

28 Valla Vakili, *Debating Religion and Politics: The Political Thought of Abdol Karim Soroush*, Council on Foreign Relations, New York, 1997, pp. 10–11.

29 Cited in Robin Wright, op. cit., p. 93.

30 The Ministry of Culture and Islamic Guidance responded by issuing new censorship rules that banned close-ups of women in movies and naming antagonists in films, plays, or books, Muhammad, Ali, Hassan, or Hussein. *New York Times*, August 20, 1996.

31 Robin Wright, op. cit., p. 53.

32 Dilip Hiro, *Iran Under the Ayatollahs*, pp. 256–57.

33 *International Herald Tribune*, November 26, 1999.

34 Robin Wright, op. cit., p. 292.

35 John Simpson and Tira Schubert, *Lifting the Veil*, p. 114.

36 Robin Wright, op. cit., p. 155.

37 This happened despite the fact that, between 1975 and 1996, life expectancy rose from fifty-five to sixty-eight, and infant mortality fell from 104 per one thousand to twenty-five. Anoushiravan Ehteshami, *After Khomeini*, p. 115.

38 Although the edict was widely cited, no one that Ms. Robin Wright of the *Los Angeles Times* met in 1998 seemed to remember the source or have a copy. Robin Wright, op. cit., p. 166.

39 Cited in Elaine Sciolino, op. cit., p. 40.

40 In 1999, the Davos Economic Forum of world leaders, held annually in Switzerland, included Massoumeh Ebtekar in the list of one hundred leaders of the twenty-first century.

41 Cited in Robin Wright, op. cit., p. 152.

42 Some Islamic scholars dispute the interpretation that the term *zinah* (adornment) covers all parts of the body, except hands, feet, and perhaps the face. Another passage in the Quran calls on the believing women "to draw their cloaks (*jalabiyah*) tightly around them when they go abroad so that they may be recognized."

43 Referring to men, Leader Ali Khamanei said, "Shaving a beard is forbidden but trimming is allowed." Elaine Sciolino, op. cit., pp. 84–85. The source of this ruling is a saying, attributed to Prophet Muhammad, which reads, "On the Day of Judgment, God will not deal with three groups of men—those who remove their facial hair, those who masturbate, and those who commit sodomy—and will summarily condemn them to suffer eternal pain."

44 By the late 1990s, the earlier practice of punishing the bad hijab women with six lashes on the palms of their hands or the back of their legs had disappeared.

45 Cited in Robin Wright, op. cit., p. 152.

46 Nikki R. Keddie, "Sexuality and Shi'i Social Protest in Iran," in Juan R. I. Cole and Nikki R. Keddie (eds.) *Shi'ism and Social Protest*, Yale University Press, New Haven, CT, and London, 1986, p. 119.

47 Elaine Sciolino, op. cit., p. 207.

48 Page 288.

OVERVIEW

1 Dilip Hiro, *Iran Under the Ayatollahs*, p. 196; and Dilip Hiro, *The Essential Middle East*, p. 340.

2 *Kayhan*, December 22, 1979.

3 Interview in Tehran, August 1999.

4 Robin Wright, *The Last Great Revolution*, pp. 62–63.

5 Cited in Geneive Abdo and Jonathan Lyons, *Answering Only to God*, p. 225.

6 Page 238.

7 *The Economist*, July 15, 2000, p. 70.

8 See further Dilip Hiro, *War Without End*, pp. 27–29.

9 *Debating Religion and Politics in Iran*, pp. 10–11.

10 Among reformists only about a third are believed to be proposing a secular set-up in Iran.

11 Cited in Geneive Abdo and Jonathan Lyons, *Answering Only to God*, p. 89.

12 Cited in Robin Wright, *The Last Great Revolution*, p. 72.

13 Geneive Abdo and Jonathan Lyons, *Answering Only to God*, p. 228.

14 Cited in Elaine Sciolino, *Persian Mirrors*, p. 293.

15 At the same time, the ten-day long celebration of *Nawruz* (New Year), a Zoroastrian custom, continues unabated.

16 The number of landline telephones is expected to reach twenty million and that of mobile telephones to ten million by 2005. *Iran Media Guide*, Ministry of Culture and Islamic Guidance, Tehran, 2004, p. 46.

EPILOGUE

1 *International Herald Tribune*, February 14, 2005. Many European diplomats privately conceded that Iran could not be prohibited from uranium enrichment while the other 187 signatories of the NPT were allowed to produce nuclear fuel.

2 Iran's Intelligence Minister Ali Yunusi said, "Most of the shining objects that our people see in Iran's airspace are American espionage equipments used to spy on Iran's nuclear and military facilities," and added that Iran had shot down some drones and discovered spying devices in them. *Washington Post,* February 13, 2005; Reuters, February 16, 2005.

3 Following the renewal of Iraq's "war of cities" in January 1987, described in Chapter Eight, Ayatollah Ruhollah Khomeini apparently removed his ban on the nuclear arms program that he had imposed immediately after the revolution. That led to contacts between the Iranians and the Pakistani group led by Dr. A. Q. Khan in Dubai later that year.

4 Agence France Press, February 8, 2005.

5 Associated Press, February 3, 2005; *Guardian,* February 4, 2005.

6 *New York Times,* February 10, 2005. Answering a question from the floor at the Institut d'Etudes Politiques, Condi Rice said that in 1947 both Greece and Turkey suffered due to civil war. A civil war in Turkey in 1947? Another embarrassing example of her poor grasp of the basic facts of the Middle East.

7 The ten sites listed by senior military sources in Tel Aviv to Dov ben Arieh were: Tabriz; Bushehr; Fasa, in Fars Province; Natanz; Dakhovin, near the Iraqi border; Saqand; Tabas, a village in Khurasan province near the Afghan border; Bonab, in the northwest; and Chalus and Neka, near the Caspian Sea. *Middle East International,* February 18, 2005, p. 32.

8 *New York Times,* March 9, 2005; *Sunday Times,* March 13, 2005.

9 See Dilip Hiro, *Secrets and Lies: The True Story of the Iraq War,* Politico's Publishing, London, p. 44 and p. 445.

10 *New York Times,* March 2, 2005.

11 Ibid., March 12, 2005.

12 *Sunday Times,* March 13, 2005. In 2004, Israel bought 5,000 smart bombs from the Pentagon, including 500 one-ton bunker busters capable of destroying two-meter-thick concrete walls.

13 Cited in *Economist*, June 11, 2005, p. 55.

14 *Economist*, June 25, 2005, p. 45.

15 Ibid., July 2, 2005, p. 42. In his State of the Union speech on January 31, 2006, President Bush called Iran "a nation now held hostage by a small clerical elite that is isolating and repressing its people."

16 *International Herald Tribune*, August 8, 2005.

17 *New York Times*, September 5, 2005.

18 August 2, 2005.

19 Agence France Presse, September 17, 2005.

20 Between the late 1970s and 1993 South Africa produced six atom bombs.

21 *Observer*, September 25, 2005.

22 *Middle East International*, October 28, 2005, p. 19. By voting with Washington, India jeopardized the firming up of its 25-year deal for the purchase of Iranian gas. Three-quarters of India's oil imports originate in Iran.

23 For the proceedings of the conference, visit www.zionot.ir.

24 *Observer*, October 30, 2005.

25 *Guardian*, October 29, 2005.

26 *New York Times*, November 13, 2005.

27 *Guardian*, January 16, 2006. Between 2000 and 2004, Germany's exports to Iran rose from 1.5 billion euros to 3.57 billion euros, and those of the European Union from 5.3 billion euros to 11.8 billion euros. *International Herald Tribune*, January 23, 2006.

28 *New York Times*, January 11, 2006.

29 Associated Press, December 13, 2005.

30 Cited in *Daily Telegraph*, January 5, 2006 and *Guardian*, January 5, 2006.

31 *International Herald Tribune*, January 31, 2006.

32 Associated Press, December 11, 2005.

33 Cited in *International Herald Tribune*, August 13–14, 2005.

34 January 20, 2006.

35 Reuters, December 8, 2005.

36 December 11, 2005.

37 The IRGC, charged with defending Iran's borders, was supplied with Shahab-3 in mid-2003. In 2005 Iran developed solid fuel technology, a major breakthrough for increasing missile accuracy.

38 *Guardian*, November 18, 2005.

39 Cited in *New York Times*, January 23, 2006.

40 For the full text of the resolution visit www.iht.com/mideast/.

41 *New York Times*, February 3, 2006.

42 *International Herald Tribune*, February 6, 2006.

Glossary of Foreign Words and Shia Islam

AH: After *Hijra*, Migration of Prophet Muhammad from Mecca to Medina on July 15, 622 AD. An Islamic year is lunar.

akbar: great

al/el/ol/ul: the

amn: security

ansar: helper

ahsura: (*lit.*) tenth; (*fig.*) tenth of Muharram

Ashura: An annual ritual of Shias, Ashura being the final day of the events of Muharram 1–10, 61 AH. The narrative of this period, recited annually by professional readers in Shia mosques and meeting halls, is mounted as the second act of a passion play of Islam, and is accompanied by grief and tears, wailing and self-flagellation in public by the faithful. After the death in April 680 AD of Muwaiya ibn Abu Sufian—the Umayyad governor of Syria who had challenged Ali ibn Abu Talib, a cousin and son-in-law of Prophet Muhammad, for the caliphate—his son, Yazid, became the caliph. Hussein, the oldest surviving son of Ali, then living in Medina, staked his claim to the caliphate arguing that it belonged to the House of the Prophet, of which he was the most senior member. His stance won him fervent messages of support from the Iraqi town of Kufa, a stronghold of Ali's partisans. When this news reached Yazid, he rushed a trusted aide, Ubaidullah ibn Ziyad, to Kufa, where he neutralized the anti-Yazid forces. By then, however, the unsuspecting Hussein, accompanied by his family and seventy-two retainers, was well on his way to Kufa. On Muharram 1,

61 AH (8 May 681 AD) Hussein's entourage was intercepted near Karbala, 30 miles (48 km) from Kufa, by Yazid's soldiers. For the next eight days their commander tried to obtain Hussein's unconditional surrender. But Hussein resolved to do battle and perish rather than surrender or retreat. He also reckoned that his martyrdom would revitalize the claim of the House of the Prophet to the caliphate. On the morning of Muharram 10, Hussein led his small band of partisans to confront Yazid's four thousand heavily armed troops. His warriors fell one by one; and he was the last to die.

ayatollah: sign or token of Allah

Babis: Followers of Ali Muhammad Shirazi (1819–50) who regarded himself as *bab* (door) to the Hidden Twelfth Shia Imam

Baseej: mobilization

chador: (*lit.*) sheet; (*fig.*) veil

daftar: bureau

daneshgah: university

din: religion

-e: of

emruz: today

faqih: one who practices *fiqh* (q.v.); religious jurisprudent

fatwa: religious ruling

fedayin: (*sing.* fedai) self-sacrificers

fiqh: (*lit.*) knowledge; (*fig.*) Islamic jurisprudence

Hadith: (*lit.*) narrative; (*fig.*) Sayings and Doings of Prophet Muhammad. As most of Prophet Muhammad's companions had noted what he said or did for their own guidance, their diligence paved the way for the codification of the Prophet's *sunna* (practice), when eminent jurist Muhammad bin Idris al-Shafii (767–820 AD) ruled that all legal decisions not originating directly from the Quran must be based on a tradition going back to Prophet Muhammad. Shias, who accepted only those traditions that were traced through Imam Ali, cousin and son-in-law of Prophet Muhammad, came up with their own collection compiled later.

howze: center of (religious) learning; seminary

hajj: (*lit.*) setting out; (*fig.*) pilgrimage (to Mecca)

Hidden Imam: The Twelfth Shia Imam who went into occultation in 873 AD

hijab: cover or screen

hizbollah: party of Allah

hojatalislam: proof of Islam

ilimiya: (religious) knowledge

ijtihad: interpretative reasoning

imam: (*lit.*) one who leads prayers in a mosque; (*fig.*) religious leader, spelled as "Imam"

inqilab: revolution

Iranian calendar: In 1925 Iran adopted a solar calendar beginning with Prophet Muhammad's migration from Mecca to Medina in 622 AD. This calendar, starting on the spring equinox (March 21 or 22), is divided into twelve months named after Zoroastrian angels.

Islam: state or act of submission (to the will of Allah)

Jaafari code: Shia Islamic legal code named after Imam Jaafar al-Sadiq of Twelver Shias.

jame: association

jebhe: front

jihad: (*lit.*) effort; (*fig.*) crusade or holy war. "Jihad *fi sabil Allah*," the full title in Arabic, means "Striving in the path of Allah." Literally, *jihad* means effort or struggle, which is waged in various forms—internal and external—and degrees, war being the most extreme.

jumhouri: republican

kargozaran: servants

kayhan: world

khalq: people

khums: one-fifth (of gains); religious tithe applicable to Shia Muslims. One of the several duties incumbent on Shias, khums, amounting to one-fifth of a believer's trading profits, should be used as charity. In practice, this means a Shia hands over this sum to his marja-e taqlid (source of emulation) whose interpretation of the Sharia (Islamic law) he has agreed to accept, and who uses it for social welfare.

kiyan: existence

koran/quran: recitation or discourse

mahdi/mehdi: (*lit.*) the guided one, leader. Twelver Shias believe that the twelfth Imam Muhammad al Sadiq, the infant son of the eleventh Imam Hassan al Askari, is their mahdi, who has been in spiritual occultation since 873 AD, but will reappear to institute the rule of justice on earth before the Day of Judgment.

majma: society

majlis: assembly. Majlis is the popular term used for the Iranian parliament since its inception during the Constitutional Revolution of 1906–07.

marja: source

marja-e taqlid: Source of emulation. A Twelver Shia often chooses a leading *mujtahid* (a cleric qualified to practice ijtihad) as his *marja-e taqlid* (source of emulation), and agrees to accept his interpretation of the Sharia (Islamic law).

martyrdom: Prophet Muhammad formalized and elevated the concept of martyrdom originating with Judaism. The appropriate verse in the Quran (3:163) reads: "Count not those who are slain in God's way as dead, / but rather living with their Lord, by Him provided, / rejoicing in the bounty that God has given them, / and joyful in those who remain behind and have not joined them."

maslehat: expediency

mujahedin: (*sing.* mujahed): those who conduct *jihad*

mobarez: combatant; militant

mosharekat: participation

mujtahid: one who practices *ijtihad*

mullah: cleric or preacher

moqawemat: resistance

Muharram: The first month in the Islamic calendar

mustazafin: (*sing.* mustazaf) deprived or oppressed

Nawruz: (*lit.*) new day; (*fig.*) New Year's Day. The first day of the Iranian solar calendar, falling on the Spring Equinox, Nawruz is celebrated by Iranians, Kurds, and Zoroastrians.

niruyeh: forces

payam: today

quran/koran: recitation or discourse

rahbar: leader

Ramadan: Islamic holy month of fasting. It was on the night of Ramadan 26–27 that the first divine revelation was made to Prophet Muhammad.

rud: river

rouhaniyat: (*sing.* rouhani) (*lit.*) spiritual beings; (*fig.*) clerics

rouhaniyun: clergy

rowze-khani: (*lit.*) one who reads *Garden of Martyrs*; (*fig.*) one who recites the tales of Imam Hussein and other revered martyrs.

sabil: path

sayyid: (*lit.*) lord or prince; (*fig.*) a hereditary title applied to male descendants of Prophet Muhammad

shah: king

Sharia: (*lit.*) path or road; (*fig.*) sacred law of Islam

shatt: river or waterway

Shia: (*lit.*) partisan or follower; (*fig.*) follower of Imam Ali. Shia/Shiat means Shia/Shiat Ali, cousin and son-in-law of Prophet Muhammad (570–632 AD). According to Sunnis, Ali was the fourth caliph (successor) after Prophet Muhammad, his antecedents being Abu Bakr, Omar ibn Khattab, and Othman ibn Affan. But Shias do not regard them as legitimate caliphs to the Prophet as they did not belong to the Prophet's family. Shias also differ from

Sunnis in doctrine, ritual, law, theology, and religious organization.

Shia Religious Titles [in descending order]: marja-e taqlid: source of emulation; ayatollah ozma: grand sign of Allah, a term that has replaced the earlier mujtahid; ayatollah: sign of Allah; hojatalislam: proof of Islam; thiqatalislam: trust of Islam; mullah: derivative of "maula," master or learned man; haajj/haaji: one who has performed the hajj

Shiite: *see* Shia

sunna: tradition or beaten path (of Prophet Muhammad)

Sunnis: derivative of "ahl al sunna," people of the path (of Prophet Muhammad)

tahkim: consolidation

Twelver Shias: The twelve Imams of the Twelver Shias are: Ali, Hussein, Hassan, Zain al Abidin, Muhammad al Baqir, Jaafar al Sadiq, Mousa al Kazem, Ali al Reza/Rida, Muhammad al Taqi Javad, Ali al Naqi, Hassan al Askari, and Muhammad al Qasim.

taqlid: emulation

ulama/ulema: (*sing.* alim) possessor of (religious-legal) knowledge

va: and

vahadat: unity

vali: guardian

vilayat: rule

vilayat-e faqih: rule of the religious jurisprudent. This Islamic doctrine, developed by Ayatollah Ruhollah Khomeini, specifies that an Islamic regime requires an Islamic ruler who is thoroughly conversant with the Sharia and is just in its application.

waqf: (*lit.*) prevent; (*fig.*) religious endowment. Instead of passing on their properties fully to their inheritors, many Muslims give part or all of their possessions to a communal endowment scheme administered by a government department or ministry in a Muslim-majority country.

-ye: of

zakat: (*lit.*) derivative of *zakaa*, to be pure; (*fig.*) alms or charity

424

Select Bibliography

Ervand Abrahamian, *Iran Between Two Revolutions*, Princeton University Press, Princeton, N.J., and Guildford, 1982.

Geneive Abdo and Jonathan Lyons, *Answering Only to God: Faith and Freedom in Twenty-First-Century Iran*, Henry Holt, New York, 2003.

Anoushirvan Ehteshami, *After Khomeini: The Second Iranian Republic*, Routledge, London and New York, 1995.

Arthur J. Arberry, *The Koran Interpreted*, Oxford University Press, Oxford and New York, 1964.

James Bill, *The Lion and the Eagle: The Tragedy of American-Iranian Relations*, Yale University Press, New Haven, CT, and London, 1988.

Robert Graham, *Iran: The Illusion of Power*, Croom Helm, London, 1979.

Dilip Hiro, *The Essential Middle East: A Comprehensive Guide*, Carroll & Graf, New York, 2003.

Dilip Hiro, *Iran Under the Ayatollahs*, Routledge & Kegan Paul, London and New York, 1985; and Toexcel Press, New York, 2000.

Dilip Hiro, *Neighbors, Not Friends: Iraq and Iran after the Gulf Wars*, Routledge, New York and London, 2001.

Dilip Hiro, *The Longest War: The Iran-Iraq Military Conflict*, Harper-Collins, London; Routledge, New York, 1991.

Nikki R. Keddie, *Roots of Revolution: An Interpretive History of Modern Iran*, Yale University Press, New Haven, CT, and London, 1981.

Ruh Allah Khumayni, *Islam and Revolution*, (tr., Hamid Algar), Mizan Press, Berkeley, CA, 1981.

Stephen Kinzer, *All the Shah's Men: An American Coup and the Roots of Middle East Terror*, John Wiley, Hoboken, N.J., 2003.

Baqer Moin, *Khomeini: The Life of the Ayatollah*, I. B. Tauris, London and New York, 1999.

Kermit Roosevelt, *Countercoup: The Struggle for the Control of Iran*, McGraw Hill, New York and London, 1980.

Elaine Sciolino, *Persian Mirrors: The Elusive Face of Iran*, Simon & Schuster, New York and London, 2000.

John Simpson and Tira Schubert, *Lifting the Veil: Life in Revolutionary Iran*, Hodder & Stoughton, London, 1995.

Robin Wright, *The Last Great Revolution: Turmoil and Transformation in Iran*, Vintage, New York, 2001.

Valla Vakili, *Debating Religion and Politics: The Political Thought of Abdol Karim Soroush*, Council on Foreign Relations, New York, 1997.

Marvin Zonis, *The Political Elite of Iran*, Princeton University Press, Princeton, N.J., 1971.

1

Index

For a name or title starting with A, Al, El, Le, or The, see its second part. A person's religious or secular title had been omitted.

Abadan, 214, 218, 219
Abbasi, Ahmad, 160
Abbasid Caliphate, 156
Abdi, Abbas, 141
Abdo, Geneive, 164, 165, 308
Abu Bakr (Caliph), 155
Abu Ghraib prison scandal, 290–91
Achemenian dynasty, 104, 107
Additional Protocol (IAEA), 282–83, 284, 285
Adel, Gholam Ali Haddad, 57, 58
Afghan dynasties, xxxiii, xxxviii
Afghanistan, xxxvii, 279, 263, 280–81, 347
Afhartus, Mahmoud, 11
Afshar, Nadir Quli, xviii,
Afshar dynasty, xvii, 249
Afshari, Ali, 308
Aghazadeh, Gholam Reza, 288–89
Agnew, Spiro, 104, 276, 277
Ahmadabad, 60, 64.65
Ahmadabad-Musafi, 64
Ahmadi, Mirza Javad, 189, 190
Ahmadinejad, Mahmoud, xiii
Ahvaz, 188, 218, 219, 224
Ala, Hussein, 97
Alam, Assadollah, 98, 99
Albright, Madeleine Korbel, xiii, xxviii, xliv, 84, 268, 271, 274, 277
Algeria, 215, 238
Algiers, xxiv
Algiers Accord (1975), 215, 217, 235
Algiers Accord (1981), 270
Ali, Nemat, 184
Ali ibn Abu Talib (Shia Imam), 23, 89, 116, 154, 158
Ali Reza (Imam), 155,
Allawi, Iyad, 291
Amanpour, Christiane, 268
American-Iranian Council, 277, 278
American-Iranian Oil Company, 192
American-Israeli Public Affairs Committee (AIPAC), 260, 274
Amini, Ali, 36
Amirabad, 305
Amnesty International, 108
Amouzgar, Jamshed, 109, 122–23
Andimeshk, 218
Anglo-Iranian Oil Company (AIOC), xx, xxxviii, xl, 34, 69, 70, 94, 96, 192, 193–94, 195, 196, 214, 342–43
Anglo-Persian Agreement (1920), 32
Anglo-Persian Oil Company (APOC), 92–93, 94, 189,

191–92
Ansar-e Hizbollah, 53, 165, 166–68, 302, 305, 307, 308, 309, 310, 311, 322, 323
Ansari, Farhad, 310
Anti-Terrorism and Effective Death Penalty Act (U.S.), 268
Anwari, Ali, 304
Arab Cooperation Council, 235,
Arab-Israeli Wars, (1967), 103; (1973) xxi, 105
Arabian Sea, xxxvii
Arabs, 138,
Arak, 118, 158, 200
Araki, Muhammad Ali, 142
Aramesh, Ahmad, 11, 83
Ardekan, 139, 172
Ardekani, Ali Shams, 202
Arco (oil company), 204
Aristotle, 172
Armenia, xxxvii, 262, 263
Armenians, 138
Armitage, Richard, 267, 287
Arvand Rud, xxxv, 207
Aryan, 94
Asgharzadeh, Ibrahim, 272
Ashura, xxii, 93, 100, 117, 128
Al Askari, Hassan (Imam), 22
Asr-e Azadegan, 53, 180
Assembly of Experts, xxiii, xxvii, 138, 316, 322, 346; (1979) 38, 132; (1990) 141–42, 177; (1998) 144, 326; and Leader, 149–50;
Association of Combatant Clergy, 19, 50, 169, 172
Association of Iranian Jurists (AIJ), 109
Association of Qom Teachers, 142, 160, 162
Aswan, xxii, 111, 130
Ataturk, Kemal, 90
Athens, 242
Atomic Energy Authority of Iran, 276, 288
Axis of Evil (U.S.), xxx, xlv, 238, 281

Axis Powers, 94
Azadegan (oilfield), 283
Azerbaijan, xvii, xxxvii
Azerbaijan province, 95, 96, 186, 192,252–53, 262, 263
Azeri Turks, 3, 13, 138, 175
Azheri, Gholam Reza, 127
Azimi, A. R., 101
Aziz, Tariq, 216

Baath Socialist Party and Baathists (Iraq), 120, 121, 216
Babis, 86
Baghdad, xvii, 80, 185, 196, 224, 255
Baghdad Pact, 253
Bagheri, Amir Bahman, 250
Bahmanshir River, 213
Bahonar, Muhammad Reza, 53
Bahrain, 257
Bakhtiar, Shahpur, xiii, xxii, 111, 129–31,
Bakr, Ahmad Hassan, xl
Baluchis, 138, 175
Bam, 287
Bani-Sadr, Abol Hassan, xiii, xxiv, xxv, 37, 42, 61, 133–35, 168, 251, 298, 347
Baqai, Muzaffar, 75
El Baradei, Muhammad, xiii, 288, 289, 291
Barkbin, Ahmad, 161
Barnaby, Frank, 282
Barzin, Saeed, 146, 179
Baseej, 18–19, 23, 139, 166, 212, 218, 220, 227, 303–4, 310, 311, 315, 337–38, 340, 361
Basra, xxvi, 136, 185, 186, 220, 224
Batebi, Ahmad, 309
Battle of Hill 270, 210–11
Bazaar and bazaaris, xxxiii–xxxiv, 1–23, 106, 108, 231, 257; and Ruhollah Khomeini, 16; and revolution, 13–14; and Iran-Iraq War, 14–15
Bazargan, Mahdi, xiii, xxiii, 42,

60, 126, 131, 132, 243
BBC, 55, 56, 147, 239, 319, 320, 322
Beethoven's Fifth Symphony, 222
Beheshti, Ali Durood, 9
Beheshti, Muhammad, 140
Beirut, 81, 254
Belgium, 29
Bemukh, Shaaban Jaafari, *see* Jaafari, Shaaban
Berlin, 147, 266
BG (British Gas), 204
bin Laden, Osama, xli, 249
Bint al Hoda, 58
Blair, Tony, xlv, 270
Blood Transfusion Organization of Iran, 222
Boll, Henrich, Foundation, 147
Bolshevik Russia, 89–90, 191
Borujerdi, Muhammad Hussein, 119, 120
Boston Globe, xxxiii
Boucicault, Nina, 186
Boykin, William, 249
Bozroughmehr, Shirzad, 317, 319
Bremer, Paul, 240, 290
Britain, 214, 231, 282, 283; and India, 5; and Iran, xix, xx, xlv, 71–72, 84, 213; and Iraq, 9, 33, 90; and Mussadiq, Muhammad, 70–74; and U.S., 84, 214
British Admiralty, 187, 191
British Empire, 275
British Secret Intelligence Service, *see* MI6
Bromley, Carl, xxxvi
Brzezinsky, Zbigniew, 111, 250
Buckley, William, 256
Builders of Islamic Iran (coalition), 57
Burmah Oil Company (BOC), 187, 188
Bursa, xxi, 102
Bush, George Herbert Walker, xiii, xxxix, 258, 259, 279
Bush, George Walker, xiii, xxxii,

xxx, xlv, 238, 341, 347, 361
Bushehr, 206, 207, 265, 275

Campagnie Francaise des Petroles, 196
Carter, Jimmy, xiii, xxiii, xxiv, xl, xli, xlii, 41, 107, 245, 246, 247, 248, 250, 251–52, 254
Caspian Sea, xxxvii
Castro, Fidel, xliii, xliv, 296,
Center for Strategic Research (Iran), 141, 142, 143, 146
Center for the Rehabilitation of Drug Addicts (Iran), 324
Central Council of Friday Prayer Leaders, 139
Central Intelligence Agency (CIA, U.S.), xxi, xxxiv, xxxviii–xxxix, xlii, xliv, 36, 71, 75–84, 96, 97, 134, 160, 195, 253, 255, 264–65, 266, 267, 343
Cesaire, Aime, 172
Chalabi, Ahmad, 291
Cheney, Dick, 261
Chevron (oil company), 204
Chia Surkh, 184, 186, 187
China, 203, 279–80, 282
Chizari, Hamid, 303
Christianity and Christians, xxxviii, 38, 40, 135, 175
Christopher, Warren, 265
Churchill, Winston, 78, 342
Clarifications of Points of the Sharia, 120
Clinton, Bill, xiv, xxviii, xxxviii, xxxix, 201, 260, 261, 262, 265, 268–69, 270, 271, 273, 274, 280, 281
CNN, xliv, 268, 320
Committee for the Defense of Legitimate Rights (CDLR), 264
Committee to Save the Fatherland (Iran), 74, 82
Communist Party of Iran, 96, 194
Communist Party of the Soviet Union, 313–14
Complimentary Law to Establish-

ment of Oil Ministry (Iran, 1979), 199–200

Concession Syndicate, 187, 189, 213

Conoco (oil company), 200, 201, 204, 261

Constantine (King of Greece), 103

Constantinople Protocol (1913), 213

Constituent Assembly (Iran), (1925), 33; (1949) 33

Constitution (Iran), xx; (1906–7), 29–31, 91, 119; (1979, amended 1989), 38–41, 44, 45, 49, 55, 133; and Leader, 149–50, 163–64, 180, 199–200, 347, 356

Constitutional Revolution (1905–11, Iran), xxxiv, xxxviii, 5–7, 84

Construction and Development of Iran (coalition), 57

Contraction and Expansion of the Theory of Sharia, 321

Contras (Nicaragua), xxvi

Cotte, Edouard, 186

Council of Islamic Revolution, *see* Islamic Revolutionary Council

Crimson Gold, xlv

Cultural Revolutionary Council (CRC), 297, 320

Curzon (British peer), 32

Cyrus I, 104

Czechoslovakia, 195

Daftar, Hidayetollah Vazir-e, 66

Daftary, Muhammad, 82

Damascus, 2, 7, 256

D'Amato, Alfonso, 262, 271

D'Amato Act (U.S.), 262

Damavand, 249

Darabi, Kazem, 266, 267

D'Arcy, William Knox, xiv, xxiv, xxx, 185, 186–87, 188

al Dawla, Hassam Khan Vossuq, 32

The Dawn of the Islamic Revolution, Volume I, 123

Dehnamki, Masoud 53, 166

Delijan, 294

Democrat Party (Iran), 69

Desmarest, Thierry, 203

d'Estaing, Valery Giscard, 111

Dezful, 190, 218, 219

Dhahran, 263

Diba, Farah, 88–89, 111

Directorate of Mosque Affairs, 139

Dole, Elizabeth, 288

Dore (fashion model), 327

Dual Containment Policy (U.S.), xxviii, 260–61, 266

Dulles, Allen, 76

Du Pont (company), 200

Ebadi, Shirin, xxx–xxxxi, xlv, 168, 302–3

Ebrahimi-Nejad, Ezzat, 302

Ebtekar, Massoumeh, 330–32

The Economist, xxxiii, 309

Egypt, 210, 235, 339

Eisenhower, Dwight, xiv, 74, 76, 78, 98, 214, 278, 343

Eisenhower Doctrine, 214, 253

Elborz Mountains, xliv, 86, 328

Emami, Said, 178–79

Enterprise (oil company), 204

Enzali, 31

Eqbal, Manuchehr, 98

Erbakan, Necmettin, 262

Esfahan, *see* Isfahan

Ettilaat, 66, 100, 121

European Union, xlv, 202, 262, 270–71, 283–84, 292–93

European Union Troika, xxxi, 283–84, 290, 292–93

Expediency Council (Iran), 43, 44, 54, 137, 149, 169, 351

Exxon (oil company), 191, 196

Faisal II (King of Iraq), 98

Faiziya Seminary, xvii, 14, 101, 121, 157

INDEX

Fallaci, Oriana, 104
Fallahi, Hooshang, 294
Fallahian, Ali, 267
Family Protection Law (1968/75, Iran), 332–33, 335
Fanon, Franz, 172
Fao Peninsula (Iraq), xvi, 210, 211, 225, 228–29, 233
Farmanfarmaian, Manuchehr, 193
Farsi Island, 231
Farzaneh, 325, 331
Fatima al Zahra, 116
Fatima Massoumeh and her shrine, xvii, xix, 101, 153–56, 158
Fear of Waves, 173
Fedai Khalq, 132, 245, 248, 296, 300
Fedaiyan-e Islam, 73, 97, 167
Fischer, Joschka, 286
Fischer, Michael, M.J., 124
Fisk, Robert, 265
Followers of Imam's and Leader's Line, 50
Foruhar, Dariush, 177, 302
Foruhar, Parvane, 177, 302
Foundation for the Deprived and Disabled, 353
France, xxxi, 111, 231, 262, 282, 283
Franklin, Benjamin, 4
Furuqi, Muhammad Ali, 68

Ganji, Farhad, 153, 296
The Garden of the Martyrs, 117, 155
Gazprom (company), 202
Geneva, 271
Georgia, 263
Germany, xxxi, 93–94, 262, 283
Ghaffari, Hadi, 165
Gharabaghi, Abbas Karim, 131
Gharazi, Jamal, 21
Giap, Vo Ngugen, 296
Gilani, Fathollah, 32, 89
Goiran, Roger, 71, 77

Goolgiri, Massoumeh, 327
Gorbachev, Mikhail, 313
Gore, Al, 279
Grand Bazaar (Tehran), 2–4, 18, 23, 73, 76, 83, 310
Greece, 267
Grossman, Marc, 290
The Guardian, xxxiii
Guardians Council (Iran), xlv, 14, 28, 39–40, 41, 45, 47–48, 54, 55, 56, 141–42, 149, 165, 173–74, 312, 322, 340, 347, 348, 357, 358
Guevara, Ernesto Che, 172, 296
Guilani, Rudolph, 279
Gulf, xxxv, xxxv, xxxvii
Gulistan Palace (Tehran), 3, 89
Gulf Wars, (1991), xxxix, 196, 236; (2003) 22, 182, 239, 281, 282

Habbaniya, 70
Habibi, Azim, 293
Habibi, Shahla, 326
Hadavi, Abdul Karim, 21
Hadavi, Hidayat, 244
Hadian, Nasser, 53
Haeri-Yazdi, Abdul Karim, 118, 158
"Hafiz," 246
Haftkul, 290
The Hague, 35, 72, 291
al Hajja, Riyad, 264
Hajjarian, Saeed, 58–59, 141, 146–47, 174, 351
Hakimi, Ibrahimi, 96
Halabja, 232–33
Haleyle, 265, 275
Halliburton (company), 261
Hamadan, 83, 129, 134, 307
Hamas, 270, 346
Hamburg, 172
Hanafi (Sunni code), 156
Hanbali (Sunni code), 156
Haqqani Seminary, 164
Heikal, Mohamed, 131
Hejazi, Fakhr al Din, 16

Henderson, Loy
Herat, xviii
Hicks, Ilah-e Sharifpour, 168, 302
Hidden Imam, see Twelfth Imam
Higglesworth, Diedre, 65
al Hilli, Jamal al Din, 156
al Hindi, Ahmad Mousavi, 102, 114, 115
al Hindi, Mustafa, 114, 115
al Hindi, Murtaza Pasandida, 115, 118
Hindus, 154
History and Documentation of Human Rights in Iran, 302
History of Masjid-e Suleiman: History of the Beginning of the Oil Industry (in Persian), 189
Hitler, Adolf, 93
Hizbollah, (Iran) 165–66, 322; (Lebanon), 254, 346; (Saudi Arabia), 264
Hobbes, Thomas, 172
Hoja, Enver, 296
Hojjati, Reza, 359
Holland, 267, 291
Hoveida, Amir Abbas, 37, 103, 109
al Hudhaif, Abdullah, 264
Hukumat-e Islami: Vilayet-e Faqih, 12, 39, 120–21, 355
Hull, Cordell, 253
Human Rights Watch, 168, 302
Hungary, 195
Hussein, Saddam, xiv, xxx, xxxix, xl, 207, 211, 215, 235, 249, 282; and Algiers Accord (1975),), 215, 217, 235; and Iran-Iraq War, 219, 220, 234, 341; and Kuwait, 235, 258; as President, 216, 235, 236, 344; and U.S., 235, 258, 345
Hussein ibn Ali (Imam), 68, 89, 153, 154–55, 158, 182, 212, 297
Husseinian, Ruhollah, 165, 357

Ibrahim, Amir Farshad, 168, 302

Imam Hussein University, 242
Imperial Tobacco, 5
Independent, 265
India, 282
Indian Ocean, xxxvii
Indian sub-continent, xxxvii, xxxviii, 5
Indonesia, 338
Indyk, Martin, 260
Inqilab-e Islami, 133
International Atomic Energy Agency (IAEA), xxx, xxxi, 282, 283–84, 286–89, 291–93
International Court of Justice (ICJ), 35, 72–73
Internews (news agency), 278
Inter-Parliamentary Union, 279
Iqbal, Muhammad, 164, 321
Iran, 15, 138; and 9/11, 279; and Afghanistan, 280–81; and "Axis of Evil": 281; and Britain, xix, xx, xlv, 71–72, 84, 213; class composition and analysis of, 59, 95, 98–99, 105–6, 122–23, 180–81, 182, 327, 339–40, 359, 361; clerics in , 90–91, 92, 93, , 95, 97, 99, 100–1, 106, 107, 119, 340, 352, 353; demography of, 317; drug addicts in, 324; economy of, 12–13, 16–17, 18, 19, 20–21, 28, 45–46, 48, 57, 69, 73, 91–92, 98–99, 105–7, 122–23, 141, 170, 171, 189, 196–200, 202, 203, 204–6, 222, 224, 225–26, 261, 349, 359–60; education in 314–15, 325–28, 336–37, 361; elections, number of, 345–46; and environment, 330; and European Union, xlv, 202, 262, 270–71, 283–84, 289, 292–93; and European Union Troika, xxxi, 283–84, 290, 292–93; and Gulf War (2003), 239; intellectual dissenters in, 171, 177, 239, 320–24; and Interna-

tional Atomic Energy Agency, xxx, xxxi, 282, 283–84, 286–89, 291–93; and Islamic Conference Organization, xxviii, 218, 237, 274, 342; and Iraq, 213–14, 238, 239, for war with Iraq, *see* Iran–Iraq War; Islamic Republic of, xxiii, 38, 357–58; Islamization of law, 335; Islamization of universities, 297–99, 314–15; judiciary in, 353; military of, xxiii, 223, 213, 234, 361; music in, 44, 313, 336; and Muslim world, 346; nuclear power plant in, 275–76; nuclear program of, 263, 265, 269, 275–94; oil and gas, *see* Oil and gas (Iran); and Palestinian groups, 226, 270, 346; power centers of, 350–51; public opinion about U.S., 293–94, 304; revolution, nature of, 339–40, 343–44; revolution, stages of, 108; and Russia, 31, 275; satellite dishes in, 318–19; and Soviet Union, 94–95, 195, 196, 236, 275, 345; state-sponsored terrorism by, 265–66, 269, 270; telecommunications of, 360, 361; and United Nations, xxvi, xxvii, 140, 170, 217, 231, 233, 259;and U.S., xxviii, xxxi, xxxvi, xli, 177, 199, 238, 239–40, 246, 269, 274, 281, 282, 287–88, 343, 344, 345, 347; and U.S. Congress, 245, 251, 252–53, 257, 259–60, 267, 273, 274; and U.S. Embassy in Tehran, premises of, 242, secret documents at, 247, seizure of, (February 1979), 245, (November 1979), 243, 246–47; and World Bank, 261; ad World War II, 8
Iran and the Capitulations Agreements, 67

Iran–Contra Affair, 255
*Iran: From Religious Dispute to Revolution,*124
Iran–Iraq Frontier Treaty, 214
Iran–Iraq Non-Proliferation Act (1992, U.S.), 260
Iran–Iraq Treaty of International Boundaries and Good Neighborliness (1975), 217
Iran–Iraq War, xxxix–xl, 14, 206, 209–239, 251, 256; Fao Peninsula, xxvi, 225, 228–29, 230, 233; Iran's losses, 226, 234; Iran's military and hardware, 221–22, 223, 226–27, 231, 234; Iraq's chemical weapons used, xxv, xxxv, 223, 233, 254, 342; Iraq's economy, 225, 234; Iraq's losses, 234; Iraq's military and hardware, 223, 213, 234; and Islam, 215, 227; and Khomeini, Ruhollah, 135–36, 137, 140, 170, 218–20, 224, 226, 233, 286, 342; Phase One (September 1980–Mrch 1981), 217–19; Phase Two (April 1981–March 1982), 219; Phase Three (March 1982–June 1982), 219–20; Phase Four (July 1982–March 1984), 220–23; Phase Five (April 1984–January 1986), 223–25;Phase Six (February–December 1986), 225–30; Phase Seven (January 1987–January 1988), 230–32; Phase Eight (February–June 1988), 232–33; Phase Nine (July–August 20, 1988), 233–34; and Rafsanjani, Ali Akbar Hasehmi, 170, 211–12, 228; and Tanker war, 198, 229, 232; truce, xxvi, xxvii, 233; and U.S., 219, 222–23, 225, 229, 232, 251, 254, 278; and "War of Cities", xxv, xxvi, 224–5, 232

Iran–Libya Sanctions Act (ILSA), xxviii, 201, 204, 262, 265, 270–71, 279, 346
Iran News, 50, 291, 317
Iran Non–Proliferation Act (2000, U.S.), 274–75
Iran Party, 69
Iranshahr, 139
Iran–U.S. Claims Tribunal, 278
Iraq, 214; and "Axis of Evil": 281; economy of, 225, 234; and Gulf War (2003), 22, 182, 239, 281, 282; and Iran, 213–14, 238, 239, for war with Iraq, *see* Iran–Iraq War; and Khomeini, Ruhollah, 215–16; and Kurds, 215; and Kuwait, xxvii, 9; military of, 223, 231, 234; and U.S., xxv, xxxvii, xlv, 199, 254–55, 257, 258, 281
Iraqi–Soviet Treaty of Friendship, 214, 220
Isfahan, 242–43
Isfahani, Abol Hassan, 90, 91
Isfahani, Jamal al Din, 6
Isfahani, Shahriyar, 242–43
Isfandiari, Sorya, 79, 97
Islam, xxxviii, 104, 137, 156, 168–69, 180, 197, 215, 227,
Islami, Muhammad Javad, 159
Islamic Associations, 38, 41, 136, 299–300
Islamic calendar, 142
Islamic Coalition Association, 57
Islamic Conference Organization (ICO), xxviii, 218, 237, 274, 342
Islamic Dress Law (1981, Iran), 334
Islamic Iran Participation Front (IIPF), 51, 52, 57, 58, 143
Islamic Jihad (Palestine), 226, 270, 346
Islamic Propagation Organization, 139
Islamic Republic of Iran Broad-

casting (IRIB), 29, 44
Islamic Republic News Agency (IRNA), 136
Islamic Republican Party (IRP), xxiv, 14, 38, 41–42, 43–44, 133, 134, 139–40, 165, 340
Islamic Revolutionary Council, 130, 139–40, 243
Islamic Revolutionary Guard Corps (IRGC), 18, 44, 55, 139, 237, 264, 265, 309, 311, 319, 340, 361
Islamic Revolutionary Guard Vocational School (Tehran), 242
Islamic Women's Olympics, 328
Islamshahr, 227
Israel, xlvi, 28, 100, 266, 277, 282, 285, 286, 343
Istanbul, 2
Izeh, 190

al Jaafar, Sadiq (Shia Imam), 156, 301
Jaafari, Shaaban, 64
Jaafari code, 30
Jaafari Shias, *see* Twelver Shias
Jacobsen, David, 257
Jalaipour, Hamid Reza, 53, 176, 177, 179
Jalaliyan, Kiana, 301, 303
Jame, 175, 323
Jamran, 17, 113, 116
Jannati, Ahmad, xiv, 55, 273, 287–88, 326, 358
Japan, 283
Javadi, Ali Asghar, 108
Jebhe, 53, 334
Jenco, Lawrence, 257
Jerusalem, 2, 7
Jerusalem Liberation Day, 225
Jews (in Iran), 38, 40, 175
Jones, Zeke, 269
Jordan, 210, 235
Jumhouri–ye Islami, 42
June 5 Uprising (1963), 100–1

Kabir, Amir, xiv, 86
Kadivar, Muhsin, 141
Kamarei, Yusuf Khan, 102, 115
Karaj, 263
Karamane, Daud Arab, 227
Karbala, 22, 89, 97, 107, 117, 153, 157, 212, 237
Karbaschi, Gholam, 174
Karrubi, Mahdi, 28, 43, 52, 54, 55, 56, 278, 279, 285
Karun River, 184, 207, 221
Karzai, Hamid, 281
Kashani, Abol Qasim, xiv, 9–11, 73, 74–75, 76, 77, 82, 83, 97, 120, 197
Kavir–e Khorian Company, 191
Kayhan, 108, 176, 287
Kayhan International, 226, 227, 331
Kazakhstan, 263,
al Kazem, Mousa (Shia Imam), 8
Keddie, Nikki, R., 95, 337
Kelaye, 263
Kelaye Electric Company, 288
Kennedy, John, 99
Kermanshah, 129
Kerr–McGee (oil company), 204
KGSAVOY, 75
Khadija, 7
Khamanei, Mujtaba, 58
Khamanei, Ali Husseini, xiv, 27, 116, 135, 147, 162; and 9/11, xxx, 279; and Afghanistan, 279, 280; on Ansar–e Hizbollah, 167; on assassinations, 178; and Assembly of Experts, 144, 151, 346; and Baseej, 311; biography of, 139–41; on factions, 148; and economy, 19; and Guardians Council, 28, 45, 47, 358; and Gulf War (2003), 240, 290, 291; on intellectual dissent, 323; and Iran–Iraq War, 226, 228; and Khatami, Muhammad, 139, 143–46, 148, 311; as Leader (1989–), xxvii, xxxiv, xxxvi, 45, 138–50,
171, 258, 340–41; on 2004 Majlis elections, 145; on nuclear program, xxxi–xxxiii, 286–87, 291–92, 293; as President (1981–89), xxv, 27, 42, 43, 140, 348; on 1997 presidential poll, 144; on the press, 54–55, 147–48, 149, 169, 181, 312; on reform movement, 314, 348; on student protest (1999), 145, 306, 307, 308, 310, 312; and U.S., 240, 258–59, 273, 278, 290, 293
Khan, Abdul Qadeer, 288
Khan, Hulagu, 156
Khan, Ismail, xxx, 280
Khan, Mirza Taqi, xiv, 86
Khan, Reza, *see* Pahlavi, Reza Shah
Khanshor River, 152
Kharg, 198, 223
Kharrazi, Kamal, 237, 238, 278, 291
Khat–e Imam, 247, 272
Khatami, Muhammad, xiv, xlv, 23, 143, 178, 180, 240, 285, 311, 353, 362; and Ansar–e Hizbollah, 166; biography of, 171–72; on intellectual dissent, 323; and Iraq, 237–38; and Khamanei, Ali Husseini, 139, 143–46, 148, 311; and 2004 Majlis, 57; as Minister of Culture and Islamic Guidance (1982–92), 46, 173; on nuclear program, 293; and students, 307, 308–9, 310; as President (1997–2005), xxix, xxxiv, xliv, xlv, 21, 28, 48, 169, 181–82, 267–68, 305; presidential election campaign of, 175–76; and the press, 177, 323, 352; and reform movement, 348; and U.S., xxviii, xxx, 268–69, 347; on women, 330
Khatami, Muhammad Reza, 52–53, 59–60, 143

Khatami, Ruhollah, 139, 143
Khazal, Muhammad, 90
Khiyat, Muhammad Ibrahim, 22-23
Khobar Explosion (Saudi Arabia), 263-65, 270, 273
Khoeiniha, Muhammad Mousavi, 49-50, 141, 173, 246, 305
Khomein, 102, 114
Khomeini, Ahmad, 115, 138, 143, 172, 246
Khomeini, Mustafa, 115
Khomeini, Ruhollah Mustafavi, xiv, xliii, xlv, 2, 5, 8, 10, 12, 23, 114-38, 141, 145, 150, 159, 162, 169, 235, 316, 320, 340-41; audi-tapes of, 107, 121; on Baathists, 120; and Bani-Sadr, Abol Hassan, xxv, 133-35; and bazaar, 13, 15-16, 17; and Baseej, 303; biography of, xxi, xxiii, xxvii, 114-16; oncivil liberties, 15-16, 166; and cultural revolution, 297; and Expediency Council, 137; on factions, 161; and Iraq, 215-16; on Iran-Iraq War, 135-36, 137, 140, 170, 218-20, 224, 226, 233, 286, 342; on Islam, 168-69; on Islamic Republic of Iran, 357-58; on monarchy, 120, 344; on oil, 197; and Kashani, Abol Qasim 120; and Mussadiq, Muhammad, 119; on nuclear power plant, 276; as Leader, xxiv, xxxiv, 135-37; and Montazeri, Hussein Ali, xxvii, 160-62; and Pahlavi, Muhammad Reza Shah, xxi, 11-12, 100-2, 109, 110-11; as a pragmatist, 342; on private enterprise, 8, 17-18, 119; as revolutionary leader, 121-32; and Shariatmadari, Muhammad Kazem, 159-60;

terminology of, 58, 303-4, 344; and Tudeh Party, 119; and U.S., xl, xli, xlii, 133, 230, 256; and U.S. Embassy, 247-48; and vilayet-e faqih doctrine, 38-39, 159-60; on White Revolution, 120; on women, 328-29, 332-33, 336-38, 342
Khomeini, Zahra, 336
Khordad, 179
Khordad 2 Front, *see* May 23 Front
Khordad 15 Uprising, *see* June 5 Uprising
Khorramshahr, xxxv, 185, 188, 207, 213, 218, 219
Khoshtaria, Akady, 191
Khrushchev, Nikita, xliii
khums, 157
Khurasan province, 191
Khuzistan province, 90, 127, 198
Kiarostami, Abbas, xlv
Kiyan, 323
Knesset (Israel), 28
Kolahi, Elaaheh, 278
Komala-e Jian-e Kurdistan, 266
Koran, *see* Quran
Kufa, 154
Kurdistan Democratic Party of Iran (KDPI), 266, 270
Kurds, 138, 215, 266, 270
Kuwait, xxvii, xxxix, 196, 198, 217, 223, 225, 258
Kyrgyzstan, 263

The Lamp of Guidance, 118
Langley, 255
Lasmo (oil company), 204
The Last Great Revolution, 338
Lavizan, 131, 282, 289
Law Enforcement Forces (LEF), 305-11, 313, 335
League of Nations, 92-93, 192, 213
Lebanon, 10, 346